Sara

Sara

My Whole Life Was a Struggle

Sakine Cansız

Translated from German by Janet Biehl

Published in German 2015 by Mezopotamien Verlag as
Mein ganzes Leben war ein Kampf (1. Band: Jugendjahre)
First English language edition published 2018 by Pluto Press
345 Archway Road, London N6 5AA

www.plutobooks.com

British Library Cataloguing in Publication Data
A catalogue record for this book is available from the British Library

ISBN 978 0 7453 3803 3 Hardback
ISBN 978 0 7453 3801 9 Paperback
ISBN 978 1 7868 0290 3 PDF eBook
ISBN 978 1 7868 0292 7 Kindle eBook
ISBN 978 1 7868 0291 0 EPUB eBook

This book is printed on paper suitable for recycling and made from fully managed
and sustained forest sources. Logging, pulping and manufacturing processes are
expected to conform to the environmental standards of the country of origin.

Typeset by Swales & Willis, Exeter, Devon, UK

Simultaneously printed in the United Kingdom and United States of America

Translator's note

This book is the first of three volumes that Sakine Cansız, a co-founder of the Kurdish freedom movement, wrote between 1996 and 1998, mostly in the mountains of Kurdistan.

In this first volume, Cansız describes her Alevi family and her childhood, her clash with traditional women's roles in Turkish society, her entry into the movement then known as Kurdistan Revolutionaries, her organizing work on its behalf, its relations with groups on the Turkish revolutionary left, its bitter clashes with fascists and with the state, and the founding of the Kurdistan Workers' Party (PKK). It ends with her arrest in early 1979. She writes intimately and candidly, as if she were talking to a trusted friend, with a compelling combination of intelligence and warmth, political astuteness, and personal engagement.

Her account of her life overlaps with the story of the rise of the Kurdish freedom movement itself. Early on she recognized the crucial importance of women to the movement, and she initiated recruiting and educating female members. She describes at great length the constraints placed on her own work by traditional gender roles, and her struggle to free herself from them. Most political activists struggle with the question of balancing a personal partnership with political engagement, and most political movements must confront challenges posed by tensions between family and sexuality on the one hand, and political commitment on the other. Cansız's solution to this conundrum, which led her into and out of a marriage, is of enormous relevance to that issue.

Cansız wrote this memoir in Turkish, in the mountains of northern Iraq (South Kurdistan), in the mid-1990s. Anja Flach and Agnes von Alvensleben translated it into German, which was published by Mezopotamien Verlag on the anniversary of Cansız's assassination. When I came across the German version, I was astounded to learn that no English edition existed. When Estella Schmid of the Peace in Kurdistan campaign recommended the book to me, I set about translating it.

Not knowing Turkish, I worked from the German. Mustafa Gundogdu then undertook the task of checking my English against the Turkish original. I am grateful to him for the corrections and clarifications he made and for the advice he gave.

I'm grateful to Mezopotamien Verlag for permitting this translation and to Havin Guneser for making necessary arrangements. Havin also corrected errors relating to Turkish and Kurdish culture. Anja Flach was helpful in answering questions about the text. Mezopotamien Verlag provided the photos and captions from their edition. Inan Asliyüce and Tijda Cansız also helped with photos, especially those that will appear in Volumes II and III.

Janet Biehl

German translators' note

For everyone connected with the Kurdish freedom movement, the world stood still on January 9, 2013. On that day in Paris, one of its most important personalities, Sakine Cansız, was killed, along with her comrades Fidan Doğan and Leyla Şaylemez, in a political assassination.

One year later an edited version of the present book, which Cansız wrote in the 1990s, appeared in Turkish. This significant document describes the first steps of the revolution from the point of view of one of its significant leading figures. At the same time, it is the first part of the life story of a remarkable woman who was a friend and model for us. So we set out to make it available to German readers as well.

The winter of 1995–1996 was very rainy in South Kurdistan. Normally the Kurdish guerrillas use the winter months for education and regeneration. But that winter the Turkish army, in collaboration with the KDP,[1] undertook a military operation against the PKK. Military helicopters circling above the Zap region bombarded their positions. Turkish fighter jets shot missiles into the narrow ravines. Wood was scarce, so the provisional tents were improvised from plastic sheeting and crooked oak logs—they were damp and cold inside. Even the headquarters, where Cansız stayed, was warmed only by a smoky potbellied stove. During this time, sitting on the damp muddy ground, she wrote her memoir on a decrepit typewriter.

She was one of the first women to join the Kurdish freedom movement, before it even had a name. She was one of only two women to participate in the PKK's 1978 founding congress. In May 1979 she was arrested, and like everyone who refused to buckle under arrest or betray her comrades, she was tortured harshly. She was the first woman from the Kurdish freedom movement to mount a political defense in court. Among the prisoners she was considered a leading personality. For 12 years in various Turkish prisons, she maintained a resistance. Soon after her release in 1991, she did legal work at the party academy in Lebanon and from there went to the guerrillas in the mountains. Starting in the late 1990s, she lived mainly in Europe. In 1998 France granted her political asylum. In March 2007 at the request of Turkey she was detained in Hamburg pending extradition, but in April, following massive protests, she was released.

The present book, a product of the 1990s, recounts the history of the Kurdish movement through the lens of the era's ideological and political conflicts. In 1979, shortly before Cansız's arrest, the idea of a freestanding women's organization and making a social analysis from a woman's viewpoint was still new. In this book she describes the enthusiasm with which she dedicated herself to the work. In 1995, when she began writing her life story at the request of PKK chairman Abdullah Öcalan, the first official women's congress was taking place. As well, the first official women's units were being formed, for which the women felt enthusiasm but also self-doubt and fear of being relegated to nonfighting units.

Today the Kurdish freedom movement finds itself in an entirely different place. Autonomous women's organizing in all areas of life is now a matter of routine. Women are regarded as innovators and have built their own institutions everywhere. Women are equally represented in all committees within the movement. Sakine Cansız shaped and propelled this development. Gültan Kışanak, mayor of the Kurdish metropolis Diyarbakır, has rightly called her the "Kurdish Rosa Luxemburg."

We personally knew Sakine Cansız as a courageous, determined, and thoroughly warm woman who shared in all areas of work with modesty and humor. She tirelessly connected with and inspired people of diverse heritages to contribute their abilities to the Kurdish revolution. Once she made contact with someone, she kept nurturing the connection. She remains for us an unforgettable model, with her self-discipline, her erect bearing, and her receptiveness to all questions pertaining to freedom.

The murders of Sakine Cansız, Fidan Doğan, and Leyla Şaylemez have not been officially solved even to this day. Numerous factors point to a contract murder carried out by the Turkish intelligence agency MİT, but no one has yet been charged, tried, or convicted. With the translation of this book, we wish to keep the memory of Sakine Cansız and her friends alive and to continue their struggle.

For their support during the translation, we thank Anja Hansen, Mehmet Zahit Ekinci, and Yusuf Başkan.

Agnes von Alvensleben and Anja Flach
October 2014

Author's preface

It wasn't easy for me to write a book using the notes I made a year ago. When I wrote it, I hadn't thought it would be published as a book: it seemed too early, and the writing process wasn't natural. I did it in a time and context marked by deep conflicts.

If I had had the energy to start with that time and then go back into the past, I could have produced a very different work. Of course both variants were difficult at the outset. I preferred the simpler alternative.

The pages I wrote during those eventful days in the Zap area [in South Kurdistan] became a burden that I sometimes carried in my backpack and sometimes in Ferda's [Ferda Çetin]. I allowed only Ferda to read what I'd written. And he shouldered it all over the area for months, along with all his press documents, partly because he had respect for the work done so far, and also partly because I insisted. We were in the middle of a war, and I admit I turned it over to him because I thought he would protect it better and would use it in case anything happened. He sent one message after another to my unit saying he was coming to pick up my text.

In September 1996 I arrived at the party academy [in Damascus] with the notebooks on my back. Abdullah Öcalan had always said how important it was for us to write it. Because he attributed so much significance to writing, it was like an obligation that I had to fulfill.

It was hard to apply myself once again to writing. I didn't enjoy it at all, and I still don't. But I'd put a lot of work into it under conditions that gave it meaning. And I had neither the desire nor the courage to write everything down all over again.

It was also hard for me to reexperience my struggles and the events that had influenced me. I tried to narrate everything according to my memory, but this book is only a fragment of everything that happened.

Further work on this book took place in a good comradely atmosphere in the house of Abdullah Öcalan. I thank all my friends for that.

Any further evaluation of this book must be the task of the reader.

Sara (Sakine Cansız)
October 1997

Translator's introduction
The 1970s political context

Sakine Cansız came of age during the 1970s, and her early life unfolded in the context of that time. Readers unfamiliar with the Turkish revolutionary left of those years may be puzzled by the many political groups to which she refers by acronyms—hence this brief sketch. I've **boldfaced** names of people and groups that Cansız mentions in her text.

Starting in the early 1960s, political and social developments in Turkey allowed for a revival of the revolutionary left. In 1961 labor union members founded the **TİP, the Workers Party of Turkey** (Türkiye İşçi Partisi). It was a legal socialist party oriented toward parliamentarianism. The trade union acts of 1963 accepted the right of Turkish workers to collectively bargain and to strike, and in 1967 **DİSK, the Confederation of Revolutionary Workers Unions** (Devrimci İşçi Sendikaları Konfederasyonu), was formed as a breakaway group from the government-controlled Confederation of Turkish Trade Unions (**Türk-İş**). DİSK's first general assembly meeting took place in Istanbul on June 15, 1967, after which a wave of labor strikes began.

The ferment spread to all the major universities, where political debating societies mushroomed, "the most prominent being the one at the political science faculty of Ankara University," as historian Erik Zürcher notes.[2] In 1965 student activists networked these societies into a nationwide Federation of Debating Societies/Debate Clubs.

In the late 1960s news of revolutionary struggles in Cuba, Vietnam, and China radicalized the outlook of these student groups. Che Guevara was particularly inspiring for young militants, in Turkey as elsewhere, with his urban guerrilla strategy. The student uprisings around the world, especially the Paris uprising of May–June 1968, further excited militant students and teachers, so that by the late 1960s, many Turkish students and intellectuals embraced revolutionary socialism.[3] In general, they came to regard Turkey as "a semi-feudal society ... dominated by the United States." To cast off such domination, many developed a program for a National Democratic Revolution (NDR), in which a broad national front comprising intellectuals, workers, and peasants, as well as progressive forces within the bourgeoisie, would work together to build a socialist revolution. Armed struggle would be necessary to achieve this revolution. Marxist journals emerged, around which leftist students formed organizations and associations.

In 1968 the NDR current took over the Federation of Debating Societies and transformed it into **Dev-Genç**, or Revolutionary Youth (Devrimci Gençlik). This organization, notes historian David McDowall, was "the cradle from which most of the revolutionary movements of the 1970s were born."[4] Among its members were **Mahir Çayan** and the charismatic 21-year-old **Deniz Gezmiş**. Dev-Genç organized university occupations, protested the U.S. military presence in Turkey, organized in solidarity with workers' protests, and fought fascists on campuses and in the streets. From June 1967 to February 1969 Dev-Genç protested the U.S. Sixth Fleet, which was then in Turkey. Deniz Gezmiş led these protests, becoming the symbol of the burgeoning student unrest.

The student protests were turning violent. In 1969, while the U.S. ambassador was visiting an Ankara university campus, Dev-Genç set fire to his car. Gezmiş and other student leaders concluded that an armed guerrilla force would be necessary to bring about the socialist revolution. In 1969 he received guerrilla training at PLO camps in Jordan. The next year he and two other radical leftists, Yusuf Alsan, and Hüseyin İnan, created an armed force—**THKO**, People's Liberation Army of Turkey (Türkiye Halk Kurtuluş Ordusu)—to carry out the struggle. On January 11, 1971, Gezmiş took part in a bank robbery in Ankara, and on March 4 of that year, his group kidnapped four U.S. servicemen stationed in Ankara. But he and his comrades were captured after a standoff and sentenced to death.

In December 1970, **Mahir Çayan** and others founded a twofold group called the **THKP/C**, or People's Liberation Party/Front of Turkey (Türkiye Halk Kurtuluş Partisi-Cephesi). THKP was the political party, and THKC was its armed wing. The THKP/C, emulating Che Guevara, began a campaign of urban guerrilla warfare.

And in 1970 **İbrahim Kaypakkaya** co-founded the **TKP/ML**, the Communist Party of Turkey/Marxist-Leninist (Türkiye Komünist

Partisi-Marksist/Leninist), oriented toward Mao's China. It too had an armed wing, **TİKKO**, the Workers' and Peasants' Liberation Army of Turkey (Türkiye İşçi ve Köylü Kurtuluş Ordusu).

These years also saw the rise of right-wing groups. In 1969, a former army colonel **Alparslan Türkeş**, founded the **MHP**, or Nationalist Movement Party, a neofascist political party advocating Turkish ultranationalism. He also created a youth section for the party, known as the **Grey Wolves** (Bozkurtlar), which functioned as the MHP's paramilitary wing. These organizations were antipathetic toward Marxists (believing them to be "racially degenerate, villains ... not Turkish") and toward Kurds (believing that "one that does not have Turkish blood is not Turkish").

By 1971, campus and street violence were the order of the day. Hundreds of thousands of workers and students clashed repeatedly with police and with neofascists on the streets. The universities were all but shut down. Students following the urban guerrilla strategy attacked U.S. targets. Neofascists bombed the homes of university professors who had criticized the government. Factory workers went on strike at a hitherto unforeseen rate.

The government of Prime Minister Süleyman Demirel seemed powerless to curb the violence. On March 12, 1971, the army chief of staff staged a coup and imposed a state of emergency to end the "anarchy, fratricidal strife, and social and economic unrest" and achieve "restoration of law and order." The army imposed martial law in 12 of the 67 provinces, especially those with cities home to universities and industry, as well as Kurdish provinces. Security forces arrested activists and intellectuals all over the country, detaining high-profile figures in Turkish political and cultural life, even some who had welcomed the coup. The public prosecutor blamed Dev-Genç for the student and street violence and sought to close all youth organizations affiliated with it and indeed to suppress the left generally. It banned even the moderate TİP for having boldly affirmed, at a party congress in 1970, "There is a Kurdish people in the east of Turkey."

But some Guevarist youth refused to be suppressed. On May 17, 1971, THKC guerrillas, led by Mahir Çayan, and his comrade **Hüseyin Cevahir** (a socialist militant and author), kidnapped the Israeli consul in Istanbul and five days later killed him. His body was found on May 23. On May 30 Çayan and Cevahir entered a house in Istanbul's Maltepe district and took hostage a young girl, **Sibel Erkan**. On June 1 police and soldiers attacked the house in Maltepe and killed Cevahir. They captured Çayan and detained him, but he managed to escape.

Çayan and his comrades in the THKC and THKO were determined to free Gezmiş, who was still in prison, and two other comrades. On March 26–27, 1972, ten guerrillas, including Çayan, entered a NATO base in the Black Sea area and kidnapped three radio technicians (two British, one Canadian), who were working there, and took them hostage. The guerrillas brought them to a hiding place in the village of **Kızıldere**, in Tokat province. In return for freeing the hostages, they demanded the release of Gezmiş and the two others. But Turkish special forces discovered the Kızıldere hideout, surrounded the house and raided it on March 30. In the shootout, all three hostages and 10 of the 11 guerrilla-kidnappers were killed.

The imprisoned Gezmiş had nothing to do with this episode, but the army decided to make an example of him as the symbol of the student movement. In advance of the execution, students massively protested. But Gezmiş and the two comrades were hanged on May 6, 1972, as Cansız remembers in these pages.

In May 1974, a new somewhat left-of-center government declared a general amnesty and freed many young militants and intellectuals who had been arrested and imprisoned after the March 12, 1971, coup.

After the amnesty, some groups from the 1960s like Dev-Genç regrouped. As the 1970s progressed, groups of the revolutionary left engaged in political violence: against the state, understanding that it offered them no nonviolent form of redress; and against each other; and against right-wingers.

During the 1970s Grey Wolves engaged in street battles with leftist militants, intent on purging "the enemy within."[5] As the leftists were fully aware, Turkish security forces were helping the right-wing paramilitaries, as, especially under the 1975 and 1977 general "nationalist front" coalition governments between the neofascist MHP and the Justice Party (**AP**), and the National Salvation Party (MSP). Türkeş himself was deputy prime minister of Turkey in 1975–1977 and again in 1977–1978. A later president

admitted that the security forces protected the rightists, believing that they were performing a patriotic duty. ... A raid on [Alparslan] Türkeş's

Ankara headquarters in June 1979 turned up guns and documents that clearly implicated the rightist party in the violence.[6]

By the late 1970s the Kurdish areas of southeastern Turkey were in ferment, as state authority was eroded. According to an April 1979 report, "A resident secret policeman in the border town of Cizre reported to the country's leaders in Ankara that all the signs pointed to a classic revolution around the corner, as 'the rug is being pulled from under my feet.'" The April 1979 report talks of "a growing fever on the southern borders ... leading to chaos. Only a brave officer will go into a village with less than 20 people to catch an outlaw. Our colleagues feel like a colonial army."[7]

As for Turkey's Kurds, the Kemalist state continued its decades-long denial of their existence, at times regarding them as Turks, at other times denigrating them as subhuman rustics. Prejudice against them was as overt as it had been since the 1920s. The Turkish left, following a strategy of trying to conciliate Kemalist nationalism, also refused to acknowledge or address the Kurdish question, insisting that ethnic identities should be submerged in class solidarity. Not even the TİP could raise the Kurdish question openly and hope to survive legally.

But Kurds were nonetheless drawn to the TİP and other socialist and labor groups because they offered ordinary people a means of organizing. Besides, "it was only on the Left that Kurds were treated more or less as equals." By the late 1960s, Kurds and Alevis were the TİP's "backbone," says McDowell.[8]

In 1969, a number of radical urban Kurds in the TİP and its milieu—youth and intellectuals—were frustrated by the refusal of the Turkish left to address the Kurdish question and demanded that attention be paid to the plight of the Kurdish minority. They left the TİP and founded the **DDKOs**, the Eastern Revolutionary Culture Centers (Devrimci Doğu Kültür Ocakları). It was the first legal Kurdish organization in Turkey, although it used the term *Eastern* as a euphemism for *Kurdish*.

Structurally, the DDKO was a network of cultural associations established in towns and villages in the Kurdish east as well as in Kurdish neighborhoods in Istanbul and Ankara. Ideologically, the DDKOs were both Kurdish nationalist and Marxist-Leninist, viewing the Kurdish question as simultaneously a class problem and a national/

cultural problem. They opposed the economic backwardness of the east, accusing large landholders and capitalists of collaborating with the United States to exploit the disadvantaged there. At the same time they opposed the suppression of Kurdish culture and language. The DDKO wanted to liberate Kurdistan from its double yoke of cultural and economic oppression. They were inspired by the Vietnamese struggle against U.S. imperialism and believed that Turkey too would undergo great upheavals.[9]

But in 1970 all the DDKO leaders were arrested and tried. In their defense they wrote a 150-page document asserting Kurdish identity and rights, covering Kurdish history, language, and society. It was the first major statement of its kind. They lost at trial, several received long prison sentences, and the DDKOs were shut down.[10]

But those who would go on to found the PKK had no "significant previous relations with any of the Kurdish political parties active in the 1970s," as Jongerden and Akkaya have argued.[11] Rather, the roots of the PKK lie in the Turkish revolutionary left, as it continued into the 1970s in the wake of the March 12, 1971, coup and the amnesty.

In 1972 **Abdullah Öcalan** was a student in the political science faculty at the University of Ankara. His sympathies lay with the revolutionary left, especially the THKP/C. After the deaths of Mahir Çayan and his comrades at Kızıldere in March, Öcalan helped organize a boycott in protest. For that, he was arrested and detained in the Mamak military prison from April to October 1972. There he encountered seasoned Dev-Genç leaders, with whom he held extensive discussions and who radicalized him further.

After Öcalan's release, a friend introduced him to two revolutionaries from the Black Sea region: **Kemal Pir**, a sympathizer of the THKP/C, and **Haki Karer** of the THKO. The three young revolutionaries lived together in the Emek district of Ankara for about a year, until the winter of 1973–1974, then dispersed to other parts of the city. They were joined by **Ali Haydar Kaytan**, Duran Kalkan, and **Cemil Bayık** to form a core group of three Kurds and three Turks. During 1974 the six of them worked together in the **ADYÖD**, or Democratic Higher Education Association in Ankara (Ankara Demokratik Yüksek Öğrenim Derneği), an outgrowth of the THKP/C and connected with the reconstituted Dev-Genç. Together they developed ideological, political, and strategic foundations. Strategically, they had seen the 1960s revolutionary parties' rapid rise and equally rapid defeat. Öcalan concluded that the problem was that their confrontation with the state had been premature: they had rushed into it while they were still inchoate. So he and his friends decided to take the time to organize slowly and prepare meticulously before entering a conflict.

Their ideology was a mix of Kurdish nationalism and radical Marxism-Leninism, designating Turkish Kurdistan as an "internal colony." Marxist-Leninists had pointed out that the West had subjected countries of Africa and Asia to imperialist domination. Similarly, "the Apocular [followers of Öcalan] asserted that the Turkish state—while itself being subjected by the West—had acted in a similar manner towards Turkey's Kurdistan, with a fascistic feudal class exploiting it."[12] The group advocated an armed struggle against the Turkish state for cultural and political rights and for self-determination for the Kurds in Turkey, an independent Marxist-Leninist state based on a fusion of revolutionary socialism and Kurdish nationalism. They took these ideas to the ongoing house meetings, indeed to any Kurd who would listen to them.

The group knew they could not hope to advance the Kurdish question by publishing a journal—Kurdish identity was banned in Turkey and any magazine would be suppressed promptly. So instead they decided to organize by meeting people in homes, where they could discuss face to face, especially with Kurdish youth and intellectuals. Between 1973 and 1977, perhaps hundreds of house meetings were held, according to Jongerden and Akkaya.

> Sometimes two or three meetings a day took place, with up to around 10 or 20 participants. The frequent, long, and intensive discussions at these meetings contributed to the carving out of a distinctive ideology, the enlisting of new recruits, and the forging of a close camaraderie.

The meetings lasted as long as they needed to. "If three hours were needed to convince people," recalled Kemal Pir, "we would be busy for three hours. If 300 hours were needed to convince them, we would be busy for 300 hours. We were working to convince people."[13] Through these house meetings, new people were recruited to the group, including Sakine Cansız, who describes it in these pages.

In December 1974 the ADYÖD was closed after a police raid that arrested 163 students. Soon thereafter, in 1975 the core group of Kurdish militants met in the Ankara suburb of Tuzluçayır, where they outlined plans to form a Kurdish leftist organization that would work to create a Kurdish national liberation movement. It would be independent of leftist groups and of bourgeois Kurdish groups. Öcalan was elected leader, and the incipient group became known simply as the **Apocular**, or followers of **Apo** (nickname for Abdullah). Later the group adopted the provisional name **UKO**, or National Liberation Army (Ulusal Kurtuluş Ordusu). They were also known as **Kurdistan Revolutionaries** (Kürdistan Devrimcileri). The core members abandoned university studies or livelihood work to become full-time professional revolutionaries.

It was in 1974 that Sakine Cansız entered the movement, so from this point I will let her tell her own story.

Janet Biehl

Born in winter I entered the world on New Year's Day in 1958, in the village of Tahtı Halil in Dersim.[14] At the time my father was in the military. He didn't register my birth until his furlough in February, so my official birthday is February 12, 1958. Did it bode well to be born in the harshness of winter? Best to start off believing that it did, that it portended happiness. So in my opinion, to come into the world on New Year, in midwinter, in a snow-covered region, was auspicious.

Our village comprised 20 households. All the houses stood along a single street. At the upper end lived the Kocademir family, and at the lower end the Duymazes. Both families were large and beloved in the village. Our house stood in the village center, next to the water source. Our next-door neighbors were Uncle İbrahim and his family. İbrahim was regarded as the most amusing and courageous person in the village, and also the bravest. Once while he was working in the fields, it was repeatedly told, he'd fought with a bear. The bear had ripped out his internal organs, but he shoved them back into place and actually made it back to the village. Much more was said of him as well. He was our village's version of Nasreddin Hodja.[15] The villagers usually went to the threshing place, below the water source, to talk. There the elders entertained one another with jokes, eliciting peals of laughter.

The village water supply was of recent construction. The water flowed there from mountain slopes in Mazgirt, several hours away. The spring itself was in the terrain of another village, so a certain sum of money was paid for it. The male villagers dug a canal and laid in the pipes. If you walked along the iron pipes, you'd reach the spring. When we were little, we found it exciting to follow the pipes, as if by doing so we'd discover something new. The waterhole itself was large and built from concrete. It had a nice-looking box-shaped basin, from which high, wide steps led upward along two sides.

It was always very clean. Xezal, a high-spirited woman from the Kocademir family, usually saw to that. Powerfully built, she had a huge face with bushy eyebrows, and her large nose featured broad nostrils. The *kofi*[16] on her head was always tidy. Her headscarf, adorned with pearls and embroidery, was blindingly white. Her skirt had smocking along the hem. Over it she wore a wrap, and under it the elastic pajama pants

1

that in Zaza we called *manıs*. The sight of her plunging her enormous copper bucket into the water was remarkable. First she'd clean the whole place with plenty of water, then she'd wash her hands, face, and feet. Only then did she fill her water container. She always repeated the same routine. Maybe that was why I observed her with fascination. All the villagers were impressed that she cleaned regardless of the weather. The village houses were normally all clean too, but Xezal and her house stood out. She had thick wrists and ankles, adorned with bands of pearls.

Xeyzan, from the Duymaz family, was the exact opposite. Her voice was husky, and her body was smooth, tall, and thin. Unlike Xeyzan, Xezal was authoritarian. Her domestic authority extended to the outside as well. The old women in the village enjoyed a certain natural respect, but hers went beyond that. She behaved cautiously around others. The young married women in the village adapted themselves to the prevailing traditions. They weren't openly pressured, but in their behavior toward the old women and men, they had to comply with certain norms. When they saw or spoke to elderly people, they covered half their face with their headscarf. That showed the necessary respect. It was also conventional not to speak in a loud voice or at inopportune moments. Infants couldn't be breastfed everywhere, or else the nursing baby was covered with a headscarf. The women who were somewhat older had it easier.

The widow Emoş, whose house stood opposite ours, on the other side of the waterhole, had a special position in the village. She had six children but was still young. Everything she did drew attention to herself and was immediately commented upon. The other women didn't like her much, treating her with overt suspicion and jealousy because she was a widow. They gossiped about her incessantly. But in general village life was harmonious, with warm bonds, respectful interactions, and little conflict. Nothing happened to seriously disrupt the peace.

I've never forgotten how Uncle İbrahim used to listen, over his huge, old-fashioned radio, to songs in the Kurdish dialect Kurmancî, which we called Kirdask. Whenever they broadcast singing by Ayşe Şan,[17] he'd turn the volume all the way up, and we heard it all over the village. Even in Şekerman, the next village over, people could hear it. Sometimes we'd hear radio sounds coming from over there. People listened to news avidly, and when something serious was happening, they were all ears. We children had no idea what any of it was about, but we imitated the grown-ups' seriousness.

2

My parents: children of the Dersim genocide   My mother and father were born during the years of the Dersim genocide,[18] my mother a few years after my father. My father still remembers the repression and hard times after the massacre. He talked about it. My mother was a daughter of Hesene Hemede Kalik, of the Kureyşan tribe. My grandfather was a tribal leader who owned several villages, mills, and shops. So my mother's family was considered well off.

By contrast, my father's family was poor. My parents' marriage was arranged, according to tradition, by their relatives. My father's mother had been married twice, and my father was the only child of her marriage to my grandfather. Probably my grandfather got the name Cansız[19] because he was tall and thin.

I don't remember either of my grandfathers—both died young. My father's family belonged to the Süleymanlı, a branch of the Kureyşan tribe—*Sılamanız*, one would say in Zazaki dialect. My grandfathers' good relations were said to have played an important role in my parents' marriage. But on their wedding night, my mother fled my father's house and returned to her parents' house in her own village. She couldn't accept his family's poverty or unexceptional heritage. But her father didn't approve of her behavior. Over the next three years, several suitors turned up for her, but he refused to let her marry any of them, telling her, "You are the bride of the other house—I won't allow you to marry anyone else." Friendly relations were important to him, and he still considered my mother to be the daughter-in-law of my other grandfather. Finally he was able to persuade her to return to my father. The incident hurt and angered my father, but he had the maturity and patience to wait for her.

At the time of the Dersim massacre, my mother was still in diapers. My grandmother hid, along with her children, daughters-in-law, and nieces, in a dense forest near the Munzur River. She never had a chance to nurse her children. My mother, the youngest, cried continually from hunger. My uncle was terrified that my diaper-wrapped mother's crying would betray their hiding place. Along the far shore of the river ran a street used by military vehicles. The soldiers sometimes took breaks there. They might very well have heard a crying infant. My uncle wanted to tear my mother from my grandmother's arms and throw her into the Munzur.

But my grandmother wailed, grabbed my mother back, and wrapped her in her arms. She beseeched my uncle and swore she could quiet my mother. So my mother was saved. Later, when my mother got angry or found life unbearable, she'd snap, "Oh, if only they'd thrown me into the water—I'd have been spared all this!" It was mostly my uncle who told stories from that time.

My father's memories of that time affected us more. His experiences were more extensive and painful, and whenever he talked about them, he seemed to relive them. He had good recall, and his memories were vivid. In later years he expressed them with his *saz*,[20] in poems, and in songs.

The Dersim genocide started in 1938 and lasted into the 1940s. Between 1940 and 1945, military units raided more villages, looking for members of Demenan tribe, and hauled the male inhabitants off to military posts. My father's memory here was a little vague, given his age, but it persisted. I wish I could recall everything he told me, but unfortunately, I retain only a little.

"I remember very well the day the gendarme units crossed over the Pax Bridge into the village," he said.

They forced the men, including my father, to assemble in the village square. There they were tied up and had to hold out in the sun for a long time without bread or water. The heat was fierce. Later everyone was taken to the gendarme station over the Pax Bridge. I wanted to go with them, but they didn't let me. I cried. My mother and the other village women cried too.

The next day a group set out to figure out what had happened to the men. I went along. We had to wait in the yard. No one paid any attention to us. Suddenly an officer ordered the watchman at the military station—a Kurdish man, native to the region—go get the documents, *evrak*, from the Şekerman village. This man misheard *evrak* as *avrat*, wife, so he rounded up all the village women and brought them to the station. When the officer saw the guard coming with a large group of women, he burst out laughing and said, "Our smart-aleck brought *avrat* instead of *evrak*," and ordered him to take the women back immediately. I was relieved, because I'd been afraid the women would be tied up like my father and the other men were and thrown into prison.

Usually when my father talked about his experiences, he couldn't hold back tears. He constantly gave us advice and demanded that we be smart and do the right thing so that we wouldn't have to go through the pain he did. "What you've experienced up to now—how are you supposed to know what life means? But look at what we went through ... "

All that repression and torture were said to be justified because members of the Demenan tribe were hiding in the village.[21] On the least suspicion, people would be rounded up, imprisoned, and tortured. I don't have to recount what happened when tribal members were actually found in the village.

"My father didn't let me go to school"   My father was among those in the village who had gone to school. He finished primary school. His schoolmates included Ali Gültekin, Kemal Burkay, and Hüseyin Yıldırım. He'd always mention those names when speaking of that time. He was especially close to Ali Gültekin because they came from the same village and grew up in the same living conditions.

My mother, on the other hand, never went to school, and in fact she never missed an opportunity to complain mournfully that her father had prevented her from attending school. She possessed a kind of authority that derived from her advantage in coming from a well-off family. Moreover my father was influenced by the Alevi culture, with its respect for women, and he behaved toward her accordingly.[22] The effect was to make her even more authoritarian.

In society in general, when people refer to a family, to its children or its property, they use the husband or father's name. It seems natural and alienates no one. Few things are referred to according to the female family members. But in our culture, people spoke of Zeynep [Sakine's mother] as much as of İsmail [her father]. My mother's family even put the emphasis on Zeynep. That was entirely normal, even necessary.

Within the tribe and the family, my grandmother too had authority and influence, but hers was different from my mother's. Hers was based on her personal strength and on her dedication to the common good.

My grandmother's name was Hatice, but we all called her Eze. She was tall and strong, with a fair complexion and blue eyes. Actually, no one could say precisely whether they were blue or green. If I say they were blue, I'm doing an injustice to green, and vice versa. In any case, her eyes were very beautiful. She was a beautiful woman, my grandmother. With her energy, her poverty, and her ability to master anything, she had a great influence on people around her. She was remarkably far-sighted. Her grandchildren, children, daughters-in-law, brothers-in-law, neighbors, and relatives, the people in her village, and everyone she knew called her Eze. She enjoyed great general respect.

After my grandfather died, her reputation and her authority rose even higher. From then on she bore the responsibility for a large family with widely dispersed relatives. For any problem that arose—whether a daughter was marrying, or a daughter-in-law was coming into a family, a quarrel or a conflict—no solution was imaginable without her. Nothing happened without her approval. She had an enormous heart. She helped anyone who needed help, valued fairness, and tried never to hurt anyone. She assisted the needy, and newlyweds, and anyone who suffered a loss.

Whenever someone's jealousy or a quarrel resulted in a crisis, or even a death, my late grandfather would turn up at the scene. In Dersim most things were sworn "on Düzgün Baba,"[23] but in my family everything was sworn on the head of my grandfather. For my grandmother to swear something on his head was to resolve all misunderstandings, and everyone had confidence in her.

She was a very strong woman, my grandmother. She excelled at whatever she undertook and was hugely talented. At night she went out walking alone, checking to make sure everything was all right. If a wolf or other wild animal came near the stables, she shouted at it with her powerful voice, and the animal took flight. She always knew who was sick or who was fighting, and she intervened. The kind of attention she gave her fellow human beings elevated her reputation.

In my grandmother's house the tea was always fresh. Her big teapot constantly simmered over a flame. Our village had one street, and so whoever wanted to go to another village had to pass through ours. Many people tired from a journey found rest in my grandmother's house. They ate her food and drank her tea. Many good friendships came about this way, and my grandmother always enlarged her circle of acquaintances.

My grandmother's qualities fascinated me. I admired her and followed her around. I especially observed how every morning she rose early with the sunrise, stood with her face toward the sun, and prayed with her palms over her face. She did the same thing at moonrise. She prayed at sunrise and sunset, moonrise and moonset. During her prayers her face looked sadder. Whenever the sun or moon was eclipsed, she prayed, cried, and entreated, making my whole body shiver. Gloom hung in the air: the darkness aroused fear and a mood of hopelessness and pain. My grandmother wanted the darkness to end quickly. And as soon as it did, she baked the kind of buttery bread that we call *niyaz*.

Another peculiarity was that she never let the fire in the kitchen go out. In the evening she buried the glowing embers under the ashes, so that at daybreak she could reignite a flame. It was considered a sin to get fire from another house or to have to pass fire along to another. If someone requested fire from us, she got annoyed and told the people to make sure every evening from then on that they'd have embers in the morning. Eze lived according to the Zoroastrian teaching. For her it was part of life to preserve fire, to find refuge in the sun and moon, and to be connected with the earth.

Learning Turkish: a unique torture   I didn't have much to do with my paternal grandmother, and I have only a few memories of her. She rarely visited us—mostly she lived with her other children. I last saw her in 1973, when she was very old. Her face and hands were wrinkled, although her body was still vital and snow white. She was highly meticulous. She always carried around with her a mat made of thin material. Before sitting down anywhere, she'd spread this mat out first and adjust her skirt. Only then would she lower herself.

After finishing his military service, my father became a civil servant. He passed the exam at the vocational school and went to work as a clerk. By then I had already learned a few words in Turkish, like "mother" and "father." Whenever I learned new Turkish words, I'd run into the center of the village and shout them at the top of my lungs, to annoy the other children my age. Learning Turkish words is one of my most vivid early memories. Nobody was forcing me to learn the language back then.

My oldest sibling was my brother [Haydar]. In between his birth and mine, my mother had brought another girl into the world, but she died at 6 months old. My brother entered school before me. I saw the city [Dersim] for the first time when I registered for primary school. In my first year of school, I ran from the village to the city every day. In the summer we could cross Harçik Creek as a shortcut. In the winter there was a lot of snow. The snowy winter evenings were unforgettable. We little ones were in the middle, and the grown-ups were arrayed in front of us and behind. During an especially heavy snowfall, there was the danger of losing a child, or we could encounter a wolf or jackal. So a vanguard always cleared the path for us and kept alert for possible dangers. On such evenings a group of men usually met us, and together we made a racket to scare wolves away. Or we sang songs together. Later I learned that that not only dispels fear but raises the body temperature, reducing the risk of frostbite.

The worst was the way our hands hurt, after we got home from school, if we tried to warm them at the stove. It hurt as much as if we'd put our hands directly on the stove. Our teacher taught us to warm our hands by sticking them in our armpits, rubbing them, breathing onto them, and running them through our hair. That way they'd warm up faster and with less pain.

My first-grade teacher was a blond Turkish woman named Gönül, who taught us until third grade. Learning Turkish was a unique torture—even though we were eager to learn, it was very difficult for us. We learned new words quickly, but our teachers recommended that we always speak Turkish after school. "If you speak Kurdish, you'll be beaten," they said. This threat, and some schoolmates who supervised us, induced us to learn faster.

My father's civil service career inevitably changed our living standard. We now could have bread baked from white flour and wear low shoes. When my friends wanted to trade two loaves of barley bread for one made of white flour, I was ashamed and did it right away. But I took only one barley loaf and said I liked cornbread the best. Sometimes I offered to trade so they wouldn't have to say anything. Sometimes we took a city-bought loaf of bread and hid it in homemade puff pastry bread and ate it that way. Later we moved to the city. In winter we'd live in the city and in summer in the village. That changed our lives. My knowledge of Turkish improved.

Our first house in the city was in the Dağ neighborhood. It was a mud-brick house—only the floor was concrete. And unlike in the village, here we had electricity.

A fight in Tahtı Halil village One summer night in the village, I awoke to a huge crash. My grandmother had a club in her hand and was screaming for the men to come and meet her in the village center. I'd never seen her so angry. Even before she started to scream, I'd heard some sounds but didn't understand what they were. A strange restlessness hung in the air. Many of those who showed up at the square had only just awakened and were rubbing their sleepy eyes and trying to understand what was going on.

My grandmother asked them where my abducted aunt was. She cursed the abductors. My father wasn't there, and Mustafa Çallı, the husband of my other aunt, acted as if he didn't know anything. He pretended—cunningly—to have only just awakened. "What's all this about?" he asked my grandmother. "It's midnight—has something happened?" With that, he became the first to feel the brunt of the club. Many others tried the same trick as he. At first I had no idea what was happening, but gradually it came out that my aunt Melek had been abducted. It was like an episode in a movie: fear, excitement, adventure, it had everything. If my uncle hadn't stepped in, it could have led to a blood feud.

A man from the Rayber tribe had wanted to marry my aunt Melek, but our family rejected him, preferring that she marry someone from our clan. But my grandmother ignored the preference of the rest of the family and promised Melek that she could have the young Rayber man. So the others decided to abduct my aunt. It was mainly men who participated in the abduction, men who worked and had a certain intellectual background. The abduction itself was remarkable. The two villages lay at a distance, and in between were several others. As she always did, my grandmother took precautions. She slept outside on a wooden bed. My aunt's abductors approached the house from several directions. They must have had helpers from the village too. They had to pull the abduction off without a hitch, otherwise my aunt would be given to the other tribe.

Since changing my grandmother's mind had proved too difficult, they'd devised the following plan. One or two people would slip into the summer stable and cry out as if wolves were attacking the herd. The panic would lure my grandmother away from the front door. The others would then use the opportunity to grab my aunt and abduct her from the house and then from the village. Deceiving my grandmother would, of course, be the hardest part.

As soon as the panic erupted in the stable, my grandmother grabbed the club and ran to see to the herd. The group that was to carry out the abduction then ran into the house and searched for my aunt. They found her under the big wicker basket that normally held yogurt and milk. They clapped a hand over her mouth and dashed off with her.

My grandmother quickly grew suspicious. The group from our village went over to her and kissed her hands and tried to stall her by talking to her, acting as if it were a perfectly normal visit.

My grandmother answered them with the club, cracking a few skulls, but they succeeded in distracting her and so won some time for the other group. My grandmother swore and then called for my aunt. When she realized that she'd been abducted, she ran off to track her down.

The village had only two roads. The abductors had planned to take my aunt from Kavun village, not to Ali's village, but to ours, to Tahtı Halil. This route had advantages. But my grandmother went to Ali's village and right away started shouting and calling out. The residents came out into the square. My grandmother demanded that they turn over her daughter, but the villagers said neither Ali nor Melek was there. Finally my grandmother believed them and came to our village.

The men who had brought my aunt to our village were hiding on the outskirts. Others involved in the affair were by now sleeping as if nothing had happened. The abduction was successful.

But it didn't end there. When my grandmother left the village, her shouting had also aroused and informed the Raybers' village. She reported the abduction to the gendarmes. Of course no one could have imagined that anyone would get the state involved. But the next day gendarme units occupied the village and searched it. They continued the search into the outskirts. Because of the complaint, they were determined to find my aunt. The result was chaos. No one had expected the state coming in with its gendarmes. That could put an end to good relations once and for all. The gendarmes clubbed several village residents, blaming them for the abduction. And they accused my uncle Hasan, the tax collector. Others guessed that the Raybers were behind the complaint.

As it all got very serious, a group from the village came to my grandmother to mediate. She still didn't realize what had happened. But when her fury subsided, she withdrew her complaint, whereupon the gendarmes left.

My grandmother's reputation suffered from this episode. On behalf of her daughter, she'd turned against everyone else and had cursed and insulted people, hurting their pride. In the end, Melek and Ali got happily married in Höpük. Later they moved to Milli, where Ali worked as a teacher. A long time after that, my grandmother went to visit my aunt and Ali and reconciled with them.

But my grandmother's prestige was greatly reduced, because she'd called the gendarmes into the village and had clubbed people. Her behavior had a seriously negative effect and astonished even me, leaving taints. It diminished my love for Tahtı Halil village and for Eze herself. But this episode also helped form my hatred of wicked and unjust fighting.

Quarrels in the village had always made me fearful, but this horrible fight in Tahtı Halil left the deepest scars in me. In Höpük, where we spent our summer vacations for several years, fighting would erupt for entirely mundane reasons. The people stopped talking to each other and had it out. Often the cause was the provocative behavior of some women, who had reacted mindlessly and emotionally to something and thereby stirred up a little disagreement into a fracas with bashed-in heads and bloody faces. Since these women had caused unrest in the village, no one wanted them around. I didn't like them either and was angry at them even from a distance. Their fractiousness seemed senseless to me.

That summer was the last time my family was in my grandmother's village. For whatever reason, we returned to our village early. A month before vacation began, we were enrolled in the village school in Kavun. The city was unbearable in the summertime, oppressively hot. And my mother wanted to bake bread in the village and make butter and çökelek²⁴ from the sheep and cow milk that she got from my grandmother. In the village everything was free. In contrast to city life, staying in the village was like having another source of income besides my father's.

My uncles and aunts also came to this village every summer. My grandmother's relations to my family were somewhat shaped by the fact that my mother was her oldest daughter by far and not so close to her siblings. My father was idiosyncratic in this respect. For him, family ties didn't transcend everything else. He valued human relations in general and was open to other people. As a lowly clerk, he was concerned with his own affairs and didn't care for deviousness and flattery. He didn't place much value on material things. He was satisfied with what he had.

Sometimes my grandmother showed greater tolerance for certain children, which my mother would make into a problem. Sometimes it even led to friction. One day an ugly quarrel broke out between my mother and my aunt Sakine in front of everyone. The conflict escalated and drew in my father and my aunt's husband, who up until then had

had peaceful relations. Chaos prevailed. Even after my mother went to do the milking, no peace returned.

The last straw came when my aunt insulted my father. Up until then my father had been involved only verbally, but now he got to his feet, and the next thing I knew, he'd fallen to the ground, bleeding. My uncle, my aunts, and my grandmother were all hitting him cruelly. I screamed and cried. My big brother was still very young, but he screeched too, threw stones, and shouted, "Stop it!" But no one listened to him. Finally Mehmet and his wife Fatma, who worked for my grandmother in the fields, stepped in and rescued my father. He looked frightening with all that blood, and they rushed him to the hospital in the city.

It was a terrible episode. All the participants in the fight were related. I was horrified. How could it happen that everyone was hitting him over nothing, as if they wanted to kill him? When my mother heard about it, she came running in with a rock in her hand, but she was too late.

Thinking of this incident still fills me with pain, and my tears rise. That everyone could gang up on my father that way affected me deeply. Inside I was furious at my mother. I also felt sorry for her, but my rage prevailed, because she was the one who had instigated the fight. But it was my father who had been beaten up, and everyone who participated was a relative of my mother.

After that we couldn't stay in the village any longer. We went back to the city right away. My father had been hit in the forehead and in the back of his head. He was depressed and went into decline. He was angry at my mother, and he showed it, even without saying much. My mother admitted she was at fault and begged him for forgiveness. My father was not one to hold grudges. Even while he still suffered from the effects of this incident, he gradually forgave everyone. He even reconciled with most of them. The relatives, including my youngest maternal uncle, understood how distressing and senseless the fight had been and showed remorse.

For me, this episode led me to think a lot about the role of women in fighting and to draw my own conclusions.

Advice from my mother: "Don't be ashamed to be Kurdish!" My father managed to get us an apartment in state housing, reserved for civil servants, for people who worked for public authorities. It was rent-free—you only had to pay for electricity and water, but we didn't have money for rent anyway. Those who had the right connections and careers under way got the bigger and better flats. Ours was in the attic and consisted of two rooms and a wooden shed. On the same hallway were two more apartments where families lived.

Living in state housing in Dersim, and working in a state institution, gave a person a reputation for being connected to the state. Our Turkification was accelerated by our milieu. We lived among families of civil servants and police, who were Turks themselves or spoke Turkish well. For us, in some ways it was like a continuation of school. Of course we thought of that as an advantage. By now we could speak Turkish well ourselves.

I pressured my family to speak Turkish at home too, so my mother could learn it faster and the neighbors wouldn't laugh at her anymore. I even said to her, "When you make mistakes in speaking, it embarrasses me." In reply, she told me not to be ashamed of my Kurdish heritage. In later years, when I was more aware of Kurdishness and the reality of

1 Cansız in fifth grade, 1970. In Turkey, the Day of the Child falls on April 23. She is seated symbolically at the desk of the National Education Authority.

Kurdistan, I would remember her words and regret my earlier shame. I had become estranged, I would realize then, from my own native tongue.

The housing where we lived had previously been part of a military camp. My father told us that in those days, he and the other kids went every day from the village into the city to go to primary school. On the way home, if they were blocked by snow, they spent the night in the camp's basement. After new military buildings were erected, the old ones turned into employee apartments. Apart from the gray walls, nothing there suggested the military anymore. The water basins in the yard were filled in with soil, and the trees were no more.

The residential block that had a view of the city center was three stories tall, while the other buildings had only two. They were like boxes stacked between rocks overlooking the Munzur River. Inside were a lot of corridors and stairways, and the paths leading everywhere. I liked the middle courtyard the best. On a nearby hill was a restaurant with a view, and beyond that an open-air cinema. Not everyone could go into the restaurant, only rich people with important guests. The view was stunning, opening out over the winding Munzur, with rows of houses in the lower neighborhood with their green yards. The streets were very good and the architecture was distinctive.

The governor's house stood just at a bend in the river. It was the only two-story house in the neighborhood. In the nearby houses lived higher-grade civil servants. The neighborhood was like a barrier that separated the state from Dersim. The governor lived there, and the district administrator, the chief of police, and other high-ranking bureaucrats and employees. It was like it wasn't really in Dersim. The neighborhood lay along the riverbank, and all the houses had gardens. It would have made more sense if people indigenous to this area had been able to use these lands. But as it was, the neighborhood was always cold, distant, and alien to us. The children there, the women and men, their language and culture, were all different. Walking there felt like intruding into a restricted military zone or a police station. Even the air there made us afraid.

And then there were the officers' quarters. They were in the military camp on the side of the bridge going to Elazığ; they were multistory apartment houses in camouflage colors.

The city had been founded on a small plain at the foot of Düldül Hill. On the far side was another hillside, a gentler slope concentrated with huts. Dağ neighborhood was on a hill alongside Düldül Hill. The Demiroluk and Hastane neighborhoods lay at the city's entrance. The city had a hospital, a high school, a girls' trade school, and a general trade school—Dersim was a city with many schools.

On the western side of the camp lay the Orman neighborhood, where more apartment buildings stood next to official installations. The buildings of the forest management and the military battalion were most prominent. The Teachers School was on the other side of the Munzur, in Kalan-Mamiki district. It was the most splendid building on the far shore, right next to the Gazi neighborhood.

The Munzur divides the city the way the Rhine divides Cologne. It flows into the Harçik River at Lake Xızır. It was used as a pilgrimage site. Especially on Wednesdays almost the whole city would make a pilgrimage there. *Xızır vo* [Zazaki for "at Xızır"] was one of the pledges we learned as children. Deep whirlpools roil its waters, terrifying us. Some young men had drowned there—maybe that was why this place was a pilgrimage site. Doesn't faith mean that people pray for something that they can't understand or control, or whose secrets they can't penetrate? Maybe that's why every Wednesday people lit candles there, and brought animal sacrifices and votive offerings.

In the place where the candles burned away, an oily layer had been built up. People attached stones or coins there, while making a wish. If a stone or the coin fell away, the wish wouldn't come true. But because the layer was soft and sticky, most of the wishes were answered. I went often to this site. Once I attached 25 *kuruş* [Turkish coins] to the spot and asked Xızır to make sure I got a good grade on a written test, which I then proceeded to pass.

In this context faith worked its influence on me. I was too young to know much about the culture and nature of Alevism. But at home a giant framed portrait of the prophet Ali hung on the wall. My father was a *pir* [Alevi wise one] and in that capacity carried on the tradition of the Kureyşan tribe. We also had a *pir* who was in charge of us. If he visited us, we lined up in a row by age with our father at the head and folded our hands. As I remember, first the *pir* knelt down and said a prayer, and then we kissed the ground, and then his feet and hands. I disliked this ceremony, so I didn't participate very often.

My father didn't act like other *pirs*—he never went to see his *talips* [Arabic for followers]. Normally the *talips* listened to a *pir*'s prayers and then handed him the desired gift. But we did just the opposite. The *talip* came to us in order to get help from my father. They brought along a pitcher of yogurt or a bowl of butter from the village, and my father gave them basic provisions like sugar, soap, and more. Whoever needed it would also get a small sum of money. I loved my father all the more for this. I always believed he performed good deeds. It touched me that he helped people. Sometimes my mother would get annoyed and say he shouldn't let the people get used to all this.

My father resisted other things. Once he criticized *pirs* who were affluent yet still came every year to demand their presents or money. Once while my father was home on vacation from Germany, a *pir* visited, and my father asked amiably,

> My *pir*, I'd like to ask a question, but I don't want to hurt anyone. I work in the homeland of the infidels, and I save every *kuruş* for my children. It's not bad for them, they all go to school, but their father isn't home. They need some affection. Have you ever asked after my children? Or handed them a little pocket money? Isn't that what a *pir* is? Immaterial values are of the greatest importance. You shouldn't remember you're a *pir* only when I come back from Germany.

I was at an age where I questioned a lot of things and was looking for answers. My father had criticized things that I didn't like either. That *pir* never came to see us again.

Pilgrimage route to Düzgün Baba   But my father's attachment to the religion was striking. Every year he made a pilgrimage to Düzgün Baba. At first, while we were living in the village, he took us along with him. We walked in the summer heat for three days. To go barefoot was considered particularly pious. That was the faith of Düzgün Baba. You couldn't get to him by comfortable paths. Many people fasted and wore mourning clothes. Their goals varied: some hoped to recover from an incurable illness, while others wished for children.

Düzgün Baba is a very tall mountain peak. On the way to the place of pilgrimage, you passed villages full of almond trees, beautiful gardens, and springs. At the entrance is the Hınıyı Xaskar, the Haskar spring, a small rocky cavern among the rocks. It was said that whenever sinners stood in front of the spring, it dried up. So those who drank from it were in a certain psychological state. Commentary wasn't permitted, but the secret was easy to explain: the water was at best only a trickle, and when many people drank one after another, little or none would be left. After climbing up the rise, people were always thirsty, so they often drank several gulps of water instead of just one, and so there wasn't enough for everyone.

And sometimes the snow that fed the spring had all melted away, so no water trickled out. Seeing it dry plunged visitors into despair. They racked their brains to figure out what sin they'd committed. They had bad dreams, and the whole pilgrimage became a nightmare. Rumors spread in the person's village. For anyone revealed as a sinner in the face of Düzgün Baba, their ideal world collapsed, and it took a long time before things improved again.

I once witnessed an astonishing incident at Düzgün Baba, involving my father's relatively materialistic mindset. A group of pilgrims arrived that included a family. They caught my eye because normally not many young people made the pilgrimage—it was more middle-aged people, or children my age, and elders who could still walk that far in the thin mountain air. Few young people seemed to seek out Düzgün Baba. In any case, this family I'm talking about came from Istanbul. They were a Turkish family, including a young man. My father struck up a conversation with him, and they got into a deep discussion. My father spoke as if he were imparting wisdom: "Now my son, we're from an old tradition, and we've been coming here for years. But you're young, a university student. Tell me, what has brought you here from Istanbul?" The young man, it turned out, had come because of his faith. A year earlier he'd been very sick, and no doctor could cure him. Finally a neighbor who was an Alevi from Dersim had suggested he make a pilgrimage to Düzgün Baba. So he came with his family, and after he got back to Istanbul, he was perfectly healthy. So after that, his family swore to make the visit once a year.

After the young man finished, my father broke into laughter. As they kept talking, everyone who understood Turkish gathered around the two of them. My father told a story from his childhood in Tahtı Halil village.

When I was 9, I came down with malaria, running a high fever. I was the only child in the family, so my parents were weeping copiously. All the villagers came over and wailed, "Oh no, oh no, the child is dying." Listening to that made it even worse for me. Later people even came from Şekerman village.

Then an old man pushed through the crowd of people, felt my fever with his hand, and said, "Take the boy to the Sogayik cemetery. Let him eat some soil from the grave of Hüseyin, and let him bathe in water from the spring there. Then he'll recover with no damage." His words revived my spirits and my own faith that I'd get better. While I was burning with fever, my parents had wrapped me tightly in multiple blankets and tried to heal me that way. They didn't realize I had malaria. But when we went to the spring in the cemetery, the cold water helped by reducing the fever. By the time we returned to the village, I was hopping and playing as usual.

My father was trying to show that healing has two sides: at the threshold between life and death, faith and the corresponding psychological state can help a person decide for life, but there is also a scientific explanation, as cold water reduces malarial fever. The young man from Istanbul had come with the faith that he would recover, but beyond that, the air and water quality at Düzgün Baba was very good. Eating fresh meat and yogurt contributed to better health. All contributed to his recovery.

My father's time in Germany had no negative impact on his faith. On the contrary, it even deepened. In Germany he wrote poems and songs of longing for his homeland. And he visited Düzgün Baba every year.

My father went to Germany in 1969, so we couldn't stay in our state housing any longer. His colleague Ali moved into our apartment, but he wanted to pick up his family from the village at a later time. Until then we could continue living there. During the summer vacation, we went back to the village. An episode from that time affected me profoundly.

It was one of these long, hot summer days in Dersim. At the cinema one evening, there was to be no film but something quite different: a theatrical production called *Pir Sultan Abdal*[5] was to be performed by the Ankara Contemporary Theater Group. The tickets were sold out days in advance, posters were hung everywhere, and there had been a lot of advertising. I'd never been in a theater before—that art form was alien to us—but I imagined it would be something like the plays and sketches we acted out in school. I knew about Pir Sultan Abdal pretty well from songs and stories. My father sang very beautiful lyrics by Pir Sultan, accompanying himself on the *saz*.

Shortly before sundown, the theatergoers walked through the streets toward the cinema and assembled there, outside. Many knew each other, some had studied together in high schools in Ankara and elsewhere. Our "leftist big brothers" were also present, which caused some tension. All that day a minibus with an Ankara license plate had been driving through the neighborhoods announcing the play, talking it up, urging residents to go see it. So now more and more people arrived. The mood in a few spots got tense. Suddenly, as people were pressing toward the cinema, a black Renault careened through. People standing at all the windows were looking down at the street. We children were waiting to get in line in a half-circle just outside the crowd. A tumult arose in front of the cinema. Everyone pushed and jostled, voices were raised. We liked the clamor a lot—it was exciting. But many of the mothers grew afraid and decided to take their children home. I didn't want to leave, though my friends were saying I should. I was 11 at the time.

The wailing sirens of the careening black Renault incited a panic. Then an announcement blared: "Attention, attention! The governor's office has banned the *Pir Sultan* play. We urge you to disperse immediately." Almost before it ended, cries of "boo" were heard, and the car was pelted with stones. Then came the words "Governor—resign!" Chaos erupted. More police arrived, and the first arrests were made. The people raised fists in the air and shouted slogans. The clashes with the police were sensational—I was afraid and excited all at once. I wanted to creep up closer and see who the police were beating up. Women and children were screaming all around.

From a distance I'd guessed it was Uncle Ali—Ali Gültekin—and I wasn't wrong. During the brawl sometimes the policeman was on top and sometimes Ali Gültekin was, as if they were wrestling. The crowd and the police were now clashing fiercely. More police came. They forced Ali Gültekin into the police wagon and drove away with him. His brother Veli had tried to wrest him free of the police hands. So now they went after him. But he was a fantastic guy. He ripped off his shirt with both hands and shouted at the top of his lungs, "Hit me, man—shoot! Whoever doesn't hit me a son of a b——!"

The police began beating Veli with clubs and gun butts. One of them sneered, "You Moscow brute! Red Communist! Who's gonna save you now! Your people from Moscow gonna come and save you?" Then Veli was dragged away too.

Veli was a brave man from the village. He may not even have known who his "people in Moscow" were supposed to be, had never hard of them. He would probably have understood if they had referred to Russians. But what did he know of Moscow! Whatever he understood, the fact was that the police had said nothing good, and mentioning Moscow and Communism was intended as an insult.

The clash was spreading. Slogans were shouted continuously, and stones were thrown. The police continued their violent attack. All of Dersim was soon caught up in it. The police filled their wagons with prisoners and hauled them away. In the meantime the crowd had started moving. As if commanded, the scattered groups took to the street and marched in a fury, shouting slogans, with raised fists. I felt sorry for my uncles Ali and Veli and began to cry. But this mass rebellion and the pent-up rage didn't leave me cold. My inchoate fear gradually eased. The crowd that had gathered was strong and fearless. For a time I ran alongside the demonstration. Earlier, when my mother called to me from the window, I'd ignored her. Now I jumped through the window into the house, scuffing the varnish on the frame. I kept thinking about the cop who had hit Uncle Ali. He lived next door to us! He was our neighbor, I knew him—how could he do such a thing? I'd been in his home with his kids a lot of times. We were schoolmates. Our mothers visited each other too. Not that we were particularly close as neighbors—they were reticent because they didn't trust us. The police just weren't very much beloved by the inhabitants. Still, up until this episode, our relations with the police family had been distant yet neighborly.

I told my mother about the situation. At first she didn't want to believe me, and then she tried to downplay it all. I swore I'd never visit those neighbors again.

For the longest time, the images of my uncles Ali and Veli and the others getting beaten up and waging a unified resistance stuck in my mind. Ali and Veli were taken to the police station. While they were still on the street, I'd seen the policeman tear at Uncle Veli's mustache and say, "I'm going to rip out your whiskers one by one. You Moscow brute!" It occurred to me that his chest was pretty hairy and that they'd tear out his chest hairs too, one by one. I was sad because that would hurt him a lot. My mother knocked on the neighbor's door and tried to soothe them. "Nothing happened—don't be afraid." But I couldn't understand it. Was it a crime to be the child or the wife of a police officer? This was the cop who'd beaten up Uncle Ali, Uncle Veli, and the others. And he'd insulted them all horribly. I came to the conclusion that all police were the same, and so were their families.

On that day the shouting of slogans never let up. The police station was in the Demiroluk neighborhood, near the MİT building. You could always hear shots coming from there. It made us afraid. My mother talked to the neighbor women—none of their husbands were at home. My brother and my uncle Hüseyin had also not come home. Then we heard something that set the whole camp in motion: Mehmet Kılan had been shot!

Mehmet Kılan was the brother of Emine, the wife of Uncle Hasan. We ran to their house. There everyone was crying. My uncle said he'd been with Mehmet Kılan just a little earlier, they'd drunk alcohol together. He couldn't believe he'd been shot. Mehmet Kılan was middle-aged—why would anyone want to shoot him? He didn't do anyone any harm and kept to himself. The news spread like wildfire.

As we later learned, a large crowd had gathered in front of the police station, demanding the release of those arrested. Then Hasan Küçükoba, a young man from our village, burned a Turkish flag. The police used it as a pretext to shoot indiscriminately, but the crowd wouldn't disperse. The unrest spread to the rest of the city, where people sought refuge from the police bullets.

Later we found out how Mehmet Kılan had died. He'd drunk a lot, it was said, and when he heard that the play had been banned, and about the arrests, he headed over to help calm things down. Carrying a white handkerchief, he was going to say,

Look, the young ones are mad because they can't see the play. Okay, so they overdid it a little. But that doesn't mean you can stir things up like this. If the play hadn't been banned, this fighting wouldn't be happening. The kids have reason to be angry. They paid for tickets and went to the theater. What did you expect, by canceling the piece at the last minute? The actors from Ankara had all arrived. The performance had official approval. The play had already been performed all over the place, so why not here?

He couldn't have known he'd be the martyr of that day ...

While he was running along the street, a cop at a window trained a gun on him and waited. As he came closer, he stuck his hand into a pocket to pull out his white handkerchief—and at that moment he was shot. So simple, and so senseless!

His death further enraged the group who were fighting near the police station. The slogan "Mehmet Kılan will never die" rang throughout Dersim. I kept wondering why they would say a dead man was alive. What did it mean? How did those who were martyred become immortal?

Later the police brought reinforcements from Elazığ and Erzincan provinces, and an indefinite curfew was imposed on Dersim. Tension and fear of more deaths persisted into the morning hours. The city center was closed off—you couldn't get through there. Gendarmes and police swarmed through the streets, searching the whole area and arresting anyone who had had anything to do with the riots. Many of the young people, trying to leave the city for the countryside, were trapped in police ambushes and carted away.

The whole night was like a nightmare. By sunrise we could see better how the curfew was being enforced. In the early morning soldiers had occupied the surroundings of the camp. As soon as my mother pulled back the curtain at the window, a gun barrel was pointed at her. She screeched and jumped back from the window. We were curious, but my mother was terrified. She began to clean the house, to distract the soldiers, so they wouldn't be suspicious of us. When I looked out the window, I saw the whole area was full of soldiers. Every two steps, a soldier was standing with a weapon at the ready. Not a civilian was in sight. Anyone who dared to step outside was immediately taken away.

Suddenly there came a loud knock at the door, and a deep voice thundered, "House inspection. Open the door! Anyone who resists will be shot!"

Our house was the third to the right of the entrance. Apparently the first house wasn't searched—the police had passed over it and come straight to us. As soon as the door was opened, they stormed in with their boots like a pack of wolves. First they asked about my father. My mother said he was in Germany. There was no other male in the flat who interested them. My elder brother was still very young, he didn't call a lot of attention to himself, but if they'd known he hadn't come back home till midnight, they'd doubtless have taken him away.

My mother murmured that she'd only just cleaned the house and why had they come in wearing shoes? The commander roared, "Woman, we wear shoes wherever we go! You are no exception." It was a threat. He was telling us not to expect any favors and to keep our mouths shut. They rushed through their inspection, tossing things every which way. What they were looking for was unclear. They even pulled up the carpets and looked underneath. Pillows, sheets, laundry baskets—everything was strewn around the floor. And they stomped on everything with their big boots. When they were finished, they slammed the door with a loud crash on the way out.

The inspection of the camp lasted for hours. The halls were full of people, some crying as the soldiers stormed around, and the sound of boots stomping didn't let up. It was an extraordinary day.

Hours later news spread through the corridors: Ali Ekber from Mazgirt—who came from the same village as Kemal Burkay—Metin Güngörmüş, Rıza, and Erdal had been arrested. What had they had to do with the riots? Their arrests could only mean that they'd resisted the police and shouted slogans. These young men had taken a stand against the state! Interest in and sympathy for them grew. Everyone speculated who might still get arrested and who had really been involved in these events. Questions mingled with tension and fear persisted for a long time.

Those arrested became like our big brothers—we loved and honored them. They were brilliant revolutionaries. Some new words appeared in our lives, sensational and dangerous: *communist, leftist, revolutionary.* Many posters bore slogans with the signature "TİP."[26] And there was something else: on the concrete base of the suspension bridge to our village was written in big red letters: "AK-PAK Günlere. TİP."[27] I didn't know what it meant, but I read it again every time I passed by. These new things raised many questions in my mind.

The police station was located in the Demiroluk neighborhood. People in the houses nearby could hear the sounds of torture. Those who were taken there during the riots were detained for a long time and tortured. Veli's red mustache really was ripped out. A cigarette was stubbed out into his chest, it was said. But after his release, he let his mustache grow back, long and strong, and he once again looked like he was "from Moscow." And he was proud and even more interested in everything than before. Veli, who had been a simple man back in his village, now studied to be a red Communist, to be "someone from Moscow." He also grew closer to his big brother, Ali. It takes a hero to stand up to the state and shake his fist at it.

During the torture, it was said, the eardrum of Ali Ekber, from the Pilvenk tribe, was torn. Once he was released, he kept sticking cotton into his ear and couldn't hear very well anymore. For days and months afterward, people in Dersim talked of ripped foot soles and wounds caused by burning cigarettes. They commiserated with the tortured and honored them as heroes.

The events affected the families. People in Dersim inevitably associated the state with 1938, for it was during that year of brutal massacres, savage repression, and deportations that they had become acquainted with the state. They had learned to distrust it, and to distrust "others," because they witnessed betrayals. People like Rayber[28] had betrayed friends and relatives. The tribes hadn't supported each other—someone who smiled at you one day stabbed you in the back the next. Promises were broken, as if defeat and capitulation were fated. Everything had been lost in 1938, whether through heroism or treachery. A line in the sand had been drawn.

A new Dersim? "For heaven's sake, may Düzgün Baba make sure we never live through such days again!" People also saw what had happened next door, in Elazığ, Bingöl, and Erzincan. There was no security and no trust. Dersim had gradually entombed itself in its own pain. That was reflected in the way people moaned, what had Sheikh Said done,[29] and what should others have done? He hadn't been able to pull it off. People like Alîşêr and Besê were only legends.[30] The people wanted never to experience such sorrow again. The state thoroughly entrenched itself. The true essence of people in Dersim was stunted. A few young people acted with the enthusiasm typical of their age, but they were ignorant, and their cockiness would only get them into trouble. This state was a traitor-state. It had never supported the people of Dersim, let alone trusted them. It had shot or hanged, one by one, even the most rotten traitors—it had no use even for the people who had turned their backs on their own heritage and cravenly delivered their own people to the knife. The state knew the people of Dersim well. Kurdishness was finally dead and buried with them.

But this new unrest caused people in Dersim to think once again of that time more than thirty years earlier. Would the state unleash a new '38? Would the young people once again be deceived? Who was behind this? These questions were on everyone's lips.

In the Demir family there were three or four young men. Haşim, the oldest, was a student in Ankara. Metin Güngörmüş also went to college. They were most influenced by outside ideas—their minds had been opened. But the children of the Söylemez family were more conventional—they were influenced by their parents and didn't rock the boat. The father was braver than the children. That was true of the Çetins as well. The young people were well educated and went on to higher education, but they'd been raised like Turkish children. Their mother was Turkish, and the father was even more Turkish than the mother.

The children of Osman Mutlu were politically right wing. Osman Mutlu, like other families living in state housing, was himself a pillar of the state. Their neighbors talked to them warily, with restraint, watching their words. They were calculating. The only ones with whom such families had good relations were their fellow pillars of the state. They behaved toward their peers and the police and their families very differently from the way they related to the natives. Many kept aloof from their neighbors, although some tried to mix. They didn't even particularly like the flatterers among the natives. No one trusted them, even if that was never said aloud.

This recent episode revealed everyone's true colors. Now people in Dersim knew who was on which side. It was like a litmus test. Dersim was fragmenting, as people chose sides. This division penetrated even into daily life, affecting visits and the distribution of sacrificial meat, aşure,[31] and other gifts. Those who were disliked were given less and thereby shown that they were valued less. Even at births, weddings, and other ceremonies, they received no gifts and no visitors. People took sides, and those on the same side drew closer together. Osman Mutlu's daughter Şenay was no longer included in our games, in jump rope, hide and seek, and our dances. As for the police families, only a few police children played with us, the children of the "good police." Their parents forbade them to play with others.

"Oh my child, Hüseyin Cevahir has been shot!" My third-grade teacher, Edibe Abacıoğlu, was chubby yet nimble. She wore glasses and was a clever teacher. She had Arab heritage and smoked like a chimney, but her purple lips broke into a lovely smile. I liked her a lot and have never forgotten her. At that time, I had beautiful handwriting, error free and easily readable, so she always let me write out the schedules and the attendance lists. I was class speaker too. When she wasn't present, it was I who wrote out the day's schedule on the blackboard. I was fairly tall and could reach the upper blackboard.

The school's director was our neighbor Mazlum Kaya. At another point Mustafa Söylemez served as director. I loved him like my father, and he was like my father in certain respects. He was also the teacher of my elder brother's class. Our families were friends. We came from the same area. His wife Ayşe worked in health services, as a nurse and midwife. She was cute, energetic, lively, intelligent, and much beloved. Mustafa Söylemez was quiet but very astute.

My class's teacher lived in the neighborhood below ours. Her husband was a government official, and they had two sons: the older was in middle school, the younger in primary school. She frankly wished she'd had daughters. My classmates Nesibe and Feride lived in the same neighborhood; they were Turks and felt close to our teacher. I liked both of them very much and we had good friendships. Nesibe was calm, while Feride was more capricious.

Our teacher was imperious. She could teach well and worked hard for us. But she was also irritable. When students didn't do their homework or came to class with dirty fingernails, handkerchiefs, and hands, she pulled their ears and sometimes smacked them with a ruler. She didn't do that often, only when she was really annoyed, and even then only sometimes.

In Dersim, we had drinking water only on certain days, usually in the morning. The other water wasn't clean and couldn't be used for drinking. In the lower neighborhood most people had domestics or hired day workers to do the cleaning. Really no one was eager to work in these houses. Certain women would go around the houses one by one and do the necessary work. My teacher had them clean her house and do the laundry. Over time I got to know her and her life outside the school better.

One day during class, she looked at her watch and exclaimed, "Ah Sakine, my child, come here." Her "ah" made everyone excited. I rushed up to her. She pulled a key ring out of her pocket and singled out a key for me.

See this key? Don't get it mixed up with the others—see, there's a T on it. Take it and go to my house. You know the house—you've been there to wish us good holidays. As you open the door, to the right you'll see a basin and a hose. Use the hose to fill the basin. Take the basin into the kitchen. Be careful the water doesn't spill, otherwise the oven will rust. Use it to fill the canisters and jars in the kitchen. Then come back here. Kamil isn't home, and I don't want to be without water when I get home later.

I ran to her house, opened the door, and filled the basin and the canisters as she'd instructed. But I noticed the house was very messy. The kitchen was unusable because of all the piled-up dirty dishes. On the shelf there were hardly any clean bowls. The other rooms were no better. Nightclothes and pajamas were strewn around, and the ashtrays were overflowing. Would it be right for me to go through the whole house without permission? I couldn't decide. It might be misunderstood. But my teacher was old, and besides, she had no daughters. I just couldn't leave the house in this condition. So I decided to wash the dishes very fast. I put them all on a big brass tray, separating the spoons, plates, and glasses. I filled the basin and rinsed everything with clean water all at once. Even though I was working alone, I got everything spick and span in no time. Then I ran back to school, where the class was half over. I handed my teacher the key. She thanked me somewhat abashedly and stroked my head, and I sat back down.

I was elated by her thanks and ecstatic thinking of the joy she'd feel, after the class was over, at seeing her clean house. I liked anticipating her delight while she didn't yet know anything about it. When I got home, I told my mother, and she was happy too.

The next morning my teacher beamed at me—I could see it even from a distance—as if she wanted to take me in her arms. She actually pressed my head against her bosom and patted my shoulder.

My child, did you do all that work? But how did you do it so fast? And what a wonder you performed! I can't clean anywhere near as well. And you put all the dishes in order. Do you do this at your house? What kind of a woman is your mother? I absolutely must stop by and congratulate her on her daughter!

She said a few more things, almost as if she were talking to herself. It felt awkward, but I was thrilled to have made her so happy. Finally I could be sure I'd done something good.

My teacher even talked about it in the staff room. She'd told her guests about it, she showed my handiwork to her husband and her children, and she praised me everywhere, as if I'd done who knew what. One day she invited me to her house to introduce me to her neighbors. I brought along my classmate Aysel Ağırcan. First she kissed us, then her other guests kissed us too, or else contented themselves with extending their hands. At her invitation, we sat down among the women and let them serve us. But as they distributed the glasses of tea, I couldn't endure it and stood up to help. They insisted that I was their guest and must touch nothing. Abashed, I ate their little dumplings with yogurt. Everyone scrutinized me to see how I sat, how I drank tea, and how I ate. That made me even more self-conscious, so I nibbled very carefully, using a small spoon for the yogurt pastries and a fork for the cakes. I managed to avoid spilling anything or otherwise embarrassing myself. This as well as being skilled at housework gave me confidence, my embarrassment eased, and I could speak more freely.

After that episode, I went to her home a few more times to fill the water canisters. Aysel Ağırcan came with me, but she didn't care as

2 Cansız with school friends, c.1974. *Left to right:* Perihan Gündüz, Cansız, Aysel Ağırcan, Zülfiye Kortik, Nurcan Gündüz, Yemoş Güzel. *Front:* Aysun Ağırcan.

much about the tasks at hand. Instead she looked around. She studied the wooden cigarette box in the guest room for a long time. And she found a music box—when you opened the lid, music played, and the female figures spun around. And even as young as she was, Aysel found the cigarettes interesting. She put one in her mouth and lit it with a lighter from the cigarette box. The first inhale made her cough. I laughed but also scolded her, because it didn't seem right to take a cigarette and smoke it without permission. But Aysel didn't stop there. She ate some of the rice pudding in the icebox and then filled the container with water, to make it look like nothing was missing. That was another trespass. I told her that if the teacher noticed, she'd never trust us again. Ashamed, I broke into a sweat. Then Aysel handed me a bonbon from a candy box that was for guests. I tried to resist, but I accepted it.

Once when I went there by myself, my teacher's husband was there. He'd just awakened. I wanted to leave right after I filled the water. But he told me to wait and wanted to put two and a half lira in my bag. I didn't accept it, but it was very embarrassing. It seemed like a reward for help. Thinking about it, it irritated me. I wasn't a servant who did housework for money. I helped my teacher because I liked her. This feeling arose unconsciously, spontaneously. My teacher never asked me to take care of the water again, since the times of water allocation had changed.

On the Aşure month, I brought my teacher and her family a small pot of *aşure*.[32] The next day, when I went back to retrieve the pot, I saw that they'd dumped the sweets into the trash. Inside I was fuming. They didn't want the *aşure* we'd made! It was a sin to throw it away. I couldn't believe my teacher had done such a thing.

My sisters were twins. That winter we kept a cow in our shed, to provide milk for them. My teacher regularly bought a half-liter of milk from us. It was hard in those times to obtain it. When she heard we had a cow, she'd asked to buy milk from us. No way could she have it for free, but I delivered the milk to her at home.

One day my teacher came to visit. She hugged and kissed my mother and asked how she'd raised me. She'd been talking about me everywhere. My mother answered in her bad Turkish. When she faltered, I jumped in. My mother's poor articulation was always a source of embarrassment for me. I could not understand why I was embarrassed, but I was. As soon as my teacher stepped inside our door and took in our large room, she grasped our poverty. But she wasn't looking for comfort—her home was simple too. We were a working-class family and we were clean. I thought that impressed her. After she made this visit, I liked her again.

In the fifth grade I learned many new things. Over the radio, news announcers were reporting on some events that I didn't understand and couldn't figure out. They often started out saying, "In a clash with terrorists ..." and ended with a death or arrest. The announcers spoke in very serious tones and gave the names and addresses of the people who were being sought.

At our house no one listened to the radio regularly or read newspapers. We got old newspapers from shops or from neighbors and used them to line our shelves. But I studied them with great interest. I spent hours at the shelves, to my mother's annoyance. One newspaper had color photos of Sibel Erkan, a young girl who had been captured by "terrorists." The photos showed the occupied buildings with the "terrorists" barely visible at the windows, and the commentary took up most the newspaper column.[33]

A young girl had been seized and was being held hostage. I didn't know why or what it would lead to. It was mostly interpreted through categories of "left" and "right." The captors were apparently leftists. They'd turned against the state—like the young people in the *Pir Sultan Abdal* affair. The news reports said the house had been surrounded, there were calls for surrender, and it would be only a matter of time before the "terrorists" were captured. That made me sad. I felt sorry for them, interpreting the events superficially based on what I'd seen and experienced in Dersim.

One day I stopped by my teacher's house, and we walked to school together. As we parted, she glanced at the newspaper and cried out, "Oh my child, that's not possible. Kamil, look, see what's happened. They've killed the young man. Hüseyin Cevahir has been shot!"[34] Her words frightened me. The police had shot him dead. My teacher asked me if I knew Haydar Koç. "Isn't he from your tribe?" Haydar Koç was from Mazgirt, from Kavun village or thereabouts. He was a leader of the Kureyşan tribe who was now close to the state, so he was regarded as a collaborator and traitor. The young people particularly disliked him.

But the Cevahirs were good people. Hüseyin Cevahir was dead, he was shot. My teacher tried to help me understand: "He was one of the captors of Sibel Erkan, they lived a floor above. There was a shootout with the police. It's too bad, they were so young," she clucked sympathetically.

On the way home from school, I couldn't get the pain in her voice when she learned of the death of Hüseyin Cevahir out of my head. In Ankara a young man from Dersim, whose family I knew, had been shot.

Everyone in our building already knew about it—bad news travels fast, and so did this news of death. Some said the body would be brought to Dersim. The first condolence visits were already being made. Every day the apartments of the city-dwelling relatives were crammed with so many people who came to express their sympathy.

For us, it was difficult to continue living in state housing. My father had already been in Germany for a long time. His colleague wanted finally to bring his family out of the village and needed space. So we moved into a rental apartment in a new building in the Dağ neighborhood.

The man who traveled the seas?   In Dağ, I started secondary school, in part of the Tunceli high school building that was set aside for it.

The radio and the newspapers reported more unrest. I kept hearing the names of Deniz Gezmiş and his group.[35] His was only one of many names, but he was mentioned the most often and attracted the most attention. At first I thought they were talking about a man who had traveled the seas.[36] I didn't understand why so much was said of this man, but more and more he dominated the news reports.

On the main streets posters were hung with photos of the group around Deniz Gezmiş and personal information about them. The people examined the images with great interest. "What a heroic fellow!" they said to each other. They really did look like heroes, with determined looks and bold postures. Each one was beautiful in his own way, and their eyes gleamed with hope and struggle. They had challenging expressions on their faces. Consciously or not, everyone was impressed by them. Not much more was known about what they'd done. They were called "terrorists" and "Communists on the run," or they were vilified as murderers, thieves, and criminals. A large reward was offered for information leading to their capture. But surely no one with a conscience could betray them. Did such callous, inhuman people really exist?

On my way to school, I looked curiously at the posters that hung on a signboard on a utility pole at an intersection. After I read the caption "Reward for information leading to their whereabouts," I noticed a crowd of people on the street. I studied each one, as if I could tell by looking who would be capable of doing that. Many of them averted their pained eyes, while others looked happy, and still others whispered among themselves what splendid young guys they were. At that moment I decided to come back here during recess with a few girlfriends and tear the posters down. Maybe we couldn't tear them all down, but there were places all around where we could. Another poster hung next to the hospital entrance. That would be simpler, since we could enter the building at the ground floor without a problem. Of course entry to the upper floors was probably barred.

At recess my friends and I got to work, tearing down as many posters as we could. They were attached with strong glue and had been posted higher than our heads. The easiest to remove were those at the hospital. But the matter didn't end there. We figured no more posters would be hung, and so none of the fugitives could be found. They were very childish thoughts.

But no! Revolt was sown in the middle of our childhood. The events under way threw our worlds of feeling and thought into confusion. We learned new things. Already in the first days of the first term of middle school, I ended up in a rebellion.[37] It was raining lightly that day, and excitement broke out in the schoolyard. As we watched, the "big brothers" ran around calling together scattered groups of people who everyone knew and loved. They met at times outside the crowd, talked in low tones, then scattered again.

Suddenly the mood changed. I heard names of Ali Yeşil, Hasan, and Metin—seniors in the high school. Had the police taken them? Suddenly police units poured into the schoolyard. Our teacher and the deputy director Şinasi Eskiçırak, acting in the director's absence, shouted something I couldn't entirely understand. Then I heard him cry to the police: "Where is my Ali, where is my Hasan? I want my students back! What right do you have to take my students away? No, it doesn't matter who gave you the order! They're students, and they've done nothing wrong!"

The crowd swelled, as everyone strained to follow the events. No one asked what happened, and no one could answer, except in one shared response: outrage.

Our teacher Şinasi, undaunted, continued his defiance. "Then arrest me!" he cried. This enraged the police, but they also lost their nerve. The students all waited in front of the school. An air of rebellion prevailed.

Even the director seemed disobedient. So the police didn't take the initiative but stood by, awaiting their chance. You could see they were afraid. Many kept their distance, watching the events with apparent indifference.

At length the police order came, and the cops arrested the teacher Şinasi, grabbing him firmly, from both sides. He struggled mightily to shake them off, in vain. Finally he said something and walked with head held high to the police van. As it pulled away, the crowd pressed into the schoolyard. We ran, I and everyone else. At the entrance Sabri Cengiz gave a speech and called for a moment of silence. Leftist fists were raised high. Then we marched along the street. Everyone moved together. Then at an intersection the police divided up the crowd to head back to their own neighborhoods, so they wouldn't have to handle the whole demonstration at once.

Our literature teacher was Halide Burkay, the Turkish wife of Kemal Burkay.[38] Her lessons were always very special. Usually she read poems aloud to us. One day she read a poem and then shared that her husband had written it. At that time Kemal Burkay was in custody. On the second day of the school rebellion, we heard that several of our teachers were to be transferred for disciplinary reasons, as well as a few students. My big brother was transferred to the Turan-Emeksiz High School in Malatya. This school was known to be "a nest of fascists." Halide Burkay was transferred to the high school in Elazığ, where fascists were in charge. One very tall teacher was also transferred, like all "leftist, progressive" teachers. Teachers and students identified as "ringleaders" were affected. Halide Burkay refused to go. Some submitted their resignations. It all created mayhem.

In the second class in middle school, the teacher Yusuf Kenan Deniz taught us literature. One day he explained something unusual to us. He drew a triangle with two long sides on the blackboard. Across the upper part of the triangle he drew a line, creating another small triangle. This upper part he called the class of the rulers and exploiters, and the large lower part represented the oppressed working class and the people. In simple words he tried to explain how exploitation and oppression function. He said the oppressed needed to organize themselves and to struggle against the rulers. The vanguard of this struggle was Dev-Genç, under whose leadership we must free ourselves from oppression.[39]

We loved our teacher Yusuf Kenan Deniz still more because he was so straightforwardly a "leftist." With just a simple drawing, he'd shown us what oppression is. As soon as recess came, we started calling out "Dev-Genç!" without knowing whether it was an organization or a person. In the second class, our teacher warned us that we couldn't just go around shouting that name, because what he'd told us was in some ways dangerous. So he taught us secrecy. Some things you just couldn't talk about whenever and wherever you wanted.

Continue learning over time ...   The Kızıldere affair set my child's leftist heart aflame.[40] The newspapers ran large color photos showing the village, the destroyed house, and the dead, as well as the survivor Ertuğrul Kürkçü, who had been hiding in a hayloft.[41] The moon-face of Mahir Çayan with his big beautiful eyes was particularly affecting. Ten lives had been extinguished. How could it have happened? I wondered as I studied the newspaper. This affair was much bloodier than the *Pir Sultan Abdal* incident. These guerrillas had wanted to initiate the guerrilla struggle in the rural areas of the Black Sea region. But then suddenly Deniz Gezmiş and his friends were to be executed. That was why they had taken people from the NATO base hostage. The guerrillas' goal was to prevent the execution. But it went awry.

On May 6 Deniz Gezmiş and his group were executed. He had long ceased to be "the man who travels the seas," but I now knew him as was a revolutionary, a militant, and a dangerous Communist who threatened the state. Not for nothing had he been sentenced to death. I tried to imagine what a gallows looked like, never having seen one.

Everywhere people talked of the executions, and the newspapers were full of illustrated stories. Our neighbors bought the newspapers regularly, especially Uncle Ali Ataman. I wished someone in my family would buy newspapers. With the little pocket change we had, I sometimes tried to buy *Günaydın* or some other tabloid that reported on the affair, but my mother was categorically opposed. She thought newspapers were dangerous, and she didn't want us involved in dangerous things. Besides, I was still a girl and shouldn't concern myself with such matters. But my mother's prohibitions, her attempts to prevent me from keeping up with events, only spurred me on. My mother had no idea that she achieved the opposite of what she actually wanted, as I tried all the harder to understand new things.

Ali Ataman's family was large. The daughter Fethiye went to the Girls Art School. Her sister Perihan and I went to secondary school together. The others were younger. Their mother Emine had more to say—the women in the family were interested in everything. They didn't put any pressure on the girls. They all read the newspapers together or listened to the radio.

Deniz, Yusuf, Hüseyin   Three names were on everyone's lips in those days: Deniz, Yusuf, and Hüseyin . . . they were spoken of all day long. The day they were executed, meals came to an abrupt end. People lost their appetite because they were in pain, or because they were concerned for their children and relatives in other cities. I remember how Fethiye and others cried. We cut photos from the newspaper and saved them. Some families even hung them on their walls. In a few newspapers, the photos and reports took up entire pages. Thus did Deniz with all his friends enter into many homes. The newspapers reported their last words on the way to the gallows. Excerpts from letters to their families were published. We wrote their names in our notebooks and composed poems. The first letter of each line was a letter from their names. The poem had to be long enough to cover their whole name. Probably we thought with our childish minds that we were accomplishing something, but it only reflected our naïve if genuine feelings. It also expressed our attitude against the Turkish state.

Ecevit as an alternative to the revolutionary left!   In the yard of the building where we lived stood a two-room house made of mud-brick.[42] In winter and especially during the school year, it was hard to find a home, especially for students. Everyone wanted to rent a flat near their relatives, or near people from the same village, or from people they knew. That was the emotional reflex of those who'd come from villages, because it promised that they wouldn't be alone. They weren't entirely wrong. City life was confusing and even frightening to people from villages.

So the landlord rented the mud-brick house to people from his own village or to students from near his village. Most were male teens. Only rarely did a female relative live there. Since the rooms were always rented out to several people, it was difficult when only one or two girls were there. Initially only a few students lived there, but their number rose over time. Mostly they went to the high school or the middle school.

The landlord's children lived in apartments on the first floor. In one of these apartments, I first got to know a revolutionary. During those feverish times, he spoke of Deniz and his group, and he showed off his tie, a present, he said, from Mahir Çayan. He recited names of some of the dead and said they'd come to his village and had spoken with him. There were also revolutionary students in Halbori, Çukur, and other villages in the area. A brother of Veli Tayhani studied in Ankara. They were Armenians, which caught our attention. One night, at a very late hour, there was a knock at our door, and a tall, powerful man asked for my brother. He was at home and seemed to be waiting for someone. The man at the door didn't come in. He just said he had to leave the city quickly and get back to Ankara. I learned he was Veli's brother. I overheard them talking.

He'd previously given my brother a large pistol for safekeeping; now he was here to pick it up and then vanish. My brother handed it over to him covertly. They hadn't noticed that I was in the living room, because I hadn't turned the light on, and it was half dark. I was thrilled that my brother was involved in illicit activities.

We had only a few books at home, bought by my brother. I remember novels by Fakir Baykurt, Yaşar Kemal, and Kemal Tahir, and a book of poetry by Tevfik Fikret. I loved it when my brother read poetry aloud. He had a gorgeous full voice. I especially loved it when he recited *Allı Turnam*. Later, much to my disappointment, I found out it was a song sung by fascists, but I still like to listen to it and sing it.

Increasingly the concepts "left" and "revolutionary" took shape in my mind. We sang new kinds of songs. Deniz, Mahir and all the others were now in our songs. My standards for movies, music, and books were changing. The films of Yılmaz Güncy weren't to be missed.[43] Showings were always sold out, and there was always a competition for tickets in advance. People would even stand during the showings, if that's what it took, and they'd applaud and cheer the films. In one film with [actor] Murat Soydan there was an execution scene. Some in the audience cried, while everyone stomped on the floor in protest and booed. Songs by Mahzuni and Zamani thrilled us.[44]

Nevertheless, these weren't conscious developmental steps based on knowledge. They were impressions that played a role in the formation of my personality. Even Ecevit[45] had some influence on us. Nicknamed Karaoğlan, he was considered a kind of savior. Although revolutionary groups had great influence, the radical left hadn't succeeded in producing an ongoing, revolutionary, militant organization. If it had succeeded in doing the hard work of building an organization that could play a leadership role, the Ecevit left would have had no notable influence. As it was, Dersim had a youthful population, and pressure to assimilate was intense. Ecevit spoke precisely to these groups and so had electoral success. His party was the CHP.[46] Of course it was nonsensical to think one could find the best alternative among the established parties and to place one's hopes on a politician who represented the state. Unable to distinguish between the revolutionary left, which opposes the state, and the Kemalist left, which is loyal to the state, the Ecevit constituency tried to have it both ways. It was a further form of alienation from the self.

During the election campaign, people wore blue shirts like Ecevit's and hung Ecevit posters. Those who considered themselves leftist but lacked political consciousness propagandized for Ecevit and took part in his rallies. Those who didn't have the strength to work illegally as revolutionary leftists entered the CHP as leftists to try to oppose the state. Ecevit was like a liberator for them. At least he was better than [Süleyman] Demirel and the others! The flip side was that the state, by promoting the Ecevit left as an alternative, was trying to bring the revolutionary left under its control. And so it was thoroughly realistic to try to draw the opposition in Dersim into the state-loyal CHP.

In late 1973, Ecevit came to Dersim. A splendid reception was prepared for him. Every van, bus, and truck was mobilized to transport people from the surrounding areas into the city. From Kovancılar over the Mazgirt bridge, from Sihenk, people streamed in. I was mad because I wasn't allowed to go into the city center. My father instead took us to the roof terrace of a hotel. We wore Ecevit blue, and his photo adorned the left side of our chest. But that wasn't enough for us. We wrote, using red letters, on the terrace's concrete pillars: "Karaoğlan comes! Karaoğlan to power!"

The hotel stood across from the city hall. We could look out over the entire square. Even before Ecevit's arrival, all the rooftops were jammed with people.

And then he came into view. His wife, Rahşan, was at his side, and when they waved, the crowd cheered enthusiastically. People shouted slogans with one voice and applauded such that the square shook. Then from the balcony of the city hall, he began, "Worthy people of Tunceli, . . ."[47] but the crowd couldn't be silenced. The whistles and slogans wouldn't subside. Ecevit talked over it all, about the rising cost of living, how expensive things were here, and poverty.

And he made many promises.[48]

My mother taught me not only to rebel but to fight　That year [1973] my father decided to take my big brother and me to Germany. I didn't want to leave school. I'd finished middle school and wanted to continue my studies. I was interested in becoming a nurse and wanted to go to Health School. I didn't know much about boarding schools, but in our extended family there were girls who attended schools with attached dormitories. The daughter of an uncle on my mother's side attended the Girls' Vocational School in Elazığ, and the daughter of a paternal uncle went to school in Akçadağ. I thought that would be better. And at the time I wanted to be far away, because I thought it would make my mother love me more.

My youngest sisters were the twins. They had the same names as my friends in primary school: Feride and Nesibe. Their upbringing was difficult. My mother always said, "Now that I can handle one, Allah has given me two!" She complained about it to Allah. But I secretly rejoiced that the twins were there. During my mother's pregnancy, when she would scold me and express irritation that I was a girl, I said: "Well, I hope two more [girls] are coming!" I had no idea that twins were on the way—I just meant, I wanted to have many sisters. When the twins were born, I was delighted. It was as if God had heard my prayer. But of course it wasn't easy to raise the two of them, and it was sometimes onerous for me.

Normally I took care of Nesibe, while my mother handled Feride. Together we changed their diapers and fed them their mush. The neighbors took to calling Nesibe "Sakine's daughter." Feride was blond, while Nesibe was darker. They were fraternal twins. Just after their birth, my mother had an appendectomy, which didn't make things easier for me. I had to manage the whole household, take care of the twins, and be responsible for the rest of the family. Even at a young age, I had to learn to do every possible task.

At the time we were seven siblings. I was the oldest daughter. Besides my big brother, the others were all younger than me and had to be looked after. I did the laundry, prepared the food, baked the bread, did the shopping, and performed all the other chores, but somehow my mother was never satisfied. The neighbors would hold me up as a model for their own daughters, with all my household industriousness despite my youth, but in the eyes of my own mother, I could never do right. She was a very prickly woman. But then, with my father being away, leaving her alone with so many children, it wasn't easy for her. The burden, in fact, overwhelmed her. She presided over the family with words and rules that she knew and understood. She is the person in my life who most influenced me, so I'll explain much more about her. Even as she made me rebellious, she also taught me to struggle. I owe her a great deal.

My father persuaded my brother and me to go with him to Berlin. It was the first time I'd ever left Dersim, my family, and my mother, Zeynep. The farther we traveled from home, the more homesick I became. I was filled with sorrow and cried sometimes.

The first city I saw after Dersim was Elazığ. But the bus didn't stop there—it continued on to Istanbul. Along the way I could see things only during the rest stops, because we traveled a lot of the journey during the night. The bus trip itself was torture. The whole trip was horrible, and I threw up. My father and my brother were used to such trips. In Kovancılar and Elazığ, I could see "MHP" written on signs and rocks. Both places were known for being home to fascists, and the label was like a confirmation. I also saw "MHP" and "AP" in Kayseri, Yozgat, and Bolu—but I hardly ever saw "CHP."

Finally we reached Istanbul. It was huge. The Bosporus bridge was still being built that year and wasn't quite finished. It was enormous and very long, and it excited me. We had relatives in Istanbul, but we stayed at a hotel. Our plane tickets were bound up with my father's ticket, so we had to be absolutely sure not to miss the flight. One of the owners of Turkish Airlines was Fahri Baba, a close friend of my father. My father had called him and arranged the booking. I was curious about him—in my imagination he was a powerful businessman. Later in Berlin I got to know him, and he was really a lovable, awe-inspiring man.

I stepped onto an airplane for the first time. It was superb—I couldn't get enough of diving through the clouds. It was like jumping into a giant pile of cotton. I saw many new and interesting things, but nothing seemed strange. I acclimated myself by watching my father and my brother. I even understood the menus that were handed to us right away.

The plane had to land and refuel in Sofia. I was in a Communist country! In history class I'd paid attention to the subject of Bulgaria because it had a socialist regime. I was curious, but we only made a stopover. What were people and human relations like here? I tried to see a difference. But only the police looked different—Turkish police stirred up very different feelings in me.

Germany was huge. We flew over Stuttgart and Frankfurt to Berlin. My father explained to us about East Berlin. He said the city had been divided, and a wall built down the middle. I'd already heard in school about the distinctive regime in East Germany. Of course, it would be something else to see it in reality, but we only flew over it.

We landed in Berlin and took a taxi to Johanniterstrasse 10, where we passed though a big gateway. We drove past a lot of buildings, then finally reached a rather isolated two-story house. My first thought was that the house was remote and simple. I didn't like it when a house had too many apartments. My father said this was the only apartment he could find. In Germany it was considered unhealthy for many people to live close together. It wasn't permitted. The three of us would live in an apartment intended for one. It had a living room, a small hallway, a kitchen, and a bathroom.

Why had my father brought my brother and me here? To a place that he himself called "the country of infidels" and that he didn't even like because work conditions were tough and his family was far away? We both had to leave school. My father had no intention of letting us work. I was 14, and my brother was 17.

My father and my brother had an interesting relationship. My brother was the oldest sibling and in my father's absence the head of the household. That gave him a certain autonomy, which my mother didn't really accept. At home he had a special status. He was very orderly, his clothes always clean and ironed. Sometimes he changed clothes two or three times a day. No sock or shirt of his was ever dirty—otherwise all hell broke loose. He was the last to get up in the morning, and then he was served breakfast. He never filled his water glass himself, even when the pitcher was right next to him. He usually didn't like the food and normally ate out. It caused my mother grief, and she also reproached him: "You go out to the restaurant and eat dirty soup, but you won't eat the clean food at home. But then, what can one expect from progeny like you?" She thought him an ungrateful son.

My mother was a very good cook. I couldn't understand my brother's habits. In the summertime he went to Istanbul, Antalya, or Ankara, where my father sent him extra money, but he pestered my mother to send him more money, or he'd go into debt and ask my father again. My brother's debts were always cleared when my father came home for his vacation. He told my brother to "fear Allah!" but he never got angry. My brother had his own principles, which he followed in his own special way, regardless of where he stayed. Even my mother had no power to change him. My father was very tolerant of him, considering him not only a son but a friend. He thought highly of him and was proud of having such a tall son, even when he was young. At first the people around us, even the German neighbors, didn't believe we were my father's children. We were both very tall for our age. My father was young, fit, and vigorous.

He was an open man and treated everyone like a friend. Most people in Dersim kept to their own kind, but not him. He had friends from Sivas, Kayseri, Istanbul, and Kars. People from different places came to visit him. He had German, African, and Libyan friends. Because he was warm and guileless, they loved him. At the same time he was close to his family. In Germany I got to know my father better and loved him all the more.

In his thoughts and feelings he was actually always with us. His frequent trips home, his songs and poems, his pieces of advice—everything flowed from his love for us. He made a cassette "Advice for my children" that was very touching when we listened to it. He wanted to show us what is right in life, step by step. We held on to this cassette for a very long time. I wish I had it with me now and could listen to it. Advice giving is a feature of Zoroastrianism—it's an expression of devotion. The cassette contained criticisms and warnings. In a certain way we were my father's world. He was different from other fathers. Many fathers didn't come home for years. Even though they were married at home, they married again in Germany. Alcohol, gambling, and affairs with other women were common, which threw domestic life into turmoil and destroyed whole families. In Dersim many men were known to have married German women. Many even brought the new wife back home on vacation. That created bad blood. Some married rich German women to be able to inherit from them.

Everyone knew my father didn't behave this way with women. He enjoyed the great trust in the neighborhood. Sometimes when men had something to do elsewhere, they'd leave their wives in my father's custody.

Normally my father was with us or else he told us where he'd be. If he had to work long hours or be somewhere else, he would call. He'd even put the people he was traveling with on the phone. He avoided doing anything that could shake our trust in him. That was his way of being, which rubbed off on us. By comparison, my brother was a bit more cunning. Sometimes he cheated, but he'd be caught right away. Considering my father's behavior, it was hard to lie to him. It isn't easy to lie to someone with such a pure heart. You'd soon admit to everything.

My father wasn't inclined to cigarettes, alcohol, or gambling. He didn't smoke. He drank alcohol only when visiting, without ever getting drunk. He couldn't tolerate much. And then he'd play *saz*, sing, and sometimes cry. His songs were always about separation and yearning. Now two of his children were with him, but that wasn't enough. Sometimes he'd stand up from the table with tears in his eyes and ask: "But what are my children eating? Did they get the money I sent? Is Zeynep still frugal?"

These constant repetitions exasperated my brother, but he'd be able to calm my father and say the right words to comfort him. Somehow I could never comfort him. I wept too, either with him or by myself. I felt sorry for my father. Around Dersim the children of the Almancı[49] were falsely thought to be rich, to have a lot of money and many presents. My father, when he came home on vacation, gave us everything we needed. He brought us presents and spared nothing to see that we were well nourished for 20 days or a month.

Once my mother said she wanted to move away from Dersim and live somewhere else. My father let us vote on it. Except for my mother and my big brother, the rest of us supported my father. We didn't want to go to another city—that held no appeal. My brother didn't really care—he was always on the go, always moving around. Sometimes I thought he was lucky. He was very orderly and clean. I learned a lot about cleanliness from watching him. So I brushed my teeth three times a day too, especially before bed.

One day at breakfast, my brother took off his shirt and snapped at me, "Get up and wash my shirt and bring it here!" I could have washed it later, but now we were sitting at the breakfast table. My father was furious that he'd barked at me and ordered me to get up.

Some weeks my father's shift duty allowed us to have breakfast together, but the other weeks he had different starting times, and we were seldom all three together. And there was another problem as well. My father didn't like my brother's lifestyle. He said so to his face and expressed it through his behavior too, so my brother was very aware of it. His late-night homecomings, his frequency away from home, his profligacy with money, and his other habits sorely tested my father's patience. On this day, my father's patience came to an end. At my brother's words, my father hurled a glass ashtray at the wall. "You son of an ass," he said, "don't you have any conscience? She does all the housework, she serves your friends and mine, she doesn't take a break for even a minute. What's your rush? You just took the shirt off. Now wait, she should have her breakfast first and wash it afterward." And he rose from the table.

The ashtray had whizzed by my brother's head and splintered against the wall. If he hadn't lowered his head, it would have cracked his skull. My brother hadn't expected my father to do such a thing. He was very distressed and cried, sobbed. He too rose from the table. Now I was left alone, but I couldn't eat another bite and left breakfast on the table. What would happen now? My father had left the apartment. I couldn't go to my brother. And it had all happened because of me. Finally I couldn't stand my brother's crying and asked him to stop. To my surprise, he didn't get mad. I knew why he was crying, and my father had been right to blow up at him, *but he shouldn't have thrown that ashtray*, I thought. My brother wondered where my father had gone and wanted me to go look for him in the park along the canal.

"The old man"—that was what he called him in anger—"lost his temper," my brother said, concerned.

My sensitive father couldn't bear it that he'd acted that way toward his beloved son. I ran from the house into the park. To my relief, I found him sitting on a bench. We walked a little way together, then I took him by the arm and led him back home. He kissed my brother, and they made up. Of course my brother apologized too. Suddenly the atmosphere was very different. Delighted, I rolled up my sleeves and began to wash the shirt. I didn't want anything to be dirty ever again. My greatest fear was strife in my family—that was a horror for me.

In Germany my father put me in charge of the finances. He handed his paycheck over to me, saying, "Take the money and do what you want. But don't do what Haydar does!"

I sent as much as possible back home to Dersim—usually 300 Marks and rarely 500, when the child benefit increased or when my father worked overtime. I gave my brother and my father pocket money and did the weekly shopping. I tried to keep a piggy bank. It all worked because I was frugal with money. But we had lots of visitors. All three of us had separate friends, and some came over all the time, taking advantage of the fact that my brother and I were always at home. As we got to know a lot of people, our expenditures rose accordingly. Hardly anyone showed understanding. We ourselves seldom went out. Our most frequent guests were the Güngör siblings from Nazimiye,[50] some of whom were stingy and almost never at home. One brother married a German woman and got two children.

I turned 15 in the New Year. My father enrolled my brother and me in a language course. German had been my second language in the middle school; my brother had studied English. My brother actually needed the language more than me, but he learned it in his daily life. He also had German friends and traveled often to East Berlin. Our fellow students were of diverse origin, coming from Istanbul, Çanakkale, Kayseri, Sivas, and Dersim. I was the youngest. My brother drew a lot of attention to himself. The young women tried to get to him by talking to me. At first they thought I was his girlfriend and ignored me, but when they realized I was his sister, they clustered around.

A few of my brother's friends were leftists, revolutionaries. When they visited us, they paid a lot of attention to me. When they talked about socialism, about the oppressed and the ruling classes, I was interested. They taught me songs of struggle. The first one I learned went like this: "Gendarmes, we're socialists / We come in friendship / Your liberation is linked to ours / Extend your hand to us." The young man who taught me that song came from Elazığ. He was older than my brother and said he was with the TKP.[51] My brother also frequented the leftist political clubs.[52]

One evening when I came home from shopping, I heard slogans being shouted in our neighborhood. I threw my bags down and rushed out to see what was happening with my neighbor's daughter, but along the way I was so excited, I hurried off and left her behind. I thought it must be revolutionaries. Nothing else occurred to me. But as I got near, I heard a fascist song. I was indignant and disappointed.

One of them in the first row carried a picture with a wolf, the fascist symbol, and they made the wolf sign with their hands. I regretted that I'd run and whispered to myself, "These rotten guys!" When I got back home, I told my father about the Türkeş demonstration.[53] My father said they had their own club and got state support.

We got some letters from Dersim, not often, but they told us about events there. In the *Hürriyet* and *Yeni Asır* newspapers, which we bought sometimes, we read about violent clashes and shootings. In Vartinik, a Dersim neighborhood, people were killed in a shooting and there were arrests. The boarding students at the secondary school and the students at the Teachers School were mostly recruited by fascists, coming from places like Erzurum and Elazığ.

There were clashes in the schools and universities. My father was glad that my big brother was with him—my other brothers were too young, he thought, to have anything to do with such matters.

I was very interested in events in Dersim, precisely because I could only follow them from a distance. Where the letters were vague, I had to speculate. In Dersim there were a lot of high-spirited young people. The name Tunceli was always associated with progress and revolution. Just say someone came from Tunceli, and it would be assumed they'd easily be won over to revolutionary work. We became revolutionary leftists almost automatically—it was part of being from Tunceli.

One day a cultural event was being held at a political club in Berlin. My brother's friends had told us about it, and I went, along with my brother and my father. The room was crowded. There were also foreigners present, Germans and others, which made the event even more interesting. My brother left us from time to time and went over to his friends, who were milling around or standing at the doors. Again I rejoiced because I thought my brother was secretly involved in these things and was just hiding it from us.

At this event a play was performed. In one scene Turkish soldiers chain a young man's hands, then beat him and lead him away. The young man is bleeding and moaning, but the soldiers keep on hitting him. I was so moved, I jumped to my feet and shouted, "Hit me, I won't die so easily / My embers have turned to ashes in the oven / In my belly is my word, for those who understand it."

Everyone turned and stared at me. They assumed my poem was part of the play. My father and my brother were astonished and wondered to each other what was going on with me. But they had to smile, and my father stroked my hair. They fussed over me lovingly and asked jokingly if I'd been drinking. At the intermission a few of my brother's friends came over and congratulated me. They gave me the address of their headquarters and invited me to visit. But their manner wasn't particularly appealing to me. They talked rather mechanically, as if they were thinking, *Okay, we've found another one.*

I just didn't know yet what being a revolutionary really meant. The theoretical-ideological dimension and the practical-organizational work were both strange to me. A few general truths had impressed me, but I lacked information and consciousness. I didn't want to become a revolutionary at the behest of others, or to join a fraction without really being convinced about it. That train of thought wasn't conscious, but that's how I was from the beginning. Still, my self-awareness was growing.

My family and friends were receptive to leftists, including in social life. The family was very close, with a culture of order and discipline. At the same time we had autonomous relationships, thanks largely to my father's democratic and humanistically inclined personality. My brother, as the oldest son of the family, encountered no problems in making his own decisions and choosing friends. Even as a girl I wasn't subjected to pressure or burdened with special prohibitions. Unlike my mother, my father openly demonstrated his love and esteem for me. I could feel it clearly.

Life in Europe, while easy in some ways, held no appeal for me. Berlin was an enormous city with huge buildings, and the people were different in all respects. I noticed a few things right way. When we stepped off the plane and were waiting at the taxi stand, I saw couples kissing out in the open. It was embarrassing for me, and I dropped my gaze, especially because I was with my father and my brother. And one time when we were going to the Turkish store where we did our shopping, we passed a restaurant for dogs. Every time I walked by, seeing the women and men who went inside would infuriate me. The women had painted lips and wore feather-trimmed hats, furs, canes, or umbrellas. On the other hand, it was nice that old people here had houses and were taken care of. Back home, no one wants to get old. People prefer "a handful of good soil" from Düzgün Baba to becoming old and frail.

As a young girl, I did what I pleased. I didn't emulate anyone and tried not to do what others did, only what I was really convinced about.

I was careful not to hurt anyone and to respect the opinions of others, but I considered my own opinion the most important. And I truly was stubborn. I was indifferent to makeup and dressy clothes. But I didn't like my frizzy hair, so I sometimes put on a wig. When my father saw me with the blond wig for the first time, he said, "Welcome, but where is Sakine?" Only then did he recognize me, and we burst out laughing. My father, my brother, and many friends liked my curls and said I looked better with my natural hair. Later, when I returned to Dersim, I was wearing this wig.

Kurdish identity and revolutionary consciousness My father and I attended another event together. It was as if a secret force were organizing us—everything seemed to unfold on its own. Our family culture was receptive to change, to the new, we weren't conservative, so we were always meeting new people. The event was organized by the KDPI,[54] and my father didn't know exactly what kind of event it would be. He just knew it would be Kurdish.

3 Cansız (*right*) in the blond wig, Berlin, 1974.

Back then we had no Kurdish consciousness. We called ourselves Alevis. No Kurdish identity was noted in our passports, IDs, work contracts, or with the state authorities. It didn't matter if you were from Tunceli, Kayseri, or Trakya, every citizen of the Republic of Turkey was denoted a Turk. And it wasn't so important—no one was looking for their national roots. Not even the revolutionary left made any such distinctions. In Dersim, Ali Gültekin and Kemal Burkay were known for their Kurdish consciousness, but they were disparaged as Kurdish chauvinists. They had a book by İsmail Cem about the Eastern Problem.[55] We came from the east, so it intrigued us. But otherwise Kurds were never spoken of.

What, then, induced my father to attend this event? He was a worker, had children and a family he was very close to. He'd gone to school—only primary school, but it had contributed to his enlightenment. He was influenced by the ways of the Alevis, was flexible, and took the initiative, even more than my brother. My brother was calmer and tried to avoid attracting much attention to himself.

The three of us went to the event. I wore my wig, a long simple skirt, and a blouse. But it was much different from what we expected. Everyone there wore national clothing. Even the foreigners had put on our traditional dress. A colorful exuberance prevailed. The room wasn't very big and reminded me of a restaurant. People were speaking Kurdish as well as German. The moderator wore a shirt, a *şalvar*, and on his head a *kefiye*.[56] We recognized only a few Kurdish words, and my father could understand only a little of the German translation.

A video about the Barzani movement and about Mahabad was shown, also discussing Atatürk, Dersim, Sheikh Said, and Koçgiri.[57] In the part about the Dersim genocide, it showed people chained together with shaved heads. Then the Peshmerga were discussed.[58] The film showed scenes of war and fighting. It was 1974, and the Peshmerga were resisting the Iraqi regime. We got a glimpse of the fascist Saddam, but Mustafa Barzani was shown more often. He was in the mountains and dressed like a Peshmerga, with *raxt* and *şutik* around his hips.[59]

My deepest impression from that evening was a song sung by a chorus: "*Bîrnakim ha bîrnakim, riya Lenin bîrnakim.*"[60] It lingered on my lips for a long time afterward. Then more Kurdish songs were performed, accompanied by a *saz*. Finally everyone danced *halay*.[61] My father couldn't be restrained, especially because his son and daughter were there, but I didn't want to dance, I felt more like crying, because I wasn't wearing Kurdish clothing. My father laughed. "How was I to know everyone would wear traditional clothing?" he said. "Even if I'd known, where would I have found a dress for you? Your long skirt is beautiful. Come on, let's dance!"

But he couldn't dispel my gloom. Why did I feel so ashamed? Why was it suddenly so important to me? Up till then I'd been more ashamed of my Kurdish heritage. It had been embarrassing that I was unable to speak Turkish well and that my mother didn't speak like a Turk. Now I was ashamed that I wasn't wearing Kurdish clothing, those colorful garments that expressed Kurdish identity, and because I felt different from everyone else. Maybe it's profane to say it, but perhaps this sense of shame somehow awakened my interest in Kurdish identity.

The owner of the house where we lived fell very ill. We knew he had a son and a daughter, but now we learned he had another daughter in East Berlin, his oldest child. One part of his family was in West Berlin, the other in the East. The two halves of the city had different governments. What would it be like to live in a socialist country? I wondered. My brother went often to East Berlin, but he didn't say much about it. From a tower on the wall, I'd peered at the East through a telescope, but I couldn't make out any differences. The ruins along the wall had been rebuilt. A broad stretch was marked as a danger zone with big signs. Running atop the wall was electrified barbed wire. That was what a border between two states looked like.

The daughter of our landlord had petitioned the consulate for permission to come to the West, and it had worked. I was curious and excited to see a person who lived in the socialist system—my first! We invited her to our house and plied her with questions. What was equality, what was freedom? What was her life like, and how had they managed to overcome the division between rich and poor? We queried her about every possible subject. In answer, she said she had an apartment and a car. Everyone worked, and it wasn't easy to overcome the vestiges of the war. The differences between her and her siblings were obvious. She seemed more mature, more earnest, and more conscious, while the others seemed more frivolous.

My father responded by cracking jokes. That's what he always did whenever someone spoke of the Kurdishness of Ali Gültekin, of socialism, or of communism. He joked about Uncle İbrahim in Tahtı

Halil village, saying "When you found a Kurdish state, make your uncle İbrahim president!" Today he laughed about our impatient questioning and our interest in socialism: "I can buy you a car. If that means socialism, well then, it's easy!" Our zeal bothered him.

We thought it was great to learn something about socialism from someone who lived in such a country. We had talked about socialism so much and had sung about it in songs, even if we had only limited information. Talking to this woman meant that it was no mere dream but could be made real, even that it was necessary to fight for it. I'd not yet read any books explicitly about it, but there was a concrete instance. East Germany lay right outside our door, and with permission one could even travel there. I wanted to see East Berlin so much, but every time my brother was about to go there, he blew me off. I didn't just want to look at East Germany from the wall. For me, the country was still a secret. It had to be different somehow, and I wanted to see it with my own eyes. That would indeed be possible, but I wasn't able to fulfill that wish for a long time. The idea that socialism could be implemented and that it was the future was alive within me.

My father worked in three shifts, which was exhausting. His health suffered. He got sick and had to go to the hospital. But he fed nine people by doing his work. It wasn't fair. Sometimes I couldn't stand it and burst into tears. Sometimes when he got home from work, it was hard for him just to climb the stairs. I cursed the alarm clock that rang every morning. Usually he left the house without breakfast. Sometimes he brought along a lunch that I was glad to fix. Cooking his favorite dishes made me happy, because then I felt like I was making a contribution. But doing the cooking and cleaning wasn't enough for me. One day I got mad and asked if I was a servant, but it changed nothing. And I really didn't want to say I minded serving my father and my brother. Many people came to visit, some of whom seemed to take advantage of us—they came for no reason. When I suggested to my father that I go to work, he refused.

What would people say! "İsmail brought his little daughter here to put her to work!" What if something happened to you here in the land of the infidels? You can see for yourself, the streets are full of vagabonds and drunks. It's out of the question.

It infuriated me.

The German language lessons we took didn't help much. I'd already learned the basics in middle school. And we mostly spoke Turkish in the class. A few of the girls attended class without really intending to learn German. Sometimes my brother got together with them, and they went out. I went home alone. When my father noticed, he got annoyed. For a while my brother had a girlfriend—an Iranian Kurd. My father liked her a lot, but the relationship didn't last because my brother didn't want to marry her. He was picky and had high standards. But he continued to see a lot of girls and often had a new girlfriend, which didn't seem right to me. Most of these ties were temporary and insincere, which wasn't helpful to anyone. Once when I told him how I felt, my brother got irritated and told me to mind my own business. My father shared his thoughts sometimes. Such friendships in Europe could easily corrupt a person.

The German wife of Ali from Mazgirt was in touch with us.[62] She knew a little Turkish, and I knew a little German, and so we could understand each other a bit. But it seemed senseless for me not to work and to do nothing. So I didn't like being in Germany anymore. Berlin was a beautiful city, sure, but the parks and the big buildings didn't satisfy me. Even the lakes and hills in the parks were artificial. There were artificial roads, artificial mountains, and artificial streams. I missed the forests and trees of Dersim. I missed the Munzur.

Of course there were also beautiful places in Berlin. I was glad that our neighborhood was near a park, with a canal running through it. I liked to run across the green fields, the clean grass and soil.

I asked our German neighbor if she could help me find a job after my German class. She agreed, and we went together to several places to ask for work. Finally we found something in a small shop in a shopping center. The work wasn't hard. I just had to stack the shopping baskets once a week and put things in order. I had a school permit, an ID, a photo, and a residence permit. All that was missing was my father's permission. How long would I have been able to work secretly, without his approval?

In those days we learned from a letter from Dersim that my mother was pregnant again. I just blew up. "It's enough!" I said to my father. "Why do you want so many children?" My brother was angry too. It was a little embarrassing for my father. He said we were right, but it was done now.

My father forbade me to work. "Then send me back home," I roared at him. "I don't want to stay here anymore!" He tried to persuade me to stay with him. He kept saying how important it was to him to come home to a hot meal and to see his children. But finally he agreed that it would be better if we went home.

Return to Dersim Deciding to return to Dersim improved my mood. I especially wanted to go back to help my mother, but I didn't want to look after small children anymore and wash diapers. It had been hard enough to raise the twins. Now we'd be eight siblings. My parents themselves were annoyed about all the children, but they kept making new ones. That infuriated me. But I was glad to be going home to Dersim at last. I could continue my schooling there—I'd been away from the classroom for 11 months.

During that year, I'd grown up. My body had changed. I'd seen and experienced a lot.

I was thrilled to set foot in the city again. I'd never been away so long—my brother was more used to it. When we got off the bus, everyone stared at us. I didn't realize that my wig and bell-bottoms made me very conspicuous. I looked like a German. I'd never thought that could happen! So people kept a chilly distance from me. I couldn't understand why, and I was disappointed.

Before we reached our neighborhood, my mother was told that Haydar had arrived with a German girl. The neighbor children, some female relatives, and my mother all came out to meet us. My mother didn't recognize me, not even when I was standing right in front of her. "Mom, it's me," I said. "Don't you recognize me?" No one had expected I'd wear a wig. And after the 11 months away, no one had expected a completely altered Sakine. I acted like everything was normal. People accepted my wig quickly, but I never put it on again and eventually got rid of it.

Dersim, for its part, had changed in our absence. After all the talk about Deniz, Mahir, and the others, now people talked about the group around İbrahim Kaypakkaya.[63] Everywhere people talked about how wounded group members had been dragged behind a jeep and their corpses shown to the people, to spread anger and terror. Much was said about torture. Ali Haydar Yıldız was killed. İbrahim Kaypakkaya, wounded, fled to the home of a teacher and community leader who let him stay in his house, but the teacher betrayed him, and the police arrested him. He was tortured to death in Diyarbakır prison. Rumor had it that his fingernails and toenails had been ripped out, and then the fingers had been cut off. He was considered a hero, who preferred to die rather than betray anyone by giving information. Songs were composed in honor of Kaypakkaya and Ali Haydar Yıldız.

At the Teachers School at Dersim, too, something had happened. The fascists, who lived in a boardinghouse, had clashed violently with the revolutionaries. Even the lower neighborhood was attacked, and the governor was hit. That was in 1974.

Freshly returned from Germany, it felt advantageous to be living at home. My mother tried to leave me in peace. But things were different than before. I was becoming a young woman, and we had to get used to it. The girls I knew had a different kind of relationship with their mothers. These mothers didn't try to force them against their will on every issue. On many things Perihan, Cemile, and Nimet, who were all my age, could make choices for themselves, and their mothers didn't insist on accompanying them everywhere, and they had their own friends, who they could even invite to their homes.

4 Cansız with school friends, *c.*1974. *Left to right:* Cansız, Elif Kiliç, Perihan Gündüz, Cemile Aygün.

My mother did realize that I'd grown up. She was glad her friends liked me, but she tried to shield me from possible dangers. She interfered in everything from my clothing to my hair. And in everything she tried to impose her will on me. We fought a lot, neither side giving in. And she talked incessantly, an aggravating habit that could send me into a rage. She didn't care if the moment or the place was inappropriate for bringing up her complaints.

Her behavior only made me more obstinate and rebellious. It got to the point that I ignored her whenever she spoke to me. Or else I would do what she wanted me to do, angrily and against my will and to my own disadvantage, just to satisfy her. But it made no difference. Say I wanted to go to the movies or do something with my girlfriends. I would have to implore her, beg her for permission, at length. Then just as I was getting ready to go out, she'd change her mind. I gave up. My friends felt bad about it. Their mothers felt sorry for me and were annoyed at my mother and even begged her to give me permission too. But I decided I wouldn't let her get to me anymore. In our remarkable relationship, we fought constantly. Perhaps she thought she loved her daughter more than the other mothers did. But when you're constantly trying to frustrate a person's will, it's not love. What did she make of the fact that so many people were angry at her? Through her behavior, she failed to nurture affection and connection with me; just the opposite— she guaranteed that my rebellious side would come to the foreground.

With my father away from home, she bore a double burden, to be both mother and father to us. We were a large family who had to be fed. All the children went to school. There was unrest all around us. It all prompted my mother to reflexively control us and protect us from "bad influences."

Caring for eight children and handling all the family's problems simply overwhelmed her. Our contact with relatives was limited. She felt better when letters from my father arrived or he came home on vacation. He could rein her in. He would talk things over with her and soothe her senseless outbursts. He tried to correct her behavior toward me.

She's your daughter—a young woman. You have to help her. Let her do a few of the things she wants to do, and don't meddle in her life all the time. We can't possibly want our children to think and live exactly as we do. That wouldn't be right. They aren't doing anything bad, and we can be proud of them.

He tried to persuade her this way, and our relations improved for a while. He didn't like it that every morning I had to get up to do the housework before school. And it disturbed him that in spite of all my efforts, my mother was never satisfied with me. "Fear Allah!" he said to her. "She gets up and does the chores and then goes to school! No other daughter does that. And yet you're still on her for her faults!" I just couldn't do right by my mother.

No one contradicted my wish to continue my education. On the contrary, my family supported it. And to that point no one had said much about marriage, not even in reference to my brother, my older sibling. But then, he didn't give anyone a chance to discuss this question—he had his principles. He had girlfriends, but marriage was not an attractive subject for him. It meant binding yourself to someone else. Who knows, maybe the existing families and relationships of people around us gave him this concept of marriage.

My aunt Sakine, for one, had a marriage that we sometimes laughed about. It had been arranged by her family, following tradition. While she was engaged, she'd wanted to see her future husband before the wedding. She couldn't leave the house, so she had to look out the window. She stepped up onto a water canister, to be able to see better. But the canister tipped over, throwing her to the floor. So she had to marry a man she'd never seen even from a distance. She went on to have seven or eight children. Her husband was a driver. They were like strangers to each other. To us, their relationship seemed empty and meaningless. They hardly spoke to each other, although they made a lot of children. We felt sorry for the kids and sometimes laughed about them. Compared with their parents, my parents had a good marriage.

My childhood enthusiasm is suffocated   Social conditions were slowly changing. Traditional values were loosening, and now young women and men didn't have to get married right away—they had the option to get to know each other first, to meet and converse. My youngest aunt, Günes, had married this way. Also Fethiye, the neighbor's daughter, met her fiancé casually, and the two decided to get married on their own volition. That much was still frowned on in those days. Rumor had it that the young man visited the family as a guest, and then the daughter had wanted to marry. They took walks together, giving rise to gossip and scandal.

The concept of dowry was on the way out. Young people in Dersim were, after all, "left revolutionaries" and had to advocate new practices. Many people approved. Meanwhile in the large cities it was becoming more normal for students to marry girls of Turkish, Circassian, or other heritage. Marriages between relatives had formerly been common, but not so much anymore. It was no longer mandatory. Betrothals that the parents had arranged for their children while they were still in the cradle lost their validity. But how much could one's fate be changed? How much could tradition be cast aside? That was the question. Even I had been chosen as a future daughter-in-law while I was still a child.

We didn't have much to do with my father's side of the family. We saw them seldom, only when my father was home on vacation. My three uncles had children my age. We didn't know one another well, we lacked the familiarity of relatives, and we stayed aloof from each other. When I was still a kid, the family of one of my [paternal] uncles had decided to make me into their daughter-in-law. My mother was indignant—she didn't get along with my father's family and didn't like them.

My mother's family was more considerate toward me, but my uncle and his wife assessed their children realistically. They'd dropped out of school and didn't work. Who would want to marry such men! But they liked me and thought that because I'd had a school education, I'd be a good match for their sons.

Whenever someone we knew got married, my father would get excited. "Ah, if only I could experience this pleasure!" He was very eager for us to marry but didn't pressure us, and rarely mentioned it. That was partly because of my big brother's dismissive attitude toward marriage. He sometimes said, "I can barely stand my mother. How could I endure a wife?"

My parents' wishes and thoughts about their children focused mostly on this subject. My mother had me work on my trousseau. She brought home highly intricate and beautiful samples of embroidery and needlepoint. While she taught me these skills, she worked hard in her own right. Many young women worked ardently on their trousseau. They dreamed of marriage, of preparing themselves for it and of becoming a candidate for it, but it held no joy for me. I'd brought home nothing from Germany for my trousseau, only presents for others. Marriage and material relationships were distasteful to me. My father's philosophy of life had got through to us. He always associated the material side of life with profit seeking, injustice, conflict, and lovelessness. Whenever the subject of material advantage arose, he would curse. But in the world we lived in, material values played a big role.

It was after I returned from Germany that my family started talking about marriage. Our neighbors from across the way, Uncle Hıdır and his wife, often came to visit. Hıdır was a large, handsome man, retired but still very active. His wife was a Turk and, in contrast to him, small and round. This old couple were very well liked. They received many visits, so they didn't suffer from loneliness. They had a daughter who was already married and had children and lived in Ankara—around this time she came to visit.

When we came home from Germany, many guests visited us to greet and welcome us. Hıdır and his family were the first to arrive and the last to leave. They took an interest in everything, but they especially liked my domestic efficiency. A young woman with housekeeping skills could enjoy high esteem as a future daughter-in-law. To me it felt strange that they considered important the approval not of the person in question but of the parents. Love is surely important in a person's life. To love someone's positive characteristics or pleasant appearance is crucial for living together. No one wants to live with a repellent personality. But here the question was handled on quite different terms.

We had been neighbors back in the military camp too. We hadn't been particularly close, and I don't remember the children well, only Doğan and Metin. Metin was tall, walked fast, and had an effervescent temperament. He was known as "Brother Metin." When we were small, we played ball in the yard. Who knows? Maybe in their eyes we were naughty, scruffy children. We'd been shouting "Brother Metin, Brother Metin," in a childish effort to get some attention. They stroked our heads while they tried to make us understand their annoyance at our impudence.

Now we'd grown up. Metin came home during vacations. When we met, I avoided eye contact with him or acted as if I hadn't seen him. I spotted him a few times on the balcony or in the street. He was just someone I knew—his existence had no other meaning for me. But I noticed how gracious his mother, his father, and his big sister were toward me.

My father's brothers were around too. Celal, the son of Uncle Mustafa, went to the high school. Haydar, the son of my other uncle, attended the Vocational School. İbrahim, Mehmet Ali, and Baki were sons of Uncle Mehmet. Mehmet Ali studied in Ankara; he'd been a Turkish Communist Party member for a long time, and even while he was still in school in Erzincan, he was known for getting into fights with fascists. Baki and İbrahim were hotheads too. We liked İbrahim the best—he always showed an interest in us. He didn't visit often, but when we saw each other, he always asked how we were doing. We had an affectionate and easy relationship. Baki went to the high school, and I didn't have much to do with him. He was only a little older than me, so I respectfully called him *abi* [big brother]. My uncles' sons were all older, so I called them all that.

Baki had visited us before, and I thought it was a normal visit this time. But it turned out to be something quite different. My big brother and my mother knew what was going on. My brother said, "She's still very young, but talk to her yourself. It'd be better if we didn't talk about it." Then he left. He'd previously suggested to my mother that she show some sensitivity and leave us alone. As everyone drifted out of the flat one by one, I caught on. I got up and started cleaning house, stalling for time. It all seemed very strange, but I was sure of myself and was glad I could make up my own mind. I was a young woman now, and my mother acknowledged my right to make my own decision. Being grown up had its advantages.

[Baki and I] sipped tea, and I rejected his marriage proposal. He told me that he'd been interested in me even in school. Our conversation was very mature. I explained that I had no thought of marrying and wanted to go to school. He said he didn't want to get married right away either, that he was also studying, but we could get engaged. I told him frankly that I had no feelings for him. That made him sad, and he left with tears in his eyes.

My mother had been waiting expectantly outside. Judging from his early departure and his sorrowful face, she could guess what my answer had been.

That evening my brother was happy. "Good! You made your decision," he said. "There's nothing more to be said." So that was that. A few of my girlfriends from the neighborhood had heard about it and were curious to know why I'd turned him down. [Baki] was after all a university student and was even my cousin. They couldn't understand me.

My own clarity strengthened my self-awareness. My mother was impressed, and I thought she'd finally stop trying to impose her will on me. When my father came home for vacation that year, my uncle's family tried again with him. My father thought my mother had probably influenced my decision and tried gently to get me to change my mind.

While my father was home, Uncle Hıdır and Aunt Tonton practically moved in with us. They came right out and said what they wanted. I'd resumed my studies and now was a freshman in high school. They even roped in their acquaintances to try to persuade my father. One day when they started talking about it again, I burst out, "How am I supposed to accept someone I don't know at all, with whom I've never even had a conversation? You can't just decide for me!" My father got angry because I'd said it in the guests' presence. He took it to mean I was spoiled. Strange, how furious he got at my entirely normal reaction! As if I'd committed a crime!

After they left, my mother talked at me for a while, then had a big argument with my father. He was mad that she had given preference to nonrelatives over his kinfolk. Their argument rang in my ears all day, and then they stopped talking to each other altogether. I was suffering as well. A little while later the subject was reopened. Uncle Hıdır was determined to pursue his plan. Whenever he ran into me while shopping or on the street, he asked how I was and what I was doing. He observed me closely.

One day, annoyed by my mother's pressure, my brother erupted. "What's this?" he snapped. "She's still so young. Are you really that desperate? Or do you consider her so superfluous? Is it that we can't afford to feed her anymore? Why are you pressuring her like this?" Then he turned to me. "Don't give in to pressure," he urged. "Make up your own mind. Marriage is not a children's game!"

His attitude elated me. Nonetheless in the following days, a decision was made. On a day when I was at school, I was promised [to Metin]. It turned out my wishes weren't so important after all. I gave up all resistance. At least I was less certain about rejecting him than I had been about my cousin [Baki]. Some of the advice I'd received got to me: "Metin is a good boy. You're crazy to reject him. He's a student. And marriages between relatives are no good. Rather than marry your cousin, accept this family." I was undecided, but my mother had decided for me and also convinced my father, even though he was still annoyed because he preferred his nephew.

When I got home from school, I was told that the betrothal ceremony would take place before Metin went back to university. Digging in my heels didn't make any sense. My cousin Cemile said I shouldn't get worked up for no reason, as it was a fait accompli.

So now I was really to get engaged to someone I'd barely spoken to and whose character I didn't know. He knew me just as little. Doubtless his mother, his sister, and his father had influenced him. Up to now he'd seen me only from afar—a girl with a blond wig!

Uncle Hıdır forged on ahead and suggested that the wedding take place right away. Then I could go with Metin to Ankara. My family was against rushing, so I could at least finish high school.

Was I living in a dream? I was aghast. What was I supposed to be happy about? If it had been happening with someone I knew and loved, that would have been different. But the decision had been made behind my back, and I was astounded. I was a girl, and my parents considered it their right to decide for me. And Metin? He was a man, and his parents were educated people. He was a student. Why hadn't he taken the initiative himself? We had neither met nor spoken to each other. He had no bad habits, and he wasn't hard to look at. You could even say he was good-looking. I was interested in him. But now I was promised to him. *Maybe it's all for the best*, I thought. All night long I wondered what being engaged would be like. I tried to picture what lay in store for me, but I had no experience and no idea how I was supposed to feel. I actually felt excited thinking about some moments we'd share together. The next morning my parents, Aunt Medine, Metin, and I went to Elazığ to buy an engagement ring.

In the car, he and I shook hands—that was all. Coming and going, we sneaked secret looks at each other. We were strangers, that was obvious. In Elazığ we went to a hotel. We bought rings, an engagement dress, some other garments, and gifts. We both said what clothing we liked. That was it. He asked my mother for permission to go with me to the movies in the evenings, but she said no. The movies were an excuse to spend time with me, talk to me and get to know me. I couldn't think that far ahead. He took the initiative more than I did.

After we got back to Dersim, I went to the hair salon and let them do my hair. I also got made up a little. Then I put on my engagement dress and went home, where the guests were waiting. To approving applause, we exchanged engagement rings, and then the celebration began. All the neighbors and relatives had a good time at my engagement party. Lots of photos were taken. It continued well into the night. After everyone left, I took off the dress and sat down. I felt empty and could scarcely grasp what had happened. It was as if a play had been performed, then everyone had gone home. The only difference was the ring that was now on my finger. I was engaged. I pulled it off and read the inscription engraved inside: "Metin Çetin" and the date. I glanced in the mirror at my styled hair and made-up face. I'd obviously grown up. I tried to wipe the makeup off but succeeded only in smearing it over my face. Later I learned you have to use cream or cleansing lotion.

My parents were talking in the living room. I strained my ears to hear. My father swore he hadn't understood my mother's signal. My mother had apparently wanted to leave me alone with my fiancé and had signaled my father to leave the room, which he hadn't done. Metin and I hadn't been able to talk all evening. We'd hardly said a word to each other! When we sat next to each other, I'd toyed with my fingers in embarrassment and straightened my dress. He warned me, quietly, that my body shape was visible when I pulled at my dress that way. At Aysel's urging, I danced *halay*, but the room was much too small, and I soon sat back down—I couldn't even enjoy the dancing. It was as if my childish feelings, my enthusiasm, and my joy in life had been put in chains, as if shyness had gripped my soul. It was like being in a vise.

The next day Metin came over to say goodbye to us. We had tea, and then he got into a conversation with my father. Once again my mother tried to signal my father with hand gestures, but once again he didn't understand. He loved these kinds of conversations. Metin and I looked at each other covertly, with mutual curiosity, but didn't speak to each other. We never got close. We sat at the table. All we had in common was the rings on our fingers. When he left, he extended his hand to everyone and bade me farewell last of all. At that moment I wondered bitterly, *Why does he have to leave already?* But of course I didn't say that. He kissed me on the cheeks and hurried out of the apartment.

He went back to Ankara, and I returned to school. My girlfriends congratulated me on the engagement. I was more mature, now that I was betrothed. I paid more attention to how I behaved. I couldn't carry on as casually as I had in the past. And my mother constantly reminded me of it—from that point on, she began every admonition with the words "You're engaged now."

We wrote to each other. Metin sent the first letter, and in reply I told him candidly about my mental state. He liked my letter, saying he was glad I'd expressed my thoughts freely.

He mailed his letters to his family, who then forwarded them to me. I wrote directly to the address he'd given me. His parents had become members of our family. They were over at our place day and night. So I was under twofold pressure. Both my mother and Metin's family were trying to control me and to set boundaries. I didn't accept either and struggled against the pressure. Whenever my bickering with my mother intensified, I threatened to take off the ring and throw it away. She knew I was capable of that, so she restrained herself for a while. She was terrified that I'd blurt out something like that to Metin's parents, so she tried to be cautious.

During the semester break, Metin came back to Dersim, and we got to know each other better. The letters we exchanged had brought us closer, if only on paper. Now for the first time we had a chance to talk about what moved us, so we grew closer.

Metin took the initiative socially and could form ties quickly. He was eight years older than me. Sometimes I felt like a child when we were together, but then, sometimes he seemed like a child. We had a limited perspective on life and didn't step outside traditional boundaries. Since we both were interested in politics, we talked a lot about current events. Neither of us wanted to marry right away. We wanted to finish school first. We wouldn't give in to family pressure. One could say that this semester break not only brought us closer but made our engagement official. We pledged ourselves to each other. Then we parted—he went back to Ankara, and I to school. My self-awareness had grown stronger because I'd taken responsibility for my life.

A lot more was happening now at the schools and universities. A clear distinction was being made between fascist teachers and revolutionary ones. One of our sports teachers, a boxer, got beaten up because he'd threatened people with the power of his punches. The fascist teachers got a little nervous. My classmates came mainly from the villages of Haceri, Çukur, and thereabouts. Most were close to the PDA[64] and a few to TİKKO.[65] The factions' names weren't often spoken aloud, but in discussions it quickly became clear who belonged to which one. But we formed a common front against the teachers with fascist tendencies.

School conditions were getting worse. There were no more fascist boarding students, but the living conditions were awful. There weren't enough teachers. Fascist teachers were usually given preference. Many demanded to be transferred, while others who were supposed to come to Tunceli didn't arrive. The school's windows were broken, and the heat usually didn't work. Conditions deteriorated in every respect. It was all an effort to suppress the political dynamic that had emerged in the school.

The German lessons with our teacher Mesut became laughable because of Zülfü [a fellow student]. The German word *Herr* means in Zaza "donkey." During an entire class Zülfü kept saying "Herr Mesut." He strung a few words in Zaza together and mixed in a few German words, to provoke the teacher. But Herr Mesut didn't give up. I was good at German, having spent almost a year in Germany. I liked the class, but sometimes Zülfü got on my nerves, because he created the same nonsense in almost every classroom. For him, being a leftist revolutionary meant opposing learning and school.

In the Turkish class, Zülfü, sitting in the back row, made a funny noise whenever the teacher, İbrahim Polat, turned his back. Who did that? the teacher asked. As soon as he turned back around, Zülfü made the noise again. I found it ridiculous and signaled to him to stop, which the teacher saw. He asked the whole class who was responsible. When no one answered, he called a few people to the front of the classroom. He considered snitching to be proof of honesty. The students he called to the front were considered upstanding and intelligent.

Why didn't we just tell him who had done this obnoxious thing? But we were silent. The teacher was actually beloved, he came from Dersim and was known as a progressive revolutionary. In the classes and during recess, we often had discussions with him. But he was still a teacher, a representative of the state. We students formed a united front. To betray someone from our own ranks would be wrong. The teacher, to punish us, rapped our knuckles with a ruler. We were in high school, and he hit us! I wept in astonishment. During recess we confronted Zülfü. I told him his behavior had been vacuous and silly. He said that it had been entirely normal and that I was angry because I'd been hit. The teacher, İbrahim, apologized, but I was hurt.

Years later I would meet İbrahim again in İzmir, and during our conversation, he made a signal with his fingers that showed that he remembered the incident and asked once again for forgiveness. He was a very worthy man, and I'd forgiven him long before. Zülfü, on the other hand, later switched sides. His behavior reflected his character. I never liked him, so it was normal that we took separate paths.

Another protest took place in our school, this time to demand improved school conditions. You can guess which factions put it together, but that wasn't important to me. The demonstration was to be an act of resistance, and the need to participate was obvious. We would march from the school to the government building.

When we passed the hospital, the police tried to stop us, so we threw stones. We had agreed in advance on what to do if the police opened fire. If they shot into the air, we would use walls and cars as shields and continue the march, shouting our slogans.

Along the route, several students were arrested, to our outrage. By the time we neared the commercial street, the crowd had swelled. Many local people watched us from afar—we called out to them, "Join us!" Some warned us to be careful, saying that our slogans should relate only to the school protest, that we should just demand windows, doors, heat, and more teachers. But others were shouting "Neither America nor Russia—for an independent Turkey!" Not everyone supported that slogan. I hesitated too, because I wasn't really sure if it was a good one. Yet it seemed wrong to hold back. So I shouted a full-throated "Down with fascism!" My voice rang out the loudest. And we demanded that the detainees be released.

As we assembled in front of the government building, still shouting our slogans, the state prosecutor appeared on the balcony. He seemed to want to intervene and tried to calm us. "The detainees will soon be released," he announced. But even hours later none of them had been freed. The protest was roiling all of Dersim. Students at the Teachers School came. At the bridge into our neighborhood, the police tried to stop the demonstration. A few people went across anyway, and others supported them from a distance. Even helicopters were deployed. We heard that the governor called to demand commando units of gendarmes from Hozat and Pülümür [districts in Dersim]. "There's an uprising under way! The Kurds are rebelling!" he supposedly said. All the police were put on an emergency basis.

The crowd was restive. Suddenly I noticed my father among them, apparently looking for something. He was home for that year, during the unrest. A peaceful vacation was out of the question for him. Now he was looking for me. With his suit and his trimmed mustache, he resembled civilian police. Anyone who didn't know him would find him suspicious. Beforehand we had been warned that civilian police would be mixing among the demonstrators to provoke or to make arrests. So everyone was paying attention to what was going on around them. My father spotted me, and as he made his way over to me, a knot of people stopped him: "Sir, wait a minute, where do you think you're going?" He said, "I'm going to find my daughter. She's got to go home, her mother is ill, she's fainted." When a brawl threatened, I stepped in.

My father stood with me for a while, then said somewhat abashed, "Let's go home. Your mother really is sick, and if you don't come, she'll die. Come with me and see for yourself. Then you can come back here." Just as he said it, people around us started roaring slogans again. My father turned to them and said,

> Girls and boys, don't shout such things. You're students—stick to your own demands! Otherwise these bastards will really let loose on you. As you've heard, they've called in soldiers as reinforcements. These bastards don't care a whit that you're young and go to school. They don't care that your demands are justified. You've got to be careful. What does this have to do with America and Russia? Wake up!

As the others sobered a bit, he tried again to persuade me to go home, even just briefly. His persistence infuriated me. Up until then, his behavior had been reasonable, and I'd tried to stay calm to avoid hurting his feelings. But now even in all this chaos, he was still pleading on behalf of my mother and trying to pry me from my friends. It was too much—no way would he separate me from this action.

> Dad, can't you see what you're doing? I'm here with my friends at a demo, we're in the middle of it. We all worked on it together. They all have parents too. I can't just run off to my mom!

My words incensed him, but his stubbornness seemed perverse. Where was his usual understanding for me? Couldn't he see how awful it would be for to abandon my friends? Finally he left, dejected.

Once again the situation reached a crisis point. We were in front of the government building in a police kettle, hemmed in on all sides.

Gendarme and police units stood with weapons in hand only a meter away. Through the windows we could see that chaos reigned inside the building. Then the governor appeared at a window, aiming a pistol at the crowd. We circulated quiet warnings to each other not to be provoked or to let ourselves be dispersed and resolved to continue even in the face of gunfire.

Some students from the Teachers School arrived. We recognized them by their clothing and by the slogans they shouted.

The danger loomed that if a shot were fired by accident, the security forces would open fire on the whole area. Suddenly the state prosecutor wrested the pistol from the governor's hand and cried, "Mr. Governor, Mr. Governor, have you gone mad? Those aren't Kurdish rebels—they're children—students! They're just trying to tell you about problems at their school! If the police shoot at them, it will turn into a rebellion!"

A while later he reappeared on the balcony. "My dear young people," he said,

> listen to me. You must stay calm. We understand you. I swear on my honor that your friends will be released within the hour. I will personally see to it. If they're not released, I'll offer my resignation. I declare that here openly, for all to hear.

His promise was interrupted by slogans, but the slogans weren't picked up. He was trying to say we should wait peacefully. A bit of calm followed. A few activists thought the prosecutor, as a man of the state, wasn't to be trusted—he just wanted us to back down. We should march on the police station now, they said. No one trusted the prosecutor, but it was also important not to let ourselves be provoked. The crowd was indecisive—what did we actually want, and what should we do if our demands weren't fully met? Because the action was unplanned and spontaneous, we hadn't decided on that in advance. Finally we decided to wait for one hour. If the detainees weren't released by then, we'd march to the police station. Word of this decision got around.

An hour passed, and there was no release, so we got moving again. Then all hell broke loose. A loud crack was heard—perhaps an explosion, perhaps not, but it was enough to transform our mood. We ran, screaming slogans, into the commercial street, while the security forces also got moving. The clashes began. The gendarmes pistol-whipped everyone who got in their way. The police attacked with clubs. We threw stones. The fighting spread from street to street into all the neighborhoods. The local people held back and watched the fighting from a safe distance. A wall of police and gendarmes stood between us and them. "Join us!" we cried, but the people didn't come over to us, and we couldn't flee to them.

Then one group shouted, "Army and youth, hand in hand!" The soldiers attacked them. *Oh, what crap!* I thought. *What's that even supposed to mean, "army and youth hand in hand"? Can't they see what the army is doing to us?* The slogan exasperated me no end. Since early morning we had been shouting slogans, but this one was from the PDA—members from the Teachers School had recently joined our action.

The demonstration slogged on with brutal clashes, then fell into disorder. When we reached the camp, someone suggested we go to the justice building, because the detainees would have been taken there. Others insisted on going to the police station. No one was in charge, much to my chagrin—all this open squabbling was helpful only to the police. The local people were watching, staring out at us from their windows. The children were rooting for us and mimicking our slogans.

The uncertainty intensified the pressure we felt. Our friends had still not been released—in fact, more had been arrested. The protest that had begun in the morning ended in the evening in this regrettable way. We reassembled in an unsuitable place. If we had been in a residential neighborhood, we could have dispersed into the streets, but here we were exposed to the police, who could easily corral us if we tried to leave.

Someone expressed just this fear, so we started moving again, heading for the school. But before we got there, as we passed the hospital, the march dispersed. Word went out that everyone was to scatter into the streets and try not to get caught. The next day when we got to school, we were all to be careful, because the police might do an inspection at the entry.

Inside the government building, the detainees were interrogated. Most of them were from the Teachers School. In a sense, it was an advantage to be high school students—we'd started the protest, but the cops came down harder on those from other schools or from outside. Under interrogation, the detainees were beaten, threatened, and insulted. Some of the young women were released during the night, but Türkan, Nurhayat, and a few others were still in custody. That gave rise to speculation that those released might have informed on the others. Rumor spread quickly that those still in custody were being treated in terrible ways. Some of the female detainees might be raped, and tortured with clubs. After four or five days, everyone was released.

"Marvelous girls!" Much was said about the young women who had been taken into custody during the protest. Rumors spread that the police had done awful things to them. Their families rejected such rumors, considering them injurious to their honor. But in general people were sympathetic to the "marvelous girls."

These events had consequences for my relations with my mother and my circle of friends. Various groups from the revolutionary left appeared on the scene, advancing different ideas and definitions, with diverse slogans and analyses of the events. These differences weren't decisive, but in every activity, we noticed the presence of ever more varied theoretical and practical positions.

School and classes, for their part, were ever more meaningless. We considered school a means to an end, something to be used—you just had to move up from one grade to the next. More important than regular participation in classes and study was the possibility of raising political developments in the classroom and discussing them there. The most progressive and revolutionary teachers allowed such open discussions, while those with fascistic tendencies rejected them, making their classrooms unendurable, but then we made it impossible for them to teach. Student attendance shifted with every hour, but lists of those who had been present in the previous hour were always marked "complete." It wasn't important to be present really—even those who didn't show up were put on the roster. Some skipped classes just because they felt like it, but most used the time for revolutionary work. The school didn't hinder anyone from doing that work, but consciousness wasn't complete, and many families reacted with anger, so we had to be careful. An extreme act could have negative consequences. Increasingly the school became a political gathering place.

To understand events correctly and choose the right side, I had a lot to learn. Leftist groups carried out many actions, underpinned by many analyses, in the name of the revolution, but none of them turned out to be what I was looking for. Others felt the same way. You didn't do revolutionary work out of politeness. Many people I knew tried to win me over to their factions. They handed me newspapers, magazines, and flyers that reflected their political views, or they tried to collect membership dues from me. I gave some PDA members a contribution and took a copy of their newspaper, even though I'd never liked or agreed with them. In fact, I found their slogans preposterous and their behavior repulsive. But whoever gave me a newspaper or flyer would then go on to count me as "one of us." Especially in the early years people acted that way. Their goal was to recruit members, but they were so transparent as to be offensive.

At home, reading books was considered dangerous. We talked about it endlessly. My very alert mother noticed that my attitude toward school had changed and that events were influencing me. Actually, they shattered my world as a young woman. My desires and my behavior changed every day. My circle of friends changed. Now we visited each other and had tea for specific purposes. Instead of dancing to music on cassettes or talking about clothes and trousseaus, we talked about the less superficial things that moved us now. We struggled to understand political events and exchanged stories about the heroic revolutionaries we all knew about. My older friends had come from the neighborhood and the school, but now I had more to do with the students at the Teachers School and the Girls Art School. My new friends and I bonded over our shared feelings and ideas. My mother watched me suspiciously, observing us. In those days, some young women took up smoking cigarettes, equating that with freedom. As if they'd liberate themselves by smoking in public! But that wasn't for us.

My mother followed me around like a shadow, always trying to figure out what I was up to. Whenever I came home after being with my new friends, she was unbearable—she even sniffed me to find out if I'd been smoking. Sometimes she made a secret mark on my embroidery, to find out whether I'd been working on it, as she later confessed to me in one of our arguments. She let me do nothing without her permission, go nowhere without informing her. I didn't lie to her, but it would have been unwise to explain all my new contacts to her. Had she shown any comprehension, I would've told her much more, but she didn't, and I didn't. Still, she intuited a great deal. She was intent on controlling me, observing me, and obstructing me. My big brother was no longer at home—he stayed mostly in the city—so I was the oldest sibling and yet a "girl." I hadn't yet joined any organization, but my mother worried because I was tenacious and stubborn, and because I had chosen the revolutionary left as my political direction, and because my commitment to it grew stronger every day. And she was afraid I'd influence my younger siblings.

Julius Fučík's *Report from the Gallows*[66] was the first book I read, then *The Mother* by Gorky.[67] Both impressed me greatly. We passed books around and read them and got together to discuss important passages, so it was as if we read them several times. Our discussions helped us understand a book's content. My neighborhood friends Perihan, Cemile, Nimet, and Fethiye were among the readers, and more reading was going on in other parts of the city. Word got around quickly as to who had which books. Many were allowed to keep books at home. Türkan Çakmak, my school friend who later went to the Teachers School, came

5 Cansız (*left*) with Türkan Çakmak, Dersim, 1974.

from a family that didn't have many rules. So she could move around more freely than the rest of us—in fact, she could go anywhere and was very active.

Our sports teacher, Ali Aydın, had finished secondary school in Dersim, then went elsewhere to study, then returned to teach at his old school. He was beloved and considered teaching to be a service to his people. He was especially interested in karate, tae kwon do, javelin throwing, high jump, and broad jump. The fascists considered karate important—but now we thought, why not learn about it from this Tunceli high school teacher? Once upon a time we would have rejected martial arts as fascist, but now we got interested in them. After all, our teacher was a Dersim revolutionary, which made him all the more appealing. And revolutionary leftists had to be physically strong and flexible for self-protection.

You could also learn to play the *saz* in school. More and more young people did so, and the classes were good opportunities for get-togethers, since our parents considered them innocuous. But all the parents in all the families shared the same fear and issued the same warning: *Don't become a revolutionary, and don't get involved in politics, because it will only lead to catastrophe.*

"There are no peoples, only one people!"   My admiration for Ecevit was diminished by his strange behavior at a certain demonstration. Some were advancing the slogan "Freedom for the peoples," and it got on his Kemalist nerves. "There are no peoples, there's only one people," he objected. He referred to the speakers as "enemies of the people and provocateurs." He stirred up the people against each other with his comment: "In Kovancılar, MHP members threw stones at me. They too are enemies of the people. They're not your children. You have to recognize them and give them no quarter."

Anyway, I didn't applaud for Ecevit at this demonstration, as I had before. I didn't write any slogans on the walls. I had gone to the demo wearing an Ecevit-blue shirt. I was still a follower of his, seeing no contradiction between that and my revolutionary convictions. But this day changed everything. With his remark that there were "no peoples, only one people," he lost my respect and that of many others. Actually it opened our eyes: Ecevit was just a representative of the system, who merely promoted, defended, and safeguarded Kemalism.

It was a beautiful sunny day. People were crammed together in front of the city hall. The square was so full that if you had dropped a pin, it wouldn't have hit the ground. When Ecevit began to speak, a group carrying banners and signs called out "Freedom for the peoples!" Peoples! Why did this phrase "the peoples" infuriate Ecevit so? Suddenly we found him hateful. Previously even his quirks had been appealing to us, but now his face seemed strange and inhuman. I first noticed it that day. His qualities that had once seemed good were transformed into their opposites.

Many had regarded Ecevit as a demigod, a savior, but by denying the concept "peoples," he wrecked this reputation. To deny the Kurds and other peoples was blatant racism. For years people had assembled here and supported "Karaoğlan"[68]—who did he think they were? Turks? No! His leftist mask fell, revealing his true face as a racist. That he rejected the MHP and Türkeş no longer made sense. His years-long conflict with them had only distracted us from reality. The slogan he now rejected had been shouted not by enemies of the people but by Dersim youth— we all knew them.

At Ecevit's order, the police attacked, ripping the sticks from the banners and using them to beat people. The provocateurs also used banner sticks to attack, not just the Grey Wolves but their own people.[69] Their view was that the banners disrupted the demonstration and had to be dismantled because they had sown chaos. In the end the state was not to be radically challenged.

This demonstration transformed me. I removed the carefully framed photo of Ecevit from the wall in our flat and threw it to the floor. My mother shrieked, "Have you gone mad?" Yes, I'd gone mad. Ecevit, to whom hitherto I'd felt closely allied, had allowed revolutionary youth who I knew to be beaten, because they'd spoken of the "fraternity of peoples"! By removing his photo, I was striking out on a new course, making a new beginning. The event induced me to ponder my real identity. With every question that arose, I undertook a new self-search.

And family pressure spurred me on even further.

Normally my siblings were favorably disposed toward me. But my middle brother Ali was rather more conventional and very close to our mother. She took advantage of that and sometimes had him follow me, to spy out where I was going. She looked for excuses to come down hard on me, so I usually exercised caution. But sometimes I took risks. She and I fought hard battles, neither of us willing to give in. She tried to bribe me materially, by offering me good clothes. In her eyes, brand-new, fashionable garments from the shops were compelling arguments. Had I been at all interested in them, she could have had reason to hope.

But my searching was still hampered by a missing level of consciousness. Slowly I edged my way toward a foundation that allured and impressed me, I couldn't resist it. Yet my mother still had far more power over me than the police or the military. She was like an organized institution, domestically. All her antennae were extended in my direction. She let me do what I wanted as long as it didn't have anything to do with politics. Yet in practical terms I didn't do anything unusual, apart from reading a book now and then and listening to or participating in a discussion. So what was she so afraid of? She didn't take things lightly. Her intuition told her she was going to lose me pretty soon. She tried to save me because she was convinced that once I found my footing, she'd never be able to hold on to me. Not engagement, not marriage, not school could stand in my way. And it was actually from her that I had learned such determination. My struggle with my mother prepared me for other struggles.

The person I was fighting was a woman, a mother, a comrade of my own sex. She was closer to me than anyone else. It's not that I would have preferred to be born a boy. She often said, "If only you hadn't been a girl!" and every time she did, I loved femaleness more. But her manner of fighting propelled me to enter a battle for which I was still far from ready. She either didn't notice or was unaware of what her behavior could lead to.

My father presumably knew about our escalating conflict. Maybe it was a conscious decision, or maybe just happenstance, but that year he decided to take my mother to Germany with him. On the way, she stopped to visit Metin in Ankara. I don't know if she intended it as advice or as actual pressure, but she said to him, "Young man, I will not be in Dersim. While I'm gone, don't go there, otherwise there'll be talk. When I come back, we'll go there together!" Maybe she thought I'd have a bad influence on Metin and entice him into political work. Surely her motive wasn't to protect my honor, since we were engaged. And his parents were in Dersim! No, it was an embargo against me.

Metin respected rules and traditions. Even if he didn't like what my mother said, during the semester break he did stay away from Dersim.

But during that time when he and I didn't see each other, many things happened. His letters to me got stranger, and more important, I decided to become a revolutionary, even if my ideas were still a bit hazy. My relationship with him wasn't at the forefront of my thoughts. This just happened by itself.

In my letters to him, I tried to explain that I'd changed and was no longer the Sakine of old. Actually I wasn't really sure how I'd changed or what I was looking for. I acted emotionally, in acts of defiance that had no stable foundation. Metin, for his part, became calmer and ever more mature. In his letters he tried to understand me and gave me advice. I should choose my friends carefully, he said, and keep away from certain people as much as possible. He singled out a few of my girlfriends, saying I should be careful of them because they could poison our relationship. I didn't like him giving me advice and judging my friends. It was irritating that he thought I could come under others' influence. So I wrote back that I was no longer a child. Of course, I was indeed influenced by the people around me, and his opinion of my friends wasn't all that wrong. My defensiveness was an overreaction. But his warnings reminded me of my mother's methods—she was always comparing me to others, which made me so mad.

My behavior heightened the differences between Metin and me. I read the letter with his warning out loud to my friend Nimet—she was one of the girls he'd referred to. How dumb I was to do that! Nimet and I were friends, we loved and respected each other, but I didn't have to tell her everything. Later, when Metin and I began to grow apart, she used the letter to widen the gap between us.

I was still young and immature. Instead of learning to cope with growing up, I rebelled against everything I heard and rejected everything I encountered. That was apparent in my fights with my mother. My struggle with her was inevitable, necessary, and incredibly instructive. It paved my route toward a revolutionary life and taught me to love women. At that time, my joy and pride in women who chose a revolutionary life was still weak. My mother had the strongest influence on me. Women who rejected their own sex and were unjust to them made me angry. I was interested in Aysel Doğan, Saime Aşkın, Türkan Çakmak, and Nurhayat, young women who studied in the Teachers School and were associated with various revolutionary groups.

6 Cansız with school friends, *c.1974*. *Left to right:* Medine Vural, Cansız, Nimet Kaya.

My family never really liked [my friend] Kıymet. She was a teacher, a profession that was considered "blessed" for women, and she was interested in politics. My mother didn't care for her appearance, or her masculine behavior, or her free-spirited demeanor. But what really bothered her was her political activity. Although my mother's values had no meaning to me, I didn't find some of Kıymet's ways particularly attractive either, but her political side interested me. When I wanted to get to know a person who was politically active, I also got to know their milieu. Over time I learned to form friendships on the basis of new criteria: not residence in the neighborhood but political perspective. As I got to know more people this way, I soon found myself in circles that were very attractive indeed.

Searching Generally you knew or could guess who belonged to which group or sympathized with which faction. The way a person moved and spoke, the concepts and slogans they used, all their ways pointed toward their political orientation and class background. People never stated their theoretical-ideological perspective explicitly, it was reflected in their daily life and in signs of affiliation. For example, TİKKO members called one another *kirve* and *bacı*,[70] and they all wore the same army parka and boots and had the same haircut and beard. They considered a scruffy look chic. The point was to make clear that they rejected the existing system and its material possibilities. Instead of working toward a renewal and beautification of life, they created a culture of helplessness.

That outlook was understandable as a first reaction, but as a foundation for a principled way of life, it was bogus. This was no way to arouse wide interest in a revolutionary life; most people would find it repulsive. When my cousin İbo visited us, my mother snubbed him on account of his appearance. He looked slovenly and stank of sweat. And it wasn't as if they didn't have time to pay attention to their personal hygiene. They neglected it as a matter of principle. The strangest thing was that they invoked Mao to justify their way of life. It's one thing to find ways to cope with difficulties and remain steadfast under onerous conditions, but to interpret Mao in this superficial and self-serving manner was something else. Basically they used Mao to justify their own inadequacy.

People obsessed over the behavior of other revolutionaries. Some of them did things only at their own convenience, as some of us who were looking for the right path forward realized. The unity of words and deeds had a pronounced effect on relationships. Sometimes a single word carried enormous meaning. In general, a revolutionary life was associated with courage, selflessness, audacity, and the ability to stand tall even under arduous circumstances. Challenging every form of injustice was a basic principle. A revolutionary personality was also energetic and creative. The first impression played a crucial role, because as yet no liberated life existed that one could point to. Everyone shared certain political theories and general truths, but not everyone had really internalized what it meant to be a revolutionary.

Most were caught up in a youthful enthusiasm; only a very few developed a comprehensive consciousness. We had no criteria for a socialist personality or a revolutionary life. People were merely reactive, yet they were passionately prepared to embark selflessly on a better life. Their life circumstances drove them—that was a law of dialectics. Development and change were unavoidable, but protests were disorganized and disjointed. We were still searching.

Joy in learning Despite the constant strife with my mother, I loved our apartment in Dağ. The beautiful things I experienced there are unforgettable, and remembering even small details always brings me joy. During that intense time, I learned about life, chafed under the strictures of tradition, and rebelled. Some part of me felt connected to conventions and wished to find a satisfying life along those lines. But another part longed for a new, more beautiful way of life. As I look back and think about it, a deep sigh escapes me.

I read a lot in those days—reading and studying delighted me. I studied for school less passionately because the pedagogy was based on memorizing things and then regurgitating them, which I found boring. I much preferred books about social problems, ideology, politics, and literature. In class, while standing up front at the blackboard, I found it very difficult to say anything. But in discussions outside the classroom, I was more relaxed and could express my thoughts. I often talked about novels I'd read and their mainly emotional impact on me. I usually got the essential points, but sometimes I lingered over details. Such minutiae then became the starting points for my interpretation.

At home, there were still six of us. My siblings were all younger than me, and I now had responsibility for the family. My mother's departure transformed our life. We did all the practical work together. Whoever was at home did the housework. We posted recipes in the kitchen. My brother Metin—I called him Meto—could cook better than I could. Life was exhausting.

In that year, we had an infestation of mites. Everyone in our family except me felt itchy. We didn't know why—had my siblings picked them up swimming in the Munzur or from other people?—but it was a horrible illness. They scratched their hands and arms until they were bloody, and then the wounds got infected. Everyone had to sleep separately. I boiled the laundry every day and bathed them every 24 hours. In addition to going to school and doing housework, I had to take care of five siblings. Almost all our money went for medicines. There wasn't enough dressing. I boiled the bed linens and sterilized them to use as bandages. I didn't get infected myself because I was always handling the medicines. My siblings were sick for a whole month and looked wretched. Depressingly they all lost weight. Given that our parents were away, my siblings' terrible circumstances could be interpreted to mean

I didn't take good care of them. But our next-door neighbors knew the truth. They felt sorry for us and tried to help.

My search for a revolutionary life made me more emotional. Being a revolutionary meant sharing cares and concerns and coping with pain. Shouldering the responsibility for my siblings and for family life was exhausting, but it made me stronger. Having to manage a situation for which I didn't have enough energy made me more conscientious.

And I was still engaged. Uncle Hıdır and Aunt Tonton[71] objected to my associating with revolutionaries and my new circle of friends. They also didn't like it that I had taken over the housework and the childcare. They blamed my parents. Sometimes Aunt Tonton brought us food after school. That was nice—and it felt awkward that an old woman thought of us and did us this service. But at the same time she and Uncle Hıdır tightened their control. By visiting us frequently, they reduced not only our isolation but their own.

They didn't interfere in my life, didn't try to impose restrictions, but then I didn't give them much of a chance. They could imagine how I'd react. While my mother was home, they'd encourage each other to criticize, but now it wasn't so simple. Sometimes they'd invoke Metin's name to criticize me indirectly. Tunceli was a small place—it was easy for the police to oversee everything. But then when Uncle Hıdır and Aunt Tonton explained to me, lovingly but firmly, that one must not attract attention and must not immediately form a friendship with every possible person, it led to a little fight between us. Clearly if I didn't draw a clear boundary at the outset, they were going to stick their noses into everything I did.

It was a sensitive subject. I couldn't allow them to consider me their property while I was still living in my father's house. They had no right to that, and I rebuffed it. [Metin and I] were, after all, only engaged. Their wish to get everything nailed down as soon as possible seemed senseless. I'd just come out from under my mother's shadow, only to face the possessiveness of two elderly people who considered themselves my parents-in-law. I seethed at their behavior but also got annoyed at myself. When I described the situation to Metin, he tried to smooth it over.

A secret we would like to penetrate   The mud-brick house that stood in the yard of our building held a magical attraction for us. I developed a new kind of relation with the students living there, and it wasn't only a matter of exchanging books. At New Year, Meto put on one of my dresses and my wig, then went over to the student house to celebrate with them. The wig and that clothing weren't important to me anymore and became a funny disguise. It was a visible sign of the transformation I was undergoing: by giving my old clothes and my wig to my brother for his pleasure, I was repudiating my old way of life.

I wanted to get to know the students in the mud-brick house better and to have a dialogue with them. Something about them appealed to me. They had a secret that I wanted to get to the bottom of. I'd go there sometimes to play *saz* or exchange books. Veli's brother Neco could play *saz* well. A lot of them played *saz*. Standing outside, we could tell, from the playing style and the voice, who was making music inside. My siblings found this student house very unusual in contrast to the apartments they knew. Through our frequent visits, a feeling of connection grew. They didn't have much money, but they were friendly and showed an interest in us. My siblings noticed how many things we had that these students didn't. They showed compassion and learned the joy of sharing.

That winter was difficult—it snowed a lot. The city's bakeries and some of the shops were closed. The options for shopping in the next city, Elazığ, were limited—there just weren't enough basic food supplies. The students were in an especially bad position, because normally families could provide for their basic winter needs in Elazığ. My mother had done all our shopping before she went to Germany. We had sugar, fat, flour, gas, everything we needed. She had impressed on us the importance of using it sparingly.

We supplied the student house in the yard with electricity. We ran a cable from our guest room, which was hardly used, through the branches of a mulberry tree. If you didn't look closely, you'd miss it. Our neighbors spotted it right away, but the neighbor from the Şavak tribe didn't care: she was good-natured and liked the students. And her own sons Mazlum, Halil, and Fazil had finished school and were now working as teachers somewhere. She could imagine what the students needed. And she knew that people involved in politics lived under special conditions and that it was a sign of humaneness to support them. She liked what we did and laughed sympathetically because in the absence of my mother, she considered us courageous and thought our close cooperation with the student friends demonstrated a greater level of responsibility in us.

It was unclear who came and went from the mud-brick house. Although the students were always careful, the people around us noticed the many visits during the daytime. The actual tenants were middle schoolers, but dozens of young people came in and out. The neighbors looked benignly on it. No one was disturbed, but they asked us about the students to satisfy their curiosity. Especially the families where the children were revolutionaries looked upon the young people with love and sympathy.

But the mud-brick house bore a secret. Its inhabitants were different. Of course, the neighbors wanted to know what kind of relations I, as a young engaged girl, whose parents and big brother were absent, had with so many young men. They knew me and trusted me, and we all went to school, but it seemed odd.

Sometimes the woman from the Şavak tribe tried to mother us. The Şavak are a large nomadic people from Çemişgezek [a district in Dersim], but this family had settled in the city. Having no daughters themselves, they loved me like their own. In my fights with my mother, they'd always taken my side. They'd only just begun to learn Turkish. After a while they set aside their traditional clothing and became city people, although their old garments were much more beautiful and looked better on them. Still, they could never get accustomed to city life. Sometimes they complained about it. Their son Mazlum was a quiet man. When I noticed that he tended toward a revolutionary life, I wanted to talk to him, but he wasn't open to conversations with young girls. His reticence meant we talked with each other only a little.

Metin Güngöze, Hüseyin Güngöze, Hasan Taş, Veli and Necati Tayhani, Yılmaz ... I met with these comrades now all the time, and others were at the student house every day. They all came often. I borrowed books from them, read them, and returned them. No one found this objectionable. They didn't want me to return the books until I'd read them. I felt that they all accepted me, and they seemed to like it that I sought them out. Since I knew most of them from school and before, our relations were relaxed. But when I met someone I didn't know, I'd invariably get shy. And the person would look surprised, because they weren't accustomed to meeting young women there. Once someone even said, "She's the classic example of the petit bourgeoisie, borrowing books and then returning them unread. She's faking it." Comrade Mazlum Doğan, who happened to overhear this comment, defended me: "Forget about the petite bourgeoisie. If you showed any concern for her, she'd become a revolutionary." He told me this, of course, much later.[72]

The arduous winter meant we had a lot to do. In the whole city there was no bread. Because of our ties to the students, they felt free to come and ask us, without embarrassment, for something. Veli was the first. He said guests had arrived, but the bakeries were closed, and if they had flour, they could make some dough and bake it in the oven. The fact that he was asking made all the difference—previously we hadn't dared to offer them anything. I'd often seen them try to satisfy their hunger with a few olives or some halva on newsprint. Afterward I'd cried. Several times my brother Meto told me about their austere meals and wanted to help them. But we shied away from offering help because we didn't know how they'd take it and feared insulting them.

But now they'd asked us. We bustled around preparing food, kneading bread, and lighting the oven. We moved quickly and animatedly, as if we had received an order that we were eager to fulfill. Every so often one of them came over and asked how we were coming along. Clearly they were hungry. So we pulled out all the stops. It was late, but none of us could sleep until the food was all ready. They'd asked only for bread, but we prepared food, heaped it onto big plates, and served it to them on a tray.

After that, we ate together every evening. Sometimes we contented ourselves with just a small morsel and gave the rest of the food to them. It made us happy. We made sure no one in the area saw us. After dark, my brother Meto would carry the food over to them on a big tray. We didn't want Aunt Tonton, or the family from Pertek who lived above us, to find out. Aunt Tonton looked for ways to help us as much as she could and didn't want me to suffer under my responsibility for my siblings.

She and Uncle Hıdır believed that since my parents weren't there, I mustn't form ties with others on my own initiative. They disregarded the obvious. If they knew we shared everything with our new friends, that wouldn't have been good. They both visited us almost every evening, which didn't make it easy. But we were well organized and arranged the food transfer quietly. If a comrade came to visit while Aunt Tonton and Uncle Hıdır were there, we brought him quietly into the back room or introduced him as a schoolmate or relative.

Haşim from Pertek was a master electrician who worked for years for the authorities on road construction, water, and power; currently he worked for all the agencies in Dersim. In addition to being an electrician and a civil servant, he had another occupation we didn't know about. He and his wife had only limited and superficial relations with their neighbors. His wife got visits from wives of police and other civil servants. We all found all that suspicious. His wife was still young and not a bad neighbor—my mother had a good rapport with her. And Haşim went hunting sometimes. As Alevis, we didn't eat rabbit, but sometimes we ate partridge. Whenever Meto went trout fishing, at least three neighbor families would have fish for dinner that night. He brought home heaps of trout. We gutted them and distributed them like sacrificial offerings to the neighbors. That was how we deepened our neighborly relations.

Some of those from Pertek and Çemişgezek were Turks who had settled in Dersim after the 1938 genocide. They lived mostly within their own culture, but in some things they'd adapted to Kurdish culture—for example, they now fasted for three days during Aşure month and cooked *aşure*. They were also influenced by conventions on circumcision and marriage, and longtime residents would even function as godfathers or best men. Pertek and Çemişgezek were where the fascists were organized. Some of those in Dersim were spies and agents, but it was dangerous to be an open fascist here—you'd risk your life. The fascists who had once been at the Teachers School and the secondary school dormitories had packed up their schoolbags and left. The few who remained took a beating. There were still individual fascists among the teachers, but they kept a low profile.

Our neighbor from Pertek was suspicious. In general the neighborhood knew who were civilian police and who were spies, and they weren't able to rent apartments as in the past. A few local homeowners had once been happy to rent to police officers, but no one wanted to do that now. The lines were clearly drawn. And the state sent out spies and secret agents everywhere.

By mutually supporting each other with food, wood, electricity, and books, we developed a pure and honorable connection with the young men, full of love and respect. In Dersim everyone referred to their own friends by well-known names to make it clear which group he or she was close to. Everyone knew how everyone else's political orientation was crystallizing. I wasn't fussy about those with whom I sympathized, but I felt a deep connection to these friends. Gradually I developed a position strong enough that those who instilled confidence in me gave me unsurpassed joy and excitement. I did not hesitate, hold back, or doubt. I didn't ask where this story would lead, who these people were, or what they represented. The answers lay in the confidence, grounded in respect and love that I felt toward the comrades because of their way of life. I was sure that over time all specific questions would be answered.

It isn't easy to describe everything, or for you to understand, without having lived it yourself. Writing can't do justice to the simplicity and beauty of those days or capture my feelings at the time. As I write, I'm experiencing them once again, with all my heart and with full consciousness. It was wonderful to arrive, so unconditionally and genuinely, through contradictions and struggles, at an ideal. It was an immense joy, and I will repeat it aloud now: *I'm the happiest person in the world because I participate in this struggle.*[73]

Conversation on a winter night   During one long winter night, D.K. was our guest.[74] That evening Meto had scorched the bean stew. What bad luck! It smelled burnt. Embarrassed, I tried to compensate by laying out pickled vegetables and brewing some especially fine tea. On this evening we were all doing cartwheels from excitement, because D.K., that is A., was coming to visit. Up to now we had spoken only briefly to each other and kept our distance. Veli and his friends visited more often. But this visit was special. I sensed that it would offer something new and unexpected.

After dinner we all took seats in the room and waited eagerly to hear what he'd say. Fortunately Uncle Hıdır and Aunt Tonton didn't stop by that night. But early in the conversation D.K. asked about them and their attitude. He knew about the situation more or less, because their constant visits made it obvious that they wanted to control me.

"There are so many of you—they can't control you," he said. "If you wanted to, you could easily shake them off. They're elderly. They don't have the energy to decide everything. Anyway, wanting to decide everything is their great mistake."

Then he asked how my mother's absence was affecting us. Before she left, my contact with revolutionaries had been more limited, since I had had to hold back. But since she left, the situation had clearly changed. To our complaints about my mother, D.K. responded: "Your mother is a good woman. The other women hardly talked to us at all, but she always greeted us and asked how we were doing." He also criticized our half-formed political consciousness.

Of course we objected, interrupting each other to name her sins. "It's great that our father took her to Germany. She was impossible and didn't let us do anything," Meto said. "She came down on my big sister harder than the rest of us. I went out in the mornings and came home at night. It's good she isn't here. You wouldn't have been able to visit so easily if she were."

D.K. laughed. He was calm, patient, and relaxed. His answers soothed us. Without being annoying, he showed us our mistakes. With simple, concrete examples, he tried to show us that every problem has a solution.

He referred to several novels that we'd borrowed from him and his friends and wanted to know how much of them we'd understood. We had recently read *Cement*,[75] and he asked what we liked about it. He commented carefully on a few passages himself, so we wouldn't feel he was testing us. We interrupted each other to share what had specially impressed us, but of course we hadn't read the book critically. D.K. explained there has to be a relationship to a socialist approach and that we must always read critically. I was embarrassed that I hadn't read the book the way D.K. interpreted it. But what were the criteria for right or wrong? *Cement* was a book about society. We thought revolutionary authors would write only what was true in their novels. But that evening I learned that you have to read every book attentively and independently of its author.

Similarly, you had to be careful about the many different political groups. They all called themselves revolutionary, but they represented different political orientations and carried out an ideological class struggle. Those who claimed to be leading a class struggle did it roughly. They all claimed to be right, but could they all be right simultaneously? No, impossible. Socialism was the only truth, and they all called themselves socialist, but did they live accordingly? That was the salient point. To live according to socialist principles, and hence according to the values you believed in, was key.

D.K. wanted to know what political orientation prevailed in the schools, in the classrooms, in the neighborhood, and among the relatives. He also wanted to know what we thought about such things. So he got to know us better and at the same time guided us in a certain direction.

My father's brothers' children all followed different political directions. In fact, almost every faction of the "Turkish" left was represented in my family: TİKKO, the PDA, the HK,[76] and the TKP. The neighborhood looked to be the same. In my class, PDA members were in the majority. My circle of friends told D.K. we didn't yet adhere to any group or faction.

He [D.K.] studied at Gazi Eğitim University in Ankara. He'd come to Dersim even though the semester break hadn't yet begun. Revolutionary work had priority for him. Metin attended the same university. D.K. knew him but didn't seem to like him much. "Metin is quiet, passive, and useless," he said candidly, "He's still in touch with the CHP milieu." That was all he said, but it made me unhappy. Obviously [D.K.] was looking for a reaction from me. I didn't say much and kept my feelings to myself.

Then we got down to the main subject. As we listened attentively, he slowly and straightforwardly explained certain issues. He defined the concepts of People and Nation and spoke of Vietnam, Angola, and Cuba. He recounted episodes from current national liberation struggles and quoted Ho Chi Minh, Castro, Cabral, Lenin, and Stalin to support the validity of his words. At times it seemed like he was telling us a fairy tale or reading aloud from a book. It was like a history lesson.

He explained in detail the Indo-European roots of the Kurdish people, their areas of settlement in Mesopotamia, and the Misak-ı Millî,[77] as well as colonialism and exploitation. He rattled off dates and analyzed the causes and effects of various developments. He talked at length about the 1938 Dersim uprising. His descriptions and analyses far surpassed the abbreviated explanations I'd heard from my father, mother, uncles, and grandmother. He vividly described terrifying massacres, the annihilation of a people. He described rapes, extermination campaigns, deportations, and betrayals.

Hearing about those cruel events made me tremble inside. We listened in breathless silence. How was it possible that the very existence of a people over such a long period of time could just be ignored? Kurdistan didn't appear in any history book. Our country was called Kurdistan, but for years we called it the Republic of Turkey.

D.K. continued his narrative, explaining the division of Kurdistan into four parts and the Sèvres agreement and Lausanne. He talked about the many Kurdish uprisings. It was endless. So riveting was his presentation, we didn't even realize when he stopped talking. In the schoolbooks we had read something about Sèvres and Lausanne. In some chapters the words "Kurds" and "Kurdistan" even appeared. But they were only words in books. Only now did we learn that our country was called Kurdistan and that it was a classical colony. That clarified many ideas for us.

Kurdistan is a colony and half feudal ... The right to self-determination of peoples is inalienable for the Kurdish people as for all others ... In Kurdistan organizations and struggles must correspond to a concrete analysis of prevailing conditions.

In his presentation, D.K. repeatedly mentioned Vietnam, which awakened my interest in that country. Vietnam, he said, was divided into north and south, and a revolution had taken place in the north. Over time in the south a struggle had emerged against a new form of colonialism, and finally a voluntary and democratic reunification had taken place. Similar processes of development had occurred in African colonies like Guinea, Angola, and Mozambique, and in many countries national liberation was still being fought for. The range of subjects became ever broader. I thought about Kurdistan. At the event I'd attended back in Germany, I'd seen a colorful map of Kurdistan. Only now did I begin to grasp that it referred to my country. And the more I understood, the more it affected me.

A handful of appealing people   I felt I'd finally found what I was looking for. Right away I forgot some of the details and dates he'd given us, but one thing constantly swirled around in my head:

Kurdistan is a colony. The Kurdish people will fight for their national liberation on the basis of their own power and with their own organization under their own leadership. An independent, united, democratic, and free Kurdistan will be founded, in which peace and prosperity will reign.

The Kurdish people would wage this struggle themselves, under their own steam. I'd never heard anyone use concepts like "their own power" and "their own organization."

The Turkish people are not our enemy. We're bound to them as siblings and friends. Our struggle will be carried out in common with them, but we will organize ourselves as conditions in Kurdistan require. A person suffering from a stomach ache isn't given the same treatment as a cardiac patient. Different methods are necessary.

In this way D.K. tried to show us what internationalism and love for one's own country were. In describing Kurdistan, he mentioned Leyla Qasim[78] and the heroism of Besê in Dersim in 1938. He said revolution isn't only a man's affair—rather, women and men must fight shoulder to shoulder for national liberation. Women were oppressed and debased, so the revolution is most important for them. As he said that, he looked right at me.

He explained all this in one evening and seemingly in one breath. It was late. We listened intently, until he finally said that was enough for now. Flustered, we felt ashamed that we hadn't known we were Kurds from Kurdistan. But it had been a pleasure to learn who we were this way. We were Kurds, and we had to fight for our own country, for our people, in alliance with all oppressed peoples. It was exhilarating. We were glad we hadn't yet joined another group.

In my mind, a few points remained unresolved. In whose name had D.K. spoken? What was the name of his movement or faction? What were we to call ourselves? He'd said that the struggle would be led by the revolutionaries of Kurdistan. Was the name so important? The question occurred to me only after he left. But more important was that we now had an analysis and outlook that we could bring to discussions as our own. We rehearsed it among ourselves, or as much as we had understood it, and thought perhaps no name had been mentioned because of the need for secrecy.

The presentation that evening became a starting point for us. In order to lead an ideological struggle, we needed a grounding in Marxism-Leninism and national liberation struggles. Learning, understanding, and knowing were all part of a revolutionary life.

At school and in the neighborhood, I talked enthusiastically about what I'd learned. First I told Türkan C., Ayten Ö., and Fidan A., but I wasn't able to win them over, so I invited them to our flat along with D.K. and Veli. During a protracted discussion, Türkan and the others became ever more agreeable. While talking to me alone, they'd stuck to their own views and disparaged mine. They were more theoretically adroit than I was, with a touch of demagogy. At the Teachers School

7 Cansız sitting, with Fidan Aydın (standing), c.1974. In the background is Cansız's brother Ali.

there was much more space for discussions, so they'd honed their skills quickly and reflectively. And they weren't under pressure at home and could move around freely. Before they left, they said they wanted time to consider a few points, and we could continue the discussion later. Fidan stayed aloof, but Türkan and Ayten wanted to think about these new ideas that seemed interesting to them, then renew the discussion. That was positive. It meant we might win over two people. Every discussion, every conversation would leave an impression. Our opinion was correct, we knew, and anyone who was really interested in a revolution would join us. It wasn't wishful thinking—we knew from our own experience how this analysis impressed people.

The ideology was only just beginning to get around, but soon everyone was talking about the new faction that had formed that gave priority to Kurdish identity. The other leftist groups made fun of it, but they were also intrigued. In discussions, the first thing people asked was the name of the new organization, which was so substantively different from existing leftist groups. Its approach was different too. The leftist groups relied on dogmatic propaganda—they wanted their names in the newspapers, they wanted to be known and to attract as many people as possible. The new ideology, by contrast, was promoted by very few people, but they stirred interest with their personalities and left an impression. Their self-certainty, maturity, and straightforward demeanor, as well as the determination evident in their speeches, gave them great appeal. Young people in Dersim had already joined distinct groups, but revolutionary work was still new to everyone, and political convictions weren't yet fixed. Everyone revered Deniz, Mahir, İbrahim Kaypakkaya, and other heroes who had lost their lives in the liberation struggle. The international left tendency had reached Turkey and Kurdistan, and people were ready to organize. Especially in Dersim, leftist groups competed to win over as many people as possible.

At the center of interest was the Teachers School. There the new group openly opposed the school's fascists and faced aggressive provocations by HK members, which some leftist groups worked to counteract. They misrepresented the incidents and propagandized against the "Kurdistan Revolutionaries," spreading the rumor that they were some louts from Urfa[79] who wanted to sow chaos in Tunceli: "They're not leftists, or revolutionaries—they're Türkeş supporters who say they're representing the Kurds. You should throw them out of the school." Their leadership cadres were teachers who tried to hold on to their sympathizers with propaganda so they wouldn't shift to another group. But in many cases their actions had the opposite effect: interest in the Kurdistan Revolutionaries was growing.

A conversation with Mazlum Doğan At secondary school, the Turkish leftist groups were in the majority. Their discussions were acerbic and often ended in fights. In my class I was almost the only one who supported the new ideology. Only Zülfü felt some affinity because his brother Kamer Özkan was in touch with the group. But he was hotheaded. Instead of making theoretical arguments, he stirred up conflicts. During the breaks, I led intense discussions with others. My arguments consisted of only a few sentences, but I constructed them carefully. Some called me a nationalist, which I hated, and I retorted that they were assimilated and uninformed and had lost their true selves, ashamed of their own Kurdish identity.

Our teacher, Abdullah, had been a DDKO[80] member who came from Muş. Discussions with him were more positive because we both accepted our Kurdish identity. As a teacher, he avoided deepening the discussion much, but he was happy about my interest in Kurdistan. In almost every class, arguments broke out, becoming heated on certain subjects. The teachers joined in. Our physics teacher, in his lab classes, criticized our grumbling:

> You've misunderstood the revolution. Physics is a science from which you can benefit. If you reject this education as bourgeois, you're mistaken. Here we have an opportunity to try new things. You're missing out on the chance to learn something theoretical and practical about explosives. It could come in handy.

At that, we conceded and performed some of the lab experiments. But our overall lack of interest outweighed it.

At home, nothing hindered our work. During a discussion, if someone showed signs of moving our way, we continued the conversation in their home. Our place was best suited—elsewhere, problems could arise. More and more people came over. After a while, we formed a group with T., A., N., K., C., and K.M. and started educational work. We met for a few hours each week. For safety, we met in a different home every time. We read and discussed classics on important philosophical tendencies, on dialectical and historical materialism, history, and class society.

On March 12, 1975, the Kurdistan Revolutionaries launched publicly in Dersim. Cadres, sympathizers, and members participated in a demonstration, marching from the secondary school to the government building, then through the lower neighborhood and over the bridge to the Teachers School. All of Dersim seemed to take part in this action, and the police and gendarmes went on high alert. It was impressive. Our slogans condemned the fascist regime that had resulted from the military coup.[81] "Down with March 12!" we shouted in rage, and for the first time the slogan "*Ji kurdan re azadî*" [Freedom for the Kurds] was heard. Comrades from Urfa brought this slogan and waved kefiyehs, symbols of resistance that I'd seen Palestinians wearing on TV and in newspapers. They used the scarves to hide their faces during airplane hijackings. The comrades shouted the same slogan over and over in strong, decisive voices, and we joined them. We could tell by the slogans who among the demonstrators were with us. C.M. marched next to me, and we called out the slogan together. One group from the Teachers School tried to drown us out with chauvinistic slogans. One PDA member screamed in my ear, "Down with nationalists!" I felt as if my eardrums would burst. I called her ignorant and said, "Aren't you ashamed of constantly attacking us?" Then I shouted again, "*Ji kurdan re azadî!*" Police were all around us, which was good because at that moment I wanted to punch her in the face, and then the situation would have escalated. This social chauvinist really got under my skin—how could she deny her own heritage so vehemently? But I didn't do anything, since we were all in the action together. The worst thing was that these people didn't know who or what they supported. I couldn't understand why they were so angry at us.

The shouting of slogans also reflected the numerical size of the various groups. We formed a bloc, but some of us chose to stay separate so that not everything could be deciphered. But the know-nothings from the Turkish left loved to make their numbers visible, as if their existence depended entirely on demonstrations and their strength was based solely on quantity.

The demonstration ended in front of the Teachers School. A minute of silence was called, and then came the speeches pointing to the day's meaning. Ahmet spoke for us, briefly in Kurdish. Then the rally dispersed, and we made our way back to the guest rooms.

There we met Mazlum Doğan—I'd never seen him in the apartment in Dağ, but now I saw him up close for the first time. We got to know each other and had a chance to converse. I asked him about a few things I'd been wondering about, mostly concerning Kurdistan's half-feudal social structure, modern revisionism, and the slogan "*Ji kurdan re azadî.*" Comrade Mazlum answered, "The slogan isn't wrong, you can use it, but it's too narrow, and it has a nationalistic tone. Ultimately we're demanding freedom not only for Kurds but for all peoples in Kurdistan."

His explanation ended my uncertainty about the slogan. But what about "Neither America nor Russia" and "Soviet social imperialism"? What was the group's opinion of those? Comrade Mazlum explained, using much evidence, why the Soviet Union could be called modern revisionism. This "ideological doping" after the demonstration was very exciting for us. Through the evening we continued to talk among ourselves. I got to know Nurhayat, comrades from Urfa including Ahmet, Cuma Tak, and S.G., and many other friends coming from different places in Kurdistan. To see them all together made me happy and gave me strength.

Alarm bells go off After the demonstration, I came home to find Uncle Hıdır and Aunt Tonton there. They had been worried about me and were angry, with grim faces. But I was in the best of moods, so I didn't take them seriously. I was elated from the terrific demonstration and my new friendships. I was taking an important step forward. Like many other steps I made that year, this one would contribute to a complete transformation of my life and my personality. Nothing would ever again be as it was before.

Even my clothing style changed. Now I wore plastic shoes and simpler clothes. Uncle Hıdır and Aunt Tonton grumbled about it. Our relatives and neighbors were surprised by my transformation, which proceeded unconsciously and unplanned. I adapted to the simplicity of the group to which I now belonged.

For me, a new life had truly begun. My rejection of all traditional ways altered me in many respects. No one told me how to dress or what to do. I voluntarily adopted the group's clothing and ways of life. My inner world reordered itself. The closer my connection with the comrades became, the faster my transformation proceeded.

The most important part of our work was education. We considered it a duty to show up punctually at the appointed place. Educational work demanded commitment, selflessness, attention, and awareness of responsibility. For a long time, II.Y. led our study group. We would read something and then discuss it. His guidance wasn't particularly lively, and he was uncomfortable teaching a group of women. Sometimes the group was mixed, but then we had to be careful not to arouse any notice in the neighborhood. The mixed groups had the advantage that the discussions were more colorful. The female friends were theoretically wayward—only a few were far advanced. H. looked up from his book only when he called on one of us. We made fun of his discomfort. Sometimes during lessons we used hand signals to refer to him. Our debates afterward were freer.

Discussions in the study group were serious: only when we all understood a subject could we move on to the next. The beauty of this work was that we all felt a thirst for knowledge and embraced the responsibility that resulted from it. Our studies took place in a comradely atmosphere and created a shared mindset. We all developed a determination to shoulder the revolutionary struggle, even its difficult aspects.

Sometimes when the study group met in our home, it was disrupted because I had to receive guests. Whenever someone visited us, the neighbors noticed right away. The doors were visible from the streets, so the neighbors could see who entered. Aunt Tonton paid particular attention and [when the study group met at our place] would come over to see what was going on. We'd act as if it were just a normal visit. It got on my nerves, though, because it made us lose time. Uncle Hıdır and Aunt Tonton could see that something had changed. They complained that our apartment had become a clubhouse where no one knew who came and went. And they noticed I didn't write to Metin as often as I had before. They heard alarm bells going off.

After we finished a few educational units, C. became the group's leader. Her father was known in Dersim as a wealthy man. Her family was large, and a few of them were teachers. Y., C., K., and K. came to us from the PDA. They all had fundamentally different personalities. Since our home was becoming too conspicuous, the study group shifted to theirs. They lived in a quiet neighborhood of middle-class shop owners, vendors, building contractors, and the like. The family had several daughters, so it wasn't particularly odd that they would get visits from other young women. We worked with great discipline and always started on time. During the breaks we smoked. At first we drank tea, too, but stopped so as not to waste time. This discipline carried over into our daily life. We sat in a formal posture, and we raised a hand when we wanted to say something. No one forced this regimen on us or said it had to be this way. It was an expression of how seriously we took our work.

The group kept growing. Soon S.K. started coming. Every day it got stronger and consciousness rose: we were the first women's group. Over time we began to point out one another's weaknesses, practice critique, and identify mistakes. A group consciousness emerged. We talked about how to behave toward other groups when making contact and discussing. We were to avoid provocative, off-putting behavior, and we wouldn't let ourselves be provoked by the other side. To win people over, we had to proceed constructively. But the other groups used a method that had nothing to do with revolutionary consciousness: they forbade their sympathizers and members to discuss with us, and they tried to prevent them from listening to our more articulate members speak. They preferred discussions in which they could use demagogy in a struggle for power. They wanted to bind people to themselves. Unfortunately this meant suppressing an open exchange of ideas. But not even this tactic could prevent our ideology from spreading. With determination, self-consciousness, and enthusiasm, our group set out to overcome all obstacles. No clashes, no provocations, and no intolerance could impede us. Our force of will was too strong. We carried on our struggle on the basis of our convictions.

It was like a divine force. Our group's members and sympathizers could hold discussions with a broad range of people, without fear and with great passion. That was what astonished everyone. Our group had no name, no newspaper or magazine of its own, and no headquarters, but everyone behaved the same way in the face of injustice. Initially we were mocked as the "three or four Kurdish supporters," but then people said "Kurdistan Revolutionaries," and finally the name "Apocu" emerged.

Our numbers continued to grow, along with an awareness of Kurdish identity and tradition. We analyzed concepts like Country, Nation, and People according to revolutionary criteria. Who was the enemy? How would we fight him? With which party and which army? Our tiny and generally scorned group with high revolutionary claims had to answer these questions. But those who sensed the group's uniqueness couldn't escape its influence.

Suffused with hope and longing on the road to reality Women and girls were part of this revolutionary process, as the ideas spread quickly, especially in the schools. Women's participation wasn't unusual in Dersim, with its specific conditions. Here girls weren't considered less valuable than boys—on the contrary, daughters were loved even more. But revolutionary work was another matter. Political activity was dangerous even for men, so this work was unthinkable for women. Social values were changing, but brothers, husbands, fiancés, and lovers perpetuated feudal structures in revolutionary groups. Only our group rejected and combated feudal relations. If two people were attracted to each other, there was no objection to them forming a connection as long as it was based on new revolutionary criteria. But otherwise they proceeded at their peril.

During that time our group still had no name and was disparaged as nationalistic or as nationalist-liberal. The enemy became aware of us, and the local people also began to notice us, and sympathy for us grew due to our radical attitude toward the police, our determined ideological struggle, and our enthusiasm. The group's name wasn't important. Even when someone tried to smear the group's image, sympathy for us expanded. Many groups that called themselves revolutionary propagandized against us, saying we were "worse than Türkeş supporters." But how persuasive could it be to deny us our identity and associate us with murderous thugs whose sole function was to destroy the highest human values through reactionary and racist politics? Even those who made such propaganda didn't believe it. Their attacks lacked any theoretical or ideological basis and contradicted left-revolutionary fundamentals. In the end, these attacks accomplished only one thing: they exposed the true face of the groups that made them.

The factions advanced differing theoretical analyses, but they were united against the ideology of national liberation. Even as the groups lacked internal cohesion, they attacked each other in ways that reflected their own lack of principles and their great volatility. They would invoke Deniz, Mahir, or İbrahim Kaypakkaya, but in competing with each other, they increasingly abandoned the revolutionary values for which those heroes had fought.

On May 6, the anniversary of the execution of Deniz, Hüseyin, and Yusuf, discussion forums took place in the schools. We participated at the secondary school. Much to our annoyance, some groups tried to claim these great revolutionaries for themselves, as if they had a monopoly on them. But only by continuing their struggle and advancing their revolutionary values could a group really connect with them. To the slogan "Long live the common struggle of the Turkish and Kurdish peoples!"[82] the most meaningful response was the one we Kurdistan

Revolutionaries gave with our ideology, our level of organization, and our actions. Only in this way could one memorialize the martyred revolutionaries and carry on their struggle.

During the forum at our school, a moment of silence was called, and then speeches were made. At the closing, slogans were shouted: "We do not forget May 6! Deniz, Hüseyin, and Yusuf will never die! Down with the fascist dictatorship!" Then the participants went at each other. But the "people's liberation front" wanted to absolutely prove its strength, so its members assembled in Dağ. That was where they had the largest base—they even called Dağ "our neighborhood." After the secondary school forum, they called another one, which annoyed everyone else. In Dersim the neighborhoods were very close together, so when a large group shouted something, you could hear it everywhere—the slogans were easily audible.

The police arrived to block off the quarter. As they approached, those who claimed to be leading the people fled, leaving behind mainly women and children. The police beat them and chased after the young men. One cop, while pursuing a demonstrator, came over to us—we were there as observers. A few neighbors and Roma women were watching the events from the street, or from windows and balconies.

Some of the women were exasperated at the young men, while others were furious at the police and insulted them. Then the police attacked them. They seized one woman and wanted to cart her off forcibly. I knew her—she was our neighbor, Elif. I jumped in and tried to pry her loose from the police, who then tried to seize me. Aunt Elif, the Roma women, and my little sisters all grabbed me to keep me from being arrested. The twins screeched, and Aunt Elif roared, "Take me! What do you want with this girl? She had nothing to do with it!" I comforted my crying sisters and gradually stepped back. The police were speechless at the reaction of Elif and the Roma women and let us go.

My admiration for the Roma Aunt Elif was a powerful woman, a widow whose children worked in Germany. After she drove the police off, she turned to me and scolded, "Go home right now! What are you doing outside at this hour? You're an engaged woman!" Then she went home. The Roma invited us to go home with them, and together we prepared a meal and ate it while sitting around a cloth on the floor. We talked for a long time. They explained how in their neighborhood in Erzurum, they'd protected young revolutionaries during a violent confrontation with the police. Today they were angry at the men:

> Those men who just looked down from the balcony—they're cowards! Their meekness only encourages these dogs, who are threatening us with another 1938. If they'd arrested you, we would've attacked them and freed you. Good thing they didn't try it.

The conversation turned to the subject of women and revolution. We talked about what women were able to do when they channeled their hatred of the enemy into organization. We praised the Roma women's courage and assertiveness. I said I'd admired them since childhood. They had sometimes set up their tents near our village, on the bank of the Munzur among beautiful willow and poplar trees. The men were skilled at tin plating. People from the surrounding villages brought their copper containers for that service. The women were collectors. Loaded down with saddlebags and carrying babies on their backs, they wandered around and begged for flour, fat, wheat, and more. They adjusted their wishes to a region's economic condition. That was how they survived. After a while they took down the tents and moved on.

Sometimes during the winter my grandmother let them live in otherwise empty houses and looked after them. They added to the village population. In spring they left, because city people came to the villages to spend the summer. The Roma way of life seemed to me very free. They moved around as they wished and never settled down permanently. On the other hand, I felt bad for them because they were poor and often encountered hostility. Whenever I could, I invited them to our house, and I got to know a few of them pretty well, as they visited often. Once when my mother was absent, I gave them some of our family's clothing.

The Roma women were beautiful, some of them enchantingly so, despite their poverty and ragged clothes. The young women cultivated a fine appearance, adorning their tresses with dozens of colorful clasps. Their swarthy complexions were alluring. Everything about them was natural, and their distinctiveness made them fascinating. "We're on your side," they said, but of course they also looked after their own interests.

Surely it would not be their fate to beg until the end of time. Maybe they didn't think that far ahead, but in an independent Kurdistan, I'd set aside space for them to have a free life. I'd seen Roma in Germany too, but they had a higher standard of living and weren't treated with such disregard as here and led their own lives. It was easy to recognize them because of their distinctiveness, and I liked them very much. The Roma weren't really free—how could they be? But they lived outside social norms and cared nothing for the existing system. They lived according to their own rules. That was what I so liked about them. My admiration for their "free" lives derived from my rejection of the social order and the family system, which boxed people in and made them unfree. In this respect I still see the beauty of their way of life.

Angry at others' mistakes, I take it out on myself   We had a serious problem with books. It was hard to get hold of them in Dersim. So my friends and I looked for new ways to do educational work. Many friends couldn't store books at home—the parents forbade them. The police, even without intervening directly, tried to spread fear, and books could serve as a pretext for repression. People in the group also had financial problems.

So some friends made bulgur wheat balls, garnished with parsley in bread, and sold them. This work also expressed their affinity with the proletariat and gave them respect. But having enough money just to live on was a problem. Hüseyin Güngöze would form the wheat balls quickly, with a cigarette dangling from his mouth, then arrange them on a tray.

Our friends' way of life was for us [the Cansız children] like a signal to get busy ourselves. My brothers Hasan and Ali sold water. Meto caught fish, delicious and expensive trout, and sold enough of them to meet our needs. He also worked as an electrician, repairman, and mover. He unloaded merchandise from trucks. We shared the money we earned with the friends, or we bought things they needed. We did it willingly, because we participated in their group and considered ourselves part of their lives. We had no fixed rules, but we wanted to share everything with them. The group was my world, and every member was precious to me.

One day when I was on the way home from school, my sister Nesibe rushed up to me excitedly: "The police want to get inside the mud-brick house. Metin told us to warn everyone to stay away!"

I was surprised. Why were the police suddenly going there? What was happening? But then I'd been afraid something like this might

8 Cansız with her brother Hasan and her sister Nesibe, c.1974.

happen. Recently I'd noticed our neighbor Haşim, the one from Pertek, observing the house. It had made me uneasy. And his wife had asked my siblings strange questions. A civil policeman lived right above us, and sometimes, on the pretext of going for a walk with his children, he'd spend hours walking around the street staring in our direction.

Aunt Tonton's excellent hearing affected our work. Once Meto and I had to spend several consecutive evenings together at a typewriter, pecking out excerpts from books using two fingers. We needed them urgently, so we took turns, typing into the early morning. But the typewriter made a racket that could be heard outside in the street. We set the machine on a soft pad and closed the windows firmly. Sometimes we worked in the back room, even though there was no stove there. Aunt Tonton was suspicious and warned us about producing "dangerous things." But the typewriter was ours. We said we were doing schoolwork. She didn't believe us.

Anyway, Nesibe's news was important—the others had to be warned. Clearly it wasn't just a routine observation, but I hadn't understood exactly what Nesibe said. Had the police already entered the mud-brick house, or were they about to? No, actually that wasn't so important— what was important was that the enemy had become suspicious and was taking action.

I racked my brains to figure out where we'd slipped up. Many people came to the mud-brick house, but mostly under cover of darkness. What had been the weak point? Maybe our home had attracted attention due to the many visitors and the use of the typewriter. Who knew? Maybe someone had noticed that we [siblings] ate dinner over there. And we'd run a cable over there for electricity—maybe the neighbors from Pertek had spotted it. Or maybe people from the Turkish left had informed on our friends. They always spoke disparagingly of the "nationalists" and named names, thereby acting, intentionally or not, as spies.

It hit me all at once. At home we pulled back the gauze curtains in our window, and Ali watched the mud-brick house, while Meto kept an eye on the street. They'd sent Hasan to the path below the mosque and told him to stay there till evening and warn anyone who passed that way.

It was winter, and the ground was snowy. Where were the friends supposed to go? From the window, Meto said he saw a man standing in the street and looking around carefully.

He was civil police. There were three of them this morning, pointing at the house and talking to one another. They waited awhile, then pointed to other nearby houses, and then to ours. Then they walked along the street. They wanted to find out if anyone was in the mud-brick house. I got suspicious. As soon as they left, I went over there. We sent a few friends away and brought their stuff over here, via the balcony.

He removed a few chair cushions and showed me three suitcases and some bags. They'd set some more bags on the balcony next to the woodpile. Meto continued excitedly,

We left the cable in place, because if we'd tried to remove it, we might have aroused more notice. It's still there. I sent Nesibe on the way to school and Hasan to the mosque. The comrades knew not to come home. Two are in the house, the middle-schoolers Ali and Necat, the renters. Otherwise no one's home.

For a moment I didn't know what to say or do. I hugged Meto. How astutely he'd behaved. But I also worried: Had he really been wise to bring the stuff over to our place? What if the police got suspicious and searched our home? Meto said he'd been very careful and pointed out that the balcony wasn't visible from the street. Still I was uneasy. I pulled out the suitcases and opened them. Inside were books, IDs, pistol clips, a chain, a knife, a map of Kurdistan, and several mimeographed papers, as well as three copiers, a typewriter, and revolver parts. Seeing it all, I got even more nervous. I had to find a solution. I couldn't take it over to Aunt Tonton in broad daylight. But on the lower floor of our building, there was a room where wood was stored. Meto took our key, climbed downstairs via the balcony, and put the key in the lock. It actually fit! Inside the room we found building materials and a woodpile. It belonged to the landlord and so would not be noticed.

Fear of the state   While we were figuring out what to do, a police van pulled up and parked. Police got out and went off to reconnoiter. Another group of police arrived from the lower road, at least 20 of them. A few scouted around, following tracks in the snow. They looked inside woodsheds and outhouses. One saw the cable in the mulberry tree and pointed it out to the others. He went over to another cop who had a radio set and indicated our home. They tried to figure out which flat the window belonged to, where the cable originated. I was getting very nervous. Quickly we thought up a plan. "I'll get the twins," I said, "and make a show of taking them to the movies. Meto, you stay inside and watch everything. Ali should go into the city center and inform the friends. Hasan is already on the path." Meto agreed. "If they get in downstairs and find the stuff, we don't know anything about it. We say our neighbors gave us books because their house was damp, then went back to the village. We don't know what's in the suitcases because we never looked inside."

I changed into my cutest outfit and put on my wig. My fur-lined jacket and my bell-bottoms were very flashy. Then I went out to the balcony and called to the neighbor's daughter, Perihan, "We're ready! Which route should we take? Nimet wants to come too. It's a good movie, it's probably sold out already. So hurry, let's get going!"

The cops all stared at me, but I stayed cool. Perihan shouted back, "Let's go this way, it's shorter!" I took Nesibe and Feride from the flat and locked the door behind me. We passed between the surprised officers and went on our way.

After we left, the cops asked the landlord who lived there. It's the home of İsmail Cansız, he said. "The parents are in Germany, and the oldest son is in Istanbul. The siblings all go to school." The cops asked about the cable. At first the landlord hemmed and hawed, then finally answered, "They're students. They all go to the same school. The kids get money for it." That was a good answer. The police groused for a while, but their suspicions hadn't been borne out, and there would be no inspection of the flat.

"They live in their own world. Didn't you see her clothes?" said one cop. Revolutionary leftists in Dersim looked very different. The TİKKO and HK members dressed in a truly funny way—they wore trousers under their skirts and wrapped their heads in scarves. "Proletarian clothing," they called it. Our friends dressed more simply. Normally we wore pants or a skirt along with a shirt or blouse. It made us more agreeable to the people that we stood out less.

In all this tumult, could I really go to the movies? After we'd been gone for a while, we went to a neighbor's home, wholly inconspicuous, and waited there tensely. I sent the children outside to find out what was going on. We heard that two students had been arrested. Nobody knew what else had happened, but the two had been beaten. When the police asked them who else lived there, who came to visit, and whether they were expecting anyone now, they answered that they lived there alone. A couple of cops dug in to wait, but when it became clear no one was coming, they left. Once I was sure all the cops were gone, I went home.

Meto told me breathlessly what had happened in the mud-brick house. Apparently they'd found a few scraps of paper for a flyer titled "To our people! Our courageous people!" It consisted of only a few typewritten sentences, but the police regarded it as important evidence about the activities of the young people in the house. Then a few pieces of carbon paper turned up. The cops were sure the house was used for some specific purpose, but they couldn't find any more evidence. Fortunately no one visited that day—it would have wrecked the whole subterfuge. The cops were frustrated. "How can this be? Who tipped them off?" they wondered. "No one's come home! Oh, they pay close attention. They noticed something, and so they didn't come." It intrigued them that the ones they were looking for had acted so cagily. "These are real fellas, not like the other groups," they said. Of course, we learned about all this afterward from the neighbors.

Slowly darkness fell on that short winter day. I was glad, of course, because darkness offered protection. Out of breath, Ali finally arrived, explaining that the friends had learned that our home was to be searched too. They'd overheard it at a guardpost. We had to scour it, but where would we take our stuff? Meto leaped into action, shrewd and practical. He brought the suitcases and bags back up, over the balcony, and took them to the woodshed. I followed with a flashlight. We put the suitcases on the woodpile, shoved them into the farthest corner, and covered them with boards. We felt better.

But after a while this hiding place didn't seem safe to me. Suppose tomorrow morning our apartment was searched—wouldn't the cops look there too? I thought of Aunt Tonton and suggested her home to Meto. Ali broke in, "Uncle Hıdır is a coward." Meto agreed. Actually I thought the same, but I thought we should try anyway.

How could they turn me down? They considered me their daughter-in-law, so they'd just have to accept this risk. "There aren't any young people in their family," I said. "They're all old. Uncle Hıdır goes to the mosque and gets along with everyone, including those from Pertek. They don't call any attention to themselves." But I didn't dare just take the stuff over there. "If they say no, maybe everything will be much worse," I said to my siblings. No, better to go over to them and explain the situation.

So I went to their home with Meto. They were astonished to see us so late at night—no one ever visited them then. Aunt Tonton said, "What is it?" as Uncle Hıdır emerged in pajamas. I said, "We have a few books at home, and today the police searched the students' apartment [in the mud-brick house]. They might come back. We've been supplying them with electricity. It might make us suspicious to them." Before they could object, I rushed on: "We get money for it, it adds to our pocket money. But the police might get the wrong idea. In our house we have books and the typewriter. We could leave them here on your balcony, then tomorrow take them somewhere else."

At first they scolded me: "We've told you several times, but you don't listen. The students' place is like a clubhouse. No one knows who comes and goes. And you all are still in school—what do you want with books? Throw them in the oven! Forget about Marx and Lenin! It's impossible, girl! Your parents aren't here, not even Haydar is here. What if something happens to you—"

I interrupted her torrent of words gently: "It's only for one night. You're right, we've got to be careful. But now it is what it is. We've got to take precautions. So what do you think? Can we bring the stuff over here?"

Reluctantly, they agreed. We ran off to get it. It was much more than they'd expected. When they saw the suitcases and bags, they got nervous. Aunt Tonton groaned, but we didn't pay any more attention to her and wished them both goodnight.

Back home, we talked about their behavior. Ali insisted they weren't to be trusted. Meto joked about Uncle Hıdır turning the stuff over to the police.

I was still uneasy and also annoyed by the inconstancy of the old couple. As soon as something didn't suit their interests, their presumed affection for their future daughter-in-law vanished. They'd internalized fear of the state. I was also annoyed at [my fiancé] Metin because he'd done nothing to influence his parents. They didn't care if the world fell apart. How was I supposed to love these people and live with them? They saw me as nothing more than a servant. If that's what I was to be, then I'd break off the connection. For the first time, I really took stock of this relationship. What did they want from me? What made them feel they had a hold on me? And what about them was I supposed to love, given that I'd be connected to them? I was also mad at my mother, even though I knew that in tough situations like this, she always thought of us first. My future parents-in-law didn't. They didn't want to take any risks or experience any inconvenience.

During the night, we got a message from the friends: "Don't worry about us, but take good care of the stuff. We'll pick it up in the morning." It was delivered by a young man from the same village as one of the friends. So the connection was reinforced. It had been a very bad day, the mud-brick house was empty, and life was at a standstill. We felt very much alone. So this message made us happy.

In the morning a little peace returned. Our plan was to leave for school as always. If nothing happened, there would be no further problem until we could take the stuff away.

But it didn't work out that way, given the anxieties of Uncle Hıdır and Aunt Tonton. After I left for school, they asked Meto to remove the stuff. Meto tried in vain to persuade them otherwise. Then their grandson from Demiroluk showed up. In broad daylight they all hauled the suitcases and the bags over to our place, which of course everyone in the neighborhood saw. Meto wept with fury, but nothing could be done. He took the bags back to the woodshed. For the suitcases, we'd tell the police the same story as before, that we didn't know what was inside. It was risky to take them to the woodshed in broad daylight, since the landlord could see it.

When I came home after school and found out what had happened, I was shaken and incredulous. To bring the stuff back over to our place in daylight—it was a blatant betrayal. I went crazy with fury and howled every term of abuse that I could think of at Aunt Tonton and Uncle Hıdır. "I'm not your daughter-in-law!" I screamed like a madwoman. "Oh, it was a mistake to trust you. You care only about your own interests. You'd even betray your own son. Don't ever set foot in our home again. If you ever dare come over, I'll throw you out with my bare hands!"

It occurred to me that they must have spoken ill of me to my parents. The last letter from my father had been strange. He'd written in my mother's name, very reproachfully. Metin's last letter, too, had contained only advice, nothing more. That old couple! What did they take me for? Did they seriously expect me to stay home and put myself at their service as a dutiful housewife? Never!

I wanted to be a revolutionary, and no one could stop me I was aghast and sobbed with fury. What a catastrophe if the stuff and especially the IDs were found! Should we sort through it all and hide some of it elsewhere—at least the writings, the IDs, and maybe the map of Kurdistan? The books weren't so important, but the ammunition had to go. Meto kept his cool and tried to calm me: "We won't touch anything. We can't hide anything in the flat, and we can't remove it either. Best to leave the flat and go somewhere else."

That was a good idea. We went to Nimet's. Of course, we tried to make sure her family didn't know anything. I explained to Nimet what had happened. She wasn't surprised and said she would have expected nothing else from my future parents-in-law. That disconcerted me even further, and once again I questioned my relationship with Metin.

I was acutely aware that Metin hadn't come to Dersim for the semester break after my mother left for Germany. In his letters he didn't mention the subject anymore. Probably it was embarrassing for him that my mother had forbidden him to visit during her absence. Our families' behavior was actually furthering our mutual alienation. We hadn't grown closer—the gulf between us had grown wider. And this after we had formed an official connection, of which our families and acquaintances were well aware. It annoyed me when anyone tried to harm our relationship.

Sometimes I wished Metin and I could have a chance to talk about everything and run away from our families. But I didn't let him know that. He only knew that something was bothering me. Moments when I thought about escaping our families made me feel better. But I didn't know what Metin would think about it, so again I lost hope. The friends didn't interfere in our relationship. Whenever the subject came up, they just said Metin was passive and that his studies were more important to him than anything else. They were careful not to hurt me.

Unconsciously I was beginning to think the relationship made no sense unless we held the same convictions, because if we didn't, nothing would hold us together. I wouldn't have thought that way if our togetherness had developed spontaneously. But as it was, the new ideology was what gave my new life direction and meaning. The relationship with Metin couldn't be separated from that. I wished he were like the friends and that we could share our convictions. But his parents' recent behavior wrecked everything. I took the ring from my finger and vowed to throw all the engagement gifts at them if they dared ever again show their faces in our home. I tried to calm down and keep from spiraling into an extreme. But then one evening when they really did come over, I didn't hide my anger. I lit into them, accusing them of betrayal and criticizing them for using their still-young nephew. I didn't say anything else for the rest of the evening. I just didn't feel like it. I wanted to throw them out. It was unbearable to hear them talk. I was furious at Metin because he was their son. In my opinion, they didn't even think about him.

The friends didn't keep their promise to remove their stuff, but I was no longer as concerned as I had been that first day. After what Uncle Hıdır and Aunt Tonton had done, my fear faded into the background. Secretly I even thought, *Let the police come and take me away. Then those two will see the harm they've caused!* It was a foolish thought, but I couldn't rein in my anger. The thought was also childish because the friends' stuff was important and mustn't fall into the hands of the police. I could go to prison if it were found with me. When I think back to those days now, I see that I already tended to turn my anger at others against myself and thereby damage myself.

Uncle Hıdır and Aunt Tonton had made a mistake, and my fury at them obsessed me. Maybe it was even good that it had happened. Such experiences bound me ever more closely to the friends and armed me against interventions from without. I no longer felt obligated to stay home. I'd simply say I had to take care of something and leave. Or when they invited us to dinner or wanted to accompany me somewhere, I said no. Uncle Hıdır and Aunt Tonton wrote to my parents about the situation and apparently very much exaggerated it, as my parents panicked and decided to return to Dersim right away. Normally my father always let us know they were coming home, but this time they suddenly showed up in the middle of the night.

One evening our cousins İbo and Baki called on us. İbo had just been released from prison—I'd visited him a few times there. As a TİKKO member, he'd been arrested in 1975, during Mustafa Timisi's visit to Dersim.[83] Timisi was head of Turkey's Unity Party. He wanted to organize the Alevi people and thereby support the state. On his way into Dersim, his auto convoy was stopped on the Elazığ bridge by protesters, which led to clashes. For years Ecevit, as a purported leftist, had tried to make use of the potential in Dersim to further his aims. Timisi followed him with the same intention, but Dersim had changed. A notable opposition had emerged, and the young people were making their anger heard. Among the protesters was Yıldırım Merkit, a comrade of ours, who was arrested and imprisoned for a while.

When I visited İbo in prison, we had had heated discussions about whether Kurdistan was a colony. Such discussions took place in other prisons as well. İbo at least admitted that he wanted to think about it, which for that time was a positive and creditable reaction. Baki was a HK member, but he'd talk about such things too. I was glad the two of them showed at least some sensitivity toward the Kurdish question. İbo had said we'd continue the conversation after he was freed from jail. It also boded well that Baki came along on this visit. After all, a year ago I'd rejected his marriage proposal. But he didn't belabor it because he was a revolutionary and such behavior would have been petty. I respected him for that but also felt sorry for him. He and his family thought I'd rejected him because they were poor and that I'd given preference to a rich, city family with a higher social position. Their resentment was palpable. İbo joked about it a little, while Baki was calmer and left a more mature impression.

The second raid That evening [when Baki and İbo visited,] Veli Tayhani and Metin Güngöze were there as well. We all had a long, detailed conversation. I was impressed by the friends' high level of consciousness and by the maturity with which they constructed their arguments. Baki was well read but knew only a little about Kurdistan. His arguments rested on theses that had been current before the October 17 [1917] revolution. He said, for example, that a Bolshevik organization would resolve the national question. The idea of an autonomous organization was lost on him and on İbo, despite the obvious differences in conditions between Kurdistan and Turkey. Toward the end of the conversation, both said they were willing to think more about the subject. "Maybe we're wrong, but it's important to speak amicably about it. We'll meet again from time to time," they said, as they left.

It seemed inappropriate for them to stay overnight, and they'd understood. Yes, we were relatives, and yes, we were all revolutionaries, but not everyone in our neighborhood got that, and we wanted to avoid gossip. Uncle Hıdır and Aunt Tonton were lurking in the background, waiting for me to make a false step. They would surely disapprove of an overnight stay. So İbo and Baki stayed with nearby relatives.

Baki was bothered that I was engaged to Metin. When we shook hands, he said, "I didn't meet your requirements, but I still call you cousin." Elif, who came from the same village as us, overheard him and spent the whole evening scolding me for rejecting Baki due to his poverty. She even brought up the behavior of Uncle Hıdır and Aunt Tonton to rub it in. That almost pushed me far enough to ask Baki for forgiveness. I felt guilty. Everyone around me was trying to paint me into a corner emotionally using my greatest vulnerability. I'd never rejected my relatives because of their poverty—on the contrary, I liked them very much.

When Uncle Hıdır and Aunt Tonton learned who had visited us, they tried to mask their disapproval. On that particular day I was trying hard to behave respectfully toward them, to avoid any misunderstandings. I felt guilty, even though it was normal for our relatives to visit us. But instead of making that point to Uncle Hıdır and Aunt Tonton, I acted as if I'd done something wrong. The subject was such a sore spot with them. If my parents had been home, there would have been no problem [with Baki and İbo staying overnight], but rumors could arise easily, and I was after all still engaged.

The evening my parents arrived home. I was out, but as soon as I heard about it, I ran to meet them. My mother acted strangely. She'd been away for a year, but instead of enfolding us lovingly in her arms, she made an inspection of the apartment. She immediately discovered the cable running from the outlet to the window in the back room. We hardly used that room except for storage, so we kept the window open a crack. My mother yanked the cable from the outlet and threw it out the window. Fortunately my father was there and calmed her.

We were so surprised, we just stood there and didn't know what to do. Then my mother started interrogating us: "What have you done with the apartment? Tell me, who's been coming and going here?" Her interrogation was endless, and the whole evening was like a nightmare. We couldn't go out, and the friends couldn't come to us. The connection between us was ruptured. My mother was agitated even about my clothing. I was wearing some entirely normal nondescript things. Around my neck I'd tied a black-patterned cloth that I liked. She started in on that. "What is that thing—are you in mourning or what?" When Uncle Hıdır and Aunt Tonton came over, I was wearing the same clothing and received them coolly, which didn't escape my mother's notice. Anxiously she turned to my father: "Something has happened with the girl. Look at her! Say something to her—she won't talk to me."

As she got more information from the neighbors and my siblings, her anger waned. My greatest supporter was, as always, Meto. He'd also helped with housework the most. We used to argue a lot, especially before I began to call myself a revolutionary. Once in the village I'd chased him all the way to the Munzur. He'd annoyed me and I tried to catch him, but he ran very fast. Afterward I was astonished how far we'd run, and how fast, over the rocky ground without falling. Meto never forgot that I'd punched him. Sometimes he reminded me about it. I was sorry about the whole thing.

My mother sometimes resorted to violence, which I hated, but then sometimes I punched too. In those cases, the result was worse for me than for whoever felt my blows. My heart always ached when I remembered how hard I'd punched Meto's back. Afterward he, by contrast, behaved respectfully. It was hard for him, but he looked at me with tears in his eyes and suppressed his rage. He could easily have hit me back, but he didn't.

My father was calmer than my mother   In our family, Ali was closest to my mother, and she gave him the most attention. He took advantage of it and tried to hold on to his position. My mother assumed that he would always tell her everything and keep no secrets. She asked him the most questions about what had happened during her absence. She especially wanted to know who I'd associated with and who had visited us. But Ali had changed. He now told her only harmless stories and never mentioned our interaction with the friends: "Sometimes guests were here, friends of Sakine, I don't know them."

My mother tried to persuade my father to take me out of school and marry me off right away, "otherwise she will have great difficulties." She was testing my reaction, but basically she was also making a threat. My transformation bothered her. It wasn't only my revolutionary convictions and my connection to the friends. I just didn't act like a normal young woman who was engaged. When she asked me about my relationship with Metin, I said it had nothing to do with her. She flew into a rage—what did I mean, it had nothing to do with her? She didn't understand the world anymore.

Once she tried to explain to me why, before going to Germany, she'd forbidden Metin to come to Dersim during the semester break. She'd meant well, she said, so I shouldn't be angry. Or had she made a mistake? She talked to herself out loud that way. She and my father had seen Metin on their return trip. He'd seemed strange to them. Maybe he too was questioning our relationship. Now my mother was afraid that she might have caused that.

She was right. If Metin had come here during the break, it might have knit us closer together. We might have shared our ideological convictions. Then again, we might also have separated sooner than we did. But he'd followed my mother's unambiguous instruction and hadn't come, and meanwhile many things had happened that changed me.

My father, calm and respectful as ever, wanted to understand what had happened. I explained that I'd been pressured into the engagement, that I hadn't felt myself at all ready for marriage. I told him that during his absence "Uncle Hıdır and Aunt Tonton treated me like a servant and considered me their property. They stuck their noses into everything. I can't live like that, the way they want or the way you want. So much has happened, everyone's busy with something, I can't just sit on the sidelines. I want to be a revolutionary. Ever since you came home, I've been trapped here in the apartment. I can't go out to see the friends, and they can't come to us here. But we're doing not doing anything bad. You live in Europe—you must understand. Mom interferes with everything and always forbids me things. Now she's got the wedding on her mind. If you really want to know, I don't want it. Several times I've wanted to take my engagement gifts and throw them at the heads of the old couple. That's not how I'm supposed to feel."

My father said, "Baki was a revolutionary, but you didn't want him." He hinted that my mother's behavior annoyed him too, then tried to persuade me: "It's Metin you're engaged to, not his family. It'd be wrong to reject them altogether—you have to accept some things. Of course they shouldn't intrude into everything. Don't make the parents into such a problem. Metin's a good boy. He's polite, he studies, and his ideas about revolution aren't objectionable. Talk to him, write to him."

Talking to my father made me feel better, but nothing changed with my mother. She watched closely to see if I came home from school on time. But on that point I let go of my restraint. I felt bound by the general family rules—I couldn't go anywhere without permission, for one. But these new rules that were now imposed to me turned my whole life upside down. I had no rights at all anymore. Participation in the educational work, the meetings, and the discussions, even contacting the friends was forbidden to me. So we took to doing our educational work during school hours. I'd excuse myself from class or just let myself be marked absent.

That's how I got around my mother's prohibitions and continued my work. The friends visited our flat sometimes in spite of her and even discussed with her sometimes, but she always said, "Leave my daughter in peace." Some of them succeeded in softening her and making her laugh. Kıymet and Türkan detested her, while she loathed their casual "mannish" behavior. Whenever they came over, the atmosphere was tense. Having failed to prevent me from seeing the friends, my mother tried a new tactic: she harped on the differences among them. She said positive things about some and went negative on others. I defended myself vehemently and wouldn't let her say anything bad about my friends. She admitted she liked a few of them a lot. She knew only those who came to our flat or the mud-brick house.

Despite everything, we forged ahead with our educational work. Some of the friends lived in state housing. Sevim Kaya was stressed by her family. When she left their apartment in the evenings, she put on a cap and hid her face in a scarf, so she'd look like a man. To avoid being recognized, she walked alone through the streets to Dağ. That's how committed she was. Yes, a revolutionary has to take risks and be able to overcome difficulties.

We learned such things through the example of the leading proponents of the national liberation ideology. There were no written rules for us to follow, no bylaws and no coercion. The life itself was our teacher. We considered family ties to be a component of the system. In those days, the family exerted greater influence than state institutions. In many families it was an ongoing struggle as the parents tried to prevent their children from learning anything about their own reality. But the revolutionary life couldn't be impeded, and all prohibitions only amplified the contradictions.

Meanwhile I no longer tried to hide it when I went out to the educational work or to meetings. First I'd ask for permission, saying I had something to do and needed to go out. My mother said no, and I'd go anyway. But it was no good for me, because the whole time I was away, I had to think about the brawl that awaited me when I got home. Meanwhile I spoke very frankly with my mother and quarreled with her. I wasn't going to lie anymore. I was a revolutionary and had to do my work. The educational work was obligatory for me, and no one could prevent me from doing it, not even my mother Zeynep. Our dissension was ongoing. Previously I'd had to let her strong-arm me, but now she couldn't forbid me anymore. I just no longer belonged to her. When she scolded me, I snapped back, "I want to become a revolutionary, and you can't stop me. You should follow the example of my friends' parents. You know I'm not doing anything bad. If you don't stop creating hardships for me, I will leave this apartment forever."

That was a threat. My mother didn't want to believe me, but then she wasn't really sure I wouldn't commit such an act of madness. So she said, "Then get married and go! I can't be responsible for you anymore."

Under pressure What was it really all about? What underlay these conflicts?

Even though our family life was rife with conflict, it was also marked by closeness, a sense of togetherness and responsibility. My father was a worker, and his views were hardly conservative, reactionary, or feudal, so we children were able to form our own ideas to live by. He really loved us, felt responsible for us, and transmitted to us an inner ideal richness. When a problem developed, he talked it over with us, and we tried to

9 Cansız with school friends, c.1974. Cansız sits at far right, next to Perihan Gündüz.

reach a solution together. His humane nature stabilized our family life. My mother was the exact opposite. It was as if they'd switched roles.

Socially, women were the oppressed sex. My mother came from a distinguished, wealthy family, but my grandfather, in his relations with others, always valued mutual esteem. He respected others' opinions and was helpful and sociable. So he was beloved, his name on everyone's lips. My grandmother was like him. She was able to solve many problems by working well with people. She had a natural authority that she exercised reasonably. My mother's authority, on the other hand, merely stirred discord. But of course, it was hard work to raise eight children.

When I was a young woman, I didn't dream of marriage. It was a socially important subject, much was said about it, and young women imagined their weddings rapturously. But in my subconscious, resistance brewed. For me, marriage meant being pressed into a certain mold and so eventually experiencing discord, conflict, and contradiction. On the other hand, through marriage a young woman could finally leave her parents' house. But then, was the new house really all that different? Just when you were finally free of your mother, a mother-in-law appeared on the scene—Mother Tonton!

Still, I thought about marrying Metin if he accepted my revolutionary ideas and wanted to live with me as I was. I wasn't wholly against it, but then I didn't find much support coming from him. We hardly knew each other. Even when we had got to know each other a little, my wishes back then had been different from what they were now. Back then the range of my feelings and thoughts was much narrower. Neither of us really knew what an engagement entailed. Much had happened since, and we hadn't seen each other for a long time. The connection between us, weak at the best of times, had lost any meaning. What was left of it, what was I to look for, and to what was I to bind myself?

Internally, due to my mother's pressure, I separated myself more and more from my family. Often I was annoyed at Metin and blamed him for the situation, even though he hadn't done anything. What did the classical family model have to offer me? I had no firm position since my revolutionary worldview was still inchoate. I lacked patience, maturity, and political consciousness. Events were moving quickly, allowing for no procrastination. I was fighting a solitary battle against my mother, the family, the neighbors, and tradition. It wasn't easy, but I was determined to solve my problems by myself. After all, a revolutionary had to be able to overcome difficulties.

The friends were aware of my situation but didn't pressure me and left me to decide, and they were right to do so. Especially those with whom I worked understood what I was going through. Unfortunately they had no solution. But what could they do? They could hardly intercede between my family and me. Other friends were having similar problems. Performing even the smallest task like going to a meeting, or delivering information, or doing research, was difficult—that was undeniable. And for women it was harder. Even the families that we considered the best obstructed us in doing our work. Even parents of male comrades were opposed to their sons doing revolutionary work, because it meant they would be in confrontation with the state.

None of the defeats or passions of the past were forgotten. Many young people had lost their lives on this road. Deniz and his friends had been executed, Mahir murdered. The survivors from that time now lived isolated in big cities and were pointed to as evidence that our undertaking was impossible. The state was strong and cruel and merciless toward young revolutionaries. Among the people, pessimism and worry prevailed.

The new groups were associated with struggle and violence. Their members, sympathizers, and cadres shared a disputatious mindset. But in our hearts burned the revolutionary conviction of the national liberation ideology.

We formed deep bonds, determined to defend these convictions at any cost. No one told us how much we should trust our convictions or put ourselves out for them. There was no pressure or strict rules. Everyone felt shame that they had so far done nothing for their own country and had been alienated from their own identity. The more they became aware of this shame, the greater their wish to dedicate themselves to the cause. That was the uniqueness of ideology. But for this same reason not everyone could promote the national liberation struggle.

People increasingly noticed and recognized this uniqueness, but the parents of those who were involved with us grew anxious. That was entirely natural and, in retrospect, an expression of the growth that had taken place. Conviction and confidence would follow in time.

Many associated the concept of Kurdistan with massacres, deportations, and betrayals. Past cruelties had not been forgotten and indeed were embedded in the collective memory. This memory wound would have to be ripped back open, as the people were reawakened. Kurdistan was like a corpse that had been buried by silence. Reviving awareness of one's own identity would unleash trauma. But in the darkness of fear and alienation also burned a light that awakened hopes.

This struggle against fear, alienation, and darkness began with the individual. Once the individual became aware, it extended into a struggle with the family, and finally it reached the schools, the streets, and the neighborhoods. Violence committed against state facilities clarified the struggle's goal and purpose. These processes were intertwined, bringing difficulties and requiring conviction, consciousness, and resolve. And they were unavoidable, since current conditions were based on a denial of reality. Our ideology called into question the prevailing system with all its relations and lifeways: it deprived the individual of personality and identity. Family ties were an expression of slavery and limitation. Those who decided to free themselves from this coercion, or even took the first practical steps in this direction, initiated a revolution.

The ideological struggle makes revolutionary violence unavoidable I still felt tied to my family, and we still argued every day. The struggle at hand had only just begun. But I couldn't be a revolutionary when I had to beg for permission every day or else be slapped and scolded. At home I had to ask for permission, in school I had to follow the rules, and in society I had to accept traditions and values—wherever you looked, things tied you down, diminishing you, hindering you. Being a revolutionary required devoting your entire life to the struggle, but I was continually prevented from giving my life, my energy, and my capabilities to it.

School was still a means to an end, although my dream of going to university after secondary school was dashed. The friends didn't want me to drop out of school. On the contrary, they considered school a place where revolutionary work was done. Nothing more was discussed. So that wasn't the problem.

I kept going to school because it offered the best opportunities for discussions, and you could meet young people, who were such a dynamic part of society. The potential for heated confrontations was great, but the friends warned, "Don't let yourself be provoked during discussions. Avoid insults and violence. They'll just distract from the content of the discussion. Stay on topic and argue knowledgeably." We argued with classical theses about the national question, colonialism, the right to the self-determination of peoples, and the principles of Leninism. Our interlocutors often resorted to demagogy and tried to change the subject, thereby denying the reality of Kurdistan and true socialism. They quoted from theoretical treatises and tried to dominate the discussions with long-winded nonsense. These groups had no interest in doing research or developing an awareness of history, and they argued vehemently against changing. So their ideological theses were inconsequential. Their lack of a realistic political analysis made their behavior seem hypocritical.

Their revolutionary claims had nothing to do with reality. In the past, their denial of their own identity had at least followed a certain logic. Turkish colonialism, with its Kemalist character, had all but eradicated Kurdish identity. By working to reclaim it from such suppression, people regained their self-worth. But many on the Turkish left refused to accept that. In the name of the revolution, they obstructed the emergence of Kurdish identity and thereby sealed their own fate.

When the Turkish republic carried out past massacres in Kurdistan, the commanders hadn't trusted Kurdish collaborators and traitors because "he who isn't a friend to his own people can't be our friend." Unfortunately this mindset had no influence on the left. In Turkey, a more effective revolutionary consciousness could have emerged if leftists had said, "In our enslaved situation, we cannot liberate two peoples and propagate the fraternity of peoples. We must first denounce our own enslavement and win back our self-worth. From such a step, fraternity can emerge." The Turkish left, however, focused on slavery and chose as friends those who wanted to push enslavement to its extreme end. They equated denial of one's own identity with "internationalism" and "fraternity" and conversely considered social chauvinism to be socialist and democratic. This logic had harsh consequences and brought much destruction.

The ideological political struggle made revolutionary violence unavoidable. Our work met with countless difficulties and required much patience, energy, sensitivity, and selflessness. We won nothing easily. The work wasn't limited to ideological discussion and political struggle. From the outset, revolutionary violence also played a role. It was part of our political analysis. In order to intensify the ideological struggle, especially in Dersim, and to give the organizing work a stable basis, the struggle had to take place on many levels. Even if others were hostile to our group, we couldn't be ignored. Objectively, we were a force that developed quickly and represented something entirely new, whether the others liked it or not.

Since the other groups advanced ideological theses that perpetuated Kemalism and opposed national liberation ideology, they often provoked us, against our will, in challenging situations, which degenerated into violent clashes. These groups were exasperated by developments that diminished their base and exposed their true positions. So they propagandized against us and incited their members to reject us. Even though the various factions had no significant ideological differences, infighting among them was constant. Basically "the left" stood against the very condition of being organized. Organizing means pulling forces together, but they didn't do that, either in the general population or among the youth. All they shared was the power to split and prevent the emergence of a common struggle for common goals, even at the lowest level. That was the sole point on which they were unified. And they formed a common front against our revolutionary efforts.

In fact, they even attacked us at the same time as the police. One evening the police were chasing our friends in the neighborhood. The friends were armed. When they asked several families of HK members to let them escape through their homes, the families refused and even showed the police the direction in which they'd run. The families closest to us were astonished: "But one revolutionary doesn't betray another!" That was a basic ethical rule, and by violating it, the HK called into question its own revolutionary nature.

The life, the conditions, and the means of struggle weren't easy. Courage and a revolutionary stance, when demonstrated in the streets, won respect. A few consciously and deliberately worked against us, but mostly the people respected the representatives of national liberation ideology, even if they belonged to another organization. This respect rested on the group's determination and its high ethical claims. Even critique and challenge won us respect. Our movement successfully presented itself as an alternative to the traditional structures. It didn't make grand promises and had little material means. Everything began with a few words and a few people in an atmosphere darkened by poverty. Our growth was surprising, and those who initially made fun of us, ignored us, or enmeshed us in senseless bickering slowly backed off.

My mother and Kıymet pursue the same strategy   At home, the mood of doom persisted. My mother wanted to solve the problem before my father came home for his vacation. But then, she didn't want to be solely responsible for me and wanted to protect herself by bringing him in. The friends hardly ever came over to our place anymore. My mother would just throw them out: "Go away—leave my daughter in peace! What do you want with my children? You've ruined our entire family!" If she ran into them in the street, she'd revile them this way. So many of them avoided even walking past our building.

That year the village schools closed early, and during her vacation Kıymet came to Dersim. In her absence, I'd told a few friends that I didn't want to live at home any longer because I couldn't progress under these circumstances. I'd even said I might go to stay with Kıymet in the village where she taught. Her response was "Let's talk about it with the friends. But your family will oppose it. There could be problems if the police find out."

Later, to friends, she suggested I marry someone from the group, and she even mentioned candidates. I was furious when I heard about it. Instead of helping me find a solution, she would look for a husband for me! Angrily I confronted her:

> I'm already engaged! If I wanted to get married, I could just take Metin! That way I'd even have a chance to leave Dersim. But as far as I know, Metin is still in the CHP Left. He is passive, and the friends say he'll amount to nothing. He'd only create problems for me.

My consciousness was still not highly developed, and I sometimes acted rashly, but I didn't consider marriage a solution. I didn't reject it altogether, since as a married woman I could still have a revolutionary life, but the precondition was that my husband would have to share my ideology and my organizational affiliation. The comrades from our group were like brothers to me. We all thought it important to maintain our comradely relations. Something would be considered a shame, a sin, a violation of unwritten rules, if it didn't have a scientific or logical explanation. And besides, I was irritated by the men [Kıymet] suggested.

Yes, all were comrades, and I loved and respected some of them from my deepest heart, but others I valued just because they were comrades. Oh, the names weren't really important—I opposed the very idea.

Kıymet, in effect, pursued the same strategy as my mother, although my mother's version actually seemed more acceptable. I often wondered whether it would be better to marry, to move to Ankara, and to work with local friends there. But how would Metin behave? If we didn't share the same convictions, would he try to obstruct my work? As my husband, he'd have the right to stop me. Well then, I'd have to separate from him! But that would be a step into the abyss. If we ultimately would have to separate, then why get married in the first place? Divorce wasn't easy. Better to stay unmarried and just break off the engagement. And divorce brought a lot of unpleasantness. I would have to take a stand against the prevailing values. Aunt Tonton, as bad as she was, would be heartbroken. But weddings were expensive, and making our relationship official would make a later separation difficult.

On this point I was intractable. I was sure of myself. No one could force me into anything. I thought long and hard but couldn't bring myself to decide in favor of marriage. I couldn't imagine how to reconcile it with my revolutionary affiliation. The whole situation made me miserable. A marital connection would create a long-term connection between two families, but I couldn't stand that even now—how was I supposed to survive as a wife? No, absolutely not. But then what else could I do?

I thought about visiting my grandmother in the village. Meto liked the idea, and my parents supported it: "You've become so thin. In the village there's milk and yogurt—it'll do your stomach good. Stay a week, and then come back here." The situation was affecting my disposition. I was very emotional and secretly cried a lot. I had many female friends, including some on the Turkish left, but none of them were in a situation like mine. A few were engaged. Fethiye, our neighbor, wanted to get married and move to Germany. None of them wanted to lead a really revolutionary life as I did. Hatun, the sister of Ali Aydın, was engaged. Güneş was engaged. But no, my life had to take a different course from theirs.

I told my friends where I was going, then went to the village. Would it be possible for me to live there and still keep in touch with the friends? Well, after only a few days I was bored stiff. The friends were in the city, and it was hard for them to come to the village and work here. There weren't even any books. Village life seemed empty and meaningless. It was only with great effort that I made it through the week at all, and then I rushed back to the city.

I fell back into my routine. The friends saw no special problem in my situation, and the family pressure was normal, in the sense that they still wanted to restrict me more than other parents did. In our study group, people even joked about it and about Kıymet's idea to find a husband for me. Someone suggested I wear a sign that said, "Seeking husband to rescue me." I laughed too—through gritted teeth. Sometimes I believed that fate was real and considered myself very unlucky. Unable to see a way out, I felt helpless yet dug in my heels and kept looking for a solution.

I talked to my father again. "I don't want to get married," I said, "and I want to give the engagement gifts back. I haven't worn anything except the ring. They can all go back. I find this relationship meaningless. And there's no daylight between my mother and Aunt Tonton. I don't want to do what my mother wants, just what the friends do."

"Okay," he said, "we won't give you away against your will. But then what will happen?" As he tried to soothe me, my mother jumped in and hissed, "It's just as I've been saying—they've seduced my daughter. Ever since Baki was here, this girl has been wearing mourning. The neighbors say so too. Since then she hasn't put on reasonable clothes, and she doesn't eat anymore. And she wraps a black cloth around herself! Baki did something to her! Tell the truth—what did he do? Why do you want to separate? Why don't you want Metin anymore, all of a sudden? There's got to be a reason! You understood each other so well. During the vacation in February, Metin was always over here, and you wanted him then! They've seduced her, İsmail! Listen to me! Oh, you're so naïve!"

So she ranted on and on. It was awful. Each one of her words was so callous, it could kill a person. I was deeply wounded in my young woman's pride. How could she just spew out such stuff? Presumably she just wanted to know the reason for my wish to separate.

I fled into the back room and, sobbing, ripped the cable of the recorder from the wall and wrapped it around my neck. But no, I abandoned that thought. I lay down and tried to compose myself. I argued with myself. A revolutionary life would be wonderful, I thought. If I read more, gained more consciousness in the educational work, and went somewhere else,

I could be of so much more use. If only it were my last year in school—then I could go to the university as an excuse to leave my family.

My eldest brother was in Istanbul. Should I go to him? But he wanted to live alone, and it was hard to get hold of him anyway. Should I marry Metin and go to Ankara? My thoughts were running around in circles. Couldn't the friends send me to some far-away place?

Annoyingly, Kıymet's suggestion came into my mind. Why didn't the other friends take any interest in my situation? Why did only Kıymet show concern? Were they just not capable of handling this kind of problem?

I thought of [my cousin] Cemile. About a year ago we had gone to Bingöl together. Metin had wanted to come along for the ride, but at the last moment my uncle didn't let him, probably because my mother objected. But I didn't end up traveling alone with Cemile, because my uncle came along himself, using Metin's ticket. Cemile had finished at the Girls' Art School and become a teacher. She'd been assigned to Bingöl, and my uncle wanted to use his connections there to find a suitable position for her. She got a job in a "radical" village, where the people were so religious they rejected teachers and sent their children to the Koran school. They called Atatürk *atakutik*.[84] They rejected not only Atatürk but teachers, medical personnel, and all civil servants. Apparently when they got sick, they didn't go to a doctor.

Cemile was afraid of these villagers whose children she was supposed to teach. My uncle joked about it affectionately—he really liked her—but he especially showed his affection when he was half drunk. Our conversation was making him nervous. When he drank, he called us "comrades" and insisted that as an AP member, he was more revolutionary than we were. When we drove through Bingöl-Kovancılar, he snapped, "They're all fascists here, they'll attack us." On the bus and in the restaurants, the men wore open shirts and chains with the insignia of the Grey Wolves. That made my uncle even more nervous. He felt obligated to protect us young women against their leering looks.

In the end, Cemile did move to this village—and taught young girls how to sew clothes for their trousseaus. Almost a year had passed since then. Now I imagined driving to her village. I knew the route to the teachers' association—surely I'd find someone helpful there. Then I realized it was a school holiday. So this plan didn't come to anything. Anyway, it could have been risky to go there.

Dwelling on such thoughts calmed me a little. Suddenly there was a loud knock at the door. My mother cried anxiously, "Sakine, Sakine, open up! Let's talk—this won't do. Uncle Hıdır and Aunt Tonton are here asking about you. It's time to eat. What do you want to eat? Your father is so sad, he's gone out and hasn't come back." I didn't make a sound. Then she screamed, "Meto, Meto! Quickly, go outside and take a look in through the window! Make sure she hasn't done anything to herself!"

So she did notice how much her words affected me! Meto, out on the balcony, was trying to peer through the window into my room, but the tulle curtains kept him from seeing anything. My mother kept crying. I didn't say anything. Meto tried to open the casement, but it was shut fast.

He called to me in a pained voice, and I couldn't stand it anymore. He was my closest friend, my comrade, my great support. Our relationship went beyond a normal brother–sister tie. I answered him, and he sighed. My mother was relieved. Just as I suspected—no guests had arrived. I knew, because if there had been guests, my mother would have tried to hide our quarrel from them.

Escape The problem had to be solved. I finally devised a plan with Meto. I'd confided all my worries to him, and he'd been sympathetic. Since my mother mistrusted Baki and his family, I wanted to use them as a vehicle for my flight. First I talked to Türkan. We invited Baki's sister Saime to come to us. She went to a boarding school in Akçadağ and was on vacation. She was a revolutionary and had three brothers: İbo, Mehmet Ali, and Baki. Each of them belonged to a different political organization: TKP, TİKKO, and HK. She was closest to Baki.

Saime was very emotional, full of good intentions and politically open-minded. Being at the boarding school, she was relatively sheltered by the antagonisms raging among the various revolutionary groups. There were many fascists in Akçadağ, and anyone from Tunceli was automatically considered a Communist. It felt good to form a connection with her, since she could help us bring our ideology into the Teachers School in Akçadağ. We met at Türkan's, without my mother knowing. We talked about politics first, and then I brought up my situation. I didn't know how Saime would react, but I thought she'd understand me. We had no special connection as relatives, but I assumed our revolutionary connection brought us closer.

After talking around the subject a bit, I finally told her my plan.

Baki is a revolutionary. He wanted to marry me, but I wasn't ready for marriage. I explained that to him, and he took it calmly. Later I got engaged to Metin, for reasons that are hard to explain—you really wouldn't believe it. I was actually still not ready, but it happened. I wanted to become a revolutionary, but my mother was pressuring me into marriage, and so was the family of my fiancé. They said I could go to school in Ankara.

I haven't seen Metin for a long time now and don't even know what he's doing or if he's really a revolutionary. I suspect not, and his family would be against it. So the point is, I want to separate from him, but I also want to avoid creating problems. His family could call the police. So I want to act as if I'm fleeing to Baki. Once the families accept it, I'll go wherever the friends suggest. We can think about where later. But now we have to be credible, and we mustn't get caught. I want to talk to your father—he's a good man, and I think he'll understand. Your family really shouldn't consider me a daughter-in-law. I trust you, and I think even Baki will understand.

At first, Saime was stunned. They she let out a whoop, embraced me, and said, "You'll be my sister-in-law!" [Meto and I] laughed—she obviously didn't understand the seriousness of the situation and was reacting emotionally. We agreed on a date. [It is May 1975.] Before then I'd have to get my ID from school. The meeting place would be the apartment of another cousin of ours in Demiroluk. Saime wanted to come along with her father and me.

I impressed on Meto that he must make sure my mother and the neighbors didn't notice anything. He promised. Then I picked up my ID. Türkan and the others marveled at my determination. They hadn't really taken my plan seriously. I wanted to alert the friends but had no opportunity. They knew my situation. As long as I lived at home, I could have only very limited contact with them. I was determined to become an active revolutionary, and no one could stop me. That was the goal I'd set for myself. It wouldn't be easy for my siblings after I left the family, but they weren't under as much pressure as I was—they could do revolutionary work if they wanted.

Meto was to say nothing at first. Only if something went awry was he to say I'd gone to my uncle's family. How many days would it take me to get to Ankara? He was to inform the family only after I'd arrived.

When I got my ID from school, the school secretary asked for the reason. I said I was getting married. At first he didn't want to give me the ID without the director's knowledge. I explained that there could be no problem with my papers. He finally agreed, and I took the ID and went home. My mother wasn't there. I put on clothes I hadn't worn for a long time, as if I were going to visit girlfriends. As I left the apartment, the neighbors were watching.

On the street, I ran into Aunt Tonton, who peered at me mistrustfully. *Am I acting strangely?* I wondered. But she couldn't possibly have noticed anything, since it would never have occurred to her that I would just up and leave. I felt sorry for her and had a bad conscience. How would the elderly couple react? Surely they'd be hurt. And what would Metin say? Maybe I'd run into him in Ankara.

After Aunt Tonton scrutinized me in silence, she asked where I was going. I answered truthfully that I was going to visit my cousin Emoş. Of course she didn't know the purpose of the visit. "Alone?" she remarked, looking at me lovingly. I felt an impulse to hug her and say goodbye. In spite of everything, I liked both of them, and I felt sorry for them because of their age. They had placed all their hopes in me. Their older children lived in Ankara, and their daughters-in-law didn't want to live with them. They had no more children at home, their daughters were married. Metin was the youngest son. With a daughter-in-law from the local area, they wouldn't have been alone anymore. Aunt Tonton smiled sadly, as if she sensed something was up. I did nothing, but inside I wished I could meet Metin in Ankara and work out the problem with him. It was an idealistic thought, but I still said a silent prayer. Should I give up my plan? Maybe Metin would come to Dersim—summer break was coming soon. He wrote to me regularly and had even asked for a photo. Maybe he wanted to send me his photo. But I'd forgotten what his face looked like. In his last letter he'd quoted from the song "Drama-Bridge":

The Drama-bridge is narrow, Hasan,
You can't cross it.
The water is cold, Hasan,
You can't drink it.
You leave behind your mother, but never her love ...

What had he been trying to say? Why had he written that? I wondered until it no longer had any meaning. I was already on my way, and I'd taken the first step toward separation. Did I feel guilty? Was I betraying our relationship? But I wasn't in love with someone else, and I didn't want to marry anyone else. Metin knew what I thought of Baki. I just wanted to get away from my family, so I could carry on my revolutionary work. My throat tightened, and tears welled in my eyes.

Along the way I encountered many people and tried to pass unnoticed. After I'd walked for a while, I stepped off the path that led past the cemetery. No one was walking here. I broke into a run, trying to erase all thoughts from my mind.

When I arrived at Emoş's home, my uncle and Saime were waiting for me. My uncle took me joyfully into his arms and kissed me. I was surprised. What had Saime told him? Obviously he thought I was responding to Baki! But I didn't say anything. I couldn't stop now. I had to push away all doubts, I could no longer live at home.

My uncle ordered a taxi, then gave Saime some money and told her to drive to Elazığ to Uncle Hasan's and from there to call Mehmet Ali.

En route Saime told me she'd sent a telegram to Baki in İzmir that morning. That depressed me. Troubled, I was silent during the ride in the car. Saime tried to get me to talk. "Everything will be fine, don't worry," she said. She was so naïve!

Meanwhile, at home pandemonium must have broken out, but I didn't want to think about it. We spent the night in Elazığ then traveled by bus the rest of the way to Ankara. It was dark when we arrived. As we reached Ulus and İç Cebeci, the sky slowly lightened. Saime, who had been there before, found the address easily.

This residential neighborhood lay right next to the faculty of political science [at the university], Saime explained as we drove past. I thought of Ali Haydar Kaytan.[85] What was Metin's faculty? I knew he was at Gazi University but had no idea which faculty. Surely I could find him if I looked for him. He'd be astonished to see me, but maybe he'd understand.

We got out of the car and walked for maybe a quarter of an hour. Then Saime pressed the doorbell at a street-level apartment. A middle-aged woman opened the door. "Does Mehmet Ali Polat live here?" Saime asked.

The woman said yes and motioned for us to enter. The flat was small, with the living room and bedrooms connected. People were sleeping, but the noise of our arrival woke them. Mehmet Ali rubbed his eyes in astonishment, then came over to us and hugged and kissed us. Surprisingly [Aunt] Medine was there as well. She'd gone to Istanbul but had clearly returned. With half-closed eyes, she asked if it was only we two who had come. It struck her as strange. She went to the bathroom to wash up.

After everyone in the flat was awake, they expressed their confusion. Medine asked more questions. I'd been living in high anxiety for days and now had to pull myself together after the journey. Suddenly I burst into tears, which astonished everyone. Mehmet Ali said, "Sakine, my child, what's the matter? Come on, let's go into the other room." There he sat me down, and I explained everything to him. "Does your father know you're here?" he asked. I said no. "We have to tell him," he said. "They'll be worried about you."

Then he tried to cheer me up. "Baki will be overjoyed, of course."

I was irritated. "But I've explained the situation to you! You're not just my relatives, you're also, and especially, revolutionaries. That's why I thought you'd understand me. I think Baki will understand, too, and behave accordingly. I haven't come here to get married. I've come to work as a revolutionary, and I expect you'll help me with that."

Despite my exhaustion from the journey, I couldn't sleep that day. Time crawled, and I kept wondering if I'd made a mistake. When Mehmet Ali came home that evening, he said my parents had called to see if I was in Ankara. So—Meto had held out. It turned out my family was very worried and even searched for me for two days along the banks of the Munzur, fearing I'd drowned myself. The friends had thought something like that too, although Türkan and the others knew better. I'd discussed it with some of the friends in advance. Maybe they'd all said nothing so as not to get involved. But the fact was that I had chosen liberation, not suicide. Meto knew everything, and he had played his role well. My role, on the other hand, was getting harder.

Mehmet Ali suggested that for now we refrain from a rushed engagement. "We don't know what's coming. Your family knows you're here. Maybe the police know too." Metin's family, he said, "might complain to the police. Once things settle down, we'll sort it all out somehow."

I cursed my own stupidity. I'd trusted him because I'd considered him a revolutionary, but now he was proposing such a solution! "No, no way!" I said. "If that's what you're going to do, I won't stay here. I'm going." I stormed out of the flat. Mehmet Ali and the others begged me to stay and asked where I was going. "I'll look for the friends," I said. "I'm sure I'll find them in the political science faculty."

Since I'd washed my only pair of pants, I'd borrowed a pair of jeans, fashionably covered with patches. I remembered it only after I was under way, but I didn't care. I slowed my steps, trying to hold back my tears and steady myself. I sat down on a bench for a moment, then entered the faculty. Scenes from Turkish movies were playing through my head, in which Kurdish girls on the streets of Istanbul look for people they knew from their home village. At the political science faculty, I asked for Ali Haydar Kaytan!

My god, had I really thought I could solve my problems by running away from home? Internally I tried to regain my cool, but I was in so much turmoil that I didn't know anymore what I'd done right and wrong. I just knew things weren't going particularly well. But I really had had to leave my parents' house—on that point I'd been right. Family life and revolutionary work were irreconcilable. To have to beg every day, or tell a lie, in order to act as a revolutionary, was inherently contradictory.

A revolutionary life meant freedom, the free unfolding of one's own will. It meant sharing with others and working socially. That was what attracted me. A revolutionary life also meant submitting to rules, but it was easy for me to commit to that with my free will. I'd adapted to these rules without even noticing. Even with all its peculiarities and even hardships, the way of life of a revolutionary was beautiful. My love for and commitment to revolution had been shaped by the simplicity and poverty of those who'd lived in the mud-brick house in our yard.

I was inside the faculty building, but which way should I go? The university was huge, and I couldn't just ask someone where the friends were. Probably I should sit down and observe the people around me. I found a suitable spot, near a cluster of activity. As I tried not to look lost, my eyes fell on a small group sitting under an acacia tree, some men and one woman.

Then suddenly I spotted a face I recognized: wasn't that Musa Erdoğan, Kıymet's brother? I knew him from Dersim, but would he remember me? I stood up and looked at the rest of the group. I realized

I'd found what I was looking for [the Kurdistan Revolutionaries, "the friends"]. One of them—I later learned his name was Yılmaz—came over to me, and I said, "I'm looking for Ali Haydar Kaytan. I was told I could find him here." How did I know Ali Haydar Kaytan? he asked. I came from Dersim, I said. He asked me to wait a moment and went back to the group. Then Musa Erdoğan came over to me, and we shook hands. "I'm Sakine," I said. "I know you—you're Musa, Kıymet's brother." He led me over to a shady patch of lawn and asked me to sit down, offering a cigarette, which I accepted.

When had I arrived? he asked, smiling to reassure me—apparently he'd noticed from my face how lost I felt. I relaxed a little, feeling as if I'd found something of great value that I'd thought I misplaced. The pain of loss was now infused with joy. I'd left behind not only my family but also my home country and the friends there. Up to now I hadn't felt that part of the loss because the conflict with my mother was so much in the foreground, as if my struggle had been only about her, and I'd won. But that wasn't so. What I'd lost and what I'd gained were still unclear. I'd broken through, but whether what emerged would be good or bad remained to be seen.

A girl runs away from home to become a revolutionary   In Dersim everyone was talking about my abrupt departure. Would other parents now exert less pressure on their revolutionary daughters? I wondered, and the thought that they might comforted me a little. Had I fled to a man? they wondered, and I'd actually let it appear to be so. But no, I hadn't been seduced—I'd left my parents' house on my own and traveled to Ankara to my uncle's family. That part of the story, however, wasn't generally known.

Oh, let them think whatever they wished! In the end I'd win them over to my revolutionary position, even my mother. Despite all the conflicts and contradictions of my situation, despite its hopelessness, and despite my own weaknesses, vulnerabilities, and fears, I felt confident. A glimmer of hope was shimmering on the horizon. True, I was distressed at the moment, but I knew I'd get over it. I no longer feared making a mistake. Of course, I had other fears, but my desire for change outweighed them. I was sure I'd done the right thing, and this conviction gave me self-confidence.

As I told Musa my story, he interrupted me a few times, saying, "Sister, I congratulate you." He patted me on the shoulder and praised my courage. Then I told him about my uncle's family's ideas. "I can't stay there," I said. "They talked about me getting engaged—oh, it's intolerable!"

Musa replied, "Okay, we'll talk about it later."

The lone woman in the group caught my eye with her demeanor and way of speaking. I guessed she was Kesire,[86] of whom Kıymet and her family had so often spoken. I was right. Musa suggested, "If you like, go talk to Comrade Kesire. You can have lunch together. The student residence is just over there."

Kesire and I met up. "Let's go inside and wash our faces," she said. We went into the women's residence and cleaned ourselves up in the washroom. Kesire pulled a hand towel out of a bag so we could dry off. She was serene and unhurried. She didn't ask curious questions, I noticed— probably that had something to do with her position in the group. Her facial expression reflected maturity, if also coolness. She looked nicer when she smiled. *She's probably not cold-hearted*, I thought, *just dignified.*

We went back down into the courtyard and sat on the lawn. She asked my name and tried to get to know me better. What was Mehmet Ali's political orientation? she asked. He was TKP, I said, adding, "Comrade Ali Haydar knows him." Mehmet Ali had often spoken of him—Ali Haydar had even visited him, he'd said.

Kesire told me Ali Haydar had gone back to Dersim to visit just the day before—much to my disappointment. If I'd been able to speak to him back in Dersim, I might have solved my problem right there, because his words carried weight with me. I fell deep into thought, saying to myself, *Whatever—this is how it is now—I'm here. If I've made a mistake, the friends will tell me. At least Musa was happy to see me and congratulated me. If I've done something wrong, he'd have told me.*

I startled when Kesire asked another question. "Musa told us a little about you," she said. "I don't understand your story entirely, but to tell you the truth, I'm surprised. It doesn't seem especially clever—you've caused a whole uproar. Yes, it's good you left your family, but now the problem has been transplanted here. Your cousin did want to marry you before, so he'll be happy. Where is he now? Does he know anything about this?"

He was in İzmir, I said, and I had no idea if his family had asked him to come to Ankara. Saime, during the journey, had mentioned she'd sent him a telegram.

"How will he deal with it?" Kesire asked.

Up to that point, I'd scarcely thought about it but blurted out, "My cousin is a good man. We've talked, and I told him I wanted to be a revolutionary and wasn't ready for marriage. He understood. If I explain the situation to him now, it won't change anything. I'm pretty sure he thinks more realistically than Mehmet Ali does."

Kesire made no answer.

I couldn't stay in this family, I repeated, if they were going to try to push me into an engagement.

Kesire said nothing. I thought she might offer to put me up or suggest a place where I could stay, but she didn't. Taken aback, I began to cry.

Did I know my uncle's address? she asked. "No," I said, "but the flat is just over there, something like 'İç Cebeci,' but I can't remember the house number."

Finally I got up and left, on legs that didn't want to carry me. I'd found no solution to my problem. The friends hadn't acted as I'd expected, or maybe I just hadn't described my situation very well. What had I left out? What had I said wrong? And what was I to do now? Should I go back to Dersim with Medine? Maybe if I did, my family would be gentler and pressure me less—after all, they'd been worried. But no, that was impossible. I'd run away, despite being engaged. Everyone would be talking. What if I tracked down Metin here and talked to him? How would he react? I couldn't guess, but then, I didn't know his address. If he'd had a telephone, I could've called him. What if I asked Mehmet Ali—would he help me find Metin? No, he surely wouldn't want me to meet up with Metin!

I wandered aimlessly, whispering the name of the woman I'd just met: "Kesire. Kesire." What did her name actually mean? Menekşe had told me about her—she'd visited Musa here in Ankara. Kesire had been the first woman to join the group, she'd said. Oh, she could have helped me—or maybe I'd misunderstood her—but she hadn't really said anything clearly. I was distraught. If only Ali Haydar were here, he would know what to do, and he even knew Mehmet Ali!

I walked till I got tired, then found my way back to the flat. In the meantime Baki, İbo, Saime, and her school friend Halide from Hatay had arrived. My heart sank even further. Baki acted very formal but seemed to be in a good mood. İbo joked, "We failed to make our cousin into a TİKKO member, but now we can go to the mountains together."

I couldn't follow their conversation, because mentally I was still back at the political science faculty. I'd met with two entirely different reactions here: one had congratulated me and praised me, the other had been startled and spoken of a "great tumult." Then I said I wanted to speak to Baki, in Mehmet Ali's presence. We went into another room. Baki was grinning and laughing, which grated on my nerves. What was there to laugh about? Was he laughing about my flight? A year ago I'd rejected his marriage proposal because I wanted to be a revolutionary and didn't feel ready for marriage. Now I'd escaped to him and was begging him for help. It was understandable that he wasn't interpreting it correctly.

But his laughter threw me off, and I didn't know where to start. Finally I broke the silence. "I've already told Mehmet Ali everything. My mother doesn't want me to become a revolutionary. Recently she's even tried to prevent me from communicating with the friends. And seeing my resolve, she's been pushing for a marriage right away. Metin is here at the university, but he knows nothing about this. His family acts just like my mother, so I don't want to marry. I had to leave home. If I'd gone someplace else, they might have called the police. That's why I talked to Saime, to be able to show the situation in another light."

I clarified [to Baki]: "When you and I talked about it before, I spoke quite candidly. The fact that you're a revolutionary friend means more to me than the fact that we're related. It means I trust you. In our last discussion, you said our ideological positions might not be so far apart. You said you'd read up on the subject and would think about it. Then I trusted you more. Now your brother speaks of an engagement and says the police could come. But that's not right. I'm 18 years old. There's no reason for the police to get involved. We're related, and I've been a guest of your family, so there can't be a problem. If you all act that way, I'll lose my trust in you. I expect you to help me."

Baki admitted I was right and said he was glad I gave priority to a revolutionary life. "We're revolutionaries, and so we're open to everything," he said. "I study and work in İzmir. İbo is with me, and Saime will come later. You can go to school there. In İzmir there are many more possibilities. We could mutually support each other and continue our conversation. So what if the police come? The engagement doesn't matter to me, I'm not insisting that it happen. If you agree [to come to İzmir], then we can talk to İbo."

He called İbo in and described the situation briefly. İbo agreed. Mehmet Ali seemed unenthusiastic but finally agreed I should go to İzmir since anything else could be risky. "It might be temporary—you can come back here to us anytime," he added. Finally Medine agreed too, saying, "We'll go to İzmir as well and take a flat there. I don't really like Istanbul."

Saime had to settle her affairs with the school and would come afterward, as would Medine's siblings. Hasan worked there as teacher, and Haydar was there too. Aynur wanted to be with Saime or go to İzmir even sooner.

Things had turned out differently than I'd expected. It hadn't occurred to me to go to İzmir, but now that everyone was talking about it, it made sense. Mehmet Ali's flat wasn't particularly inviting—he lived there with his wife, two children, a sister-in-law, and his parents-in-law, like a family during the Ottoman Empire. The flat was small, and I didn't care for the familial relations. Mehmet Ali was a TKP member. Baki and İbo belonged to other factions, but I felt closer to them since they worked and studied. I pictured myself working too and continuing to educate myself theoretically until I could once again reach out to the friends. I wouldn't be idle. I was glad to have finally found a solution.

A painful break, and my time as a worker We left for İzmir right away. At the last moment İbo decided not to ride with us. "I'll be there in a day or two—I want to stop in on the friends first," meaning his comrades in TİKKO.

I didn't inform the friends I was leaving. Would they hear about it? I told Mehmet Ali to tell them where I was going, if they should ask for me.

I talked to Baki the whole trip. The day we left, I'd cut my beautiful long hair—he asked me why. He talked about the past. While I was in middle school, and he'd been a high school senior, he said, he'd already been interested in me. He said he considered it his great good fortune that I'd finally come to him. His behavior and his way of speaking were different now, I noticed. The day before, he'd spoken earnestly of a revolutionary friendship, but now that earnestness had disappeared, and he acted as a man does with his beloved. I was disappointed and felt I'd been naïve. I'd gone to him voluntarily, so I couldn't blame anyone else. So I was irritated at myself, and my pride was wounded. I tried hard to believe I hadn't debased myself, since that could only weaken me.

Eventually we ran out of things to say, and I withdrew into myself. When we arrived in İzmir, he suggested we go to his workplace, but that didn't seem appropriate to me. So we went to a family in Bornova, where I stayed awhile. Harun, the family's son, was an HK member. There were two daughters and a very nice mother. The family was large and had many visitors. I stayed there for almost a month. But I found it boring to live with a family with no activity. It couldn't last.

After İbo arrived, we looked for work together in Konak and Alsancak. We got a job offer in a restaurant, but it seemed unsuitable, and the pay was bad.

Baki came over on weekends. İbo lived in a bachelor pad with Hasan and spent his time with his friends. We decided to rent a flat together. Some people Baki knew in Gümüşpala helped us find one. It had a living room, a bedroom, and a small kitchen, and it was unfurnished. İbo and Baki procured the most essential items from their friends, old secondhand objects: a rug, a pair of mattresses, some blankets, a few plates, and a small teakettle. We were like children playing at being grown-ups. For a while we made do with only two spoons.

Baki's salary wasn't enough to cover our living expenses. He studied architecture at Ägäis University and worked in a tourist restaurant in İnciraltı. In other words, he worked while we lounged around, which was unbearable. İbo sometimes got day jobs at construction sites. Somehow we scraped by.

I continued to look for work. İbo and Baki weren't enthusiastic about it, but I insisted. Baki urged me to find a job as a nurse or secretary, but I preferred factory work. İzmir was an industrial city, and there were factories everywhere. I imagined that as a worker I could do trade union work. I thought of my father and also of a book by Mithkah Grabcheva, *Ognjana: Memories of a Bulgarian Partisan*. I'd read it back in Dersim, where there were no possibilities for such work. I hadn't even been thinking about wage work then, but now I had to because I didn't want to be economically dependent. It bothered me so much that I insisted on looking for a job.

Baki and I visited a family in İzmir-Hatay. The husband and wife both worked, and they had three children. Baki said I could take care of the children while the parents were at their jobs. They were in his circle of friends, were revolutionaries, and had a well-stocked library. I surveyed their book collection. That evening we stayed up for a long time talking.

The family seemed strange to me. Their lifeways and manners were those of a typical bourgeois family. Even staying with Mehmet Ali would have been better than staying with them. So I said to Baki, "I wouldn't last an hour here." Then I added, "But they're rich in books—we should borrow a few from them." We went back to our rented flat.

İbo found a job as a lathe operator. I kept looking.

On the road to Çiğli there were a few factories owned by one family. Finally I got a job in a chocolate factory there. It was in a valley with a beautiful courtyard. Most of the employees were women, mainly Bulgarian immigrants who lived in Aşaği Çiğli.

I was thrilled.

I had to get up every morning at 3.30 to catch the bus that brought the workers to the factory. Since I didn't have a clock, I trained myself to wake up at the right time, but I always had to run to catch the bus anyway. I ate lunch at the factory, and in the evening I came home. Sometimes we had to work overtime. Only a few men worked there—it seemed like a women's factory. My simple clothing set me off from the other girls—they looked like they'd stepped out of a fashion magazine, or a fashion show, wearing a different outfit every day, with makeup and blow-dried hair. They acted like they were attending a wedding or some other celebration.

A woman known as "Kurdish Fatma" worked in the factory's cauldron area. She was small and plump, dark-skinned, and looked worn out. The work with the cauldrons was some of the hardest in the plant. Lifting even an empty cauldron required a huge effort.

The owner's five children worked in the factory. On my first day, I talked to one of the sons for a while. He noticed from my ID that I was from Tunceli and asked me why I wanted to work. I explained that I'd dropped out of high school, was visiting relatives, and had to earn a living. He was a little skeptical. The factory owners were careful about hiring new workers, and the ones who said they'd dropped out of school were often the most suspect. When workers organized in a factory, usually the students played a leading role, and they were promptly dismissed. Some factory owners circulated the names of activists among themselves, to prevent any organizing among the workers. I'd been warned against jumping into organizing right off, since I'd probably be fired in a heartbeat. After seeing the factory conditions, I realized that even conversing with the workers wouldn't be easy.

First I tried to demonstrate that I could do the actual work. I tried to learn every activity and carry it out faultlessly. During the probation period, I had no fixed work area. That was fine—I could get to know the workers in every area. I socialized with them, asking when they'd started at the factory and what hours they worked.

I asked the Bulgarian immigrants about their home country. In 1973, while flying to Germany, our plane had made a refueling stop in Sofia. To establish a bond with the Bulgarians, I exaggerated a little and said I'd been in Sofia. Most of them had fled the country before the revolution; only very few had returned afterward. All said they were working to support their families and to pay for personal needs like a trousseau.

Living standards in Aşaği Çiğli were relatively high. The state provided the Bulgarian immigrants with nice houses with gardens. The neighborhood was clean and neat. There was no unemployment: all the residents found work as soon as they arrived. A few were employed in state institutions, while others were independent. The families weren't large. The factories were glad to hire Bulgarian Turks since they were considered good workers who didn't cause trouble.

The other workers were mostly Kurds, even though only Fatma identified herself as such. I recognized them by their bad Turkish and their rough appearance. My colleagues were surprised when I told them I was Kurdish, saying, "You don't look it." My proficiency in Turkish contradicted that prejudgment. But they became more sympathetic to the Kurds as we got to know each other better. They found me interesting, and many times they came over to talk to me about their problems or to ask me something. That was a positive development. It was also important to gain the sympathy of the foremen, since they were closest to the employers and passed on information about the workers that could be used in terminations.

Every day in the factory, I learned new things. I tried to understand why the girls dressed like models just to stand in front of a machine. During a break, Fatma whispered to me, "That one over there—she's involved with the boss's son. And that one over there always comes home late, because she supposedly has to work overtime. They're almost all … you know already. You may not pick up on it, but be careful with them."

I hadn't really known, although I'd suspected. Their interactions with their male colleagues were superficial. They took every opportunity to meet and talk, but not collegially. I talked to the men too. A few were older and looked as if they'd been working for many years. It was easier to talk about working conditions and living standards with them—they listened. I was relaxed with them, while the others were more flirtatious. Some of the young workers came with me when I went to talk to the male co-workers.

At lunchtime, the same people always sat together. As the cooks served the food, they looked at each woman awaiting her portion, and as they dipped the ladle into the cauldron, her degree of flirtatiousness influenced her food ration. Whether it was meat or fruit, the women who flirted got more of it. They related in the same loose way with the boss, the foremen, and even the drivers and gardeners. It was disgusting to watch the young women compete to please the paternalistic boss and his flirtatious sons. I lamented their behavior, which seemed to me to be a surrender of their personality.

But I also got angry at the situation, which hollowed out the very concept of the working class. The words *working class* and *proletariat* were sacred to me, and I'd rejected other jobs in order to become a factory worker. I dreamed of organizing a working-class resistance, but my experiences in the factory were something else. I understood Mithkah's book better now. He'd worked so hard to organize the former village women who were exploited in factories under terrible conditions. Thinking about it, I pulled myself together and vowed to be patient.

Normally we worked eight hours. The tea break lasted 15 minutes, the noon break was half an hour. No one seemed to care about the quality of the food, or social insurance, unions, workers' rights, or organizing. But the packets of sweets, distributed on holidays and special occasions, inspired great delight.

Sometimes the workers were taken on outings, which were supposed to strengthen their loyalty to the factory and ease any dissatisfaction with working conditions. And once a year, or as a reward for outstanding performance, they were sent to the seaside for a few days' vacation.

After a while I began to visit some of the workers at home. Aşaği Çiğli was an important neighborhood because many immigrants lived here. I wanted to get to know them better. A few of the young women were open to conversation. They didn't like the working conditions either, or the behavior of the boss. Their dissatisfaction was my starting point for organizing. These workers had no union or social insurance. Some of them had been severely injured when their hair or an arm got caught in a machine. A few still had persistent pain. There was absolutely no insurance. No compensation was paid. Safety precautions were taken, but otherwise everything was left to chance.

In our conversations I cautiously mentioned the minuscule pay for overtime hours, and the exploitation of their labor power and the women's bodies. From their answers, I inferred that these Bulgarian immigrants didn't believe in socialism. They considered themselves Turks and their fatherland to be Turkey, which justified their flight from Bulgaria. The Turkish state had accepted them and provided them with housing and work. They were grateful for that and ready to let the negatives pass in silence.

In this situation, it was difficult to raise their interest in Kurdistan. I tried anyway to explain, roughly, where we came from and what had happened in Dersim in 1938. They contented themselves with listening to me. I continued to visit them. At the factory we now spent our breaks together. I harbored a secret hope of being able to initiate, with much patience, a small group to talk about work issues and, eventually, a common solution. But the factory was small, and even if a workers' resistance spread across the country, it would have only a little impact here.

At the factory exits, workers had to undergo intrusive searches. Hayriye, a heavy-set woman who acted like a prison warden, rudely rummaged through their purses and bags. I didn't carry a purse, so when my turn came, she said, "You can pass on through, my son." She called me that because of my short hair. The inspections, which were supposed to prevent anyone from stealing the product, made me angry.

But then, whenever one of my colleagues ate a chocolate or bonbon from the factory, I was astonished. Knowing as I now did how the candies were produced, they disgusted me. Management paid no attention to sanitation, and ingredients that fell to the floor were just thrown back into the cauldron. The cleaning of the cauldrons was superficial. They were interested only in appearances and packaging. The tablecloths for the bonbons and the bulk chocolate were really disgusting. For a long time after leaving the factory, I ate no sweets at all.

This factory and its chocolate products, let it be said, were famous. That was laughable. Probably all factories were this way, I thought.

Quality and cleanliness were unimportant. For the owners, only capital accumulation, profit, and accelerated production had any meaning. And the workers were only concerned about their income. Their own health meant nothing to them. They too thought only about their own advantage.

The work was strenuous. I set out in the morning without breakfast and had to run to catch the factory's shuttle bus. That was my daily exercise. If I missed it, I had to take a regular bus and spend 150 *kuruş* on a ticket.

To save money I sometimes hitchhiked. It was risky, because you could end up with sex traffickers. Many women who stopped cars also sold their bodies. Standing alone on a street and flagging down drivers could give the wrong signal. When I discovered that, I was more careful. But sometimes I just didn't care, since in such situations a person's behavior can make the difference. Even if someone with bad intentions picked me up, I could head them off by maintaining a serious demeanor. On the way home after work, I usually sat on the sidewalk for a little while to settle down. The factory bus didn't go all the way to our flat, and the last leg of the journey, which I had to walk, was uphill. It was exhausting to work all day standing up and then have to negotiate that hill.

Eventually I got used to it. I was glad to be working, and it went well for me. At home, however, there were problems. For a while I lived alone with İbo, then Baki gave up his job in the restaurant and was always there too. Neither of them had permanent work—I was the only one with regular employment. This situation wasn't easy for them. "This isn't working out," İbo said. "The sister toils away, and we're living off that." Baki said nothing.

We shared a flat but not our goals   I spent all my time at work. I couldn't read books or keep up with current events. On the positive side, the work kept me from ruminating about my personal situation, but that was no solution. I worked six days a week. I spent my Sundays reconnoitering the area and visiting the various political headquarters. In Kemeraltı the HK and the DDKD had meeting rooms. In Bornova there was Dev-Genç. All called themselves "democratic cultural associations." I read their newspapers and magazines and followed their political activities. Their articles contributed to our ongoing conversations at home. Neither Baki nor İbo fulfilled the promise both had given in

Dersim. Both defended their own positions, although Baki read books on the "national question" and took notes.

We differed on the question of whether Kurdistan was a colony. For hours we sorted out basic distinctions between new and classical colonialism. It pushed me to read more. Back in Dersim, when I ran out of arguments, I'd been able to turn to the friends. But now in İzmir, where no one but me claimed to come from Kurdistan, it was harder. Büyük Çiğli was home to people from Varto and Hınıs who had arrived after the earthquake there.[87] With them I could savor Kurdish culture, which I missed intensely. Many Kurds also lived in Gültepe and Gümüşpala. But no one here talked about Kurdistan as a colony. The Turkish leftist groups had already organized all the younger Kurds.

At home, Baki's behavior became a problem. In our discussions he kept trying to produce a minimal ideological commonality, but that rang hollow to my ears because in spite of his research, he hadn't changed his organizational affiliation, and he persisted in the same ideological mentality. It made his connection to me less than straightforward. He wanted an emotional bond with me, sometimes he even verbalized that, but I wouldn't allow it unless we had a shared ideological and organizational affiliation. I got irritated, ended the discussion, and reminded him of the agreement we'd made.

Often I was evasive or even got polemical, which admittedly wouldn't persuade anyone. Over time I softened. My escape from my family played a role: I lurched between extreme rejection and a fatalism that resulted from knowing that I was to blame for my own situation, from which Baki benefited. Aware of my own shortcomings and helplessness, I still refused to be defeated or to behave according to the wishes of others. Anyway, I worked. The flat wasn't really the issue—I now had many acquaintances who would put me up at least temporarily. Even renting my own flat wasn't excluded. I tried not to lose my confidence and to trust that I could resolve the situation through my own force of will.

I'd fled Dersim in May, and it was now August. Along with my aunt's son Haydar and his sister Aynur, we were now five. Saime hadn't come. We rented a different flat in the same neighborhood, where coffeehouses and meeting rooms were frequented by fascists. We chose the area on purpose, to inconspicuously observe the fascists from close up. Baki confided this "internal to the organization secret" to me.

Since we were now five, we needed more money. The flat had two rooms and a living room. The rent was normal. Haydar and Aynur found work in a grape-processing factory, so things improved financially. We lived collectively and divided up the chores. Whoever was home went shopping, cleaned, and cooked. In the evenings, those who wanted to read sat in one room. We decided to avoid political discussions since we all belonged to different factions: TİKKO, PDA, HK, and Kurdistan Revolutionaries. The others labeled me a "national," a name otherwise unknown in İzmir. In discussions at the political clubs, when I was asked, I replied, "The name isn't important. I'm a Kurdistan Revolutionary."

Haydar was clumsy, so much so that he had trouble doing housework. He'd burn the food or ruin it some other way. I wrote down recipes and hung them on the wall for him to follow. Each of us did our own laundry, except the bedclothes, which we did together. İbo was slovenly and didn't wash his feet or his socks or his hair. In İzmir it was oppressively hot. Sometimes the stench of sweat became so pervasive that I avoided the flat altogether. I fought with İbo about cleanliness and suggested he make a point of washing his feet and his socks every evening. When he didn't do it, I said, "Give me your socks, if it's so hard! I'll wash them." Then he'd stand up and say, "No, sister, no way." As I'd intended. I really didn't want to wash his socks, a touchy point.

Whenever my roommates' behavior reminded me of the allocation of roles in the classical family, I climbed the barricades. But normally we interacted respectfully. It was just in discussions that nobody obeyed any rules. If someone initiated one, then everyone else jumped in. Our debates got heated, and extreme positions were often taken. They always ended with the others allying against me.

Haydar began and ended every contribution by referring to Soviet social imperialism. He wasn't well versed in theory and didn't read much. We had made individual reading a duty, but he shirked. When I asked him about a book, he'd mention a few pages or say he hadn't had time. In discussions, his analyses were superficial, and he just repeated things he'd memorized.

İbo was a man of action, and in this respect he earned trust. He often quoted from Kaypakkaya, whom he revered like a god. I liked this about him and respected him for his loyalty. He loved weapons. Once when we were in a village together, he'd let me shoot his revolver. "If you come over to us, I'll let you have it as a gift," he said, as if he were enticing a child with candy. He behaved as if his faction [TİKKO] were the only struggling revolutionary group and sometimes joked, "Sakine can only become a TİKKO member—she has a rebellious personality." I retorted that ultimately he'd come over to us, since he was a revolutionary deep inside.

Aynur wasn't as outgoing as she had once been, having grown more mature. She hardly participated in our discussions. She and Baki understood each other, and he often asked her questions to stir her interest in a subject or to teach her something. But she was more interested in life in the big city, and even though she'd finished primary school, she had trouble reading.

Baki introduced me to many of his friends. Some were illegal cadres who didn't go to the political clubs but visited us at home. Baki often insisted that we could overcome our political differences by marrying. "Ideological differences between revolutionaries are temporary. We mustn't deepen them unnecessarily. Marriage would speed up our ideological convergence." I objected vehemently and accused him of unseriousness. He knew I'd seen through him and recognized how insincere his supposed ideological convergence was. We decided not to discuss it further, since it only exacerbated the conflict.

Letter to Metin   I wrote a long letter to Metin, in which I candidly described what I'd been through. I reproached myself for separating from him without telling him. I tried to explain the circumstances that had led to it.

> Our relationship exists as a result of our families' wishes. At first we developed a certain closeness. We both felt bound to traditions, but our love had no basis. If things had developed in a different way, we might have continued our engagement. But the fact is, I've changed—something both our families tried to prevent. My only choices were to bend to our families' wishes or else give up the relationship. And you were not very helpful. You always advised me to be a "smart girl." That was what our parents wanted: a smart daughter and daughter-in-law.
>
> If we'd had a chance to talk, maybe things would have turned out differently. When I was in Ankara, I wanted to see you very much. I've felt guilty that I didn't try to find you, and I have a bad conscience that we didn't meet. Who knows, maybe I was afraid that you might persuade me to change my mind. Then there would have been no more problem. But

I was stubborn. I was furious at my mother and told myself, "She's not going to keep me from being a revolutionary, and she's not going to just marry me off." Now I'm in İzmir. I work in a factory. I don't want to say much more about it. I still have a few problems, but I have to solve them myself, since I'm the one who caused them. If you'd like to write to me anyway, you surely can. We can correspond in all friendliness.

I didn't tell him about my problems with Baki. Metin knew about my past with him, but this situation was truly absurd. I'd fled to a man I didn't want—how was I supposed to explain that? It was a huge contradiction that cast doubt on my own honor. Unfortunately, others would see it that way too and make unbearable comments. But objectively it was true,

Baki read the letter, and it annoyed him because he inferred from it that I still loved Metin. He didn't say anything but let me know how he felt through his behavior. I didn't care what Baki thought. I would have been remiss to blame everything on Metin—I'd written the truth. But I couldn't remember Metin's address, and since I didn't want the letter to fall into anyone else's hands, I never mailed it.

None of our roommates or acquaintances knew the exact nature of the relationship between Baki and me. We didn't share political views, and we weren't married, but we lived together. Our conversations always ended in arguments. Even on subjects where he'd once been flexible and had spoken of agreement, he now wouldn't yield an inch. He valued his position within the HK organization and took care not to violate its internal rules. In truth, he felt the HK's position on the national question was contradictory, and the more he thought about it or discussed it, the more the contradiction deepened. But he was so tied to the organization that he wouldn't change his opinion and didn't dare openly articulate his real view. A typical feudal, petit-bourgeois perspective!

Within the HK, this rigidity prevented open discussion. The Kurdish cadres in particular stonewalled: in the name of internationalism, the HK denied the existence of Kurdistan, which obstructed any positive development. For the HK, the greatest virtue of a revolutionary was to take refuge in banalities like "the fraternity of peoples." But based on what criteria? In whose name, for which peoples, and in which fraternity should the revolution be made? Turkish leftists initially influenced Kurdish scholars, who demonstrated openness to all revolutionary, democratic, and progressive developments in the universities and participated in them. But political analyses and orientations on fundamental questions of the revolution had to be straightforward and correct.

What was the revolutionary task, and on what basis could it be executed? No one asked that. The various groups all participated in practical actions, and they demonstrated courage and commitment. But their ideological foundation couldn't advance their strengths and abilities, and they lacked the class characteristics necessary to become a vanguard. In 1969 and in the early 1970s, revolutionary activity had consisted mainly of generating slogans, propaganda, and agitation. The leftist groups had competed in those efforts. But in the mid-1970s, it wasn't clear which groups championed the revolutionary ideology of THKO and carried on the tradition of Suphi[88] and Kaypakkaya.

I was most irritated by the Kurdish members of these groups. What did they get out of them? No, I wasn't hostile to the Turkish people. All my life I'd enjoyed close relations with Turkish schoolmates, neighbors, and teachers. I liked them, and we got on well. We were all influenced by Deniz, Mahir, and the others who'd advanced the revolution. How could I forget that? But the revolutionaries of an oppressor nation had different tasks from those of an oppressed nation. How could anyone try to make a revolution in another country, when they rejected revolution in their own country and ignored the concerns of their own people? On this point, I had no confidence in them and couldn't be persuaded otherwise.

Everyone sides with Baki In discussions with Turkish comrades, I could tolerate to some extent their arguments on the subject of Kurdistan, but among Kurdish friends I couldn't stand it. These discussions often became highly confrontational, and people made false allegations, but I charged on ahead without knowing much. I was actually just a sympathizer, lacking knowledge and political experience. When I spoke in our group's name, I didn't stop to consider whether what I said would be right or wrong in their eyes. I was isolated in holding these views, even though I promoted them everywhere. Still, I gained self-confidence and strength. I would read an article in a magazine and then hold forth about it in one of the leftist clubs.

The Marxist classics, from what I'd read of them, validated our political outlook. It wasn't important whether the name Kurdistan was used: the national question as formulated prior to the October Revolution, the developments afterward, and the successful national liberation struggles in many countries were all important sources that I could interpret and analyze in the light of our group's ideological theses. Even though I lacked knowledge and experience, I didn't hold back. Our ideology was correct, we were right, and that was enough for me. If you believed in it, you defended it and tried to spread it everywhere in all situations. I didn't need any official position or organizational tie for that. I was far away from the friends now, and my contact with them had been broken. *I'll get in touch with them again sometime*, I promised myself.

Yusuf Metin, from Ovacık [a district in Dersim], lived in our neighborhood and often stopped by for intensive discussions. The flat where he lived belonged to his organization [HK], and it housed an archive of books and magazines. He said the HK movement discussed the national question and would soon publish its official opinion in the HK newspaper. "We're still discussing certain differences of opinion," Baki told me. "If I try to advance a different position, they'll oppose it. I'm not the only one to hold this opinion—there are many Kurds among us who have certain expectations." That was the truth.

The national liberation ideology influenced discussions [among leftist groups] everywhere, especially in Ankara but also in Dersim, Kars, and Antep [Gaziantep]. No one could stay aloof from the battle over political ideology. Now all the leftist groups had to take a position on the subject of Kurdistan, lest they lose members to the Kurdistan Revolutionaries. They clearly worried about losing their Kurdish cadres. I could see it even in my own circle. Baki had influence in his group, so his comrades proceeded cautiously with him. If he were to develop a contrary position, it would have repercussions with his people. He was in charge of our neighborhood, but he wasn't trusted as much as he'd once been, and he could advance the political direction in only a very limited way.

Yusuf Metin played the role of a mediator. He was evidently very interested in the Kurdistan question, having recently arrived in İzmir. He now worked and studied here. He'd been in the THKO since its founding, and his group wanted to continue its tradition. Yusuf comported himself calmly and respectfully in discussions. We spent time in his flat, reading books and talking with him and Haydar and

Aynur. We read texts on the right to self-determination of peoples and on the history of the Bolshevik party. It was a kind of educational work.

I didn't think much of limiting oneself to reading the works of only one group. I wanted to read, discuss, and learn—and I didn't care with whom or where. The goal was to find points of connection on the issue of national liberation. Baki spurred me on. He couldn't always be present, but he found our work meaningful. Yusuf seemed more interested in Kurdistan than did Baki, and he seemed more important in the HK. I was happy to observe this contradiction, and I assumed some HK members would break off. The more who left the HK for ideological reasons, the better. That prospect gave me hope, so I decided to stop taking Baki's behavior so seriously, suppressing my impatience and cooling my temper when he pressured me emotionally.

I didn't dismiss Baki entirely. I began to think it might be possible to be with him after all, if we could reach ideological and organizational unity, and I told him so up front. Ideological-organizational unity was terribly important to me. And why shouldn't I want to transform my flight from my family into a meaningful companionship? Back in Dersim, the friends had stressed the importance of winning over İbo and Baki in particular. Now we had a close-knit group of ten people who were committed to a revolutionary life. Belonging to the same movement could have been so beautiful, and it would have helped us influence other groups.

Yusuf Metin advised me not to underestimate Baki's revolutionary personality. I didn't—he had a genuinely militant side, which was why I wanted him in my group. But his ineffectuality prevented me from having confidence in him. Without openly stating it, he insinuated to me that marriage could accelerate an ideological convergence. His and Yusuf's comrades knew how strongly committed I was to my own ideology, and they weren't against it themselves.

One day Sarı Ertan came to visit. He belonged to the leadership cadre of THKO and was one of those arrested on March 12[89] along with the chairman. "I was arrested along with Apo—he knows me," he told me.

We don't consider the national question to be a side issue. We have no problem that you organize yourselves separately. If an organized struggle develops and a split becomes necessary, we won't hold it back. Our task is to support you, even if a nationalistic basis develops. But to deepen the contradictions between you and Baki unnecessarily—that wouldn't be right.

I liked what he said and found his analysis realistic.

But Baki was getting on my nerves. Why did he have to bring over his HK comrades? I could make my own decision. Why did he involve Metin, Ertan, and others? Their position and their revolutionary personalities meant nothing to me. Mehmet Ali came sometimes too. He disapproved of my working: "It's just too arduous. You grown men can solve your financial problems yourselves. I can help you. Sakine should stop working." I disagreed and refused to let it become a question of masculine honor. Then he got to the subject of marriage:

> It's your affair, but it's not good to impose a hard and fast condition. Baki has been a revolutionary for years, he and I have also differences of opinion, but we're still both revolutionaries and we like each other. Why don't you put your disagreements on the back burner for a while? I don't believe there are any points [between you] where agreement is excluded. We all come from Kurdistan and want nothing else. But the problem can't be only the group's, you can't look at it that way. My sister Sakine errs on this point. The Kurdistan question can't be overlooked, that would contradict the conclusions of political science.

That was how he tried to persuade me to marry Baki. He meant well, but once again he was guided by his emotions.

Where revolutionary criteria, principles, and strength of will are the basis, there can be no force. The will of others will be respected, and guidelines for a common struggle will be set. Comradely relations will be strong and free, and collaboration will be possible. In our social life, to be sure, we had collective and democratic structures, but political differences and individual characteristics obstructed the formation of revolutionary personalities and relationships at a good level. The system's influence on us persisted. Feudal, petit-bourgeois institutions and a social-chauvinist ideology were reproduced in the men. For my part, I was inexperienced in organized political struggle. As far as romantic relationships were concerned, I was simultaneously searching and fleeing. Since I couldn't free even myself from traditional influences, I failed to develop an effective position for the long term. I allowed myself to be guided by my feelings. I wanted with all my being to dedicate myself to struggle, but my ideas of how an organized person lived were very confused.

What would one have to sacrifice for it? Of course the old reactionary ties, but I sacrificed many things without regard for time or place. I was firmly committed to leading a revolutionary life under all circumstances, but I wasn't sure exactly what it required. Mostly I let my emotions guide me. I had set a goal and vowed to pursue it at all costs. The national liberation struggle was for me a source of inspiration—in this respect I was neither vague nor hesitant. But I didn't know where my personality fit in. I tried to overcome obstacles but never seemed to gain traction—I always seemed to face the same problems all over again.

Every effort I made opened up new problems that made me stumble. These futile attempts certainly taught me to fight, but even the smallest mistake was used against me and caused damage, for which I was responsible. All my hard work failed to bring success. I would fight up to a certain point and then lose patience. I failed to govern my feelings. I'd get stuck on certain points and lose when I needed to win. I was conducting a difficult, multilayered struggle for which I'd had no preparation. I learned only through practical experience.

I had run away, which everyone judged according to their own standards. Back then it was understandable that a young woman who wanted to be a revolutionary would run away from home. It was also no loss for the group [in Dersim]. I could have married—nothing was preventing me, and circumstances were pressuring me to do just that. But I didn't want to constrain myself that way. I'd already broken off one relationship unilaterally. Normally it was the man who initiated a breakup—with me it was different. But then I'd fled to a place where I ended up in the same trap. Everywhere it was as if there could be no other life [for a woman]. Even in struggle, you had to bind yourself irrevocably to someone. No young woman could remain unattached—there were strict provisions against it. I wasn't even free of this traditional mentality myself. But a life in which revolutionary work had to accommodate the traditional family seemed to me wrong and even repugnant. It had no place in my dreams and longings. On the contrary, I'd run away from it.

I had many social contacts, a colorful mixture of companions. I continually met new people, getting to know a lot of different people and groups. Some of them had influenced me, but I had no fear of losing myself in them. I always preserved my singularity, even in my current life. I had no fear—nothing and no one could break my courage, and I wouldn't allow myself to depend on or be directed by anyone. I had my own principles that I advocated everywhere. I rejected subordination and refused to be considered solely as a woman. I fought on.

[Baki's and my] relationship, which mostly consisted of pressure from him and the occasional yielding on my part, was a flirtation but not a marriage. Our differing ideological standpoints stood in the way. How could I marry someone from another political group—a stranger, so to speak? What would we have in common? What could our love, our passion, and our intimacy ever really build? The prospect of merely sharing a house and a bed was horrifying. It contradicted my ideology, according to which a companionship should actualize a common struggle. We would live together but have different goals. If we went anywhere, we would speak different languages. Baki was committed to an ideology and organization that rejected a revolution in Kurdistan. With me, it was just the opposite. The abyss between us was acute, and even if the issue was dismissed as a "contradiction among leftists," my ideology diverged from the very fundamentals of the traditional left. Yet Baki continued to insist that we could come to ideological unity and reproached me for being blinkered and dogmatic.

Even though I didn't believe in it and was right not to, we finally got married.

Does it make any sense for me to say that I didn't want this marriage and was coerced into it? It was actually true. The hypocritical engagement ceremony took place in a small group. Mehmet Ali was delighted. As the others danced *halay* [Kurdish folk dance], I was crying. What did I have to be happy about? A bond was being celebrated that I didn't want. It was happening only because everyone else wanted it, and because Baki wanted it. If Baki had really tried to build a political collaboration and a common struggle with me, and if he'd been a little more candid, I could have tried to be open to it. But Baki was trying to please both me and his organization. That had nothing to do with my narrow-mindedness or my zealousness. Was I to be patient about that?

That day my self-awareness was shaken. My old battle-readiness dissipated into a depressed silence. I didn't want to talk to anyone. I wandered aimlessly through the streets. I didn't want to go back to the flat. Through their emotional behavior, the others had all played a role in making this thing happen. We had differing political outlooks, yet I was like a sister to them. Our interactions were natural and trusting. I had an especially heartfelt, open relationship with İbo. He'd defended me more than once to Baki: "You can't force anything—leave her in peace. She has to be able to decide of her own free will. Don't start in again on this subject." When I'd talked to him, he'd admitted I was right. But in the end even he had acted emotionally. He trusted Baki and believed that nothing could really prevent us from living a revolutionary life together.

Class consciousness imported from outside In those days certain factories were going on strike. I absented myself from work and went to the Kula Mensucat textile factory, where I spent the night with the striking workers. İbo had told me about it. Everyone who worked there participated in the resistance. They'd built a tent in front of the factory. The strike was accompanied by *halay* dancing and drum and oboe playing. The stewards wore white aprons. The area was hung with signs saying "For better working conditions," "No to yellow unions,"[90] "Those who don't get justice take it for themselves."

Many leftists were there. The mayor of Gültepe, Aydın Erten, showed up. As a friendly gesture, he had fruit and vegetables brought in in an official car. The workers applauded and shouted slogans. A group of people who were to be terminated without compensation went on hunger strike. They drank sugar water at certain intervals. I helped prepare it and talked with them, which happily distracted me from my own problems. In my factory, it would be difficult to organize such a strike. We talked about working conditions in the various factories and about how to mobilize the working class. Some thought it was mostly impossible, that the workers would have to go out on strike themselves. Many more, however, thought revolutionaries had to come in from outside to organize a strike.

"Class consciousness has to be imported externally," Lenin is supposed to have said. That seemed about right to me. The working class could not achieve political consciousness on its own steam. But in my workplace no one was bringing it in, otherwise I'd surely have known.

I stayed a second day. On the third day Saime and Baki came to pick me up, and Saime stayed with me. When she hugged and kissed me, she called me "sister-in-law." I asked her not to call me that. She was a typical young girl full of the kind of crazy ideas that always circulate in boarding schools and to whom her own culture had become strange. Her language and behavior were childlike. We lived a long time together in a flat.

One night there was an incident in the Ülkü-Bir Club in our neighborhood. Baki and his comrades had organized an attack on the fascists. Our flat was exposed, and we had to leave immediately. We didn't dare return for our things for a long while. Not that we had all that much. Finally we moved into two different flats. Haydar and his sister Aynur lived in one, and the rest of us in the other. Our flat was in Bayraklı. I found work in a textile factory in Alsancak. A few students from Bornova University also worked there—I knew them from meetings. They were HK cadre and had gone to work in the factory on the orders of the organization. I was glad to see them because I assumed we could organize the other workers better together.

It was a big factory with diverse work areas, for cotton, rinsing, and cloth. I started out in the thread department. The work made me happy. I watched with delight as the bobbins filled the rows and the thread turned. But there was no time for enjoyment. Torn threads had to be reattached immediately. Empty or half-full spools had to be pulled out. The foremen supervised us constantly. They stood where they could see the whole department. If a spool broke or stopped turning, you risked their wrath. Of course they didn't all act the same way. They snarled at those who struck them as particularly wretched. They leered at most of us snidely, and when they insulted others, we knew they also meant us. We winked at each other and secretly mocked them. When we went to the bathroom, they counted the minutes. Many went there to smoke. We used the toilets to talk about certain things, careful not to arouse any notice. At the machines, conversation was forbidden. The foremen were like police. Even in the cafeteria they acted like bloodhounds.

The resistance at Kula Mensucat had drawn in a few other textile factories. That had induced the employers to relent on a few points. Most of the demands were economic in nature. Many workers walked out of the yellow union of the Türk-İş association and joined the DİSK labor confederation. From the point of view of the employers, the danger was that a spark could spread into a conflagration. In İzmir there were factories everywhere. In Aliağa and Tariş masses of workers lived together.

In the candy factory where I'd previously worked, the supervision hadn't been so strong, but in the textile factory every step was scrutinized.

Gülnaz, a woman who had started at the factory at the same time as me, left flyers and HK newspapers in the cubicles of some of the other female workers. A few of them became fearful and handed them over, unread, to the foreman. After that we were watched even more closely. The factory also employed men who were HK cadres, albeit inexperienced. Sometimes during the breaks they held meetings, which management noticed. I pointed out to them that they were being watched with suspicion. Our employment at this factory was soon over: we were fired before the week was out, without explanation. But we knew the reason. We raised our voices against our arbitrary firing, pointing out that the employers couldn't just change the terms of employment at will. We might have seemed a bit menacing, but as we were being summarily booted out, they told us, "We've shared your photographs with all employers. You'll never set foot in a factory again. You're all terrorists—it's clear from the way you look and behave."

Gülnaz and I laughed all the way home, but we also discussed our mistakes. The biggest was our inexperience, which had compromised me as well. Together we went to the [HK] club in Kemeraltı, where I met Haşim Demir, a former neighbor, and others from Dersim. We withdrew to a quiet room to talk.

They too thought the HK would change its position on the question of national liberation. I said it could be stalling, but they objected. [The HK] was clearly looking for change, they said. If their recommendation were overridden, they said they would come out unambiguously. I was glad. Before we parted, we made another date to meet and continue the discussion.

I kept meeting new people and going to meetings.

Finally I find the friends!   The family of Ali the teacher moved to Bayraklı, I ran into his daughter Aysel by chance at a bus stop. When I left Dersim, Aysel had still been in high school, and Yüksel was at the Teachers School. Her mother was the aunt of Mazlum and Delil [Doğan], who in Dersim had tried to win over this family. Yüksel was affiliated with us—she was a comrade. She'd finished the Teachers School and worked as a substitute teacher. Her father meanwhile had retired. He'd insisted on moving to İzmir even though the rest of the family wanted to stay in Dersim. He was afraid for his daughters. Ali was a fervent adherent of Kemalism but presented himself as a democrat. In this respect he resembled my uncle Hasan, who when he was drunk insulted the state and called himself a radical democrat and called us "comrades." But when sober he warned us to be reasonable, since the state was relentless.

I suffered from being so far from home and the friends there, so I was buoyed to see Yüksel. My mood improved dramatically, and we spent a lot of time together. We walked around discussing and conversing. I learned a lot from her. She gave me Türkan's address, and I wrote to her, explaining my situation. At the end of the letter, I wrote that if Baki and I couldn't reach ideological unity, I'd separate from him and go back home. A little later came Türkan's reply: she'd read my letter with the friends, and she supported me. It filled me with joy. It was wonderful to resume contact with her.

Yüksel explained that a brother of Mazlum was now in İzmir, in Bornova. He belonged to the *Özgürlük Yolu* group.[91] We visited him and had a long discussion. He was very conservative and a fervent adherent of his faction. It wasn't so good talking to him, and we decided not to press him further—after all, he was Mazlum's brother. But we wanted to stay in touch, and I assumed we could win him over sometime.

I was unemployed and had enough time on my hands to visit the various political clubs with Yüksel. At the DDKD in Kemeraltı, we met a man named İbrahim who seemed interested in Yüksel. Others were friendly to us. In a discussion I led at the HK club, the DDKD adherents got called nationalistic. On the door hung a sign with the inscription "Entrance for Kurds only." That was of course highly exaggerated, but that was the DDKD. To us they said, "You're different. Your organization's name is hardly known, but at least your movement has content."

This assessment, however patronizing, was true—we really were different. I understood the Turkish left better after I got to know the DDKD members, whose behavior reminded me of a feudal village community. Most of them were students, but their interactions seemed very feudal. All spoke Kurdish. Right off the bat they asked us whether we were Kurds. İbrahim, who knew Yüksel's family, said, "Of course they're Kurds. They come from Dersim." Then he looked at me questioningly. I said in Turkish, "That's right, I'm also from Dersim."

They asked, "Don't you speak Kurdish?" to which I responded, "I speak Zazaki."

They restrained themselves since we were also the only women in the club. Later a dark-haired woman approached me, who spoke Kurdish. We knew each other—I'd met her a few times when I visited Ägais University in Bornova. She'd mainly seen me with HK members, so she thought I was one of them. Back when student dormitories were being occupied, I'd visited the occupiers. The universities were home to many movements, but members of different factions stuck together. The PDA isolated itself entirely and accused other groups of opportunism. Its members participated in no actions and did no outreach.

As we talked, I noticed a piece of paper on the wall. I stood up and read:

Two people have been participating in our [the DDKD's] various activities. It recently has become known that they have ties to a group called "National Liberation," meaning they have left the ranks of revolutionaries. We will discuss their position. We invite them to discuss the matter openly and do a self-criticism.

I had found my friends! I had to restrain myself from shouting—not that I cared how anyone would react. My friends were here! That was all that mattered. I waved Yüksel over to read the text. Seeing our interest, İbrahim felt it necessary to explain: "It's about two students, Celal from Nizip and Haydar from Suruç." Where could I meet the two of them? I asked. He told me their areas of study, adding that he didn't think they'd attend the meeting.

I rejoiced. And why should they hold themselves accountable to the DDKD? The only purpose of the meeting would be to denounce them.

Around that time, there had been an earthquake in Lice.[92] Various groups were collecting funds for the victims, in a fundraising campaign under state supervision. As with any earthquake, propaganda is made while assistance is collected. During our first visit to the DDKD, the campaign had been discussed. A few groups had been in the earthquake area and were to report on what they'd done. Yüksel and I had looked around the busy space, wondering if our presence there was even desired. The members' behavior gave us the impression they'd prefer we left. But the group at the next table had just returned from Lice, and we wanted very much to hear their report, so we listened to their conversation.

They referred to "nationals" and the "UKO,"[93] saying that in Lice these groups "threw everything into confusion, which gave rise to conflicts among the people." Impatiently I waited for them to say more. They were maligning the friends, but I actually didn't care—it meant our activities were spreading. If we were being talked about everywhere, raising the hackles of other organizations, that was a positive development.

The meeting began, with a panel of people from the group who had been in Lice. One by one they spoke. When we didn't understand, we asked them to speak Turkish and explained why.[94] Our suggestion was accepted. Their presentations repeated themes that had been discussed in two-party discussions.

First we worked as a joint committee, but when it came to distributing aid, the UKO acted opportunistically. They set themselves apart, organized distribution according to their own discretion, and thereby created divisions between the people. The people nonetheless found each other. At first we didn't have the situation under control, but later we intervened. Our activities were positively accepted. We sensed in the people a great interest in us. They saw that we spoke their language and fought for them. They were angry at the UKO, who didn't speak their own native tongue, the language of the people. The people didn't trust them.

I nearly fell off my chair. I wanted to interrupt the speakers, but that wouldn't have been good. It was normal for them to malign other revolutionary groups, and it corresponded to their character. So I let them finish, then spoke up.

Don't take it amiss, but I don't know Kurdish. I only know Zazaki, so I'd like to speak Turkish. I'm glad you're reporting on these developments, and I've listened with interest. I now know more about the earthquake in Lice, so I won't add anything. But the friend has repeatedly blamed and defamed others. His very one-sided report raises doubts about his objectivity. If the opposite side had been able to present their position, the issue would be more understandable. I'd like to criticize that. And the language problem is very much in the foreground. In my opinion, what's important is not whether someone can speak Kurdish. Revolutionary standpoints can be expressed in other languages too. It's a mistake to set that as a decisive criterion. And I don't believe that distinctions were made in the distribution of aid.

Then I sat down.

At first there was silence, which the moderator broke by explaining that references to facts were not accusations and had nothing to do with defamation. Then he declared: "If the friend knows otherwise, can she tell us? We'd like to hear what the UKO has to say." He looked straight at me—we were from the UKO. But we didn't have to talk about where we stood politically just to satisfy the curiosity of the others.

I'd expected the meeting to discuss the two other friends, but because they didn't appear, that agenda item was postponed. It would have been better for us if that discussion had taken place, but we'd already heard a lot. After the meeting was over, we sat for a while, and then when we left, we said we'd come again. "But of course, our meetings are always open to our Kurdish sisters," they said, as if they'd be glad to see us. Who knows? Maybe somehow they really were glad. Two women from Kurdistan, so far from home, had visited them. Probably no one who didn't belong to their faction had turned up here for a long time.

Later I did go back, sometimes with Yüksel, sometimes alone, and sometimes with Baki and the others. They knew Baki, and he knew them all distantly. I looked for Celal and Haydar, the two that the announcement had said they'd be discussing. Baki helped, asking for them at the university. He set up a meeting.

We met Celal in a coffee shop in Kadifekale, near his flat. He came from Nizip and was married to a female student from Cyprus. He'd got in touch first with the DDKD, he said, but then when he got to know the friends in Antep, he broke it off. "I had no special connection with them," he said. "It's a Kurdish club, everyone there is from Kurdistan, and our relations were warm. But I never had an organizational connection. The other friend is from Suruç." We gave him the address of our flat and explained how to get there.

Celal assumed that Baki and I were from the same organization, which annoyed me. Baki had introduced me saying, "We're married." Celal knew from the university that Baki was HK, so that confused him. The coffee shop wasn't suitable for further explanations, and for reasons of security, we didn't want to stay there any longer.

Were there other friends besides Haydar in İzmir? I asked. "There are a couple of sympathizers who we're in conversation with," he said. I mentioned Yüksel and suggested we meet more often, but he said he might be leaving soon. I didn't ask any more questions, and we parted.

As Baki and I walked along, he spoke critically about Celal. "He's with a girl from Cyprus. I'd never have thought he'd have anything to do with the nationals. He always hung around with DDKD-ers. They're all children of large landholders and extortionists. Such types can't fight for Kurdistan."

"Yes, you're right about the DDKD," I said. "But why are you talking that way about Celal? He's not with them anymore. Do you think everyone except the HK is petit bourgeois? Are the HK the only proletarian revolutionaries? What's important is not the individuals but the ideology. Besides, we've only just met Celal." I stoked the disagreement: "And why did you tell him right off that we're married? That was entirely unnecessary and inappropriate."

"It's the truth," Baki said. "Why shouldn't I say it? And why are you ashamed of it? Aren't I good enough for you?" He was incensed, and we argued the rest of the way home.

"What, do you just want me to sit at home, now that you've found your friends?" he seethed. "What kind of revolutionary responsibility is that? We're responsible for each other, and we're bound to each other."

"No, we're not bound to each other!" I exploded. "I don't see anything that ties us together. As long as we have no shared ideology and organization, you can't speak of unity and partnership. You've been dishonest on this subject from the beginning. You pretended to be grappling with it so this marriage could happen. But it's been the same thing for months now. Your relationship to the HK hasn't changed— you defend it everywhere, always. If that keeps up, we can't stay together. Our marriage is not carved in stone, and this situation is bad for me." I couldn't think clearly, I was so enraged. I didn't care what effect my words had on him.

"Okay, I get it," Baki said, then fell silent to avoid setting me off again. "But isn't it still way too early to reach this conclusion?" he resumed. "You're not thinking about yourself or others. You exaggerate such small differences so unnecessarily. You should think a little bit before you go through the roof. There's a difference between a revolutionary solution and interim solutions."

This argument was typical of our relationship.

We decided to go to Dersim together. The day before we left, we visited a family of Bulgarian immigrants in Karşıyaka. The two daughters were classmates of Baki, and I knew them from political meetings. My whole time in İzmir, I'd always worn the same pants. I didn't have another pair. I just changed my shirt now and then. We had just enough money to meet our daily needs and nothing more. Often I had to put my clothes back on right after I washed them, while they were still damp. I couldn't go to Dersim with these things. Baki said I should borrow some clothes from the two women. We stayed overnight as guests and got going the next day.

We drove directly to Dersim, without stopping in Ankara, and from there we went to the village. Meto, Türkan, and the others came out to greet me. We had a long conversation, including on the subject of marriage. We talked about how they'd acted toward me at the time, what had gone wrong, and why I'd concluded that escape was the only solution. I explained in detail what I'd already written in my letter to Türkan, and I added that the problems between Baki and me were as unresolved as ever. They talked to Baki for a long time too—he showed himself to be insightful. He noticed how the situation in Dersim had changed in our absence. Our ideology was on everyone's lips and had become a force to be reckoned with. The conversation with Türkan and the other friends had a good effect on Baki and me. They thought we could make it.

Meto meanwhile cracked jokes and made us all laugh. "Sister, Baki will come around to our position if only to keep from losing you!" He wasn't entirely wrong, but my dear brother and comrade oversimplified the matter. What kind of political unity would it be, if it existed only for the sake of preserving a relationship? I still felt uneasy.

Türkan, Meto, Nimet, and I wanted to visit Kıymet in Güleç (Derexag), where she was now a teacher. Since the village was nearby, we set out by foot and talked the whole distance. "I wish Baki had come along with us," Türkan said. "Kıymet would have been able to win him over."

But I'd opposed him coming. Had I made a mistake? Were they right? Had I seen a problem where none existed? No! There was very much a problem. Achieving unity as a basis for coexistence—that was no trifle. But the issue was being distorted or treated superficially.

I asked Türkan about organized marriages.[95] She said the subject was much discussed.

I said, "The main thing is that a relationship has to rest on free will. Love can't thrive unless it's built on shared work." I mentioned an example from my own relationship.

Türkan said that if she were told she had to marry a comrade, she'd refuse.

"Why?" I asked, my voice raised. "How do you figure?" It had to be a joke or a distortion of the facts. "You can't mean it."

We talked about many other things on the way to Kıymet's village. When I told them about İzmir and my work in the factory, they couldn't believe it and asked if it had really been necessary for me to work there. I explained that it was and that the workers' resistance and the labor struggle interested me. "Work is good. Without work you can't live in a big city."

Türkan, who had an anarchistic streak, said she wanted to go to İzmir. She was good at things—she knew how to ride a bike and a motorbike, and how to drive a car. She knew how to swim. She learned quickly and had developed herself theoretically. She couldn't sit still—she gesticulated when she spoke. Even while she was sitting, her arms and legs were always in motion. But her personality wasn't yet mature. She took things all too casually and couldn't keep perspective. Wherever she was, the atmosphere couldn't be serious.

Nimet, who had come with us, worked for the municipal administration. She asked me many questions out of curiosity, even though there was nothing new for her to learn. Her comments were superficial and banal. The intensity of my conflict with Baki surprised her. But I didn't want to exaggerate the problems unnecessarily: an immediate separation would be nerve-racking, I wanted to talk about it first in a smaller group. That was why we were going to visit Kıymet.

Actually it was strange that Kıymet's opinion was still important to me. When I'd spoken to her previously, she hadn't been able to solve my problem. In fact, she'd made a suggestion that led the others to joke that I should wear a sign around my neck saying "looking for a husband." If we'd found a reasonable and sustainable solution back then, I wouldn't be in this situation now. My marriage was damaging and unnecessary. After only a few months, we were already talking about separating. If we couldn't solve our conflict, divorce was inevitable. What would our acquaintances say to that? Presumably some would find it disconcerting, but I'd manage.

Kıymet welcomed us with delight. Her house was next door to the school. In the village there were many young people, but they sympathized with the Turkish left. Kıymet had been a teacher here for five years, but she apparently hadn't tried to organize people. That struck me as odd—as a teacher, she could have won the entire village over to us. When I asked her about it, she said, "Many have expressed interest, but a few dogmatic types keep them away from me." That seemed strange. In the evenings Zülfü, a young man from the village who played *saz* very well, came to visit. He played a few pieces for us and sang. I especially liked the songs by Sılo Qız, whose name means "little Suleyman." He played at weddings, engagements, and circumcision celebrations, I'd heard him perform once. His violin playing was gorgeous and sentimental.

The next day we visited the classroom. The usual ceremonies at the beginning of class didn't happen, and the Turkish flag wasn't hoisted. Kıymet taught reading and writing, using words and sentences with revolutionary content. The children were delighted. They absorbed whatever was taught them enthusiastically and were happy if sometimes embarrassed.

Kıymet dealt with my marital problem quickly:

> You must try in every possible way to win him over for us. These groups are important, having many young people among them. The people from the Kureşan tribe are all in the Turkish left. If we could bring a few of them over to us, it would have an impact on the others.

Afterward we embraced and bade each other farewell.

Meto wanted to take me home to our mother, but I worried about how she would behave. "She'll complain at first," he said, "then cry, and finally accept you. She'd be hurt if she found out you'd been in Dersim without visiting her." He was right.

I visited my other relatives in the village, and everywhere political discussions were taking place. Şah Haydar was now with the HB.[96] Was the entire political spectrum represented among my relatives? I teased my cousins: "PDA, TİKKO, HB, HK, TKP—that's about as many factions as there are!" All my siblings were influenced by their big brother. When talkative little Ali Cemal said he was for the HB, we all burst into laughter. He was still a child and babbled about things he'd heard. It had nothing to do with revolution. The parents were concerned: "Who brought in all these revolutionary ideas, and why does everyone have a different opinion? One of these days, we're afraid our children will all be fighting each other."

One of my uncles was interested in my political orientation. "I've heard you're advocating Kurdishness," he said. He'd obviously heard his children's counter-propaganda.

Ali Gültekin and Kemal Burkay preceded you, and they're gone now. They live in big cities. Ali Gültekin failed to win over even the people from his own village. Hasan, Gülabi, and Ali all now work in state institutions as teachers or engineers. They don't have anything to do with politics anymore.

He didn't want to say he shared his children's opinion, but he distrusted all revolutionary ideas.

Uncle Mustafa said,

It's all well and good, but what's with the constant talk about America and Russia? These people don't have a single soldier here—there's not one Russian or American on our mountains. The head of state here is a Turk, his generals are Turks, and his soldiers are Turks. We speak Turkish. Our children are confused.

But he didn't contradict my remarks and even called them reasonable. His daughter-in-law, on the other hand, said, "Let's found an Alevi state, I'll help with that." That was a widespread point of view, which my father also held.

Baki's father got annoyed at his son. "I'm for Sakine's party!" he said, and his wife agreed. Both said to their children, "You should all be for this party. Day and night you discuss, and nothing good can come from it!" They knew about the conflict between Baki and me and wanted to prevent a separation.

Later we drove to the city. First we visited relatives there, who urgently advised us to marry officially, to avoid suspicion. Maybe they were right. It had no meaning for me, but the police might use the missing piece of paper as a pretext to create difficulties for us. Baki took our IDs and photos and went off. Through his acquaintances, he succeeded in getting a date—all the civil servants in the registrar's office were his acquaintances or relatives. Our official marriage took place only on paper, but it changed my surname: Cansız was replaced by Polat.

I got in touch with my mother. At first she refused to see me but agreed only after relatives intervened. One evening we went there, and at first she wouldn't offer her hand and held back, but then she hugged me and cried. Clearly she'd suffered. We sat down together and paged through old photo albums, with photos of my first engagement. I pulled them out and tore them up, not in anger but because they had no more meaning. When someone wants to keep a memory alive, it means a connection is still there. But I was now in another situation and didn't want those strange, sour memories. My mother also gave me Metin's letters, among which was a photo of him. I hadn't heard from Metin since I ran away, but he'd continued to write to me. I looked at his photo sadly and felt ashamed, as if he were standing in front of me. I tore up his letters without reading them. I let out a sob and wished none of it had happened. Baki watched me in silence, perhaps fearfully. After all, our relationship was in danger too. My mother looked at us both wanly, with neither joy nor pain.

"What's this? Don't you have a bag or a suitcase?" she asked.

"It's in the village." It was a lie—I owned nothing at all. The clothing I was wearing belonged to the Bulgarian immigrants. Even the shoes were borrowed from them.

My mother asked a lot of questions, and I answered evasively. "We both work," I said, "it's going well." By "work," she thought I meant a civil service job. It would never have occurred to her that I worked in a factory. My father had been a worker for years—my mother had been with him in Germany and seen it. But for her and her friends, it just wouldn't have been proper. I didn't try to explain—it didn't matter what she thought.

She opened the closet and pulled down a suitcase. "Take your things with you," she said. I didn't really want to. For three or four months, I'd managed with one pair of pants and one shirt. It was more comfortable that way, better than dragging a suitcase around. After a moment of hesitation, I said, "I'd rather leave my stuff here." My mother, taken aback, burst into tears. I've never forgotten the sight. Had I expected too much of her? Actually we both felt pain, and we both suffered that my engagement to Metin had been dissolved. I'd torn up his photos and letters, but Metin's parents still lived across the way, and I was looking at the clothes I'd worn then.

The whole evening my mother tried to bring the conversation around to Metin: "He's promised never to come to Dersim again. He hasn't been here once. I heard he's now in your political group." But I didn't want to talk about Metin—it was too painful.

Finally I did pack a suitcase. We also took a few things that we could use for our flat—spoons, knives, and such. I left my trousseau untouched, since I wanted nothing to do with that part of my past. It was exhausting.

My mother spoke to Baki only out of courtesy—she was still angry. Baki felt it and whispered to me, "Your mother doesn't like me." "Good that you noticed," I answered. "She's never liked my family," he said reproachfully. "We were poor, we were peasants. But since we were honest, she couldn't start up with anything."

It was true, my mother had never liked my father's family and always kept them at arm's length. My father's mother had visited us only once, during the year when we were in Germany. In all those years, my father had been able to persuade her to visit us exactly once during one of his annual fourteen-day vacations. She died while we were in Germany.

Baki had had enough of Dersim. He had to get back to the university and didn't want me to stay any longer either. "Let's go back together," he said. But to me, it made no sense to return to İzmir without having solved our problem. I wanted to leave with a solution in hand. An interim solution didn't exist. I'd told Kıymet and the others that I'd set a deadline for Baki. If he didn't change his position by a certain time, I'd end the relationship. I still had to take the secondary school exams—I could use that as an excuse to stay in Dersim. Then I'd have a chance to talk to my girlfriends again about the problem and find a better solution. But Kıymet had had enough of it. She'd said she'd tell the friends about my situation and see that they got in touch with me. She didn't know I was already in touch with friends in İzmir. "If you want, you can get in touch with the friends in Ankara," she said. Meto said he wanted to come to İzmir later, which made me happy. But no immediate solution was in sight, and no one had suggested an alternative.

Just at this moment, Kemal Pir came to Dersim.[97] I was told to go to the "upper house," a small attic flat that the friends used—it belonged to Kıymet's family. I immediately headed out. Çetin Güngör (Semir) talked to me first. "I've heard about your situation," he said, but then he didn't seem to know anything. I'd always known Çetin to be talkative. Especially in ideological discussions, he got very lively and tried to impress everyone. I once took part in a seminar on Soviet modern revisionism that he moderated. It was very lively, with much participation. But now it was hard for him to talk about marriage and separation. Why?

Kemal had left the room, and when he returned, he noticed what was happening. "Come on, Sakine, let's go talk in another room," he said. We went off, and he said,

Tell me all about it. I've heard you want to separate, but I don't know much more, only that it's an ideological difference and that he's with the HK. Or, let's start from the other end and talk about what's to be done.

He said he wanted to hear me out, but he kept on talking. That was actually better. I guess he wanted to make it easier for me. I wasn't embarrassed, but my problem was so all-consuming that it really was hard for me to talk about it. Kemal had noticed.

I summarized the situation, from my rejection of the engagement that my family had pressured me into, to my marriage to Baki. Without beating around the bush, Kemal said,

Okay, you've made a decision, and that's good. But you have to be careful that the issue doesn't lead to disharmony between the families. Best thing would be for you to go to Ankara and talk to Kesire. You could stay with her awhile.

I didn't want to be rushed—I wanted calm consideration—but Comrade Kemal kept leaping to his feet, pacing a few steps, then sitting back down.

When we parted, I felt stronger, as if the problem had been solved, but I wished I'd been able to speak in more detail or that I'd had Kemal to talk to from the beginning. Did he know about Kıymet's suggested solution? She'd thought I should find a husband! I got annoyed at myself because I felt so helpless and so naïve. A revolutionary solution had to be entirely different from an "interim solution."

I took the two high school exams I'd missed. The teachers knew it was just a formality to get to the next class. I tried to think about the situation more calmly. The ideological differences between Baki and me had been grinding me down unnecessarily. My own impatience had worsened the problem. Whatever I did, I had to weigh the consequences. It wasn't good to show my feelings always and everywhere. I couldn't expect every suggestion someone gave me to be correct. Advice that was superficial or untimely could arouse false hopes.

The friends now knew my situation and saw I wouldn't just hand myself over to my fate. It was senseless to concentrate all my energy on this one problem. There were many possibilities: Baki could return to İzmir. I could return later. I could talk to the friends one more time in Ankara. If necessary, I could stay awhile longer in İzmir. I would not let the whole thing oppress me any further. Yes, nothing was concrete, but at least I was much more open to a constructive solution. I felt better.

In İzmir, before we came to Dersim, some land in Cumaova had become available. As a result of local elections and interparty conflicts, city residents had the ability to obtain land for themselves. Baki had managed to grab a piece. He wanted to build a little house there, to save rent. His father had promised him financial support. So he went back to İzmir, and we agreed I'd return later with my uncle.

When [my uncle and I] finally got under way, we drove to Ankara first. Baki had stopped there as well and was still there. He took it amiss that I'd lingered so long in Dersim. We had a long discussion. He was opposed to my meeting with Kesire and said I didn't make enough time for him and acted inconsiderately. It was much too early for a separation, he said: "You're not even trying to win me over to organizational unity. If you were, you'd be more patient with me. The whole thing isn't simple. Honestly, I think about it a lot."

My uncle and Mehmet Ali witnessed our quarrel. Our constant arguments and the prospect of separation disconcerted them. "Why do you make such a big fuss? You're both revolutionaries. Don't make everything so difficult!" They criticized Baki for his fanatical adherence to the HK, and they criticized me for unnecessarily magnifying the differences between us.

Finally we drove back to İzmir together. I tried to avoid discussing the problem further, resolving to find a solution myself. I'd go to the friends and tell them the problem was solved. To Baki, I said:

> You're partly right with your criticism. But you have to be straightforward, too. Don't always think only of saving our marriage. Think about what organizational unity really means. I don't want this unity to suffer a separation. I really do want to have comradely relations with you.

"Kurdistan is a colony" Back in İzmir, I looked for work again and soon found a job in a fig factory in Alsancak. It was a small processing facility that employed mainly young women. Baki and I tried to cope with our conflict. I made a suggestion: "Let's live separately until you're finished with your reflections and have reached a decision." İbo and the others supported that idea, but Baki didn't. "No one has to know about it," I said. "We're just back from Dersim. Our families will be sympathetic. Talk spreads quickly, that wouldn't be good, so we'll keep it to ourselves. Only the friends who have something to do with us have to know about it."

I'd talked to Haydar from Suruç, who said I had to know what I was doing. He wanted to help Baki and talk to him often. That was a good idea, a way to keep it from always turning into an argument.

It made no sense for Baki and me to share a flat anymore, as that only stressed our relationship. Reluctantly he accepted my suggestion to meet now and then. This decision shouldn't prevent us from seeing each other, discussing with each other, and even sometimes working together and helping each other. It should, on the contrary, strengthen the foundations for mutuality.

Baki moved in with a family in Çiğli. They came from Varto. He could have gone to Haydar and Aynur, or stayed with İbo and Saime in the flat. He was free to go where he wanted.

At work, when the noon break arrived, we normally ate lunch in a part of the factory that was designated the lunchroom. But no food was served; we brought lunch from home. Outside there was a restaurant where you could order toast, pita, *lahmacun* [Turkish pizza], and the like. We could get tea from a nearby teashop.

One day I'd just started my lunch when the foreman told me I had a visitor, waiting for me in the restaurant. *It must be Baki*, I thought. I rose reluctantly and stepped outside, wearing a headscarf and a green work apron, wiping my hands on it. Suddenly I was standing across from my big brother [Haydar]. Totally surprised, I hugged and kissed him. Tears welled in his eyes as he said, "Do you really have to work here? You look so pale, and you're so thin." "Yes," I said, "I have to earn my living. But I'm happy to work here. I could have worked other places, but I didn't want to."

Haydar was studying law in Istanbul now and had got my address from Meto. He'd come to İzmir to have a little vacation, he said, but I knew he'd come mainly to see me. We chatted over a meal in the restaurant. He pretended to eat but actually didn't get anything down.

He chewed every bite a long time, then made a strange noise while swallowing. It made me uneasy. Baki joined us, but he was quiet too. What was going on?

I asked Haydar a few questions, but he gave evasive answers. He didn't want to talk about Istanbul or his studies. His thoughts were elsewhere. Before he met up with me, he'd been in a flat where Baki was temporarily living—we'd previously lived there together. It was a poor flat, furnished only with an old carpet, a few mattresses, and some cutlery. Surely Haydar's bachelor flat in Istanbul was much better equipped than ours.

Well, what had he expected? Had he imagined I lived in a luxurious apartment? I wouldn't even want to live in such a place. And even if I did, what would it change? Would it have made me a happy housewife? No, luxury had no meaning for me, and I felt no desire for it. But how could I explain that to Haydar? *Let it be,* I said to myself. *It's normal that he's bothered. It'll pass, and soon he'll understand.*

But Haydar was tense. "Take a day off and let's go out," he said.

I agreed and took the rest of the day off. While my brother paid the bill, I asked Baki what he thought [about the poor flat]. "Well, Aynur's is better," he said. Haydar's behavior still puzzled me. What was going on? Had someone told him something untrue? Questions buzzed around in my head.

We took a taxi to the pier. At the pier, Baki shoved through the crowd of people to buy tickets. But my brother didn't let him or me pay, just waved us off without saying anything. We went out onto the deck of the ferry, and my brother gave Baki a look that said he wanted to speak to me briefly alone. Then he put his arm around my shoulder, and we walked a few steps. He asked, "Are you happy?"

I was astonished by the question. What was he talking about? Was I happy? I murmured something and acted as if I didn't understand. If he was referring to my marriage, my answer would of course have been no. But I found life beautiful, even under shabby, routine, and inadequate conditions. The revolutionary struggle made me happy and gave me strength. It gave me *joie de vivre.* Without it I'd feel very alone. Life here wasn't like in Dersim, where I knew everyone. I had self-confidence, feeling neither helplessness nor pessimism. My whole life was a struggle, at every moment. This knowledge gave me the strength to stand on my own feet.

But how could I explain my marital problems to Haydar? Ultimately I couldn't separate my married life from my revolutionary life. One gave me strength, while the other was unbearable and threatened to suffocate me. Giving up the struggle would mean resigning myself to a fate as a woman who had capitulated.

I couldn't lie to my brother—he knew me too well and would see through me. "Let's go home. We can talk better there. I'm fine. I work, and it suits me. I'm happy to work. I have friends I see often. The friends in Ankara will soon be in touch with me." It didn't answer his question, but I talked around it.

Haydar tried again: "No, I'm asking about your relationship with Baki. In other respects, I believe that you have no problems. You always did find your own path."

I responded to his candor with candor. "We discuss with each other, and we disagree on some points. We have no ideological unity. As you know, he's HK, an HK cadre. Since 1975, he says, he's wanted to engage with the Kurdistan question. He said that even back in Dersim. But he's indecisive. We don't work together and have different sets of friends. That naturally affects our relationship. It's a problem, but maybe everything will work out. He's promised to do thorough research and to find clarity on the question."

"Is it such a large obstacle?"

I nodded.

"And what about the work, isn't it strenuous? You've lost weight. Why don't you come stay with me for a while in Istanbul? My apartment is big enough. It'll do you good."

I said without thinking, "Sure, why not?"

"What—you can decide that by yourself?" he asked in wonder. "Don't you want to ask Baki first?"

"Why shouldn't I decide for myself?" I said. "You're my brother—what's the problem? I don't need Baki's permission."

Haydar nodded slightly, as if to tell me he understood.

He wanted to know more about my current life. I had no reason to hide anything from him, but I was careful. On the way to the flat where Aynur and her brother Haydar lived, we stopped for groceries. All three of us had bags in hand as we entered. Baki and I had never bought so much food at once, as we had to watch our spending so carefully.

The flat with its two rooms, narrow corridor, and kitchen, was indeed poor. I rolled up my sleeves and went into the kitchen to avoid more questions from my brother. Alone with Aynur and Haydar, I asked, "When my brother was here, did you talk to him about my situation? He didn't seem to be in a very good mood."

"No," they said.

A short time later, my brother called to me.

"The meal is ready, I'll be right there," I said.

Suddenly he exploded: "Enough! Don't play games with me, Sakine! What's going on with you? You aren't Sakine anymore. You've changed." Infuriated, he slapped me in the face.

Seeing stars, I staggered. I was struck less by the force of the blow than by its complete unexpectedness. Had Haydar gone mad? Where had this anger come from? What had people told him?

He continued relentlessly, "You're not the old Sakine anymore— you're lying to me. Did you think I wouldn't pick up on it? I know all about you! Were you working when you still lived in our father's house? Did he let you work? Now you're a factory worker. What does that do for you? You don't need it!" He forged ahead without interruption, weeping.

"It's true," I roared back, "I'm not the old Sakine! You see me only as a little sister, but you have no right to act this way. I have not lied!" I pointed to Baki: "He's the liar! He hasn't kept his word, and he's been telling you bullshit! I'm sure he's told you everything from his point of view, to stir you to pity him. If he'd been honest with me from the beginning, it wouldn't have gone this far. Just so I'd marry him, he agreed to the very points that separate us now: 'I'll think about it,' he said. But he was only stalling so I wouldn't leave him. You asked me [if I'm happy], and maybe in that moment I couldn't answer clearly. But now I can. No, I'm not happy. You all know that very well. I'm married to someone to whom I'm tied neither organizationally nor ideologically. We share only a bed. That's all that's left. And I can't stand it anymore. I'm not the only one who's evasive and tells lies. Now you know—we live separately. We belong to different political camps, and that leads nowhere!" I was crying as I shouted. Then I stormed out of the apartment.

The last bus hadn't yet departed. Baki ran after me: "Sakine, don't be silly, there aren't any more buses today. Come back here and calm down." I blocked out everything he said.

The alley was empty. I dashed over to the main street and barely caught the last bus. It was peaceful inside. I bought a ticket, and the seller looked me over. As he handed me my change, he looked me in the face, then shook his head. Apparently he'd noticed something there. I touched the side where my brother had hit me. It wasn't bleeding. But when I saw my reflection in a window, my face was bright red from crying.

In the bus I tried to pull myself together and not think about what had happened. But tears poured down my cheeks. Only after I got off and walked for a while did I feel better. I wished the route were longer. When I came to the flat where I lived, the family was already asleep, except the housewife, who peered at me curiously. "We can talk about it later," I said.

The next morning a big demonstration against the state security courts was to take place. I had to be in İç Konak in Kemeraltı at 7 a.m. I'd promised to meet Haydar and Celal at the HK club. All the groups were going to participate in the protest, even the other organizations, with all their members. It was a big deal. The prospect of meeting the friends and being able to talk to them soothed me a little.

But still during the night I tried to settle myself. It wasn't appropriate for me to cry so much. These things happened. They too were a kind of struggle, one of the most arduous. They would continue. Haydar saw himself exclusively in the role of big brother, but at home he hadn't been so tough. Baki must have stirred him up. He must have thought he could come in here as a kind of savior, unifying us in a harmony, taking a stand for his country Kurdistan, and finally producing a common ideological foundation. That was probably why he had become angry.

Of course I'd made him angry back when I'd rejected Baki earlier and then got engaged to another man. Then I'd run away and married Baki. And now we faced a separation. Besides, I worked in a factory. It angered Haydar that it had all gone so far.

I knew my big brother very well. He didn't want to make a mistake, and he was angry because he loved me and was thinking about me. His reproaches to me were actually harmless compared to those he made to Baki:

In a revolutionary life there can be no insincerity, no dishonesty. What do you really find in the HK? You've attached yourself to it and you run with

it. At the university, they're just using you. You have your own country—
why aren't you fighting for it? You're the one who's making the problem
worse. Your love for Sakine is phony. If you loved her, you'd share her
political views. I know you, you're ineffectual, always worrying about what
others might think or what the HK would say. What's revolutionary about
that? Your whole family is like that—İbo, Mehmet Ali, Haydar, Celal—you
all chase after the social chauvinists. I don't belong to any organization,
but the Kurdistan Revolutionaries are right, and they're going to keep on
growing whether you like it or not.

It was beautiful, what he said. So I couldn't stay mad at him. And
the sound of him crying was pounding in my ears. He'd cried when my
father in Germany threw the ashtray at him. My problems must have hit
him hard. Was he still in the flat? I wondered. But then where would he
have gone in the middle of the night? These thoughts occupied me all
night. I lay with my eyes wide open till morning.

That morning everyone stared at my face. I looked into the mirror,
but only a light redness was visible. "I tussled with my brother. When we
were kids, we played like that. He thought we were still home fighting for
fun." Everyone believed me and laughed. Only Hasan looked dubious.
He knew about my fights with Baki and probably assumed Baki had
hit me. But he said nothing, just took in a deep breath, as if to say, *I'll
show him*. His temples pounded with strain. We gulped down breakfast
and went out. "Why isn't your wife coming with us?" I asked, then
remembered their children were still young and couldn't be left alone.
Finally we reached the main street and walked on in silence.

Hasan was understanding and, to spare my feelings, didn't ask any
questions. He was working for Tariş, enjoying the respect of his peers.
He and his wife had three children. They'd come to İzmir after the
big earthquake in Varto. The HK had recruited these very nice people
for organizing work in Çiğli. They assumed it was a revolutionary
organization, so they made regular monthly contributions and
bought political newspapers. Later the HK even brought them into its
neighborhood committees. But they valued their Kurdish distinctiveness
and listened attentively whenever the Kurdish question was discussed.
They and I understood each other well. The friends came to visit
sometimes.

Konak Square was full of people. At the pier, we turned toward
Kemeraltı. The streets were normally lively, but today they were packed

so tight that a falling needle wouldn't have touched the ground. Workers, students, women, and many others had gathered at the rallying point. People from Gültepe, Çiğli, and Kadifekale often took part in such protest actions. Revolutionary groups found it easy to organize people in these neighborhoods, including Kurdish residents.

The HK headquarters was overflowing. With an effort I pushed though the crowd and reached the room on the upper floor where I'd promised to meet Celal and Haydar. They were already there. Two young men there were introduced to me as "some of us." "Yüksel and the others wanted to come too," I said. No one responded. Haydar looked at me strangely, as did others in the room. Yusuf Metin pointed to my face and asked softly, "What happened?" "Forget about it, it's nothing," I said. Sema looked at me questioningly, and I wasn't sure what to say. "It's nothing. Besides, there are so many people here. Let's talk later. It's not serious." I tried to ease the tension. Haşim arrived, and I introduced him to the others. He asked, "Are they nationals too?" When I nodded, he was glad. We were becoming a group. Finally Yüksel arrived with her sister Aysel. "We had a fight with our father," they said, accounting for their lateness.

We were now some ten comrades—and that in İzmir, in Turkey! It was wonderful. I was proud and happy. I'd forgotten all about the slap of the night before. Only the people looking at my face reminded me of it.

Everyone was running around frenziedly. A couple asked us to step aside so they could finish painting a banner. We went into the salon, where I explained to Celal and Haydar, "I argued a little with my brother. Don't misunderstand. I wouldn't let him hit me." They laughed a little, then asked seriously, "What kind of person is your brother? When did he arrive? Is he a comrade of ours?"

As we talked, my elder brother Haydar, Baki, my cousin Haydar, and his sister Aynur arrived. My brother looked around searchingly, and when he saw me, he shoved his way through the crowd.

He grabbed me by the arm and kissed the place where he'd hit me the night before. "Sister, I'm sorry," he said. "Forgive me. Let's talk later."

It was a little embarrassing that he hugged me and begged forgiveness in front of all these people. Worried what others might think, I kept saying, "It's okay, brother, it's all okay." I wanted the people around us to know he was my brother. I introduced him to Celal and the others.

Baki laughed, openly enjoying the scene of reconciliation. I imagined my brother had spoken to him in detail. He came over to us and shook everyone's hand.

The whole room, I realized, was filled with members of our group. "What slogans shall we shout?" I asked excitedly. "Down with colonialism!" said Haydar. We decided on a few generally antifascist and anti-imperialist slogans. "Even 'Toward an Independent Turkey' would be fine," I said. The other groups would trot out all their favorite social-chauvinist maxims. We assumed there'd be no slogans for Kurdistan. Celal said, "The preparations committee wants to broadcast the slogans from loudspeakers and have everyone shout them." We had to limit ourselves to the predefined slogans.

The DDKD, the TKP, and Kurtuluş didn't take part in the demo. Our participation made a good impression. Many, pleasantly surprised, considered it positive that a Kurdish group had taken part. News of our differences with the DDKD hadn't yet gotten around, but people were interested. I said to Halit of the HK executive, "As Kurdistan Revolutionaries, we participate in all anticolonialist, anti-imperialist, and antifascist actions. We do it out of principle, as our task. This demonstration takes place in Turkey, and through our participation, we support it." He approved, but we didn't talk anymore. We didn't want to ask for permission to shout our own slogans.

Without waiting for the organizers, we looked for a place in the march. At the very front were workers, mainly from the Kula textile factory. Then came a large bloc of HK, strong in numbers. We pushed our way among them. The march was to begin in Basmane and end at Republic Square. It started moving before everyone had found their place. Gradually more groups with banners joined, following the instructions of the preparations committee, which had to deal with obstructions by the police. The demonstration was approved, but a mass demonstration with antifascist political content would annoy the state.

The police seemed to have mobilized every available force in İzmir. Along with uniformed field forces, civilian police searched for the "ringleaders" among the demonstrators. The state didn't allow any opposition. Its fascist-colonialist character was apparent everywhere. İzmir, as a large industrial city with many students, had great potential to develop a radical revolutionary movement. That was one thing I liked about it.

In Basmane, the participants arranged themselves in orderly rows with their banners and placards. It was a splendid sight. I wished I could have watched the march from above. It was just beautiful to stand united with so many different people against fascism: workers and farmers, women, laborers, Kurds, Turks, and Laz.[98]

To be sure, the participants differed on important subjects like social chauvinism, socialism, the revolution, and colonialism, but the very existence of an opposition gave all of us hope. Class struggle was a strange thing: it couldn't be carried out by good intentions alone. *If only this mass of humanity could be organized under a unified leadership!* I thought. But the left was fragmented, as various factions accused each other of opportunism, or reformism, or even of holding a counterrevolutionary position.

Only in their attitude toward revolution in Kurdistan did most of the groups agree. In fact, it might have been the only point on which they agreed. They weren't inclined to fight social chauvinism, but engagement with the Kurdish question could have led to groundbreaking developments toward revolution in Turkey. Even the smallest step, just a supportive gesture or slogan, could contribute to a huge transformation. That would reveal the internal class vanguard, and history would be guided along the right lines, corresponding to the reality of the people. But instead the Turkish left persisted in dogmatism. In the 16 Soviet republics, there was only one central party, the Bolshevik Party. China was a half colony and half feudal, but it too had only the vanguard of a sole party, the Communist Party of China. Always it was repeated that a half colony couldn't be colonialist.

During the demonstration, the HK bloc shouted, "Down with the national oppression of the Kurdish people!" That also appeared on one of the banners. Other groups had similar slogans. But for them Kurdistan was a side issue, to be addressed after the revolution, and it was not to be treated as an issue of a minority. As always, there were signs bearing the slogan, "Freedom of nations, unity of the peoples." We enlarged this one and shouted, "For unity by choice."

Other slogans said, "Shut down the state security courts," "Neither America nor Russia—toward an independent Turkey," and "Workers— to the general strike!" We were as enthusiastic for them as for all the others. Workers raised their fists and shouted, "Down with the fascist dictatorship. Down with the oligarchy!"

We joined in with these slogans. Then came a brief pause, and we shouted, "Down with colonialism!" Even though we were only a few, our voices could be heard clearly. The rows of marchers ahead of us and behind joined us. Joyously we repeated the slogan many times.

The stewards with their red armbands went into a panic, running around and trying to figure out what part of the march had originated this slogan. A few cried, "Don't shout out this slogan. Shout only the agreed-upon slogans!"

We got into a discussion with the stewards. "We're revolutionaries and Kurdistan Revolutionaries, and we have our own slogans. That was a very general and yet important slogan. You can't prevent us from shouting it." We tried to persuade the stewards, but they wouldn't hear of it. More and more stewards showed up, and the discussion got heated. Haydar, Celal, Yüksel, and I talked to different people.

One of them said, "The preparations committee decided that only the agreed-upon slogans could be shouted. Even if you're Kurdistan Revolutionaries, you have to stick to the overall program."

They threatened us with growing aggression as the police watched from a nearby spot. An acquaintance came over, identified himself, and said, "There was a general resolution that we all adhered to. All the organizations agreed to it, and it can't be overridden."

I said, "You're saying that we can voice our demands only when you've previously approved them? What does that have to do with revolution? Revolutionaries from an oppressor nation need not behave that way. We're doing our part. We're calling out all the general slogans alongside you. We've even joined in the call 'For an Independent Turkey.' But now you want to ban 'Down with colonialism' and are even threatening us instead of joining us? You have internalized chauvinism."

One of the stewards came at me menacingly: "Now you've gone too far."

At that point the police intervened. My brother and others couldn't stand it anymore. A fight broke out. Enraged, I shouted again, "Down with colonialism!" Others joined me, and finally a hundred people were shouting the slogan. I said to the stewards, "You might as well shout 'Long live colonialism.' You should be ashamed of yourselves, you're worse than the police!"

Their behavior was intolerable. They conferred with each other, and the tumult ebbed a bit. Finally, even their own cadres started shouting the slogan. The stewards tried to silence them, saying, "What are you doing? Do you want to form an organization within the organization?" Our friends warned, "Don't be provoked any further!" I was still furious. "I don't care what you do! But we're sure not going to beg you for permission to shout a slogan! You don't have a monopoly on this square. Revolutionaries are demonstrating here!"

My brother was walking in the demonstration alongside me, and arm in arm we'd shouted the same slogans. The fight had actually brought us closer together.

I kept turning back to look. I knew most of those who had shouted "Down with colonialism" with us, including Baki, Haşim, and Hasan Ali. A split had emerged, initiated by their own people. What was the point of trying to ban the slogan? Once again people shouted "Freedom of nations, unity of peoples," and we responded with "For unity by choice." They didn't attack us again, and we didn't provoke them.

At the Atatürk monument on Republic Square, signs bearing demands were everywhere. Here the rally began. Speeches were made, and slogans were shouted. We shouted our own. When a speaker referred to the situation in Eritrea, Celal cried out in Kurdish, at the top of his voice, "Long live the liberation struggle of the Eritrean nation!" Then in Turkish: "But why can't you see Kurdistan? It's right on your doorstep!" We supported him by shouting, "Down with chauvinism, social chauvinism!" Maybe our unambiguous position wasn't a big deal, but it was still revolutionary.

Toward the end of the demo, Haluk from the HK executive came over to us with Baki. "That was awful," he said. "We didn't have anything to do with it, and the friends didn't recognize you. The DDKD didn't participate in the action. The friends thought it could have been a planned provocation. That's the first time that slogan was shouted. It's true, we don't accept the slogan 'Down with colonialism' in our program, but our response here wasn't good. We've called a meeting for tomorrow where we will officially apologize, but I'd like to apologize now in the name of the friends."

We were content. That was how revolutionaries should behave. To each other, we said, "It's a good thing this incident didn't lead to anything further." My brother was glad too.

It was great that we'd participated in the demonstration and positioned ourselves there. At least we were being discussed. We had aroused interest in the Kurdistan Revolutionaries, whether positive or negative.

The HK was most afraid of a split within its own ranks. Yes, they insisted they respected our position, but their concern was primarily for the fact that their own Kurdish cadre had not adhered to the organization's decision. Superficially the discussion was about the slogan, but more important to them were their members' differing positions. If a slogan didn't correspond to the political line, those who had shouted it must be challenged, as their behavior would create an "organization within the organization." Baki was aware how serious the situation was—they were most angry with him. It had set in motion a development, and contradictions had emerged that might lead to clashes. Maybe Baki would finally decide where he stood.

After the demonstration, we went out to eat together. It was my last meal with my brother. Celal and Haydar from Suruç came too. My brother wanted to continue our discussion from the day before, but this time we spoke calmly and showed the meaning of happiness, love, and unity.

"I've made a lot of mistakes," I explained.

When I ran away from home, I had to go somewhere. I wanted to cut myself off from traditional relationships, but I entered a new relationship that was no different from the traditional ones. It wasn't easy. I was looking for something. Baki didn't help but instead took advantage of the situation. I wanted to free myself, since I'd lost my way, and I couldn't find a solution by myself. The reactions of people I knew influenced me. Sometimes I thought I was against everything and everyone, without thinking of the consequences. Too often I've let myself be guided by my feelings. When I noticed I'd ended up in a cul-de-sac, I was right to reverse course. Problems developed. But it's better to recognize a mistake and then limit the damage as much as possible. Now here I am at another dead end, and the price is very high. With me, the price is always high. I usually seem to make a problem worse. I could have gone to you in Istanbul, or I could have stayed with the friends in Ankara. Then I wouldn't be in this dilemma now.

My big brother answered that he respected my choices, no one could force me to do anything, and even Baki would finally have to come to an honest decision. Haydar said, "We'll talk about it more. We'll find a solution. The problem shouldn't be magnified unnecessarily."

That evening my brother said goodbye. He was planning to drive to Ankara to meet the friends, then continue to Dersim to try to mollify our family. It was important for him to understand, since the rest of the family would probably follow his lead. His visit bolstered my self-confidence.

I gave notice at my workplace in Alsancak and began work in a grape-processing plant on the Bornova road. Inactivity wasn't good for me, and I also needed the money—sometimes I didn't even have enough change for the bus.

The day after the demonstration, we went to the announced meeting at the HK headquarters. Halit explained that the first part of the meeting would be open to the public, and internal matters would be discussed later. "As you all know," he said,

> a demonstration took place in which all the factions except the DDKD, Kurtuluş, and the TKP participated. It was to be a large demonstration open to all antifascist forces. Thousands participated, threatening the fascist powers that be. It denounced the state security courts, which prosecute both Turks and Kurds, people who devote their lives to the revolutionary process. No revolutionary movement can ignore the fact that the state oppresses the Kurdish people. As HK, we've introduced the national question into our program and conducted an in-depth discussion about it. We will publicly announce our position on it very soon. We can also discuss it with the friends.

By which he meant us.

"Our demonstration, apart from a few small problems, came off successfully," he continued. "There was a preparations committee, consisting of representatives of the participating groups. This committee made clear its will throughout the event. It decided in advance which slogans would be shouted. Groups also shouted their own slogans."

He went on, referring to "a few Kurdish friends." He knew the name of our group perfectly well—by calling us that, he made clear that we didn't count as an organized force to be taken seriously.

> A few Kurdish friends shouted their own slogans. "Down with colonialism" is not an incorrect slogan, it has general application. Frankly, our friends in Ankara also shouted this slogan. But the central resolution wasn't conveyed to us. It didn't reach us. So we didn't use this slogan. That was correct—

it's how our organization functions. But a few friends got very emotional and formed, so to speak, a group within the group. To these friends, we will transmit our critique in another place, and we'll take a position as is necessary. But the behavior toward the Kurdish friends wasn't correct. The stewards who were in charge of controlling the march could have reacted more reasonably. We think that those who overreacted were friends from the other group. I'd like to apologize in the name of the friends.

We asked to speak on this agenda item. We called attention to the tasks of revolutionaries of oppressor nations, pointed to our expectations, and explained our wish for solidarity. We criticized the DDKD for not participating in the action—to preserve its class characteristics and thereby not represent the Kurdistan revolution—while we wanted to combat petit-bourgeois nationalism. The meeting continued without any untoward events. Among ourselves, we agreed that this meeting, regardless of the HK's goals, was a positive step.

Then Baki made a strange contribution:

> I've criticized the [stewards'] behavior toward the National friends. This is a positive meeting, and I don't have much more to say about it. As for my behavior at the demonstration, I'd like to say that it was really purely emotional. Objectively, it's true that we formed a "group within the group." And it contradicts our bylaws to shout "Down with colonialism," before the discussion of the national question has been finalized and a decision made. I find the slogan not incorrect, and I think [the HK] will reach a positive decision about it.

Was it really necessary for him to say that? It had been announced at the beginning of the meeting that an internal discussion would take place. What honor was Baki now trying to save? His behavior enraged me. What was he trying to do? "I behaved emotionally and shouted a slogan"—what nonsense! Was it only a matter of obeying bylaws? What were the political ethics of Baki and his comrades? They had traveled far from the reality of their own people, but it was unclear where they were going. They'd turned their backs on their people—that was their ethic and their revolution. To declare oneself in favor of something at the time and place when it was most necessary—they considered that immoral!

For revolutionaries of the oppressor nation, no form of thinking, feeling, or behaving along social chauvinist lines was acceptable. What did they have to lose? Their careers? No, they took on every menial task. With their pragmatic approach, they managed to be active everywhere yet hardly gained any respect. It wasn't a matter of their careers. Why were they so hypocritical? What were they so afraid of? It was hard for me to comprehend.

We didn't stay long—there was no sense in listening to this nonsense. But before we left, we discussed the situation. All agreed the meeting had gone well. The fact that different content had been discussed was positive. And we'd got a glimpse of the tensions within their group. It was normal that they'd want to clarify the issue internally. Baki and the others presumably were waiting to hear the HK's official standpoint on the national liberation question.

Haydar said, "Maybe there'll be a break. Baki was acting politically."

I had a different opinion—after all, I knew Baki very well.

Before we went our separate ways, we decided to stay in touch with the HK.

The first workers' resistance and hunger strike I learned a lot from these clashes and contradictions in İzmir. Far from my country and cut off from my organization, I defended both, under all circumstances, as best I could. I felt part of the organization and spoke up for it everywhere. In İnciraltı and other places, I met with some of those who had formed "a group within the group" in the HK, to read together and discuss. Most of them came from Dersim. Through reading, research, and discussions, my theoretical knowledge became more systematic, although it still wasn't enough to be useful to the movement.

Finally the HK, in its magazine, made the long-awaited announcement of its position on the national question. Baki had already given me some unofficial brochures to read, but the official version in the magazine was tightly argued to preclude a wide-ranging discussion. But the HK's critique now had a concrete basis. The HK thought the national question had to be resolved by referendum.

As I read it, it felt like a fatwa against Kurdistan. A people who considered themselves enslaved were demanding to be able to choose freedom—but this critique contradicted that social reality. It felt like a blow against the spirit of socialism. Revolutionaries of the oppressor nation were maintaining their social-chauvinist carte blanche.

The announcement was much discussed at the political clubs, in homes, and at the universities. Baki began to have second thoughts about his Kurdish honor. He continued to discuss within the HK, while trying to figure out how serious a problem it was between him and me. He insisted that a closer relationship with me would be a good influence on him. I'd set a deadline for him, but we got back together before it arrived.

Mehmet Ali, my uncle, İbo, and Meto all came to visit. We rented two rooms in the home of a family from Ovacık in Nergiz. They used one room themselves, and the rest were for common use. It was cheaper for us, and we also stayed inconspicuous. The house looked luxurious from the outside, but inside it was more or less empty.

Our new roommates were two young women, Sakine and Zahide, and their younger brother. Their parents lived in Germany. Zahide sympathized with TİKKO, so İbo treated her like a comrade. Sakine, the younger sister, had no special interest in politics. We worked together briefly at the grape-processing plant. It was hard to organize the workers there. I wanted to find a workplace where I could lead a workers' resistance, an idea I pursued with passion and enthusiasm.

Finally I got a job at a factory on the Bornova road that fit my ideas. I started work there along with Gülsüm from the HK. Baki, who knew where workers were needed and where organized resistance was possible, found it for me. The factory was a German–Turkish co-production site, with well-functioning work processes. There was a dressing room with lockers for everyone. We put on a white apron and headcovers before we entered the factory floor. The tea break lasted 20 minutes, the lunch break 25 minutes. We'd run to get at the head of the line for the food distribution, then wolf it down. Those last in line always went hungry because they didn't have enough time to eat. There was only one cafeteria for all the personnel. That was new for me—in the other factories where I'd worked, the managers ate separately from the workers.

Over time I learned which cadres of which groups worked in the factory. There were women and men from the TKP and TİKKO and especially the HK. We talked about mistakes organizers had made in other factories, so we wouldn't repeat them.

Every morning I ran from the house in Nergiz to the main street to catch the work shuttle bus. I liked my new workplace much better than any so far. Ümran, Gülistan, Mahmure, and I shared a goal with other revolutionary workers: Resistance! Mahmure, a Bulgarian immigrant, had blond hair and blue eyes—she was a beautiful young woman and quite talented. She had worked in the factory for a long time and risen to the position of forewoman. That had many advantages. We assumed that if we were careful, we wouldn't immediately blow our cover. The HK members had lousy relations with the TKP members. Nesrin of the TKP wasn't radical, and her ideas about union struggles were evident in her interactions with us—she didn't have much to do with us. Her concept of resistance was conspiracy.

In the area where I worked, we sewed pieces of fabric together and gave the garments form. Afterward they were packaged and readied for sale. The workers in every area were supervised, so this system did not allow us one free minute. Someone would sew a piece of fabric, then pass it over to the next table. All the workers were paid for eight hours of work and extra for overtime. After a while a new system was introduced, however, in which workers were paid by the piece, which plunged them into a competitive struggle. Everyone tried to produce more. But quality was important too, and those who did bad work got their daily wage reduced. The wage, paid out weekly, was usually between 240 and 300 lira, never more.

The workers were members of the Teksif union, which was part of the Türk-İş union confederation. So many deductions were taken out of the paycheck—for the union, insurance, food, and other things—that little was left over. Many workers had been in the factory for ten years. No one was satisfied with the working conditions. There wasn't even a full half hour for lunch. The workers toiled, and the owners profited from it. The supervisors got "hush money." As at my other workplaces, they also played the role of "mini-chiefs." But some participated in the organizing, as I learned during the short tea and lunch breaks.

Some of the workers were open to politicization. They were aware of the problems and of the general workers' movement. It was easy to get to know them. I met many new people, most of whom had never heard the words *Kurd*, *Kurdish*, or *Kurdistan*.

I explained candidly to the cadres active in the factory that as a Kurdistan Revolutionary, I considered it my role to contribute to the workers' resistance and that I was ready to do everything necessary for it. My goal was less to organize the workers in the name of the Kurdistan Revolutionaries than to help them see their problems in relation to the ruling class. In that way I hoped to bring them closer to the reality of the

Kurdish people and allow an awareness of solidarity to emerge. I said to members of the other groups, "Let's work together according to this principle." I tried to counteract their social chauvinism and to remind them of their duties. Naturally everyone held the current viewpoint of their own group, but my way of working surprised them and induced a few to come over to work with me in solidarity.

The prospects for organizing a strike weren't too bad. The challenge would be to channel the general dissatisfaction, consider the interests of all the workers, and win a lot of them over. A few factories had brought in scabs to break strikes. So the class characteristics of the participating groups as well as their views of the social struggle and the workers' resistance were of considerable importance.

As everywhere else, the differences among the leftist groups became pronounced in the factories. Instead of seeking unity, they denounced each other and amplified their ideological differences. That divided the workers, and uncertainty grew. Under those circumstances, you could no longer think of raising awareness among the masses, or organizing them to take action; you could only talk about economic demands. Political goals were reduced to slogans, as the groups competed for numerical superiority. They couldn't act that way toward me, since I'd made clear from the beginning that I was for solidarity and a common struggle. I participated in all activities with enthusiasm as great as their own. So they indulged me, and my reputation and popularity grew.

Normally we met on the weekends to analyze the situation. I didn't go to the other groups' meetings, but they discussed the same things with me. Sometimes they invited me to their meetings, where they assessed the political work in the factory and made plans. Our main issues included workers' membership in the textile union of the DİSK union confederation and shop committee elections. The other groups had some cadres in the unions, and we coordinated with them.

Around this time I had an unexpected visitor. I had expected the friends to get in touch with me, but I hadn't imagined that they would send Şahin Dönmez to İzmir. One day, along with Haydar from Suruç, he was waiting for me outside the factory. I was busy at the gate collecting signatures for joining the textile union. A worker told me I had a visitor. I looked up and recognized the two of them. I handed my paper and pencil to a friend and hurried over.

I expressed my joy openly. The arrival of a friend from Kurdistan meant that I now had a direct connection. We took the bus to the house in Nergiz. When Şahin saw the exterior, he said, "Very luxurious, your home." But once inside he was disappointed, since he'd expected a fully furnished apartment. There was only a piece of worn-out carpet on the floor and some mattresses. He took back his first impression, saying, "It's really more of a workers' apartment. It looks like a bachelor flat."

Haydar had already told him about our outreach and activities. During our conversation he asked us about it several times. He told us about the developments in the country and said every day more people were getting involved in the political work. The friends were now active in Antep, Batman, Urfa, Mardin, Dersim, Kars, and Diyarbakır. Many young people, he said, were coming over to us from other groups. I mentioned the dissensions within the HK and a conversation where some had thought about crossing over to us. I named Haşim and a few others.

Şahin asked about Alişan and Hüseyin Demir. I knew them from when we'd lived in the state housing in Dersim. They were dogmatically rigid HK cadres, but if Haşim came over to us, we might influence even this family, I said. I mentioned the brother of the friend Mazlum as well as Yüksel and her family. I didn't mention my problems with Baki. Şahin asked Baki directly, "What's İbrahim doing? And you, are you still with the HK?" Baki answered evasively, "I wouldn't say that. We're discussing a lot, especially with Sakine. We actually have a lot in common. Belonging to separate organizations is really no obstacle. We can talk things out."

I had no desire to return to this topic, knowing Baki would go on about the same old things, and then Şahin would leave thinking he could win Baki over to us, without grasping the background. But Şahin said he wanted to discuss it fully. Baki's mood turned sour. As we fixed a meal, Baki whispered that he didn't like Şahin much, that he acted provocatively and might not view our relationship problems objectively. "We should trust each other and solve our problems ourselves," he said. "When others get involved, it's not usually constructive."

I was annoyed. "Stop prejudging my friends! You've brought so many of your friends over here, and I've discussed with them. I want to talk about everything with my people, and I want them to know about the problems between us."

Baki said uneasily, "As you wish."

Alone with Şahin, I told him what I'd gone through in detail, starting with Dersim. Sometimes he tried to change the subject, but I wouldn't allow it:

Please, hear me out, I want to tell you everything because I want you to know how I've spent this time. It's good that you're here. I've decided to return to the country.[99] If you hadn't come, I'd have gone by myself. I still work in this factory, but my bags are packed, I've just been waiting for the right moment. I don't know where to go. I thought about driving to Ankara and then going to the country with the friends. But I've had enough here, it's very tedious to think a problem is solved and then go through the same difficulties all over again.

Şahin was surprised to hear about my problems and my wish to go back to the country. He said my position was "generally positive" and we could "win" Baki over. But he seemed reluctant to get involved in our relationship. "We'll talk about it more later," he said, "and come to a decision." End of subject. But more was going on here than a delayed decision. Would he really consider a separation to be wrong? My reasons for wanting to separate from Baki were obvious: our ideological differences. But apparently that was highly unusual.

The next morning Şahin talked with Baki for a while. Baki shared his fears with him, and Şahin replied, "No, we don't want to cause anyone to separate. The friend must make her decision herself. But we want to win you over."

That evening in İnciraltı, Dev-Genç and HK had organized an event about social imperialism. Other groups wanted to participate too. Speakers from both groups were coming in from Ankara, and a thorough discussion was anticipated.

That day Şahin didn't want me to go to work in the factory, but psychologically I was there the whole time because the resistance was beginning. No, the machines weren't yet silent, but they were stopping. We had gathered signatures to elect a workers' representation. The other friends had worked hard on the preparations. But now it felt like I was setting myself apart from the resistance. How would the others manage if I didn't show up? I wondered. And how could Şahin keep me from going there? It wasn't right, but I didn't contradict him.

That evening we went to the meeting. The room on the İnciraltı campus was overflowing. It began at 4 p.m. The first speaker, from Dev-Genç, spoke in sweeping terms about modern revisionism, referring to the October Revolution, the Stalin era, Brezhnev, and Khrushchev. During his talk, I remembered how the friend Mazlum had talked to us, at the Teachers School in Dersim, about modern revisionism. He'd talked about class foundations: it wasn't class domination but a distorted form of Marxism. On this point both descriptions agreed.

Next the HK speaker made a comprehensive presentation, defining social imperialism in terms of changes in the Soviet Union. He criticized the previous speaker, took up various questions, and read quotations to support his analysis.

The discussion afterward was animated, and many participants spoke up. I took notes. From time to time I glanced over at Şahin, expecting him to say something.

The national question was being discussed, to my delight. Many young people were present. This would be a good place to talk about Kurdistan and present our ideology. If we didn't say anything, the Kurdish question would only be criticized. Both groups considered the Misak-ı-Millî agreement to be legitimate. They bandied about words like "oppressed nation," "people," and "state." The HK speaker said,

> Kurdistan consists of four parts that have developed differently. So you can't think of it as a single nation. What would that even mean? Each part has to organize itself and struggle along with the nation in which it is bound. That's the only way it'll ever free itself.

The Dev-Genç speaker talked about a new kind of colonization and explained that in our era there were no more classical colonies. He talked about the Kurdish bourgeoisie, integrated into the state, saying they had the quality of national compradors.[100] In Kurdistan there were objectively no conditions for revolution, he said, and so no revolutionary upsurge was possible in practical terms, "even though a few small bourgeois groups insist that Kurdistan must do its own organizing." He continued, "We should keep an eye on them and not oppose them but denounce their nationalist character."

Invoking Lenin, the HK speaker explained that "we can support them even though they're nationalistic." It was hilarious! They could support even a national-bourgeois leadership but could not conceive of a proletarian leadership! These leftists were so strange, using Lenin for their rationalizations.

I whispered to Şahin, "Say something! Raise your hand! They want to dismiss the national question. We're the only ones who can counter them." But he ignored me. I couldn't believe it and repeated, "Stand up and say something! This is the moment. Everyone's waiting for us to speak. We've got to answer them." Haydar agreed with me, but Şahin still ignored me.

Internally I swore. Then finally I couldn't stand it anymore and raised my hand and got to my feet. Furiously and excitedly, I started talking without really understanding what I was saying. Many were curious to hear what this woman, who'd leaped up so spontaneously, had to say. Yes, I was angry at the speakers, but I was more angry at Şahin, and I raised my voice.

Both groups, I said, had assessed the national question incorrectly. They considered it a side issue, dismissing it as just one programmatic point among many and legitimating it with their support for the Misak-ı Millî agreement. But that contradicted the spirit of internationalism and the revolutionary task. The people of Kurdistan sought to determine their own fate, and whether the groups liked it or not, the Kurdistan Revolutionaries would organize according to conditions in Kurdistan itself.

I didn't talk long, but it felt good to challenge the other groups' incorrect statements, even with a few sentences, and to present our position. Şahin glowered at me. "Was that really necessary?" he snarled. "I deliberately didn't say anything. What use is it to talk to these people? They don't understand anything. Okay, let's go."

But Haydar grinned at me and nodded, as if to say, *Well done!* I was still pissed. Şahin was leadership cadre—why hadn't he said anything when it was needed? All day I puzzled over this question, and my relations with him cooled considerably. Naturally he was annoyed too. I had chosen unilaterally to speak, while he preferred to stay silent.

When someone fails to perform a task because they expect someone else to do it, that means they approve of the other's omission. But a revolutionary must not behave this way. The Kurdistan Revolutionaries do what others neglect. Even if I was laughed at and not taken seriously, I had still been correct to intervene in the discussion instead of letting the false analysis stand unchallenged.

The meeting went on until 4 a.m., lasting some 12 hours. By the time
we got home, dawn was breaking. Two female colleagues were waiting
for me. Excitedly they explained that I absolutely must go to the factory.
My absence had had a negative effect on the resistance, since the workers
had chosen me as their representative. I said I'd been sick. I knew it had
been wrong not to go. But I'd had to decide, and Şahin Dönmez was
part of my organization's leadership cadre. So I had to heed him. He
should have insisted that I carry on my political work in the factory. I
felt guilty about leaving the workers in the lurch. Everything was upside
down! I wished Şahin had arrived either earlier or later but not when he
did. Today yet another meeting was to take place, at a place by the sea
at İnciraltı. On the way to the meeting, Şahin had pointed to it—"It'll
be here."

I invited the two women inside—they were revolutionaries and were
among the organizers of the resistance in the factory. I explained that
I had to take care of something urgent and would be there later. They
responded, "The workers told us we absolutely must bring you back
with us. Everyone has been wondering about you, and some were even
worried you'd been arrested." I said I was sorry and they had to believe
that I'd absolutely be there. They left in dismay.

Sighing, I said to Şahin, "If you weren't here, I'd have gone. It
wouldn't have impaired our other work. For me to not show up just
before the strike began—that wasn't good. I have responsibilities there,
and the workers are easy to influence, and it's important for me to hold
on to their confidence."

Şahin shrugged. "Let it be. You said you wanted to go to Kurdistan.
Others can carry on the workers' strike."

So we went to İnciraltı. All told we were seven, including Yüksel.
It was our first official meeting in İzmir—we were happy to be seven.
Şahin began to talk. "The enemy does everything to divide us and
disperse us in all directions, but see, now we have come together here."
He continued, "In the future we will work in İzmir and other big cities.
There are many young Kurdish people here who we have to organize."

I couldn't help thinking about yesterday's meeting. His behavior there
was still incomprehensible to me. *If it's a matter of organizing young
people from Kurdistan, then why didn't you say something yesterday, when
so many of them were present?* I only thought it—I didn't say it out loud.
I had a strange feeling about Şahin. I didn't like him. With many people,

when you get to know them, you develop a warm relationship, and you feel an affection and respect. But Şahin was becoming noxious to me. Then I felt ashamed, as if in thinking that secretly, I'd done something wrong. Among comrades, such antipathies shouldn't exist! Half-heartedly, I tried to suppress my negative feelings toward him.

After Şahin's introductory speech, we raised questions about our relationship to the Kurdish left. We described our discussion with the DDKD and asked about our organization's relations with the *Özgürlük Yolu* group. In their magazine they'd written about the penetration of capitalism into Kurdistan, and we wanted to know what that meant. Şahin hemmed and hawed, then tersely bit out, "I'll forward that question to the friends. Haydar will take on the tasks of our representatives, but that's not official, since the friends may assign someone else or send someone. Maybe we'll take Haydar away from here. Suruç is an important place for us." To me, he said, "I'll talk to the friends, and we'll keep you posted." Then he left İzmir.

Baki was resentful and upset. "Şahin might be leadership cadre, but he's not constructive. Instead of solving the problem, he's made a solution even more unlikely."

His dismissive tone irked me: "That's enough. Stop blaming others. If you have a problem, talk to me." I added that my own decision to leave had nothing to do with Şahin's visit, as he well knew. He knew how strong my commitment to the organization was. If I were asked to die for it, I'd die. And if someone told me I had to go, I'd drop everything and hit the road. That was no exaggeration, as Baki was fully aware.

The next day I went to the factory, accompanied by Baki. I was late. The situation was unclear. Baki had experience with such contexts and could guess how the enemy would proceed. He tried to hide his worry, saying, "Be careful, don't get caught up in a discussion at the entrance— try to go right in." Before we separated, he said he'd wait for me outside.

At the gate, I was stopped. The gatekeeper went to the director's office. In front of the gate stood a white car. I was told to go to the personnel office, where the head of personnel awaited me with a notebook and a list in hand. "I was sick for two days and couldn't come. I was just released from the hospital, so I wasn't able to get here on time," I explained.

But he cut me off. "You don't work here anymore. Here's your termination notice. You aren't the only one—other workers are affected as well. You can go." And he showed me the door.

"No, no. It's not that easy," I countered. "What's the reason for my termination? I'm employed here as long as I work, but suddenly when I'm sick, I'm fired? Where's the boss? I want to talk to him. Where did he get the right to throw me out at will? I'm not going anywhere."

As I was talking, the boss entered. I'd been yelling, so loud it drowned out most of the noise of the machines. He said softly, "Please, woman, do you want to tell me something?"

"Yes, I was sick for two days and had to go to the hospital. If necessary, I can provide proof. Today I came back to work—and received my termination. For what reason? Why am I being let go? And I'm not going anywhere unless I receive compensation. So many deductions are taken out of the wages that hardly anything is left over. And I've worked here for a long time. What about that?" I was shouting.

"Please calm down," he said. "Don't scream at me that way. I don't have to give a reason for a termination. Anyone who doesn't show up at work is let go. You must know that."

I raised my voice again. "I demand to see my colleagues. I'll wait here, I'm not leaving."

The boss left the office and came back a little later. "One more minute," he said, then went to a corner to rifle through some papers.

"Your name is Sakine Polat?"

"Yes." The softer he spoke, the more I raised my voice.

"You come from Tunceli?"

"Yes."

"You went to the high school?"

"Why are you asking me these questions? It's all in my personnel file. You wrote down all these details when you hired me. Why are you asking me again?"

He grimaced. "I don't have any bad intentions. Why are you so beloved by the other workers?" I realized where he was going. "You're an intelligent woman, you have talent, you do good work, and the foremen are satisfied with you. Why don't you work somewhere else? Factory work is pretty hard, isn't it?"

Spitefully I answered, "That's my concern. I'll work where I want to work."

It was almost time for the lunch break. I absolutely wanted the other workers to see that I was in the factory—that would be enough for me. But no one from the factory floor looked in through the window, and a tulle curtain blocked the view anyway. My nerves were stretched to the limit, and this guy's questions were so irritating.

I imagined what he'd say to me—and then he said it. "Look, we don't want to let you go. We want to give you a different job. You graduated from high school. You can work as a secretary—"

That was the last straw. I interrupted, "Oh, so you want to buy me off? No, I'm a worker. You can hire your secretaries elsewhere. I stand with my colleagues, and firing me won't change that. On the contrary, we have a right to our unions and workers' councils. You can't stop us. All the many workers here are capable of advocating on their own behalf. Firing me won't change anything at all for you." I was yelling at the top of my lungs and moving toward the exit.

Suddenly three or four people came in and grabbed me. "Police! You're coming with us."

I shouted, "You fascist boss! You didn't bring police here when you hired me! Let me go!" Struggling with all my might, I managed to break free. My own strength surprised me.

I fell to the ground and tried to grab something. After a lot of wrangling, they dragged me out to the car. I braced a foot against the side so they couldn't push me in. I tried to jab the police with my elbows. One of them hit me on the back of the neck, grabbed my hair, and tried to bend my head back to force me into the vehicle. It felt like he was breaking my neck. He was trying to get me to shut up and get me away from there fast. They knew the lunch break was only a few minutes away, and they didn't want the other workers to see me. I wanted to delay, and so I put up a superhuman resistance.

With a last burst of energy, I grabbed the door and screamed, "You pack of fascists, let me go!" Finally some of the workers came out of the factory. When I saw them, I screamed louder. Surprised, they didn't know what to do at first, then came over to us. That made the police nervous. I seized the opportunity to extract myself from their grip and ran over to the workers. "Down with the police! The fascist police" I cried, and the workers joined in. Outside the factory, too, a group started shouting slogans. I recognized Baki among them. So he was still there. He'd brought along a few friends from Bornova University.

The factory grounds were surrounded by a high wall topped with barbed wire. On the other side was a canal. They'd done well to come from outside to support us, and get this far.

We all went into the lunchroom. I climbed up onto a bench and told what had happened and also said the boss wanted to buy me. People booed. In protest we all refused to eat, turning our plates over. Instead of eating, we sang protest songs and shouted slogans.

The resistance had begun. We made it clear that we wouldn't leave the lunchroom until the police withdrew. Then the stooges from the yellow unions arrived. A few were also from the textile union, but they all spoke the same language, especially about the great readiness of the Turkish worker to sacrifice. But they also talked about the right to strike, about class-consciousness and class struggle. The proletariat had nothing to lose but its chains. In other words, they gave voice to what everyone already knew.

Every sentence contained the phrase "Turkish worker." That was provocative and infuriated me. I turned to Mahmure, who was next to me:

Won't you say something to these chivalrous men? Something about the oppression of the Kurdish people? This is the right moment. The tasks of the working class have to be framed correctly. I don't want to speak here— that's your job.

A bit later Mahmure took the floor and spoke briefly about the role of the working class and international solidarity, and mentioned briefly the fraternity of peoples, especially the oppressed Kurdish people. It wasn't very impressive, but better than nothing.

Together we went to the shop floor and continued the resistance there. The machines were silent, and we sat on them and sang workers' songs: "We'll break the chains, we'll whack the fascists ..." We beat the rhythm on the worktables, increasing the excitement. Then we sang a song about the first of May and shouted slogans.

We considered this day a warning that would accelerate the preconditions for a strike. We said this to the boss, who demanded that we calm down and talk to him. He mentioned my name and said, "Send me your representative. Let's talk this out and clear everything up."

I remembered his words from the morning. "He wants to make me a secretary!" I said. "He's offered to hire me as a secretary, so I'll be quiet and give up the resistance. He wanted to buy me!" I turned to the boss: "We have nothing to talk with you about. You're the one who called the police instead of talking to us." He stalked off the floor in a rage.

Our action lasted until the end of the normal workday. Meanwhile we discussed how to proceed. Not all the workers were satisfied with the way it had gone, and in some departments they kept on working. We called a meeting for the evening. After more discussion we decided to go on strike. We divided up the tasks. One group would write slogans, and another would explain the purpose of the strike to the workers and try to get them to participate.

Management had compiled a list of workers who were to be fired without compensation—some 75 people. This list was to be posted on the gate the next day. Some were new hires, and some had worked in the factory for a long time. The housecleaning had begun with me.

In spite of my official termination, the next morning I got on the work bus to the factory. The sight of me visibly disturbed a few of the employees, but they said nothing. Without skipping a beat, I delivered a speech about the working conditions, the union, the terminations, and the police.

Today we're the ones affected, but tomorrow it will be others. The company is only about reaping profit. During work hours they don't let us have one free minute, and whenever we try to bring up our basic rights, they smash us with police violence. We won't take it anymore. We aren't slaves, we're workers. We have the right to a union and to choose our own representatives. We demand a longer midday break—that's our natural right. And so many deductions are taken out of the wages that the little that's left is hardly enough to live on. What are all these deductions for? There are many questions and problems that have to be solved. So today we're declaring a strike.

My words were greeted with tumultuous applause. A few didn't clap, but I didn't care about them. The point was that no one *had* to applaud, but the general tendency was unmistakably in our favor.

We had previously decided that the factory bus shouldn't cross the factory grounds. The workers who arrived first were to form a human chain in front of the gate. I asked the driver to stop, and we got out. A few stayed in the bus, mostly employees. Banners were hung. The buses arriving after ours were received with applause. After a while some drum and oboe players came, who raised morale. A few people began to dance. Another factory bus arrived. It didn't stop, but drove at high speed across the grounds. A few of those who got out wanted to come to us but didn't dare to.

Of 350 workers, almost half participated in the strike. The others got down to their work. Not bad for the first day. Optimistically we assumed that more workers would join the strike. But the opposite could also happen. If we failed to broaden participation in the strike, some of the strikers would change their mind and go back to work. So the whole operation had to be brought to a standstill. Even only a few machines running would encourage the boss. We racked our brains as to what to do. When the workers went for lunch, the strikers called out slogans to them. We had conversations with a few to try to get them to participate.

We went over to talk to the university student group stationed at a remote spot. They were to protect the strike, presumably with pistols. We were sure the police would attack, so we asked the strikers to remain with the group. Our position wasn't especially good. On one side of the factory was a canal, and on the other a high wall. The other factories were far away. We were next to the wall, some 200 meters from the factory entrance. For the police it would be easy to surround us.

We had brought food and drink, and at midday we sat down and ate. The organizers mingled, reminding everyone of the purpose of the strike and emphasizing the importance of sticking together.

After the workers' lunch, as they went back into the factory, we tried again to persuade them to participate. We were about 50 meters away, so we had to shout to make ourselves heard. While we were standing before the bars of the gate, a police bus barreled up and screeched to a halt followed by a minibus and a car. The police surrounded us, while the civil police walked around the property and observed us. The boss and a few of the employees pointed to us.

Some of the more experienced workers came up to me. "You'd better step back a little," they said. "The police are pointing at you, and you're the first one they'll arrest. Don't make it easy for them to grab you." They were right, but for the success of the action, I had to stay out front and to risk arrest. The workers were tense since the police arrived. I couldn't just hide behind them—that would have wrecked their confidence. No, we had to take this risk. It might mean a violent clash with the police, but so be it—that would be the only way to overcome the fear.

We shouted more slogans. The other side debated which of us was responsible, then suddenly went on the attack. The civil police attacked

me, Alik, and Ekrem. Mahmure and Gülsüm were also in front, but
Ümran had disappeared when the resistance began. A skirmish erupted.
I tried to free myself from the police. Next to me, the cops were having
a hard time capturing Ekrem, so two of the ones who were holding me
loosened their grip and went over to help. I took the opportunity to
disentangle myself from their grasp. Then I ran off. But around the
corner, two more cops appeared in front of me and grabbed me. The
cop behind me shouted, "Hold her tight, this one … she's the leader,
and besides, she kicked me!" He unleashed his fury on me. Two held me
solidly by the arms, and another grabbed my hair and yanked my head
back. A terrible pain ripped through my neck. He attacked my legs with
a club. Obviously he wanted to take revenge for that kick I'd delivered.

They dragged me to the bus. A cop radioed, "Yes, she's here, good.
That's enough now, the bus is full." They let go of my hair, but I couldn't
move my head for a few minutes. "Get in," said one of them. In the bus
doorway stood a cop who looked like a thug. As I tried to step into the
bus, he clubbed my back. The second blow knocked me over. Another
cop stepped in: "Stop, that's enough." Then he demanded that I get up.
Since I couldn't stand up by myself, he grabbed me by the arms and
raised me. In the bus there were two people sitting in every seat. Some
were bleeding at the nose, others had swollen eyes or tangled hair. We
smiled at each other. One of the police mocked, "Sure, laugh, you all
look so gorgeous."

There were about 20 of us. They brought us to the police station in
Alsancak, which was near the sea. It had become cool, and it was even
colder inside the station. All the fighting had made us sweat, and now we
were freezing. We women were to stay in a different room from the men.
For a long time nothing happened. The police had brought our banners
along. Even on the bus we'd conferred in whispers and decided to make
only very limited statements. "We'll state the reasons for the strike, and
we won't answer any questions about it. And we won't talk about the
others at all." We were all targeted for arrest anyway. Among us were
a few workers who were aware of the problem. They were upstanding
people, and none of them would give information to the police.

I was the last to be interrogated. The interrogations took place in two
different places. The commissar read out the words on the banners and
asked what they meant. "It's obvious what they mean," I said. Another
cop said, "I come from Tunceli, too. I'm Alevi." He was looking at my

ID. "Tahtı Halil was right next to my village. I think I know it." He acted as if he were trying to remember. Then another interrupted with a tough voice, "All the others said Sakine is the leader. It's obvious. Is there anyone from Tunceli who isn't a Communist?"

The other police had withdrawn. I stayed silent and impassive. "Why did you initiate an unapproved, illegal strike? Why did you stir up the workforce? Isn't it bad enough that you've caused them to lose a day's pay?" He kept talking. When it was my turn, I mentioned the working and living conditions of the factory workers as well as the deductions from their wages. Then I stated our demands and explained why we'd started the strike. We were demanding our rights, I said, one of which was the right to strike. To his question about the ringleader, I responded, "Everyone acts according to their own will. No one can be the ringleader for the others." Mahmure had begun working in the factory before me, but now they tried to pit us against each other. After my interrogation, they called Mahmure in again and said to her, "You're the ringleader— Sakine told us." She caught on to the game immediately and laughed. She was a joyous person anyway. Then she said, "There are strikes in every factory. Everywhere workers choose their advocates, as you know very well."

We spent the night at the police station. In the morning we were released and went together to the factory. An official notice in front confirmed that we were dismissed. Then we went to a place where we could talk. A few went home. We agreed that these events had to be publicized. Some 75 workers—no small number—were being sacked without compensation. If nothing was done about it, more workers would in the future be dismissed even more heedlessly, and it would harm the worker organizations. One friend suggested a hunger strike. Most of those present were ready for it. We decided to prepare for one day, then four women and five men would start the hunger strike at 5 p.m. in front of the Hasan Tahsin statue.

I finally went home, having hardly slept the last few days. Baki and Yusuf Metin came over. Yusuf Metin said with his usual warmth, "Looks like you've really taken a beating. I wish you a good recovery." I'd discussed with him a lot in my early days in İzmir. He was more experienced than me both theoretically and practically. Compared to him, I was an amateur, but I'd defended my views vehemently. I didn't advocate a banal Kurdishness—I felt myself to be a revolutionary.

I wasn't yet capable of representing the movement well, but my convictions were unshakable, and I was ready to do anything for it. In İzmir I didn't work exclusively with Kurds—on the contrary, I discussed with all kinds of people and joined the workers' resistance in the factory.

Yusuf Metin liked that, and he agreed with our decision to initiate a hunger strike. He was a very special person within the HK. Later, like Metin Yıldırımtürk, he'd be executed in an organization house by a shot to the head, news that filled me with sorrow.

The prison in Buca It was March. The next day at the club we prepared banners and signs. We wrote slogans on cardboard: "Down with chauvinism, social chauvinism! Down with colonialism, imperialism, and backwardness!" And we listed our demands. At first, the others objected to the slogans I suggested, saying they had nothing to do with the hunger strike's goal. But I was able to overcome their doubts.

On Konak Square that afternoon, there were supposed to be support groups with us. It was quitting time for the workers and employees, and the square would be busy. The ferry berth was near the square. Gülsüm and I dressed like workers: a shirt, a skirt, pants underneath, and an embroidered scarf. Mahmure and Esma wore normal clothing. We met up at different places on the way to the square. We all carried banners, signs, and batches of flyers. We wanted to inform the public in detail about the developments in the factory, the terminations, the police attack, and the arrests.

Ekrem would speak for the men, and I was chosen for the women. At exactly 5 p.m. we took up our positions before the monument and raised our banners. I began to speak, but before I could finish even my first sentence, the police attacked. I kept talking as they dragged me around. Some in the crowd shouted slogans—the police attacked them as well. Curious passersby stopped and watched. Even passing cars stopped. A few people pushed their way to the front to get a better view. The police blocked us off from the crowd and herded us into the prisoners' transport bus.

Even though it all happened very fast, people understood what it was about. Our slogans and the banner with the caption "Hunger Strike" took care of that. We were taken back to the station in Alsancak and were received by the same police as before. One by one we were questioned. They were most interested in the sign that said "Down with chauvinism, social chauvinism." "This came from you," they said to me. Only now did I notice that in our hurry we'd made a spelling mistake.

Our hunger strike disturbed them the most. "We understand the factory strike and even the slogans. But why a hunger strike? Why are you damaging yourself? Eat something right now!" they said. In our previous arrest, they hadn't given us anything to eat, but this time they put out food for us.

We hired a lawyer. On the evening of the second day, we were taken to a magistrate, who briefly read out the arrest warrant, and then we were transferred to the prison in Buca.

Not long before we got there, the Buca prison had been home to a revolt. Prisoners had set their cells on fire, we heard. And they'd been tortured. One torture method was especially sensational: prisoners with bound hands and feet were put in a sack. Then a wildcat was let loose in the sack, it was closed, and the sack was beaten with clubs, whereupon the cat attacked the prisoners. A few newspaper reports about it had appeared, under the headline "Prison revolt." That's what we knew of Buca.

My prison experiences to date were limited to my few visits to İbo that time in Dersim. I didn't know any other prison. In movies I'd seen how nonpolitical prisoners were treated. The women's cells were especially interesting.

The closed prisoner transport bus resembled a hearse. We ended our hunger strike, stopped the vehicle, and let them get milk and biscuits for us. The hunger strike had lasted only a short time but had achieved its purpose. Several regional newspapers carried reports about it. It was even written that we'd been arrested and beaten.

From the outside, the prison looked like a huge factory, very different from the one in Dersim. At the first block we turned to the left, where the intake procedures were done. There were soldiers and wardens. The external security was the domain of the military, while the internal administration was civilian. I had the impression that once these wardens read the reasons for our arrest in the warrants, they behaved more respectfully to us. The fat chief warden glanced at the newspaper we'd bought. We wondered if we'd be able to meet each other while imprisoned. The friends said, "Relatives and prisoners from the same proceeding can meet. We've seen to that." We knew there were political prisoners in Buca, but we didn't know whether any of them were women. A little later a female warden turned up. She was fat and had a red face. "God forbid!" she said, and led us through several corridors to the women's cells.

When the door opened, we heard laughing and clapping from inside. Surprised, we looked at each other. The warden waddled her fat body to the lower level. "Girls, the politicals are here!" None of the prisoners paid any attention. By the time she succeeded in getting their attention, we were already down below. The scene we encountered there sent us into shock. A half-naked woman was dancing on a table, while the others applauded her. "Evidently we have come not to a prison but to a madhouse," said Mahmure. The warden shouted to make herself heard, then pushed through the women to the table and grabbed the dancer by the skirt. The dancer calmly got down from the table. Suddenly it was quiet. Everyone wondered, "Who are they?" The warden repeated: "These are the political girls." Hearing these words, the women became serious and said, "Good evening, may Allah protect you."

The lower level was for eating and recreation. We rifled through the newspapers and read what had been written about us. The headlines announced: "Factory workers on hunger strike" and "Police clubs against hunger-striking workers." There were photos of us being beaten and thrown to the ground. "Seventy-five workers were sacked without compensation," read one article. All the newspapers commented positively on our action. So both the strike and the hunger strike achieved their goals—for that, we all rejoiced. Our arrest was less than joyful, but nothing could be done about it. Three or four students had been arrested along with us—they'd called out slogans supporting us during the police attack. All together there were 12 of us.

The other prisoners confirmed that a prison rebellion had taken place. And we learned that the only female political prisoner had been transferred recently to Manisa. From the men's block, Orhan Bakır[101] sent us a short account of the wardens and asked if we needed anything. He was from TİKKO, an Armenian from Karakoçan. We knew his name and were glad to have his news. The next day I was able to glimpse him briefly. The others had explained to him that I wasn't HK but a Kurdistan Revolutionary. That sparked his interest. During our brief meeting, we discussed the question of national liberation.

I'd always associated the name Orhan Bakır with revolution. Before I got to know him personally, I'd often wondered what kind of person he was. I thought of him as a revolutionary who embodied İbrahim Kaypakkaya's spirit of resistance and continued his struggle. Without knowing exactly why, I'd felt a certain closeness to him because he was Armenian. Maybe it was because both our peoples were oppressed and had experienced genocide.

Most of the female prisoners were there because of theft, adultery, or murder. The Roma women quarreled every day, which was unbearable. Sometimes they pulled each other's hair and threw cutlery at each other. They maligned each other with unrepeatable insults. Then in the next moment, they sat at a table and ate together. They weren't petty criminals or simple thieves. Their assets were so great that during their time in prison they earned a living and were even able to feed their families. When their men were imprisoned, they took good care of them. They always got fresh fruit and vegetables and prime meat. Within the women's block, they were the "princesses." Even the wardens and the poorer prisoners tried to get along with them and didn't get mixed up in their quarrels.

The "adulteresses" were a group unto themselves. Those who had been charged with murder due to honor or a property dispute tried to get closer to us. We had to organize our coexistence with all these women, so the passing of time would be more bearable. Above all, we had to organize our own lives.

After a while Sema from Edremit came into our cell. I'd worked with her in the factory in Basmane—we'd been fired together. I'd once traveled to her village with her. She, as well as her brother and her sister-in-law, were in the HK. She always treated me respectfully and had a good character. Later Sema joined Dev-Genç. Including her, we now numbered six. The presence of us "politicals" changed the mood in the women's block.

We formed a commune, in which we included a few of the women imprisoned for murder. We set up a complete schedule for every day. In the morning we exercised. We performed all the incidental tasks collectively. We read books and wrote articles. We watched the TV news in absolute silence. Not all of us could receive visitors, but the club sent us money and everything we needed.

The others wrote articles for the HK newspaper. They asked me for my opinion and if I wanted to sign. "If you write it the way it is, that's not a problem," I answered. I was a Kurdistan Revolutionary and insisted that my name be used only in this connection. I had to remind them about that several times. Then they amended the texts where my name appeared.

We truly were a commune, although we had sharp disagreements that sometimes deteriorated into mutual political insults. They would call me a "petit-bourgeois nationalist," and I'd accuse them of "social chauvinism." That accusation wasn't empty—they really did behave chauvinistically, especially Gülsüm from Manisa. Mahmure and Esmehan were more open-minded and willing to discuss. We had a lot of debates about the analyses in their magazines.

I got a visit from my brothers Meto and Haydar. Baki, İbo, and other relatives came too. One day Çetin Güngör (Semir) visited, along with Haydar from Suruç. I was as surprised and delighted as I had been when Şahin first arrived—I jumped for joy, savoring any direct tie to my organization. They brought me up to date on various subjects. Şahin had told them I wanted to return to the east. I summarized what I'd gone through since then. "My bag is packed, and I'm just awaiting the word," I said. "As soon as I get out of here, I'm on my way. If no one comes to pick me up, I'll get on the bus." My accounts of the daily routine in prison made them roar with laughter. They were glad I was doing well and standing my ground. "As for our legal process, there's nothing new," I said, as visiting time was drawing to a close. "We stand by our statements that as workers we went on the hunger strike to call public attention to our problems." As they left, Çetin Güngör said, "We'll be back."

Finally came the day of our trial. My brother Haydar, as well as Haydar from Suruç, were there. I loved my brother all the more for it. His presence did me good. After our fight, he'd promised to be there for me, and he'd kept his word.

The day of the trial, Gülsüm and I wore *şalvar* and embroidered headscarves. The other prisoners and the prison personnel were surprised that I'd deliberately put on Kurdish costume. As the prison transport buses hauled us away, we shouted slogans and sang fight songs. From the outside, we must have sounded good, since pedestrians stared at the bus as it passed. The HK prisoners had decided to make it a political trial, since it would be public and would have many observers. I agreed with their decision.

We sang together but still called out different slogans. I couldn't do much about it, but still I shouted. Many people had gathered in front of the courthouse, and they shouted slogans too. When I cried, "Down with colonialism," I was surprised to hear some supporters. Then I was delighted to spot my brother Haydar, Haydar from Suruç, and others—so I wasn't alone.

We had to wait in the basement for the trial to begin, so we sang fighting songs there too. The soldiers said nothing about it. A lot of the employees and visitors wanted to see what was going on, out of curiosity, but the guard on duty didn't let anyone through.

The trial was brief. After verifying personal particulars, the statements were repeated and the indictment read. Then the proceeding was postponed. The lawyers entered a motion that we be released, which was rejected almost before anyone realized it had been made. The indictment referred to resisting the police and the unpermitted demonstration. The lawyers affirmed the right to strike and explained that the goal of the hunger strike had been to call public attention to the unjust terminations. Far more than was stated in the indictment, many police had applied force, as was visible in their clients' bruises. But the presiding judge showed no interest and simply adjourned the trial.

It was my first court appearance. It felt strange to be accused of a criminal offense. What would be the verdict? What would have to be worked out? I'd read excerpts from the court proceedings against Deniz Gezmiş and others, and I'd read books about the torture of prisoners after the March 12 military coup. Although I'd been very impressed by the descriptions of the resistance, they remained abstract. To experience these things oneself was something different.

As we were leaving the courthouse, we shouted slogans again. Haydar called out in a voice so ringing and forceful that even the HK group joined him. To my delight, here in İzmir, in front of the courthouse, the slogan "Down with colonialism" resounded.

The prison personnel now treated us more respectfully. The wardens who'd taken us to the courthouse told the others how we'd behaved and how many people had come to the trial to support us. I guess they'd been afraid of us, since we'd shouted slogans even in the courthouse and were defying the state. So afterward their behavior toward us changed a little. Of course, they also took greater precautions and stepped up their oversight as to who came to visit us, what they brought, and what we talked about.

On visiting days, the racket was so unbelievably loud, as we sat in the booth, that we had difficulty making ourselves heard. Visitors and prisoners were separated by a thick pane, and we had to yell to make ourselves heard through the perforations. The wardens could hear our conversations, so when we had to say something secret, we wrote it down and held the paper up for each other to read.

The days crawled by, and May 1 [1977] approached. We decided to celebrate the workers' holiday here in prison and discussed the program. In the outside world, preparations were running full steam ahead. In Istanbul all the leftist groups were planning to demonstrate at Taksim Square. I wondered how May 1 would pass in Kurdistan. Surely the friends would participate in the action at Taksim Square.[102] In Kurdistan, police attacks were usually much harsher. I suspected there would be clashes.

On May 1 we put on our best clothes. Red carnations had been sent to us from outside—we put them in cans and arranged them on the cabinets. At 9 a.m., out in the courtyard, we started with a minute of silence, then shouted slogans together. We heard slogans booming from other cells as well. We were loud even though we were only few in number. "Long live the first of May!" we cried, and in Kurdish: "*Bijî Yeke Gulanê!*"

Then, tensely, we turned on the TV news. State television was reporting mostly on police security measures, but sometimes it switched to showing crowds streaming into Taksim Square. Hundreds of thousands were marching with raised left fists and roaring slogans. It was a splendid sight, strengthening our belief that this mass of humanity could really carry out a revolution. We all murmured with excitement at each new camera shot. Never had I had so much confidence in the working class and the prospects for revolution in Turkey. I was fired up, even as I ached with longing for Kurdistan.

The announcers reported in detail about the demonstration. There were other programs, too, but mainly the coverage was about Taksim Square. The sight of workers in smocks and overalls was impressive. Occasionally they showed footage of the leader of the DİSK revolutionary trade union confederation, Abdullah Baştürk, and the chairman of the TİP, the Turkish Workers Party, Behice Boran. I listened carefully for the slogan "Down with colonialism" and scanned the crowd for banners saying "Kurdistan Revolutionaries."

Suddenly a commotion broke out. The live broadcast showed

everything as it happened. We were riveted to the TV, and a few women screamed. At first we didn't understand what was happening. The newscaster gasped that shots had been fired from the roof of the Sheraton hotel. Official announcements referred to a "clash between leftist groups." Then we saw armored vehicles rolling into the square, and people lying on the ground. Taksim Square had become a battleground.

Banners, flags, and flyers flew through the air. Panicking people tried to flee, and some got trampled. It was horrifying. Our joy vanished, replaced by sorrow and fear. Before our very eyes, a massacre was taking place. There had been half a million people on the square, and now water cannons were deployed against them, and smoke bombs made it hard for them to breathe. The newscaster said "at least 20" were dead, then 30. Then it rose to "36 dead and many wounded." Thousands were arrested.

We communicated with the men's block about how to respond and decided on a three-day hunger strike. At a predetermined time, we shouted all together: "We demand justice for the fascist murderers!" "The martyrs of Taksim Square will never die!" and "Accountability for May 1." Within our limited range of possibilities, we protested the May 1 bloodbath in Istanbul.

The other prisoners behaved soberly in those days. They left off their usual quarreling and eyed us. A hunger strike was something new for them. At certain times we drank sugar water from tea glasses, and we smoked a lot. The others were careful not to eat in our presence. When one of us inadvertently walked into the room while they were eating, they tried to hide the food in embarrassment. They considered it a sin, if such a thing was possible, to eat while others were fasting. A few sat down to ask us about our action, and we explained.

In general, however, their interests lay elsewhere. A certain culture prevailed in prison. Women were trafficked among prison personnel, as even the bourgeois media reported. Staff were paid for conveying letters and arranging meetings between women charged with adultery and their fellow-defendant lovers. The staff even sold hashish and sedatives to the prisoners. Some were real professionals, earning ten times the salary that the state paid them. They acted like despots, being served by the prisoners. These criminal activities extended even to the prison administration and the prosecutors.

It was easy to find out which prisoners were involved with this business. We didn't get mixed up in it, just tried to get them to observe the rules of living together. We couldn't have changed anything by intervening anyway—it would only have turned the other prisoners against us. They knew only a reactionary, dead-end culture and way of life. They all had problems, and there were even a few suicides.

Hüsniye was one of them, a beautiful blond Laz woman from a remote village near the Black Sea. When she was 14, her father had sold her to a women-trafficker. The man had married her, even though he was already married, then forced her into prostitution. Together with his first wife, Hüsniye had murdered the guy. They were both in the same prison, but they didn't get along and bickered most of the time. Hüsniye was drawn to us and said, "Make me into a revolutionary too." She was looking for something to give her life meaning. She was a very attractive woman. A few men wanted to marry her. Even in prison the wardens were out to exploit her. They saw her as a source of income and buzzed around her like flies.

We warned the female wardens that we knew about Hüsniye and others, and about their operations, and we threatened them with consequences. The wardens became more cautious. After several failed attempts, Hüsniye would finally succeed in committing suicide with an overdose of pills. I learned about it only much later, from the newspaper. It was sad. There were so many Hüsniyes in this world.

One day at the educational institute in Buca, a bloody brawl broke out between fascists and revolutionaries. We read about it in the newspaper. They used chains, clubs, and knives. That night three students were brought into our cell. They didn't look like revolutionaries, and none of us knew them. We suspected they were fascists. When we asked, they answered, "We're leftists." Presumably someone in the administration suggested they tell us they were leftists, "otherwise they'll kill you!" and they had followed the advice out of fear.

We did a lot of physical exercise in prison. Mahmure had a black belt in karate and gave us lessons. Previously I'd observed my big brother working out and imitated him. But he'd got angry and said I should stop since muscles are ugly on women. So I gave it up. But in prison, we exercised regularly.

We were sure that the new arrivals had a fascist orientation, so we resolved: "These fascist girls attacked revolutionaries outside, so we'll beat them up now." But it would be no ordinary fight. Inconspicuously we prepared ourselves for a nighttime attack and stayed alert. The warden with the red face was herself a right-winger and wanted to protect the women. During the night she suddenly whisked them away. It happened so fast, we couldn't attack. When she came back, four of us said to her, "Why are you protecting the fascists? You keep saying here that you're only doing your job. But see what you've done!" Her eyes got big with terror, and she rushed to explain that the women had been afraid and asked to be moved elsewhere—she was only a poor widow and was protecting no one. We let her go, since we felt sorry for her. In the future, if another such situation arose, we'd act right away.

The days flew past. On May 13, at my suggestion, we held a memorial for Leyla Qasim. Orhan Bakır had made a drawing of her from a photograph taken at her execution, and sent it to me. Along the bottom he'd written in Kurdish: "Leyla Qasim will never die." I loved the picture and hung it over my bed. At home, before I was arrested, I'd received several placards from friends and hung them. One was a photo of Leyla Qasim. That was the first time I'd heard of this Kurdish fighter who had been executed. Her dignified posture had touched me profoundly. It's said that her executioner offered to spare her if she expressed remorse and asked for forgiveness. She spat in his face, saying, "I'll never ask for forgiveness. If anyone must be asked for forgiveness, it's the Kurdish people, for whom I've not fought enough. You can kill me and obliterate me, but my death will awaken thousands of Kurds." She was a legend to me, a hero. In the photo she carried a weapon and a bandolier. Women and weapons, women and war, women and the struggle for national liberation, women and death—that had a special significance. Kurdish women would free themselves from their enslavement by fighting.

Leyla Qasim's struggle was at the same time a struggle against Kurdish collaborators. In her search for freedom, she stood as an example for all Kurdish women. She'd considered the liberation of the people to be her own liberation and fought on the front lines against reactionary, feudal, and misogynistic social structures. The Kurdistan Revolutionaries too had, from the outset, attracted women to the struggle for national liberation. Women could obtain their freedom only by an active participation in the process. There had to be many more Leylas.

At the memorial, I explained everything I knew about Leyla Qasim. Then we read aloud messages from other friends and sang a few verses of songs that evoked Leyla. In remembrance of the martyrs, we reaffirmed our common commitment to continue her struggle.

Not just May 1, but the whole month of May was unusual: May 6 was the anniversary of the execution of Deniz Gezmiş, Yusuf Aslan, and Hüseyin Inan. On May 13 and 18 we commemorated İbrahim Kaypakkaya. And unknown to me at the time, Haki Karer—a splendid man and a valued comrade—was shot on that very day.[103] We read aloud a text that Orhan Bakır had sent from the men's block. On the cover was a picture of İbrahim Kaypakkaya in a peaked cap that I liked very much. This day, too, we sang fighting songs.

At the end of May came our trial. It was election season, and our lawyer successfully made use of the CHP milieu. We were released on bail.

Upon our release, my brother Haydar and Haydar from Suruç took me to İnciraltı. They said I should get to know more friends there. We went to the campus, and on the pane of the front door hung a large placard. People were standing in front of it, gaping at it curiously. When I passed through the door, I saw pictures of Haki Karer and Aydın Gül[104] hanging on the wall, with the caption: "The great internationalist Haki Karer—May 18, 1977." Underneath it read:

Nothing is as precious as independence and freedom.

Comrade Haki Karer, heroic son of the people of Turkey, a great internationalist, member of the leadership cadre of the Kurdistan Revolutionaries, was murdered on May 18, 1977, in Antep by the agent organization Beş Parçacılar.[105]

Down with colonialism, imperialism, and every form of reaction! Damn all spies and provocateurs! Long live the internationalism of the proletariat! Kurdistan Revolutionaries.

I couldn't hold back my tears. The caption swam before my eyes. I pressed my hands into fists and had difficulty standing. The HK had murdered Aydın Gül. "Those bastards," I whispered. He was the first of us to lose his life for the struggle. HK members had shot him in the name of the revolution! Why had I heard nothing about it? How had the friends been able to conceal it from me? I was married to an HK member!

I wouldn't remain in İzmir a second longer. I didn't care that I didn't have permission, I wanted to leave immediately. I couldn't wait any longer. That damned prison had set me back three months, a long time. I read the caption over the picture of Aydın Gül: "Brave fighter for the national liberation of Kurdistan." I remembered him. He had been very young, an understanding, quiet comrade. Sometimes he'd visited us with Meto. What had happened? I couldn't believe it. Under the photo it read:

In the homeland the lions don't have to hunt foxes. / The fascists cannot destroy the flower of Dersim. / The path to revolution is tied to him. / Kurdistan Revolutionaries, March 8, 1977.

I didn't want to see Baki anymore. He realized my situation and stayed away from me. We didn't speak to each other; he just watched me. Later he said to me, "It wasn't the HK." He didn't want to believe it. Then he said, "We'll research it." Once again that sentence! I flew into a rage. What was there to research? A revolutionary had been assassinated—he'd find nothing about that in his books! If he could just stretch his mind a tiny bit, and check his heart and his conscience—that would have been enough, if he'd had only a particle of love for his people and his country. His "research" always took him in the wrong direction. With typical petit-bourgeois cunning, he'd intone about "differences among revolutionaries" but hypocritically refused to face the ideological, political, and practical consequences. His group just ignored the reality of Kurdistan. A people that organized based on their own power—the HK considered that separatism and nationalism. They had always propagandized against us, and now they were using violence. That could hardly be considered simple and normal.

In the light of these developments, I doubled down on my decision to return to my own country. This time I wouldn't run away secretly—I wanted to make an open break. I said to Baki,

Without ideological and organizational unity, our relationship can't continue. We've discussed it often but have never come to a solution. This movement is open to everyone. If you really wanted to, you could participate—no one would stop you. But you have to be convinced and to do it not just to save our relationship. We'll see each other again and discuss it some more. You can find the friends anytime, you know some of them already.

Then we shook hands.

The residents of the house watched in astonishment. As I spoke, I was packing my suitcase and crying. Baki cried too. So it was that I left our poor home in Çiğli. I was exhausted by the time I reached the main street, less from the heavy suitcase than from this last conversation. I was alone. I went to an address in Konak that had been mentioned to me. It was the flat of Cuma Karakoçan and Kemal Coşkun, known as Bozo. They were surprised to see my suitcase. "Let's leave right away," I said to Bozo. At first they thought I was joking. "Wait a minute, we've only just arrived in İzmir. What's going on, what's happening with Baki?" Bozo asked.

"What should be happening with Baki?" I answered mockingly. "Let him stay in İzmir and make a revolution in Turkey. They won't be able to do it without him." They both realized that something had happened. They told me I was clearly very upset and shouldn't do anything in haste. "No," I said, "Baki isn't coming with me. There's no connection between us anymore, and actually there never really was one. It's my fault I ended up in this situation, and I've been trying to extricate myself from it for a long time. I'm sorry, he's very sensitive. I hope he'll be able to put all this behind him. I've tried to convince him it's better this way. We didn't part with ill will."

"You've separated in such a civilized way," said Bozo.

I laughed even though it hurt inside. The friends didn't know much about how it had really come about. They didn't take it seriously, but it was serious. For months I'd been struggling with myself, with the people around me, and with my family. It had also been an ideological and political struggle.

We ate at the flat, then Bozo and I left and bought bus tickets for Ankara. We had just enough money for them.

As we traveled, I was lost in thought. Bozo tried to cheer me up. We talked about Dersim. Bozo was known there because he'd snipped the ears of the village headman. Ever since then, he was wanted in Dersim and couldn't be seen there.

Sitting in front of us was a man who looked like a businessman. He seemed tense, clearly disturbed by Bozo, who couldn't sit still and kept banging on the seat in front of him with his hands and feet. We were speaking Zazaki to each other. We didn't look like tourists, so the businessman must have realized we were Kurds. That was fine, as long as he didn't think we were "terrorists." When the bus pulled over at a rest stop, we had no money, so we didn't get out. Nor did the man, who had been clutching a bag like James Bond. He thought he was alone in the bus and opened the bag. It was full of bundles of money. Bozo whispered to me, "Let's grab that money and disappear." That wasn't a bad idea, but it was too risky. Bozo was a vibrant, anarchistic man. The money attracted him intensely. The businessman got off the bus as soon as he noticed us. He finally disembarked in Polatli and disappeared.

In Ankara we took a taxi to a dormitory where friends lived. We were penniless, so Bozo told the driver to wait and ran in to get money from the friends. Since it was a men's dormitory, I stayed outside.

Bozo returned with Muzaffer Ayata, who I met for the first time, and then Baki Karer came out. They took me to the home of a large family. One of the daughters, Mediha, was a student and a comrade. We didn't talk much that evening, since I was tired from the journey. The next day I talked with Baki Karer. Bozo had briefly explained my situation, and Baki Karer wanted to know what had happened more precisely.

After he heard me out, he criticized me: "You left the door open for the guy, by saying you weren't ending the relationship completely." I repeated that the relationship remained friendly, but he seemed unconvinced: "When you make such a decision, you have to be unambiguous," he said. "Otherwise you'll regret it later." It was too much for me. Irritated, I said, "I am unambiguous. I've made a decision, and I'm here now. Nobody forced me. If I hadn't landed in prison, I'd have come sooner. I told Şahin that too, he knows about it!"

Had Şahin told him something different? I wondered. If I'd come sooner, I could have explained everything myself and decided what was to be done, or been told what to do. The resistance in the factory had kept me away—I'd put a lot of work into organizing that strike. I'd had to see it through to the end.

Baki [Karer] asked, "And what do we do if he shows up here?" He was right—he well might. I knew Baki [Polat] wouldn't give up. He might even say he'd become a Kurdistan Revolutionary. But what could I do? What would a more unambiguous decision look like? There was no more connection between us.

I stayed with that family only briefly. Kesire picked me up and brought me to her family's home. We talked along the way and continued after we arrived. She told me that after our first meeting, "you suddenly disappeared. We hadn't even talked about you among ourselves. It's not that we were indifferent to you, but it wasn't easy to think of a solution right away. And then you were gone." Her words had a critical undertone. I explained that I'd gone to İzmir and recounted what had happened there. I told some episodes only sketchily, others in greater detail.

Finally I had a chance to get to know Kesire better. I also made the acquaintance of Şenay, who Kesire introduced to me as a "Yugoslavian friend." She lived in a dormitory, but we women were to move into an apartment in Etlik, where male friends were already living at that moment.

Kesire was nothing like the friends in Dersim. Her family's home gave the impression that they all belonged to the organization. Her mother did nothing without Kesire's approval. Her father was quieter and mostly worked in his shop. Their behavior toward each other went beyond a normal father–daughter relationship. One of her sisters studied at the ODTÜ, the technical university. Then there were twins, a girl and a boy. The boy was called Ali Kemal. Kesire was the authority in the family and also among their relatives, who, when we visited, clearly thought very highly of her. I admired her that even as a young woman, she was recognized by all as an authority.

In these days Şenay's elder sister came to visit from Yugoslavia. We showed her around and made visits. It seemed strange that Kesire had time for such things.

One day Mehmet Ali called and asked to meet me. Apparently Baki [Polat] had shown up—Baki Karer had guessed correctly. Mehmet Ali came to Kesire's home, and we talked in her presence, which in many respects was good. I criticized him for the way he'd behaved after I came from Dersim to his family. If he'd just arranged for me to stay with them, I wouldn't have gone to İzmir, and everything would have been different. He was a little responsible for that. My critique was embarrassing for him. My separation from Baki depressed him. Kesire's presence made an impression on him, as ultimately the separation was politically based.

Mehmet Ali explained that my uncle, out of worry, had suffered a facial paralysis. I couldn't pretend it didn't move me. In fact, I had a hard time with it. Yes, in discussions I blamed Baki and his relatives, but I felt responsible myself. It exhausted me. Just as I'd thought it was over, new difficulties arose, and I wondered if I'd ever see the end of it all. I kept asking myself what I'd done wrong. What had been my error, my weakness? And then I thought that I'd made everything right, or as much as was possible. My uncle was sad, and his wife would cry, Baki would go crazy, and so on. But what about me? No one showed any interest in my thoughts, feelings, or wishes.

Mehmet Ali kept referring to my uncle's malady. He wouldn't relent—he was looking for an interim solution, one that, somehow, would satisfy everyone, but that couldn't work. Kesire cut to the heart of it:

> You're acting like you want to make peace between two combatants. But the friend has made it clear, and you were the very first one she talked to. It's you who could have helped her the most. But you thought only about Baki. Now you're looking for a solution that will also satisfy the rest of the family. We can't force the friend to do anything. You have to explain that to your father. And Baki shouldn't always just plow on ahead.

Her words relieved me greatly, but Mehmet Ali left us dejected, only half convinced.

I moved with Şenay (who now called herself Nadire) into the apartment that had been arranged for us, which was near Kesire's family's home. For a while Şenay's sister lived with us, which was good because it made us seem less suspicious to the neighbors. Sometimes the friends came to visit. After a while Şenay's sister went back to Yugoslavia. But for me, a new era began. I was looking for balance and had enough perspective to better recognize where I'd erred and where I'd been right.

The events had left their mark on me. Escape, marriage, prison, fighting, and then having to make a decision all alone ... What a lot I'd been through! But I didn't consider it my fate—instead, much more that I'd defined my own fate. The thought that this situation represented a new beginning comforted me.

During this time I grew closer to the friends. We read and discussed a lot. After a while we resumed the educational work, meeting in the home of a friend from Mardin who had been married twice. We read books like *The Right of Nations to Self-Determination* [Lenin, 1914], *The National Question and the Problem of Colonialism*,[106] and *Left-Wing Communism: An Infantile Disorder* [Lenin, 1920]. Our group consisted of Kesire, Nadire, and a few other friends. Kesire led the educational work, but in the actual discussions she spoke the least. She also didn't say much in daily life. When Nadire wasn't there, I stayed overnight with Kesire.

I respected all the friends who were part of the movement or who led it. Comradely relations were an extremely precious bond of trust. That was the first thing we learned. So I tended to revere the friends and to consider everything they did as right. Maybe not everyone. But Kesire wasn't just a comrade—she was also the beloved of our chairman [Abdullah Öcalan], who wouldn't have entered such a relationship with just anyone. I don't remember anymore whether the chairman was there that first time in Ankara, when I stumbled into the group in the political science faculty's courtyard. But then I wouldn't have recognized him, since I'd never seen him before and his name had not been mentioned. I met him for the first time with Kesire and others at a discussion in the law school cafeteria.

After this intensive period full of rebellious and rash feelings and unexpected conflicts, I found myself once again in Ankara, where I met the chairman directly.

We were known to others as *Apocu*. At first the name irritated me, since it was wrong to designate a movement by an individual, and besides it held risks for the chairman. But ultimately the name wasn't so important. Apo was an individual who stood for principles, revolution, internationalism, love of country, and an unremitting struggle. Yes, we were Apo-adherents. Basically I liked this label, and it made me proud even before I met the chairman for the first time.

Mostly I was impressed by his skill in listening to people and understanding them. He never talked about a subject directly and in his analyses didn't refer to an individual person or event. But whenever he spoke, I felt he was putting into words exactly what I was thinking. When he articulated something, he opened up new horizons that affected us all: the collective life, the future, the struggle, and what we as individuals had to contribute to it.

He didn't talk like the other friends. His manner of speaking was natural, simple, full of content, and unique. Many of the friends to whom I'd been talking had limited the conversation to my flight from home and my separation. But the chairman never even mentioned that, yet answered all my questions by explaining connections across different subjects.

My most beautiful moments in Ankara were those I spent listening to the chairman in the law school cafeteria. People from various leftist factions came too, and he carried on a dialogue with them.

As for Kesire, it occurred to me that she was ordinary yet thought highly of herself. She never set out to achieve something but expected everything would come to her. In Dersim, Kıymet had gossiped about her: "She's the daughter of Ali Yıldırım, she's cold and conceited. Not even the chairman accepted her at first." This rumor had seemed to me implausible, and why the reference to her father? I didn't get it. Now that I experienced her close up, I found her impressive. Her relations with her family and their respect for her was positive. *It's good that as a revolutionary, she's recognized by her family as an authority*, I thought to myself.

I compared her to the young women in Dersim and especially to Kıymet, whose authority was based on money and her profession. But Kesire's family wasn't well off. Kıymet meddled in everything and talked ceaselessly. Her ways of living, even of smoking cigarettes, were curious. She was no revolutionary authority who preserved her distinctiveness as a woman, but rather a girl who walked like a man. She knew no limits or standards. Of course through her behavior, she still made an impression on her family and her acquaintances.

Because of the rumors about Kesire, I observed her all the more carefully. Everything she did seemed preprogrammed. In that respect she resembled Cemile a little. I compared her to all the women I knew from the Turkish left. No, Kesire was different, and that made me proud.

Şenay—influenced by student ways of life—was kind of disorderly, whether it was eating, sleeping, or cleaning. She just considered many things unimportant. She regarded cleaning as unnecessary toil and thought it normal to wear the same clothes for a month. Her pants were baggy, and her shirts were rumpled. Ironing was a waste of time, in her view, yet she often spent time on much less important things. That bothered me.

She was educated and a member of the movement, but her outlook on life somehow didn't reflect that. She reminded me of the Turkish left in its early years. I'll never forget how the color of İbo's pants would change during washing. For her, a revolutionary life was tied to a scruffy appearance. I never understood that. Maybe I didn't understand many things, but I at least knew that a pure spirit and ethic, and a certain orderliness, were part of a revolutionary life.

Şenay changed during the time we lived together. On the subject of order, Kesire proved I was right. My relationship with Kesire remained distant, due to my respect for her. Nonetheless sometimes I succeeded in generating a little closeness between us. Sometimes she seemed quite natural with me. For example, everyone said Kesire never laughed, but I got her to burst into raucous laughter several times.

The first wife of the friend from Mardin, in whose home we conducted our educational work, was a beautiful woman. She was tall and had a dark complexion. When she put on her traditional clothes from Mardin, she was even more attractive. One day she went shopping with her in-laws. In her long, sparkling dress, a white silk scarf wrapped around her head, and her gold jewelry, she drew general notice to herself. She wore a stunning necklace, a golden belt, and golden earrings, and her arms were half covered with bangles. She could have been a mannequin.

One day the TKP women, in the name of the Association of Progressive Women, were protesting price increases and were holding up empty pots and plates in the air. As the demonstrators shouted slogans, this woman called in Kurdish *"Bimre Koledarî!"* [Down with slavery]. Everyone stared at her in surprise. Her in-laws nervously tried to pull her away: "Come on, let's not get in trouble with the police." She said, "The others shouted slogans, and I can too." Finally she gave in and went home.

When I told this story, exaggerating only a little, everyone broke out into laughter. Kesire laughed so hard she cried. She knew the woman and her idiosyncrasies. Once she'd seen the woman go shopping in the cold of Ankara—in a dress with half-length sleeves. Probably it was the tragicomic situation of a brave Kurdish woman, who in her youth had had to accept existence as a second wife and who never ate at a table with men, that brought us to laughter. There were many such dramatic, tragicomic situations in Kurdistan and in the big cities.

In Kesire's family's home, a large photo of her hung on the wall. It was taken while she was a teacher, she explained, and pulled out her photo album. Her mother looked like a typical aristocrat. She hadn't changed in the city—judging from the photos, she'd already looked that way in Karakoçan.

While we looked at the photos, I asked Kesire a lot of questions, all of which she answered, but I refrained from asking her about her relationship with the chairman. I wanted to get to know her better, but she still kept her distance.

Normally she wore a shirt and pants, but one day she changed into brown-patterned corduroy pants and a checked blouse. She was lively and joyous like a child. Obviously she was expecting someone, because she could not stop smiling, ever since receiving a phone call that morning. No one besides us was home. I guessed the chairman had said he was coming over. When the doorbell rang, she leaped up and ran for the door, but it was someone else. Her buoyancy ebbed. No one came to visit that day.

One day we drove together to Tuzluçayır and made a few visits in Natoyolu. At the first house, we found educational work under way. Dr. Ali Rıza,[107] Bezar, Gönül Atay,[108] and the Serik sisters were there. The doctor was running the class. Gönül kept trying to call attention to herself. During the discussion she didn't let anyone else talk. From the first moment, she made a poor impression on me. Kesire said almost nothing. After a while we left the house, and I said to her, "Gönül is garrulous. I didn't care for her behavior." Kesire laughed. "Yes, that's how Gönül is. She's engaged to Rıza." Then we went to Rıza's home. I'd spent a few days there before I went to Kesire's. Later Bezar and Gönül arrived.

Mother Hatice, the housewife, was an adorable woman. She behaved very respectfully toward Kesire. She was elated at our arrival, as if the chairman himself were there, or at least a piece of him. Whenever Kesire was present, everyone always pulled themselves together and paid more attention to their behavior, even Bezar and Gönül. Only Mother Hatice retained her natural easy warmth. At that time Bezar was working as a court stenographer, and Gönül was a student. Bezar acted like a just-hatched chick whose eggshell hadn't cracked properly. The education work had had an effect on her, but she carried on like a spoiled child, even though she was an oldest daughter and employed. She hardly noticed me.

Gönül was full of herself. She thought of herself as an "outsider" among us and rated that as something special. My first impression of her never changed, and as it turned out, I was not mistaken. Later we later spent a long time together in prison, and I got to know her well. I find it important to analyze her personality in detail. We fought many battles, which revealed her hateful ambitions and complexes and where they'd lead.

The days in Ankara passed colorfully and pleasantly. They gave me an important opportunity to read, discuss, and further educate myself. I was with people from whom I could learn a great deal. Slowly I worked though my previous experiences. After three or four months, the time came for me to return to the country. I was to be sent to Urfa, but there would be a language problem, and Saime Aşkin (Delal) was already there. She was a teacher and an active organizer. She'd learned Kurmancî in Urfa. I was impatient and just wanted to go to Kurdistan—I didn't care where.

The day before I left, Kesire said she'd accompany me to Elazığ. I was surprised but gratified. How fine to travel with her! I didn't ask many questions. It was unclear, at least to me, when exactly we'd leave. In the final days, a mood of leave-taking prevailed. Kesire's family members gathered around her. Kesire, who was a dressmaker, had sewn a skirt for her mother. Impressed, I thought, *A revolutionary has to be able to do everything.* Kesire was for me then an outstanding comrade by whom I oriented myself. Her family loved her. She was a revolutionary woman but so humble that before her departure she made a skirt for her mother. Everything she did felt positive to me. I could find no flaws in her, or maybe I just didn't want to. Of course, I noticed some aspects of her that she didn't display everywhere, and sometimes contradictions in her behavior surprised me, but none of that altered my high esteem for her.

That last evening her father was somber. As he spoke, he got all choked up, as if he were about to cry. Her mother cried openly. Her sisters and Ali Kemal oscillated between sadness and joy. The moment came when Kesire would leave her home and Ankara. I had already experienced many farewells, but this one was special. I observed everyone and was infected by the mood. Kesire stayed calm and relaxed. She comforted her family with a few words—"We'll call each other. Don't worry, I'm not leaving the planet." That was all.

Do they know where we're going? I wondered. I guessed they did, which was why her departure affected them so deeply. The girls and Ali Kemal drove us to the bus station, where we all said goodbye. Kesire and I boarded the bus. Vastly different emotions coursed through us. During the journey we alternated between silence and conversation. For a while we passed time by reciting poems. Kesire had a beautiful voice. At her home, I'd heard her singing along with a recording of a Kurdish song. On the bus she was carrying a book of poems by Nâzım Hikmet.[109] I read some of it as well. We talked about poetry for a while, especially the poem "Sis" (Mist) by Tevfik Fikret.

Our shared journey ended in Elazığ, at the Fevzi Çakmak neighborhood, where I disembarked. Kesire continued on to Amed.[110] I would not see her again until the first congress.[111]

A typical woman from Elazığ: Mother Zencefil   Finally I was back in Kurdistan! Would it mean the end of my year-long adventure, or would it mark a new beginning?

In Elazığ I went to the house of the Sarıkaya family, which stood above the canal. I asked for Mother Zencefil, a typical woman from Elazığ.

I'd already heard much about the Sarıkayas, and the Fevzi Çakmak neighborhood was just as well known. It was said that the police didn't dare venture there and that revolutionaries could go around armed. The Sarıkaya family gave everything for the party. The friends praised Mother Zencefil and her daughter Saniye in the highest terms.

Zencefil, the head of the family, was a tall, forceful woman who spoke both Turkish and Kurdish. The house, made of mud brick, had only one story but many rooms. Some of the family members worked in Germany. More siblings lived behind the house. They were poor and lived modestly.

Whenever anyone talked about women from Elazığ, I would always think first of Mother Zencefil. She embodied these women's quintessential traits. Neighborhoods like Yıldızbağları, Kırkdutlar, and İstasyon were full of people from Dersim. Most of the women wore a *şalvar* and either slippers or plastic shoes. The women were out in the streets in this neighborhood.

The houses had no plumbing, so the inhabitants had to retrieve water from various points in between the neighborhoods. The women spent a lot of time on the water supply and exchanged news at the waterholes. It was an organized water culture.

Formerly at the waterholes they had exchanged gossip, but now they debated revolutionary politics and whispered news. This verbal transmission of propaganda played an important role. They kept one another informed about groups and actions and about who had done what, and who adhered to which political orientation.

Saniye, the daughter of the house, was well known. The friends in Dersim had commended her courage and military-style discipline. The group considered the political-ideological struggle to be the most important activity, but they inevitably also organized and planned revolutionary actions.

Elazığ was home to many fascists. The MHP had a broad base locally, and many of its militant cadres came from here. The polarization between right and left necessarily politicized many of the people. Leftists in Elazığ defined the fascists as the enemy. They regarded fascist institutions, which were supported by the state, as different from the state itself. That was why in Fevzi Çakmak it was accepted to go around armed as a revolutionary militant, to keep watch or to hold rallies. For all the leftist groups, the neighborhood was their most important arena of struggle, where they sold magazines and newspapers, distributed flyers, and made propaganda in the coffeehouses.

Saniye was the family's only daughter. The friends had visited the family often, which left an impression on her: she sympathized with the movement. She had received the same education as her brothers, and she could move around freely. We gave her jobs like transporting documents or revolvers. This work required planning and courage, and Saniye excelled at both. Her family kept their doors open to the movement at all times. This openness could be strained when local cadres used the rooms almost like a coffeehouse.

They almost made it too easy. The family was hospitable and never turned down a request, but even if no one noticed, the constant visits disturbed them, especially those that had no set purpose. I realized this after a few days, and it bothered me. I pointed it out to some of the friends, but they didn't believe me: "You don't know this family or Mother Zencefil at all. You're just wrong." The family treated visiting cadres differently from the local ones. They watched us closely. The friends from outside were more cautious, as they were seeking long-term use of the home and a lasting relationship with the family.

Behind the Sarıkaya family's house was a two-story house, where the friends rented the upper story. The apartment was large but empty and didn't have a stove. It was used for important conversations, and occasionally visiting friends from other places stayed there overnight. Dilaver Yıldırım lived there at first—he was in charge of the region. A deaf man named Metin and Hamili [Yıldırım] were there, and a few other friends came and went as they traveled from place to place.

Another two-story house belonged to the family of Ali Dursun, which was used less often. It was at the edge of Fevzi Çakmak, bordering the

Kultur neighborhood. Ali Dursun was a regional cadre. His wife Cemile was a teacher. Both were originally from Birvan village. Their daughters were Roza and Helin, and their parents lived in the upper story. Ali's siblings Saim and Semra were sympathizers. Financially the family wasn't doing badly, they were middle class. They drew two salaries and also received income from their village's agriculture. Dev-Genç had considerable influence in that village.

I stayed with the Sarıkaya family for a while, then in other homes, and then with the Dursuns. Later Nurhayat arrived from Dersim, and I introduced her to the acquaintances in Elazığ with whom we did educational work. One of them was Sakine Kırımızıtaş, whose family came from Mazgirt. One of her older sisters was a teacher. One of her brothers was involved with the Stêrka Sor organization, which we didn't know at first. Once Alaattin Kapan[112] came to visit with a woman named Gülay. Sakine didn't know the organization, as it was still relatively unknown, and thought they were just normal friends of her brother. In reality the organization was involved with the murder of Haki Karer, which Sakine couldn't have known at the time.

Saniye's political convictions were superficial. She didn't grasp the seriousness of the situation and sometimes acted on a whim. By contrast, Sakine was more mature. She was trying to broaden her ideological knowledge and took the organization very seriously. Also in our first study group in Elazığ was Fatma, a relative of comrade Zeki Budak; Leyla, a Sarıkaya relative; and a few other young women sympathizers. Some went to school, while others stayed with their families. We ran educational work on specific days at specific times. It wasn't easy, as a few of the families created constant problems. Not everyone was like Mother Zencefil, who said nothing and just opened her house to the organization.

Nurhayat, like me, had run away from home. She joked, "So now my mother will grab your mother, Zeynep, by the collar and blame you." I finished the joke for her:

> And then Mother Zeynep will say, "What does my daughter have to do with it? Everyone's responsible for their own child. But all the mothers whose daughters run away now come to me. Oh, Seko,[113] Seko, what have you done to me?" And then she'll cry and curse.

Meto told me that our mother sometimes complained about the photos of Marx, Engels, Lenin, Stalin, and Mao that hung on the walls, and blamed them for causing me to run away. Of course, she couldn't pronounce the names correctly, and she laughed and cried simultaneously.

Nurhayat had been in our first study group back in Dersim. That was when she and I became friends, based on our shared political views. So in the neighborhood I recognized her even from a distance.

We had first made contact through her older sister, who had been with TİKKO. After she came to us, her connection to TİKKO continued in that she was engaged to a man from TİKKO and insisted she'd win him over for us.

Nurhayat was more active than her sister. Coming as she did from one of the first groups, she was seriously prepared for ideological struggle. She was highly emotional but not very militant. She had an air of permanent helplessness, so she wasn't taken seriously. She bent to the existing order and showed little initiative. But in the educational work, she was articulate and tried to pass on to others what she'd learned and so influence them.

Before I arrived in Elazığ, I had been much talked about. My escape from home was described as if it were a movie. The Sarıkaya family knew about it and made sure the whole neighborhood did too. At our first meeting, I'd introduced myself as "Fatma," but Hamili burst out laughing, "What do you mean, 'Fatma'? We all know you as Sakine Cansız. We knew about you before you got here and about your escape from home, everything up to your separation." Deaf Metin confirmed it.

I was surprised and a little uneasy. I didn't really mind personally, but it felt strange to be talked about in my absence, since it didn't seem right for my own work and for building relationships. The people with whom we worked were inclined to exaggerate little things and spread them around. And everything we did could be used against us.

Clearly the name Fatma wasn't going to work for me. Some people called me Fatma, while others stayed with Sakine. A few assumed there were two different people. Over time I got accustomed to both names.

Baki [Polat] didn't give up—he came to Elazığ. Wherever I went, he would follow, then look up the friends and find them. He explained that the differences between him and me were really not as insurmountable as I said. We could share a common struggle anytime, and an organizational commonality could emerge—it just needed a little time. So he tracked down the Sarıkaya family and said these things to Dilaver and the others, and they believed him, and then they tried to bring me around to his view. No one found Baki's behavior disconcerting. They even called him "our friend." No one thought to ask for more information.

A few comrades were of the view that ideological differences didn't justify separation. "If only ... ," they said. But then what? They glossed over how this relationship had come into being: I'd run away from home to devote myself to the struggle but had had to enter into a marriage that lacked any basis. I'd stipulated that the future of the marriage depended on ideological and organizational unity. If such unity had emerged, I might have continued it, but I'd entered the marriage due to social coercion, not out of love. Now there was no realistic prospect of continuing our marriage.

Baki's concept of marriage included a claim to ownership. But I wasn't logical, patient, or mature enough to articulate this struggle over unity and separation in positive terms. I'd behaved rashly and emotionally and had thereby allowed my weaknesses to be exploited. The result was a tragicomic "life adventure" that had become an endless problem. I struggled harder to put it behind me, especially to overcome the pain I felt.

For myself, I'd actually solved the problem. Yes, the story had left its mark on me, but in the meantime things had improved for me psychologically—just as the issue of "reconciliation" was back on the table. Viewed from outside, it all might seem simple. And many of the friends thought the problem was an entirely normal one that could arise in any marriage. A few even thought I was sulking and wanted to flirt. They cracked jokes: "Wherever you go, this guy's never gonna give you up!"

For a woman, it wasn't easy to work as a professional revolutionary. But for the male friends, it wasn't a problem—they could stay overnight anywhere. Women couldn't. Women could stay with families, but not for long, even with the best ones. And it was also problematic for women to live together with male friends. The society was just too reactionary. We had to pretend to be a group of students sharing a residence or a family home. Anything else stirred too much notice. The male friends had it easy—they could say, "Then we'll have a different home!" This way of thinking was relatively common, but efforts to solve the problem conclusively were weak.

When I left İzmir, yes, I'd left a door open for Baki, so he didn't consider our fights decisive grounds for separation. He thought differences between revolutionaries could be transcended like differences between people. It's true, we didn't stand wholly opposite each other, but our differences weren't to be overlooked. They had started in early 1977 and led to violent clashes and deaths. Baki himself was full of contradictions, but ultimately he was a cadre of a movement with which mine had a serious rift. And I was a sympathizer and aspiring cadre.

What was important was the nature of the struggle and how individuals developed within it. Those who lived the way they liked, joined others voluntarily, and fought a little on the side, were not true revolutionaries. Anyone could do that. In Kurdistan, the militant struggle demanded more, and to be a Kurdistan Revolutionary was of a whole different order. Society, individuals, and classes were undergoing a process of dissolution. Contradictions and transformations were growing. First one must undergo a mental enlightenment, then embody it more and more in life. The process was tough and painful but also meaningful and beautiful.

Women: more reliable than men   I was ordered to go to Bingöl. The female friend there needed support, so one of us—either Nurhayat or me—was to go. The friends decided it should be me. Along with comrade Delil Doğan, I got under way. The ebullient Delil could hardly sit still as we sat in the bus. He talked constantly and tried to get me to talk. His incessant joking cracked me up. Sometimes he'd say where we were. Since it was nighttime, I couldn't make out anything and learned names of places as we were whizzing by. "If only we were traveling by day! I know Kurdistan so little," I moaned. Still, the change of scene made me happy. I was ready to go anywhere the organization wanted to send me—I didn't care where. It was exciting to get to know a new place. Delil described the social and political scene in Bingöl. "Religion is dominant, and feudal values are in place. The women all wear the chador and veil their faces. For the work, you'll have to dress that way too." I was astonished but then realized it was a joke. Delil laughed fiendishly—he'd just wanted to see my reaction.

We drove to the home of Mehmet Karasungur,[114] a high school teacher who lived in school housing. When we arrived, the friends were all in a meeting. What a lucky break, to meet all the area cadres on that first day! They were some 15 male friends: Mehmet Karasungur, who everyone called "teacher," his brother Haydar, Zeki, Abdullah Ekinci, Resul Altınnok (Davut), and others. Since the meeting hadn't ended yet, we had to wait awhile.

Afterward the teacher Mehmet came over to Delil and me. Delil introduced me as his "friend from Ankara," and I think Mehmet mistook me for Kesire. He asked in a low voice for my name, my hometown, and where I'd just come from. "Fatma," I said, but then Delil jumped in with my correct name: "Sakine Cansız." It was getting late, the teacher said: "Let's send the sister to a suitable place." A few of the male friends thought I could just stay here, but the teacher said, "It isn't appropriate. If the neighbors see it and tell Mediha, it won't be so good, and we'll have to take care of it." Later I found out he was married and his wife Mediha was on vacation with their son Devrim.

Awkwardly, the teacher turned to me and explained, "You're tired, but it's not far. You'll go to my aunt. She has daughters, and you'll get to know them. The aunt will accept you, although she hid her daughters from us." He spoke facetiously, but after I got to know his aunt, I understood that he hadn't exaggerated.

My first meeting with the aunt was tainted a little by the fact that it was the middle of the night, but Haydar Karasungur, who escorted me, explained, "We have a visitor from Ankara, a female friend. If you could look after her, we'll come back tomorrow and talk about everything." His aunt patently adored him, looked at him lovingly, and laughed at his jokes. Those who had been sleeping awoke and slowly got up. The house seemed full of young girls. They were four sisters, whose father was in Europe, I later found out. The girls went to middle and secondary school. I could tell from their behavior that they had nothing to do with politics. The mother was the domestic authority.

"I left my suitcase somewhere else," I said. Actually I'd brought nothing at all with me, but it was noticeable that I'd come all the way from Ankara with nothing for my personal needs. A family's first impression of me was very important—I'd have to be more careful in the future. I looked all right, and was always meticulous.

Now I tried to be considerate and weigh their reactions to my behavior. The aunt was a sly woman who intervened right away whenever she thought her daughters had done something wrong. Aysun, one of the middle daughters, asked questions at every opportunity about things that interested her. As her mother watched us, her facial expression told me she didn't want to hear about "dangerous things" or unsuitable questions. Haydar had already explained the basics. "Don't ask so many questions," [the mother] interrupted. "She's come a long way and has to sleep now."

The only way to win over these young girls would be to first win the heart of their mother. She was a forceful woman who seemed to soften when you treated her with intelligence and respect.

I stayed as a guest for a few days and was successful. It would be easy to maintain contact with them—they were as good as won over. Yes, the girls had their idiosyncrasies and still had no idea of Kurdistan, but that had been true for me, too, before I came in contact with the movement. So it wasn't hopeless. I had no difficulty staying in touch with people and usually left a mostly positive impression.

After three days, the male friends took me to the home of Ali Güngör in the Üç Katlar neighborhood. Ali Güngör came from Nazimiye in Dersim, and his wife Fethiye was from Karakoçan. He was a civil servant, she a primary school teacher. Their small daughter Roza lived with her grandparents. They opened their apartment to the friends. I knew İbrahim Güngör from İzmir, and I'd also met his relatives in Germany. The family was large. I was meeting Ali now for the first time, but knowing his relatives made it easy for me to start talking to him.

When the two of them went out to work, I stayed home alone. For a while I couldn't open the door or go out onto the balcony. Police lived directly across and on the first floor, so I had to be careful. During the daytime I had to make it seem that no one was in the apartment. That was boring but necessary, so I wouldn't be exposed. I had a lot of time to think.

For the political work, committees were being formed. Up till now there had been only representatives. The committee secretary was in charge of organizing the committees, which were allocated for military affairs, women, youth, and workers, thereby ensuring a division of labor. Since we were still at the very beginning, the plan wasn't implemented very systematically yet.

My work wasn't strictly specified. It was easy for me to build relationships with women, but there was still no theoretical concept for woman-specific organizing. It was just part of the general work. "Women will be free when they participate in the national liberation struggle and assume roles in every area." I tried to formulate such maxims to bring our general truths to women so they could put them into practice.

Since women were the most oppressed, they also had the best prospects of becoming revolutionaries. We knew this from the outset, so we attributed importance to women. Other women's movements influenced us and gave us ideological strength. But we were not yet aware of the core problem since we hadn't yet confronted the historical, social, and day-to-day aspects. There was still no organizational and practical means for the participation of women in the Kurdistan revolution and no concrete goals. We were not yet a party, we had no charter or program, so the woman question was folded into the general aims.

The Education Institute in Bingöl was like the Teachers School in Tunceli. It had a lot of fascists too, but also a great potential for organizing young people. Similarly, at the high school, where comrade Mehmet Karasungur taught, fascists murdered a revolutionary and thereby incited revolutionary developments in young people. The murdered person had Sunni roots, and the enemy had intended to widen the divide among the different beliefs. All the more reason for us to attend the burial and organize a great protest demonstration.

Mehmet Karasungur well knew when and where to apply revolutionary violence. He had the necessary consciousness and put it into practice. In clashes with fascists, he was always in the front line and so had the stature to influence others. That day Hamit, a crazy young man from Bingöl, pulled his knife on a fascist, and as he stabbed him, he shouted, "*Ji kurdan ra azadî*" [Freedom to the Kurds]. That was the kind of transformation the city was undergoing: to weaken the left, it tried to widen the breach between the Alevi and Sunni communities. But at the burial, the interfaith unity was palpable in a ceremony that we brought about. It showed that our movement could reach many people and that it had active force. Everyone saw it.

At such crucial moments, inexplicably, Davut withdrew. No one could understand why. Usually he went to a park, a very open place, and interacted with a wide array of people. But sometimes when discussions took place among groups who knew each other, Davut just spontaneously withdrew. He'd refuse to leave the house, and whenever the doorbell rang, he'd slink into a back room. We made fun of him. He also was known to use the Güngörs' apartment for his retreats, which was bound to worsen his mood. I laughed about it, it seemed so strange to me. One day when the doorbell rang, he squeezed his giant body in between the cupboards in the bedroom. He looked so funny, I burst out with a fit of laughter. It hurt Davut's feelings, and for a week he let me know how insulted he felt.

He lived in a one-story white house that we called the "White Palace." We had given him the nicknames "Kung Fu" and "Amca" [Turkish for *uncle*]. Sometimes he joked that he came from the Far East and wasn't Kurdish at all. Other friends lived with him. He was probably home the least. Staying overnight with families was his greatest pleasure—and he just stayed there. Strikingly, his whole demeanor—the way he sat, stood, talked, drank tea, or ate—was disgusting. Some of the male friends had coarse sides, they understood nothing of aesthetics or chose not to, but ultimately their more appealing sides outweighed their coarseness and made it bearable. I do Davut no injustice to say that absolutely nothing about him was at all bearable.

Unlike Elazığ, Bingöl also had petit-bourgeois nationalist groups. *Özgürlük Yolu*, especially, tried to organize in the city center, near TÖB-DER. They had a base in the tribes that corresponded to their own class characteristics. They did not struggle or try to extend their influence. So their building was located in peaceful proximity to a fascist club.

Fighting the fascists in Bingöl had the effect of accelerating the development of revolutionary patriotism among the people, and it laid the groundwork for our organizing there, as we developed our local organization with depth and breadth. The groups with so-called "democratic institutions" couldn't keep up.

The focus on ideological political struggle, combined with revolutionary violence, revealed individual personality characteristics. Davut, for one, always opposed the exercise of revolutionary violence against fascist centers. I saw that several times, and some of our discussions about it got very heated. I criticized Davut for his behavior, but he always made excuses. Ostensibly he criticized the friends' haste and lack of planning, but in reality he opposed taking any action.

Selim Çürükkaya[115] was always in the opposition. He behaved individualistically, deflected criticism, and tried to muddy things as much as possible. He and Davut talked all the time. They denounced each other polemically as scaredy-cats. No problems were solved this way, yet nothing was done against it.

Around this time Mehmet Karasungur was having problems at home, having to cope both with Davut and with his family. His wife wanted him to come home on time and to tell her everything, but that wasn't always possible. In fact, Mehmet Karasungur did the opposite—he devoted himself increasingly to political work. His teaching was becoming only a formality, as our work was extending into neighboring areas and we discussed sending cadres there.

Davut was always at the home of the Karasungurs or the Güngörs. He seemed to exacerbate the women's discontents. Even though he was in charge, he didn't do any work but let other cadres do everything.

How could we begin to create the conditions for a lasting revolutionary work that included women? What role did Bingöl's social and political social structure play? Knowing I had to consider this, I acted with extreme caution. For a long time I didn't leave the apartment during the daytime. Davut's conspiratorialism had an effect on me. For four or five months I left the house only in the evenings. This concern about being exposed meant that my work time, and therefore my work, was considerably limited. Sometimes I was home alone all day. But it seemed necessary for the secret organizing work, and I told myself, *The organization must work patiently and secretly, and we have to abide by the rules.* But that caution was actually exaggerated.

The woman work demanded great sensitivity, alertness, and infinite patience. Bingöl was a small, backward city, and it would not be easy to organize the women and bring them into the struggle. The Education Institute and the other schools held the greatest potential, but we lacked the necessary connections. We could do outreach there only indirectly.

Comrade Hüseyin Durmuş would go over to the secondary school and sometimes come to the apartment where I was staying, which was when I got to know him. At first I didn't know his surname and so didn't realize he was Hayri's brother. We didn't ask such questions, and it wasn't necessary right away. Over time we had opportunities to get to know each other. Hüseyin said he was busy with a few girls in his school but hadn't yet succeeded in organizing them.

I got to know Yıldız and Kadriye. Yıldız was a natural for politics, she was interested and eager to learn. But Kadriye was still under the influence of religion. At home she followed the family rules, but in school she was feisty and courageous in the fights with the fascists. Evidently no other young woman was subjected to the kind of family pressure that I was. I asked them about the situation in their families and how they could free themselves from it. Of course, I wasn't calling on them to flee their families. If they'd known about my situation, they might have been wary—that was no way to solve problems.

Kadriye immersed herself in dialectical materialism and also fasted. Yıldız was more agile and succeeded better in evading parental oversight. We took a girl named Hüsniye into our group, whose family was with *Özgürlük Yolu*. Through her we reached her family. Kadriye and Hüsniye were in the same class at school. Hüsniye was adventurous and liked that the friends fought the fascist students and teachers. And she was guided by her teacher, Mehmet Karasungur. Many young people admired him and wanted to adopt his politics. Kadriye was an anarchist. When fighting fascists at school wasn't enough, she went over to the Girls Art School and beat up a fascist teacher there. She had a clear goal and a pugnacious character, but she needed a conscious and organized framework.

I began the educational work in Bingöl with [these] three young women. I was careful to use the apartment where I was staying as seldom as possible. I asked the female friends to find us a suitable place. That was an important part of the work, since it was no mean feat to meet, read, and discuss for a few hours, without the family and the enemy noticing.

Everyone realized I wasn't originally from Bingöl. When I visited families by myself, I soon formed good relations. I benefited from my experiences with my own family.

Kadriye's family was large, rich, and prominent in Bingöl. They owned the only park in the city and several hotels. The father was uncouth and a drinker. The oldest son, Mahmut, was a teacher and was in contact with us. All the others were a little nuts. For a while we used their house for our educational work. The mother even asked me to stay on and become a "daughter of the house." All that made it easier for Kadriye. Her contradictions diminished from day to day. As a young girl, she had studied the Koran closely and now concerned herself with philosophy.

One day during a discussion in the study group, she acknowledged her contradictions. Afterward she tried even harder to grasp the basic principles of philosophy. She was determined and scrappy by nature. Her whole family was disputatious. They fought all the time, yet were very close-knit. They all complained about the father, who was important to them but whose drinking was embarrassing and irritating.

We wanted to transform at least a couple of members of this family into revolutionaries. Some male friends were in touch with the men, and there were almost always young women around who could be drawn into the revolutionary work. Their work was mostly superficial and was limited to reminding them of their oppression and giving them tasks that required secrecy. A few of the male friends held the view that politics was not a matter for women, so they ignored them. It was not easy to turn women into revolutionaries, but these guys made it easier. And when we succeeded, the revolutionary transformation affected the whole family.

We continued the educational work without interruption. Yıldız was most eager for it. I got to know the Durmuş family when I visited them in their two-story house. Uncle Isa interrogated me like a detective, asking who I was, where I came from, and what my purpose was. When I told him I came from Dersim, he told me a story about some people from Dersim who had tried to steal some *pestil*[116] in Bingöl. The residents of a certain house had laid their *pestil* to dry on a tarp on the roof; then they lay down around it and went to sleep. The would-be robbers tied a string around a cat and tossed it onto the tarp. The cat sank its claws into the tarp, and the thieves yanked on the string. But it woke the residents, who opened fire, so the robbery failed.

So Uncle Isa didn't like people from Dersim, and furthermore he was annoyed by "Kurdish advocates" and found them dangerous. But at least he tolerated Davut, even announcing, "This Davut is one who will spread Kurdishness."

Uncle Isa also respected Mehmet Karasungur, saying, "He's got a job and earns an income, but he's always out on the front lines. One day the police are going to grab him, and that'll be too bad for him."

His wife, on the other hand, was sick and didn't get around much—she just sat on a cushion in a dignified way. She kept interrupting Uncle Isa and saying to us, "Don't listen to what this crazy man says."

But gradually this family changed their attitude toward the movement. Not that they agreed with everything—in fact, they had many objections—but their interest grew, in a struggle that offered a new way of living that they couldn't ignore.

Hüsniye's elderly mother didn't get involved. Her brothers and sister-in-law were with *Özgürlük Yolu.* At first we just let it be, as they didn't obstruct Hüsniye in the work. The more Hüsniye developed, we knew, the easier it would be for her to influence her people. In everything we did, we had to consider the consequences. To bring a young woman into the revolutionary movement was a great achievement.

Over time our work group grew so large that we split into two. In the second group we accepted Fethiye and Mediha. By now we had more than 20 young women sympathizers. Our organizing work was talked about in the schools and in the neighborhoods.

The other factions had only the occasional woman in their groups. But then their cadres tried to build an alternative to us. Actually that made us happy, since we'd rather see women and girls involved with other groups than have them out of politics altogether. Once they got into politics, it would be easier for us to influence them. Sometimes we participated in the other groups' seminars and meetings. The groups always propagandized against us, but when we participated in their discussions face to face, we were able to win over many young women.

The apartment where I was staying bustled with activity when friends from different places stopped by, and we talked and discussed. Then it would be quiet for a long time. Only Davut was always there. He fought a lot with Selim, which seemed asinine to me. Selim, I knew, was a demagogue—he could hold forth about anything for hours, all day long. He didn't like Davut and made fun of him. But he didn't make a serious critique, and that kind of talk bothered many friends.

Davut, for his part, accused Selim of being an ineffectual windbag. Mutual criticism among the friends was normal, but if it got out of hand, we had to stop it. I didn't like this fight because both parties were leaders in the organization. It was important for me to step in and object to their mistakes. But I still lacked professionalism, a truly revolutionary personality, and political depth. I had only a narrow and superficial view of the organization. Just adhering to certain criteria and having good intentions wasn't enough to solve problems. You couldn't carry out a class struggle that way.

Selim had won over Aysel Öztürk, a woman at the Teachers School, for us. We talked a lot about a relationship between Aysel and Selim. Selim said he was going to ask her family for her hand in marriage. In Dersim the rumor reached Aysel's relatives, who were annoyed. The friends caught wind of it and wanted to know if there was any truth to the rumor. Busiest of all in this affair was Davut, who joked about it.

Selim was not a man who held on to relationships and adhered to principles within them. His easygoing and democratic manner concealed a weak personality, and daily interaction with him revealed his sexism. Some of the male friends had a feudalistic or petit-bourgeois mindset, yet a comradely, relaxed interaction was still possible with them.

But Selim came across everywhere as oppositional. We were used to it—"that's just how he is," we said. If someone criticized him, he would recriminate for a month and repeatedly try to vindicate himself. He considered himself the organization's best advocate. Whenever he met someone with obvious weaknesses, he turned the situation to his own advantage. Davut's presumed cowardice was fodder for him.

We all regarded courage as essential to the revolutionary spirit. Our movement was known for its members' courage—that was how it emerged. Our members had to possess courage, but Davut didn't meet this requirement. Everyone, from rank and file to cadres, knew it, but he could discover not the slightest imperfection in himself. In this respect he mirrored Selim. In general, the friends didn't exploit members' shortcomings. They scrupulously avoided unresolvable conflicts and baseless accusations.

Our interpersonal relations were marked by the warmth, attentiveness, and love that a shared struggle engenders. We placed the highest value on comradely relations. We didn't permit intrigues. Behavior like Selim's and Davut's only led to alienation and rejection. Our critique of them should have flowed from a broad analysis of personality seen against the social-political background. Yes, we talked about class characteristics and antiquated personality types. But still, we handled the issue at hand only superficially, limiting our critique to specific cases.

* * *

In the winter of 1977, our work was better organized. Hayri and a few other friends had arrived, although at the time I didn't know who they were, since their identity was confidential.

One day after returning home from a study group, I found Ali Güngör sitting at a table with three pistols spread out before him. It was rather unusual to see three pistols all at once. I absorbed the scene with intense interest—I had a special fondness for taking weapons apart and reassembling them. "What's going on?" I asked, excited. "Is there going to be an action?"

"Yes, we're gonna rob a bank," Ali replied calmly. At the look of surprise on my face, he confessed he was joking. Then he said he was going to repeat the joke to Fethiye, who was due back home soon. "Let's see how she reacts," he said. "Don't let on that it's only a joke."

I agreed. "Actually in Bingöl, it'd be easy to rob a bank," I said. "It's not the kind of action you can do only in big cities. In Bingöl such a thing has never happened. I'd participate—in fact, it'd be better with women involved. Can we propose it?"

"Why not? I bet we could pull it off," he said.

A little later Fethiye walked in. She looked even more surprised than I had been. Touching the pistols, she asked softly, "What's going on?"

Ali murmured, "Stay cool. There's gonna be an action. We're gonna rob a bank. You'll come along. We've just discussed it with Sakine—women are less conspicuous. Hüseyin from Karakoçan, a good friend, will be driving the car. We've got to get ready. I'll probably be the fourth."

Then, in all seriousness, we rehearsed. We barged into the room with weapons drawn. Ali submissively handed us something from the table drawer, and then we left, watching out for each other. The action was successful! We ran through it several more times and had a lot of fun. Of course, we also might get arrested. What would we do then? We decided that if we were caught before we got the money, we'd deny everything. If we were caught after, we'd say we were revolutionaries and were seizing the money in the name of the people.

Then we took a break and prepared some food. While we were eating, we kept talking about the action. Fethiye was into it—she was on fire. She hardly ate anything, saying she didn't care about food at that moment. Ali finally mentioned their daughter Roza: "If you end up in prison, take her with you." He was testing her reaction.

The longer the joke went on, the crazier it got. I urged Ali to confess the truth: "This has gone on long enough! Fethiye thinks it's for real. We have to tell her it's a joke, otherwise she'll be hurt."

"Okay, I'll tell her soon," Ali said.

That evening the three of us slept in the apartment. Early in the morning we left, all carrying pistols. We were supposed to deliver them to Mehmet, and then Ali and Fethiye would go to their work. Ali still hadn't told Fethiye and kept talking excitedly about the supposed bank heist.

When we got to Mehmet's, he took us into the back room. He'd been waiting for the weapons. In the living room were two male friends: one was Ali Dursun, and I didn't know the other—he wore glasses, and I brushed by him. In the back room, the joke was continued, even with Mehmet.

Mediha followed the conversation curiously. When she understood that a bank robbery was being planned, she insisted on taking part. We were acting like children. When the time drew near for Fethiye and Ali to go to work, I pressed Ali again to tell her the truth.

Meanwhile Mehmet got the other male friends involved. Mediha repeated that she wanted to take part in the action. Apparently she thought it'd improve their chances.

When I came back into the living room, I greeted the male friends. Confused, I took in who was sitting there. Before, seeing him in passing, I hadn't recognized him, but yes, it was the chairman. I'd been distracted by the excitement over the pistols, but now I finally had to put an end to the joke.

Turning to Mehmet, I said, "Let's not drag this out any longer." Then I explained how it had all started.

The chairman cut to the core of the matter. "Of course women can do an action like that just as well as men—why not? The group just has to be well prepared."

Ali Dursun added, "I'm new here—the police don't know me, I can join you."

Suddenly the whole affair seemed serious. I was confused. Had it been real all along? Had Ali only been pretending to me that it was a joke? "A joke shouldn't be dragged out so long. Tell the truth, at long last!" I insisted.

The chairman responded, "What kind of joke? Is that how you go about the work here?"

Fethiye grabbed her bag and sobbed as she left the room, "I get it! You didn't trust me. You wanted to test me! Am I your guinea pig?" Ali's admission that it had all been only a joke, to test her reaction, had hurt her deeply.

Mediha agreed: "It's always the same—you don't trust us."

The chairman tried to figure out what was going on. It enraged him that such a serious matter had been made into a joke. "What do you mean, women aren't to be trusted? What are you doing, putting women to the test? I'll tell you one thing. With us, women will be trusted much more than men. It's more important than anything else to make women into Kurdistan Revolutionaries and to bring them into the revolution. We're not going to proceed by way of jokes. So pull yourselves together. Go ahead, rob a bank. Women can do it just as well."

We felt miserable. The joke had begun with the cleaning of weapons, but where had it led? I tried again to explain. "I told Comrade Ali not to drag out the joke any longer. But I've made a mistake, too. I could have overridden him and told the truth. It was perverse that Mehmet jumped in and even got other male friends involved."

Mehmet admitted his mistake.

Ali said, "The mistake was mostly mine. Fethiye thought we didn't trust her and so didn't bring her in on things. It really bothered her, and I just made everything worse."

He left for work. Mediha went shopping. Mehmet and Ali Dursun got ready to leave. What was going on here? I would be alone with the chairman. At the door, Mehmet turned to me and said, "Stay here—the friend wants to talk to you."

It didn't register. "He's right with his criticism," I said. "We shouldn't have done it. It didn't go well."

Mehmet repeated, "The chairman wants to talk to you."

"Really?" I cried, leaping to my feet. But I didn't trust myself to go back into the living room. The meeting had been atrocious—how could a conversation proceed after that?

I was agitated and embarrassed by my own behavior. For a few minutes, I stood in the hallway, unable to open the door and go into the room. Then I pulled myself together.

The chairman was pacing back and forth in the large living room. First he asked me about the work. "How is it going? Are there problems? What is the general structure?"

I described the basic work since my arrival in Bingöl, especially the woman work.

"How many women are you working with?" the chairman asked.

"Between 25 and 30," I said.

"Really? That's good," he said appreciatively. "Even in a reactionary place like Bingöl, it's important to bring young women together and educate them."

Which female friends showed promise? he asked. I named Yıldız, Kadriye, Dilan, and a few others. "If you handle them right," the chairman said, "if you're a role model for them and keep educating them, more women will join, even in a neighborhood like this."

Then he brought up my marriage to Baki. "No one can endorse slave relations. I'm stuck in such a situation as well. Many people have pointed out that Kesire is the daughter of a Kemalist collaborator." He asked for my opinion. "Other rumors have it that Ali Yıldırım is an agent [for the MIT]. You stayed with the family for a while. What's your view?"

I answered without hesitation. "The authority figure in the family is Kesire," I said. "Her family loves and values her very much. Maybe her father is a Kemalist or even an agent, but his daughter is a revolutionary."

He said, "That's the best rebuttal to Kemalism and collaboration: to make the daughter into a revolutionary. That's the foundation of our relationship. I'd never try to force a relationship on someone, and I don't accept slave relations. Relationships must be equal and free. Our Ali Haydar has married Cemile. I assume that's all right. You know both of them—what do you think?"

I was delighted to hear this news and said I wasn't surprised, as the two were suited to each other. I trusted Ali Haydar Kaytan the way other people believe in a god. I loved and respected him. Cemile was a young woman from Dersim who had taken on important organizational tasks and was ready to get things done. I considered their relationship a positive.

We talked more about relationships: one was ruined and had to be ended, another was based on a common struggle. I rejected mine and was ready for a separation, but I supported the other relationship and was even happy about it. The chairman's words gave me strength. He didn't come out and tell me what to do, just noted the general circumstances. "You can't force a relationship," he repeated several times, which made me feel that my decision was correct, even if he didn't say so openly. And he said he was sure I'd make the right decisions in the future. That was enough for me. No more agonizing—only the revolutionary work was important for me, and Baki couldn't keep me from it. If he wanted to pressure me some more, then I'd tackle the problem at its roots. It did me indescribable good to talk to the chairman.

The chairman called an evening meeting in Bingöl in a house we called our "white palace." I went there with Mehmet Karasungur. Mediha caught wind of it and insisted on going, but the teacher objected: "That's not going to work. The friend has to be somewhere else." Once again Mediha was hurt, as was Fethiye. They influenced each other and took it out on me, since I'd taken part and they hadn't. They considered it another instance of mistrust of them.

The meeting started late in the evening, as the friends arrived in small groups at different times. It was wintertime, it had snowed, and it was cold inside the house. The chairman spoke for hours. In preparation, he'd asked the friends what he should talk about. He evaluated the political developments and talked about the history of Kurdistan, our ideological orientation, the specificity of our revolution, the situation in Bingöl, the leftist Kurdish groups, and our position on them. Finally he made observations about our work. All the male friends took part in the meeting, since they were trusted. I was the only woman. Concerning the woman work, the chairman said, "The participation of women in the revolution has especially great meaning under this social structure. It will accelerate the developments. Bingöl's backward, feudal structure is not an obstacle. We have to bring to it the necessary patience and attention."

Similar meetings had already taken place in Karakoçan and Dersim. The one in Dersim was held downstairs in the building where our apartment was. We had hidden the friends' illegal things there, so I liked the idea.

The meeting had a positive effect on the participants and expedited the work. The chairman also talked about the revolutionary radicalism of young people in Bingöl and said their struggle against fascists and reactionaries would make them more militant and better organized. I saw it that way too.

The leading fascist in Bingöl was the mayor, Hikmet Tekin, a favorite of Türkeş. His co-workers in the city administration were mostly young fascists. Tekin traveled often to Germany and to Ankara, where he secured the ideological and material support to hold his local cadres in line. Our actions against the fascists had impeded the work of the MHP, and revolutionary violence had dealt them a blow. Bingöl was no longer as it had once been, and the fascists could no longer move about so freely.

I moved again, this time to the home of Zeki Yıldız, which was more suitable. He'd just married a conventional girl from his village who, in his words, came "from the same class." The family was large—even his deaf-mute stepmother lived with them. Zeki's beloved father had been killed in a work-related accident. He talked about him often, saying, "He was a worker, a proletarian." Ten people lived in the household, including his step-siblings, all warm, vibrant people. Zeki was an endearing comrade who carried on the revolutionary work passionately. At the same time he was sensitive and emotional, as I could tell from the things in the room where I stayed. He loved Kurdish music and especially admired Aram,[117] whose songs broadcast over Radio Yerevan he collected. Zeki's interest in art, culture, and learning was obvious. Apart from a wooden bed, the room contained only shelves lined with cassettes and books and magazines. It was a tiny room, but its richness took me on journeys, and I loved it.

Zeki's deaf-mute stepmother was highly sensitive: when the doorbell rang, she could not only sense it but knew, from the way it rang, who was there. Her senses were highly acute. We communicated with her through hand signs and the few tones that she could produce—this defined her world. Zeki had wonderful conversations with her this way.

After Zeki married Emoş, his stepmother became depressed, thinking he didn't value her anymore. Emoş wasn't exactly her ideal daughter-in-law. Even though she was a villager, she was a little spoiled and wanted something better. She was good-natured and intelligent, with a lot of potential, but she dreamed of a world different from the reality surrounding her. Zeki was unlike the other men in the village, and she had known he was a revolutionary. He treated her respectfully and didn't pressure her. Instead he tried to teach her. His idea was that he'd married a woman from a revolutionary class, so his goal was to bring her into the Kurdish revolution. Emoş wasn't aware of that. She thought all the beautiful ideas Zeki related to her were just abstract daydreams.

Zeki had imagined the marriage differently. Problems arose right from the start. He had to carry out his revolutionary tasks and at the same time try to meet his wife's expectations and those of other family members. He tried to do both but just couldn't. Often I saw tensions surface. And sometimes his stepmother was rebellious. Zeki's efforts to manage the situation were complicated, and his good intentions didn't suffice. His father's death left him responsible for supporting the whole family, which limited his activities for the struggle. He often expressed his thoughts openly and complained about his unhappiness. He was prepared to take on any task that was assigned to him, but if it involved work in another region, he had to consider his family. It hurt his pride when he had to say no to the friends, even though his objection was justified. But his determination, persistence, and care inspired confidence. Despite his family conflict, he was hopeful and vivacious. And after all, a revolutionary must be able to handle difficult situations.

The poverty in that house Friends from outside often stayed overnight at the house. One day Baki Karer arrived and spent the night, and the next day we went to Ağrı together. Carlos, a tall stocky friend, came with us. His name was unusual—he was probably interested in the international terrorist Carlos [the Jackal]. He was unconventional, walking briskly in a long black cloak that hung from his shoulders. We drove to Bulanık, Patnos, Malazgirt, and Ağrı. I brought some literature and a revolver with me. Women were seldom subjected to inspection. If police got suspicious, they brought in female officers, but normally they only checked ID. So [in the movement] it was mostly women who handled courier duties.

It was a good chance for me to get to know other parts of Kurdistan. The legendary Mount Ararat, the mountains in Karlıova, and Akdamar Island in Lake Van—it was super to finally see them with my own eyes. Discovering the beauty of Kurdistan gave the homeland new meaning for me. I was happy and proud to be part of the struggle for this land.

But its obvious poverty sometimes drove me to tears. In Malazgirt we stayed overnight with a family who epitomized this reality of the Kurdish people. A cow slept in one corner of the house, the wife and children in another. The window was made of plastic film. Family life was pervaded by the stench of cow dung, the mooing of the cow, and the crying of the children. I spent the entire night slapping at fleas. By morning the white bedcover was full of blood spots, as killing fleas is an art unto itself. For breakfast I was served, along with homemade cheese, one single egg, which had been cooked over a fire made from cow dung. The table was set only for me—the children stayed at a distance. Apparently the egg was something special, reserved for guests. But how could I eat it, when the children were all staring at it so covetously? It wasn't the first time I'd seen such poverty, but it affected me deeply. The wife urged me to eat the egg, but I just couldn't, so I said I couldn't tolerate eggs. Once we got on the road again, we stopped to eat. I couldn't stop thinking about the looks of those children, and I still couldn't take any food.

Driving along the winding road to Patnos, I thought of some Kurdish children who I'd gotten to know on the fairground back in İzmir. They were 9 or 10 years old and sold sesame rings. I learned that their families came from Mardin and Siirt. When I said I wanted to buy a sesame ring, all three came running over to me. One of them shoved the others out of the way, and they jeered at each other in Kurdish.

"Stop fighting! I'll buy something from each of you," I said.

They were stunned, and we began to talk. One had run away from home in Mardin because of his stepmother. Another, Ömer, said he couldn't stand it at home because his father always fought with his uncle. The third boy, Ali, from Siirt, had come to İzmir to work for relatives, but the apartment was crowded to overflowing, so he ended up on the street. The children slept in the park or, if they found a job temporarily, on the floor of their workplace.

They'd all three grown up in extreme poverty, like thousands or millions of children in the same situation. This was the core of our struggle. I couldn't save them by buying a sesame ring. The way they fought and competed with each other reflected our primitive social reality. They all shared the same problem.

In simple language, I explained to them about Kurdistan and our struggle. They had to close ranks and work hard together, I said. Then gave each of them money for a sesame ring, and we ate them together.

Later I saw them again, a few times. There were now five of them, and they worked together without fighting, as they told me, laughing. Every day, they said, they came to the fairground hoping to see me. When I said I'd been there only by chance, they fell silent. Then: "Okay, but we'll still come here anyway." Straight from their children's hearts, they expressed what our brief moment of connection had meant to them.

The sight of children in pain, poverty, and oppression always agonizes me. I had the same reaction to Zeki's younger sisters. Their father was dead, and they had only their deaf-mute mother to care for them. With their beautiful Kurdish names—Berivan, Zozan, Rojda—they didn't yet know the onerous circumstances they'd face as they grew up. In Kurdistan, poverty and suffering were part of life. That it affected children made it all the more unbearable.

Driving from Malazgirt to Patnos, we crossed a barren, dusty landscape. In Patnos, for about 3 kilometers along both sides of the road, we drove past a restricted military area. Here everything was green—the terrain was planted with evergreens. Every 10 meters stood a camouflaged armored vehicle. This beautiful place was enclosed with barbed wire, watchtowers, and officers' quarters. That was the reality of the enemy.

But outside the barbed wire, the land was parched. The mud and stone houses, funnel-shaped with small windows, resembled miniature Egyptian pyramids. Small ponds had been dug by the roadside, but there was no other water—the drought was obvious. The minibus stopped at one of these ponds, and the driver announced that whoever wanted to drink could get out. Mules, donkeys, oxen, cows, and chickens drank from this same water. Children played with sticks in it. But the people got out and drank from it anyway.

In Patnos, large areas were under cultivation, but there were no plows, let alone tractors. Baki Karer muttered about what we were seeing. In *Rizgarî* magazine, I'd read an article called "The Development of Capitalism in Kurdistan," arguing that now that capitalism had developed in Kurdistan, its feudal structures were undergoing dissolution. I mentioned it to the friends. Baki Karer scoffed, "Let them come here and take a look. It's easy to sit somewhere else and analyze Kurdistan. This place doesn't even have plows—what kind of capitalism is that!"

When we reached Ağrı, it was cold for April. Or was it the sight of the snow-covered summit of Mount Ararat that gave us a chill? This mountain, where the snow never melted, looked severe and cold from every angle. The climate made the people who lived here rugged and tough.

We went to the home of Salman, a teacher. Actually the house wasn't safe, since it had previously been exposed. As we entered, we were watched, and Baki Karer panicked: "The enemy saw us," he repeated several times. We hid the literature and a cassette we had with us in the bathroom light fixture, much to the relief of the teacher and his wife. They taught at the Girls Art School and asked us many curious questions. [My old friend] Nurhayat was in Ağrı—she'd come here when I'd gone to Bingöl. We hadn't seen each other for a long time.

The next day was May 1. The friends told us a demonstration was to take place that day in Doğubeyazıt, and more actions were being considered. Baki said, "We have to write a flyer right away," then duplicate and distribute it. He told me to get some paper and a pencil, and we began with "To our heroic people." He dictated it to me. Sometimes as I wrote, he asked for my opinion and asked whether I wanted to add or change anything.

Long into the evening we talked to the teacher, who filled us in on the situation in this area. When it was time for bed, he asked Baki softly, "Who will sleep where?" He assumed we were married. When I was alone with his wife in the bedroom, she said bashfully, "My husband and I've talked about it, and I was right—you're not married." She had a great need to talk. I'd told them earlier that I was from Elazığ, but she said my accent sounded more like Dersim. She didn't want to ask directly. She said of Nurhayat, "She's very striking. You notice right away that she isn't from here."

I told the wife she should participate actively in the work. She would find the woman work easy, I said, since she had the advantage of knowing the local women's problems, and besides, she was a teacher. She had contact with the friends, and her husband was with us, which made it even simpler. And she was from this area and knew it well. I said it wasn't right to remain passive. I made her a little uncomfortable, but she seemed unwilling to change anything. She had influence with her husband. Women like her could contribute a lot to revolutionary work, if only they wanted to. But by not participating, they actually had a negative effect, especially on their husbands. This woman was educated and knew about the problems, and she had no financial difficulty since both worked. Both of them could have made good contributions to the revolutionary work, but their petit-bourgeois outlook made them unreliable.

She reminded me of Ali Dursun's wife in Elazığ. She too was a teacher, educated and articulate. If she'd wanted to, she could have developed a militant position. But under pressure from the people around her, she wasn't willing to get involved in the revolutionary work. And she too had a negative influence on her husband. She didn't prevent him outright from taking part in the work, but made clear he had family duties. In those days there were many such families, and it was uncertain how they'd develop.

[While we were there,] I definitely wanted to visit the friends who were in prison. They had been the first of us to be arrested, and a few of my old teachers [from Dersim] were among them. When I expressed this wish to Baki, he said, "Okay. They know we're here, and anyway they've asked for someone to come, because they want to tell us something."

I went to the prison, bringing along some family members. It was surrounded by three rows of tall barbed-wire fencing. During the visit everyone was visible to everyone else. There were 12 of them, and almost all had been arrested in connection with the murder of Mustafa Çamlıbel.[118] They told us about the episode. The action hadn't been well prepared. After Çamlıbel was shot, they'd fled to a nearby village. The enemy had invaded the village and arrested all of them.

One of the friends explained, "The enemy is trying to figure out the political context [for the murder]. I testified that it was a personal issue and took responsibility. The other friends will get out, but I'm not sure about myself." Then he whispered, "We'll escape, but it won't be that simple from here. We've asked to be transferred to the prison in Doğubeyazıt. It's smaller, and the security isn't as strict. But if we're not transferred, we'll try it here. The friends should know that." Then they gave me a written message and some money. When no one was looking, the tallest friend threw a roll of coins over the barbed wire, which I immediately stashed in my bag.

I hadn't seen some of these friends since Dersim. They asked how I was doing and about my marriage. I brought them up to date. They listened with interest, sometimes laughing, sometimes looking embarrassed. So much had happened in the past year: marriage, separation, associated problems. They were glad I was still active and had gone to work professionally. Back in Dersim, they had explained to me about Kurdistan and had put a lot of effort into educating me. For a revolutionary, it is most gratifying to be able to win someone over to the revolutionary struggle. I'd chosen this path. Yes, I was like a child who'd only just learned to walk, but what was important was my determination.

As I told them my story, and I got to the parts about my own weaknesses and errors, I had to swallow hard. I was still dealing with my marriage. Every conceivable sacrifice must be made for the revolution, no matter how painful, even to grapple with a marriage and subsequent separation.

Actually I'd figured out myself that I had to limit my concerns about what others might think. It was better to have a horrible end than an unending horror, so that's how I behaved. The separation was unavoidable, as I'd decided to dedicate my life wholly to the revolution. I'd learned many things and had developed a certain serenity that allowed me to bring greater enthusiasm and self-confidence to the work. Still, I wasn't free of the feeling that I'd lost a part of myself.

Bidding farewell to my friends was bittersweet. Gazing at the barbed wire, I said, "You'll be with us again soon." When I left, I wasn't searched—the message and the money stayed with me.

On the return trip home, I thought about these conversations. The time in Dersim had been beautiful in its way. Now I was in Ağrı. The revolution had no fixed location and no homeland. Part of its beauty was to find it everywhere.

Baki Karer stayed in Malazgirt, while I went back to Bingöl with Erhan, a student at the Tunceli Teachers School. He was lively and talkative. We agreed that if we were inspected, we'd say we knew each other from the school and had visited his family in Malazgirt. But we encountered no problems. Back in Bingöl I set about looking for a new home.

The struggle continues Various actions were planned in those days. Mayor Hikmet Tekin was an important target, since he propelled the fascistic organizing. To disrupt it, some influential cadres had to be attacked. An attack on Hikmet Tekin himself would surely have positive consequences, but the action would have to be well prepared, as the man was cautious and protected himself. We looked for an apartment across from his house in Bahçelievler, from which we could observe him. We found one and rented it. I pretended to be a newlywed, explaining to the landlord that my husband would arrive later.

The apartment was on the fourth floor. In the apartment next door lived Sami, of *Özgürlük Yolu*. The landlord was from the same village as Zeki, who had found the apartment for us and had introduced us as the relatives of friends. We bought only the necessary furniture items. The neighbors didn't particularly wonder about the sparse furnishings since I explained that my husband had to move around a lot for professional reasons and we didn't want to burden ourselves with heavy furniture.

Then again, perhaps we were too cautious and no one was really paying attention. But the planned action was a very serious matter. Zeki had taken every precaution. After I moved in, I stayed very observant about my surroundings and the neighbors. I was friendly to them but distant, to keep them from getting them involved in my life, or stopping by, or noticing my visitors.

My most important task in the flat was to observe Hikmet Tekin. I had to note what time he left home, when he returned, how many people accompanied him, which door he normally used, and other such details. His house had two entrances and two yards. Sometimes Zeki came over to observe as well.

During this time the educational work and the meetings continued. New members were assigned to groups according to their education level. While I was in Ağrı, Mediha, Fethiye, and Mehmet Karasungur's female cousins had established a separate study group, on the grounds that it was unnecessary for them to read the same book with every new person or to discuss the same subject all over again. I let them do as they liked.

The woman work wasn't easy. Some of the women wanted to fight their oppression, to educate and transform themselves, but others acted counterproductively. Actually that was to be expected, as in Kurdistan there was no precedent for a women's movement. In many places in the world, women had already been organizing to demand their rights, but in Kurdistan equality and women's liberation were foreign concepts. The creation of the national liberation movement had the effect of slowly awakening the women, but at this time consciousness was still lacking, and most women remained as resigned to their fate as ever. We had our greatest influence on women at a certain intellectual level—the others didn't question gender roles at all.

Türkan, Sevim, Ayten, Gönül, and other female friends were taking short courses at the Educational Institute, learning to become teachers. Students came here from all over, so the school was well suited for disseminating the national liberation ideology. A few female friends were always to stay at the institute, and those who were not considered suspicious were assigned this task.

But the friends from Dersim weren't always careful enough. One day Türkan, Sevim, and Ayten arrived at my flat, carrying an important document that Şahin Dönmez had just handed them. When I got home, they had opened it and were reading it. I was astonished that they'd broken the rules of secrecy so negligently. I glanced at the text. Who gave this to you, I asked, and why had they read it without permission? "Şahin gave it to us and didn't say anything about it being so important," they answered contritely. How could Şahin have been so careless?

The first part of the text was about current political developments. But the second part detailed people's real names and code names, codes, and allocation of tasks. Now the three friends knew who was active in which area under what name. Yes, Türkan's curiosity and lack of discipline were known to me, but it was an important principle among us to respect confidentiality. I shouldn't have had to berate them for that expressly, but it was a question of trust and commitment.

Türkan didn't think it was all that important, but then she was defiant by nature. Ayten was calmer and more careful, but she could be influenced easily and reacted like Türkan. Sevim, for her part, had principles but lacked the strength to adhere to them. So this simple episode exposed each of the friends' weaknesses. I was furious and let them know it. They told me they understood the seriousness of their breach, but in reality they didn't care.

Şahin arrived to pick up the document. "You should have told the friends the text had nothing to do with them!" I criticized him. "Now they've read it. That's not right. You're too lax. In this respect you're a bad model for the friends." He was hurt. Davut and other friends were present too. Şahin was a leading member, and my unexpected criticism annoyed him, but afterward I felt better.

I remembered that meeting back in İzmir-İnciraltı. Now Şahin had disappointed me for a second time. I no longer trusted him. He acted with indifference toward basic principles of the organization. Did he do it on purpose? I wondered. Why didn't he behave the way his position required? His practice seemed to contradict his political analysis.

Instead of taking my critique seriously, he flopped down into an armchair. "You don't have to tell me what conspiracy means," he said. "They have to know it themselves. No one told them to read the text." I was outraged. Now our mistrust was mutual. No more would I treat him with the warmth I showed other friends, and he let me feel he didn't like me.

Was I prejudiced against Şahin? I wondered. My brother Haydar once told me about a long-ago fight he had with him, back before the movement gained a foothold in Dersim. A sister of Şahin was a prostitute, and [Haydar and Şahin] had beaten each other up. Haydar didn't trust Şahin for another reason as well. They and some others had been arrested in Dersim after an attack on a police station. The police beat them up, then soon after arbitrarily released them. Haydar had found Şahin's behavior toward the police disgusting: "He is such a coward. He all but fell to his knees and begged the police not to hurt him." This story contributed to my wariness of him.

Now I remembered this long-ago incident and looked over at Şahin. There was no need to answer him. He noticed something was off, and to break the tension, Davut cracked a few jokes. Then they left, and only Ayten and I remained in the apartment.

Ayten and I were doing educational work together. She stayed in Bingöl for a while and then would return to Dersim. Her father was strange, a true Kemalist. He spoke highly of us to Mehmet Karasungur: "The friends in Bingöl are smart people with good manners and maturity, but those in Dersim are uneducated, unteachable, and very young." He worked at a bank, drank a lot of alcohol, and gambled. He'd only come to Bingöl to check up on Ayten. He was trying to keep her from the political work.

After Ayten left, I lived with Zozan, a sister of Zeki. One night Baki [Polat] suddenly showed up, saying he had to finish a few classes and would then return to Kurdistan. Apparently he'd left the HK and come over to us.

He had previously sent me a strange letter, saying he was having a hard time with his classes and could I come back to İzmir for a while to help him? Dismayingly, he claimed me as his property. He said he wanted us to have a child to bind us together. That was the world according to Baki. As for organized political work, he was as ineffectual as ever, yet still managed to persuade the friends that he was something he was not. His ideal life conformed to a typical petit-bourgeois worldview: he wanted a normal life, with a wife and children, and to do revolutionary work only on the side.

I let Mehmet the teacher and the others read this letter. They realized they'd deluded themselves about him and gave up trying to persuade me to reconcile with him. The problem could not be solved, either with patience or with force. This letter was the last straw. It was all over, and now I would burn my bridges. I was so mad at myself. When the friends had said we had to win him over to our work, why hadn't I defended myself? After all, I knew him.

I answered his letter, and a little later he arrived unannounced in Bingöl. Blind with jealousy, he behaved like a crazy man, delusional. At first I didn't even want to let him into the flat. We screamed at each other. Zozan, terrified, cringed in a corner. Baki wouldn't listen to me. He surveyed the flat, as if looking for something. It was as if he weren't himself. Finally he said,

> You love someone else. I know you do, otherwise you wouldn't act this way. I'm a revolutionary, too. I'm even more revolutionary than you are. I already was doing this work long before you came along. What's the problem? We don't always have to have the same opinion. What's wrong with my wanting to take you back to İzmir? We're revolutionaries, not robots. Even revolutionaries have children.

A stream of such nonsense poured from his mouth.

I couldn't stand it anymore and got a bread knife from the kitchen. It was new and sharp and almost unused. There was no other weapon in the flat. If I'd had a pistol, I'd have shot him—that was what I wanted to do at that moment. But I grabbed the knife and went at him. He hadn't expected this. I had the advantage, standing in the doorway of a room where there was nothing he could use to defend himself. "Sakine, drop it," he said. "I said all that because I'm angry and love you so much. I'm sorry."

I hardly heard his words and felt about to explode. How dare he? It made me crazy that he'd released all his pent-up anger that way. "Get out of here, you scumbag! How dare you talk to me like that?" I swung the knife and thought I'd hit him, but he held up a hard cushion in front of himself for protection.

Zozan cried, "Stop!"

Our fight could be heard in the neighboring flats on the top floor. A neighbor named Zeytun rang the doorbell, which made me snap out of it. I faltered.

"Don't do this," Baki begged me. "You'll only hurt yourself this way. I'm sorry, I really shouldn't have said all that."

I went to the door. Baki, terrified, went into the other room and closed the door. I tidied my hair and straightened my clothing. I was still quivering from rage as I reluctantly opened the door.

A concerned Zeytun asked what was going on. "Nothing at all," I said. She looked at me with astonishment, then left.

I turned back into the living room and in a fury smashed everything I saw. Then I said to Baki, "Go—get out of here. I won't say it again."

He picked up his suitcase and left the flat. Sami, another neighbor, saw him leave. Sami knew about our fights from our earlier conversations. Once when Kemal Burkay visited, Sami had asked him about us. Maybe he'd found out our true identity that way. In any case, he suspected something was not as it seemed. His mother gazed at us with concern. She didn't know the reason for our fight, but she noticed I'd thrown Baki out. Of course she didn't dare ask.

Zozan normally stayed with me at night, then went to her family during the day. But the next morning we left the flat together and locked the door behind us. I had to talk to the friends. I had a headache. I was so exhausted I could hardly walk. I barely made it to Zeki's. He was surprised to see me. "Come here. Now I understand what you've been going through," he said. "I almost shot that dirtbag myself. I pulled out a weapon and threatened him with it, which got him to leave."

I thought he should have said to Baki, *Sakine is right, and we did her wrong by trying to persuade her to reconcile with you. She knows you better than we do. We tried to win you over, but you're a solitary nuisance. Get out of here, at long last! If you ever annoy our friend or us again, I'll shoot you!*

Baki now grasped the seriousness of the situation, yet still he stayed in Bingöl and looked for an intermediary. He wanted to meet me for one more conversation. But now for the first time, [the friends and I] acted in unity. It just happened. Everyone more or less realized what had happened and were now unanimous that enough was enough. "If we had given this much attention to a fascist, he'd have become a comrade a long time ago!" they said. Zeki joked, "Even when Kurdistan is liberated, Baki won't give up on you." In the end, Baki left the city.

Once again, no unity could emerge as long as there were deep differences of opinion. It was important for us to discuss this issue. The idea that everyone could undergo a revolutionary transformation and turn every marriage into a revolutionary relationship seemed unrealistic—I saw no positive example of it.

Around this time, Hüseyin Durmuş was planning to marry Yıldız, a girl from his village. Both families had approved it. Yıldız was a student who did effective revolutionary work. But Hüseyin's mother was ill and needed caring for. Her daughters were still very young, so she needed a daughter-in-law to manage the household. That was the underlying premise of the marriage-to-be. Zeki experienced problems in his marriage, which could have been as counterargument, yet everyone still assumed marriage was no obstacle to revolutionary work. Davut was ambivalent, sometimes rejecting marriages, other times approving all of them.

I was to travel to Dersim with Davut and bring a revolver. For safety, we took a taxi from Kovancılar to my family's flat, where I was to turn the revolver over to Hamili. Neighbors noticed our arrival and wondered, who was this bulky, rather odd man who'd driven up in a taxi? A rumor spread among the neighbors and friends that Apo had arrived. My mother shared this suspicion at first, but she had keen intuition and didn't like the way he looked. *No, this man can't be Apo,* she concluded.

Warily, she asked who he was.

"He's a friend. Why do you ask so many questions?" I huffed.

"The children are saying he's Apo," she said, "but I don't believe it. *Ti vana gayê Qers o.*"[119]

"Don't talk that way!" I shot back.

She hadn't expected such stridency. "I didn't say anything—he just looks a little odd," she said, distressed.

The next day Davut and I went to the Merkit family's home, as rumors still swirled around him. We asked to talk to Aysel Öztürk. I didn't know her personally, but she was at the Teachers School and had been with the HK, and she had attacked our movement. But under Selim's influence, she'd become a Kurdistan Revolutionary. The two of them had developed an emotional connection. There were discussions and rumors, and I was assigned to get to the bottom of it. Davut suggested she'd be more candid talking to me.

I picked Aysel up, and we went to Dağ, talking along the way. She explained that she'd been an HK member. When the Kurdistan Revolutionaries at her school gained strength, and the factions clashed, she began to have doubts. After she got to know Selim, her interest in his ideology grew. "We discussed it all the time. Then we noticed we were interested in each other, too. We confessed our feelings to each other. Sometimes we walked to school or walked home together. Sometimes we sit down and talk along the Munzur riverbank. That's the state of our relationship."

"What do you mean?" I said. "The friends say your relationship is now so far advanced that it's aroused notice." Davut had insisted that

I ask this question. What was I to do? This kind of inquiry was, for me, extremely unpleasant.

She rejected the criticism. I believed her—her frank description seemed sincere to me. I also thought she would be more effective than Selim in Bingöl. Her family knew about the relationship and wanted to make it official.

Also around this time I went to a meeting in Cemile's village. They discussed the overall picture, then criticized a few friends. If my memory serves, Ali Haydar Kaytan talked about Kıymet:

> In the village of Gülec, there are many young people, but they're all in the Turkish left. Our friend Kıymet has been teaching there for several years, but in all that time she has succeeded in organizing only one person, and she married him.

This person was Zülfü, the man who had played *saz* for us when we visited that time. I was startled—Kıymet and Zülfü! But Zülfü was just a sympathizer to the movement, while Kıymet was cadre! Her choice of him seemed even stranger considering that she looked down on most people except other cadres. Her marriage reminded me of my cousin Cemile's—she had married someone in the Bingöl village where she worked as a teacher. Both women had chosen from among the village men and married the one who, in that limited pool, seemed most suitable. But how had they made these choices—on what criteria? Based on what needs? Had some particular characteristic of these men attracted them? Kıymet's great superciliousness had turned into its opposite. I just couldn't reconcile her mannish demeanor and her revolutionary talk with love for an entirely conventional village man.

But internally I had to smile. Ali Haydar Kaytan hadn't brought up the subject for nothing. It was actually a very serious criticism.

In the evening a few of us returned to the city and stayed overnight at Cemile's. The next morning Yıldırım brought me to my childhood home. It was astonishing how much my mother had changed. In the past it had been a problem if I wanted to leave the apartment for a few hours. Now she just said, "We were worried when you didn't come home at night." We visited a few people together. She liked the friends, she told me, noting which ones had visited, and describing how she'd cared for them. She eagerly told me about the May 1 demonstration, in which she'd participated.

> I wish you'd come back home. You know, other daughters carry on their revolutionary work from home. See—I'm not like I was before. If I'd known what it would lead to, I wouldn't have been so hard on you. I'm uneducated, and I was always afraid something would happen to you or the police would grab you. What would I have done then? I thought I was making sure you fit in somewhere and cooled off, but just the opposite has happened. Now I see I drove you away. Come home, my daughter, work here in Dersim. Believe me, I won't get in your way again.

"Don't worry," I soothed her,

> I'll come back to Dersim from time to time. I'll come home. The bond between you and me will never be broken. My flight has actually brought us back together—you understand that now. But revolutionary work isn't for men only. If my Haydar had done what I did, you wouldn't have created so many problems for him. You wouldn't have been able to. But you had other expectations for me, and that wasn't right. I was already grown up, but your behavior put me in an impossible position. As you can see, we don't do anything wrong. For me, it's no problem to stay in Dersim, but it's not my decision. If the organization says I should stay, then I'll stay. But there are many friends here, while in other places there's a great need, so it's better if I go there.

My mother was also sad about my divorce. I wanted to finish the proceedings—I'd filed for it through a lawyer I knew. I'd have preferred to let him handle it, but the court demanded my presence. When I went to the courthouse, I ran into my uncle, who cried and begged me to withdraw the divorce petition. I tried to reassure him.

Baki didn't show up, so the hearing was postponed. How tedious. How had it come to this? First my flight, then the marriage, and now I was bogged down in these divorce proceedings. Wasn't there a way to do it that didn't require my presence? The answer was negative, since Baki didn't consent to the divorce. Yet he'd promised not to create any difficulties for me!

I returned to Bingöl, then after a while drove to Elazığ with Hamili [Yıldırım]. The chairman and a few friends were there for a meeting. That evening the chairman talked to me again. One of the rooms in the house had beds, and the others were empty. It was wintertime and very cold. I leaned against the wall, while the chairman paced back and forth. We talked again about marriage. I explained the details of my situation and about the friends' attitude up to now.

The chairman chuckled now and then. He said the subject of free and revolutionary relationships was not simple, and then he talked about our struggle and the organization. His loud voice boomed in the empty room. The friends in the next room thought he was shouting at me and wondered why. Worried, one friend opened the door a crack and warned that they could hear us. Later this friend told me, laughing, that he'd been worried about me, "so I peeked in. When I saw the chairman speaking normally, I was reassured." Another told me, "We thought the chairman had hit you!" That cracked me up.

Yes, for the second time, the chairman had had the sensitivity to talk to me about revolutionary relationships, their preconditions, and efforts to achieve unity. The other friends had not thought this question, so important, but the problem wasn't limited to me alone. All along I'd discussed it with the friends and tried to find a solution with them. But because my way of doing it was so clumsy, I'd kept failing. So the problem persisted, and I couldn't stop running around in circles.

How much I'd been through in one year! Now back in Elazığ, I was to begin a new phase of the work. Elazığ offered good prospects for our still-incipient struggle, and despite all the hardships, the work excited me.

Much had changed here. The national liberation ideology was now widely accepted, and the other groups were losing members to us. At this moment, the chairman wanted to meet with all cadres and sympathizers. He kept the meeting secret until the last moment. Only a few friends knew about it, although others guessed. Once the news was out, it spread quickly enough in Elazığ.

We drove in small groups to the village of Birvan. Dev-Genç was active there too, but we had more influence. The meeting was to take place in the primary school. In addition to our friends, members of Dev-Genç participated. The room was filled to overflowing.

The chairman spoke first. His speech was like a manifesto, analyzing history beginning with the first human communities. In simple language yet on a scientific basis, he described the multilayered reality of Kurdistan and discussed the concepts of socialism, revolution, imperialism, internationalism, and patriotism, illustrating with concrete examples.

Everyone listened, riveted. Bülent from Dev-Genç took notes and, to prepare for his own speech, rifled though books and magazines and underlined passages.

Our friends' eyes had been glowing ever since the chairman entered the room. Most were seeing him for the first time. On the table before him were scattered some blank pages. Those who couldn't see that they were empty assumed he was reading something. Sometimes he rearranged the pages or smoothed out the tablecloth. Then he raised his head and adjusted his glasses. He worked with intense concentration. His speech was clear and moving and not the least bit vague. Listening to him strengthened the spirit and the soul. It was one of those joyous moments when one wants to leap into the air and take flight. I was proud and jubilant to be part of this movement. The chairman was a remarkable person in his manner of speaking, his gestures, his entire demeanor, even his appearance. All the comrades were valuable, but the chairman was something else. Before I saw him the first time, I'd imagined what he'd be like as a person. And now here he was sitting across from me and analyzing history, society, the individual, and class. Our movement had as yet no concrete organization and was little known. But the chairman's analyses corresponded to my own thoughts and strengthened my confidence in him.

The second speaker was Bülent of Dev-Genç. The table in front of him was covered with his notes, magazines, and books. That wasn't surprising, knowing the Turkish left—they always slipped quotations into their speeches. They would even cite the book and the page number. Sometimes you wondered if they ever had any thoughts of their own rather than thinking in formulas.

Bülent argued that Kurdistan was not a colony, a country, or a nation, using logic that would have made the old social theorists spin in their graves. He was a skillful and knowledgeable speaker, and he talked longer than the chairman. But he sidestepped the reality of Kurdistan and Turkey. He rejected the national liberation movement emerging from circumstances particular to Kurdistan. As a demagogue, he was really good.

The chairman rose to speak again and rebutted all of Bülent's theses, showing how perverse his approach really was. He said the revolutions in Turkey and Kurdistan were closely connected and showed how conditions could emerge for a common struggle. It was illuminating for those present, as their beaming faces showed. All were impressed by the meeting and wished it could have gone on longer.

For security reasons, everyone had to leave the village by a different route, since the enemy could have been informed about the meeting. We went to downtown Elazığ, where we dropped the chairman off in Ali's family's flat for a brief time—Ali and I had to stop by Aytekin's to take care of something involving a meeting with Rıza. Cemile took the children to another flat upstairs.

This flat, which was on the ground floor, had a door to the street and another to the yard, which one could also reach by another route. We explained that to the chairman and left him a revolver with 12 rounds. We had told Ali's family that no one should enter the lower flat. We wanted it to look as if no one was home. The curtains were so thick that light couldn't penetrate from outside. And from outside, you could barely tell that an indoor light was burning.

It seemed strange to leave him, but the chairman said, "It's okay—go!" As we left, we felt uneasy. "We've made a mistake," we said to each other. "At least one of us should have stayed with him in the flat." But it was too late, and the chairman had warned us not to linger and to return quickly. On the way, we repeated that we'd made a mistake. At the Aytenkins' several friends were visiting. We talked to Rıza, then we talked some more, and lost track of the time. When I glanced over at a clock, I leaped up, and we rushed out of there fast.

When we reached the flat, the light was turned off. The chairman laughed,

Oh, so that's what you call fast? The police passed by. When I saw them, I turned out the light and took up a position at the back door with the revolver. But they didn't come in—they went into another flat, and only briefly. So we're all right this time.

Ali and I looked at each other, horrified. We had been feeling guilty and now were deeply ashamed. If the police had searched the flat and found the chairman with a revolver—the very thought was terrifying!

The next day we talked about our mistake. Ali knew this area—we could easily have taken the chairman to a more secure place. We could still do that. Ali thought of a sympathetic family in town, the chairman asked him about the members, and we went off. This apartment was really much better suited, and the family accommodated us graciously. Only two daughters still lived at home.

The chairman said,

> I don't think it was a coincidence that the police turned up so soon after the meeting in Birvan. Maybe they were informed, or otherwise caught wind of the meeting. Maybe nothing stays secret around here. But we pulled it off, regardless. How did it go, in your opinion? What results do you think the meeting will have? It must have given people food for thought. We have to step up our ideological struggle. Here in Elazığ, it could have a good impact.

The meeting really had left an impression. We soon won over many new members. Our potential was growing, and now we had to organize that potential.

A little later we rented a basement apartment in Fevzi Çakmak, in the home of a man from Pertek. The friends used it to store things we needed for our work. The apartment had blinds—good for security. For a long time no one even noticed that we were there. I told the landlord, "My elder brother is a student, and I work." The friend Cemil Bayık stayed there with me for a while.[120] We had many visitors, and in this respect the friends were very incautious. It was like at the Sarıkayas' except that here we also stored books and weapons—an Uzi and a few revolvers. The friends were always taking the weapons around, to Bingöl, Dersim, Amed, and even Ankara.

I had met Cemil in 1977. He looked younger then—evidently in the past year he'd aged. He spoke Turkish with an Elazığ accent—that stuck in my memory, although we had hardly spoken when we met.

The Fevzi Çakmak neighborhood was like a liberated zone. The friends kept watch at certain points, especially along the route to the police station. Cemil often didn't come home till after nightfall. He hid the Uzi under an overcoat draped over his shoulder. We had only one key to the flat. I was usually out during the day doing educational work with a group of women. I knew a few of the female friends from before, but there were also many new ones. I got to know another group of women when I went to a meeting led by the friend Aytekin in İstasyon neighborhood.

Some groups had to be organized from the ground up. At the Sarıkayas, I met with some old friends from secondary school to set up a schedule for educational work. Among them was Nadire Turgut. Cemil came too, under the impression that it would be a discussion meeting. But I thought he would make a speech to the new friends. So we were both silent. Then Cemil said, "What are you waiting for? Why don't you get started?" I was surprised and couldn't think what to say. In my excitement, I'd mentioned the meeting date. The friends were baffled and finally stood up to leave. Uncomprehending, Cemil asked, "Was that it? What kind of a meeting was that?" Then he jumped in and began to talk about the political situation. That made me feel even worse, since he didn't say anything special—I'd previously given the young women a much more detailed assessment. Why had I failed to communicate with him in orderly sentences? Normally Cemil didn't make me nervous or self-conscious.

Finally Cemil rose to leave, "Be careful when you go home," he said. "Inspections are under way in the neighborhood. We have to take precautions and scrub the flat." They'd taken the weapons someplace else, but I went to check the flat myself. I found a few notes, which I burned in the stove. And we had hidden a few copies of a recent brochure, "Understanding the Right Path," in a hollow space under the staircase. Since it was dark, I couldn't search the space thoroughly. There were also a few IDs there, which I left for now. I burned some photos. The books were still there.

The crackdown went on for a long time. Our flat was on the edge of the neighborhood. Most of the houses had three or four stories. The buildings to our right and across the street had already been searched. As the police got close, I threw the IDs into the stove. What would I say? I'd state my identity openly and tell them I'd separated from my husband and settled in Elazığ. My family supported me financially. The books were available on the free market, and as an educated woman, I liked to read. I lived alone, but sometimes my siblings came to visit—the men's clothing in the flat belonged to them. This story seemed plausible. As I was still thinking about it, the searches came to a sudden end. I was glad for that but regretted that I'd burned the IDs.

Later we looked at the hiding place under the stairs. It was very obvious—anyone could see at a glance that something was hidden there. If we'd been searched, we'd have been exposed instantly. The next day we removed the brochures from the hiding place. They were damp and smelly. I was busy until the following morning drying them page by page and then tying them into a bundle. I gave them to Kurdo, who was to hide them someplace else. So now there was nothing in the flat to raise questions during a search. I heaved a sigh and collapsed into a peaceful sleep.

For over a year now, I'd been doing revolutionary work in Elazığ, in Bingöl, and then again in Elazığ, in efforts that were as amateurish as they were intensive. I'd traveled around with different comrades, I'd got to know other regions and their unique features and seen new aspects of our struggle. At the same time I continued to examine myself and openly discussed my experiences, the progress I'd made with my comrade Cemil, and weak points that I'd discovered in myself and tried to overcome.

After I left İzmir, I had challenged others on certain issues, but much became understandable over time. Figuring out why something had turned out the way it did didn't require such great exertions as it once had. In this early period of my revolutionary life, I had been drawn into episodes that cost me a great deal. I'd been through so much in just this one year, I astonished even myself.

In Bingöl I spoke up about things that bothered me, in a limited way. Under our work system, people discussed and solved their problems among themselves. That's the way it had to be. On the other hand, some problems didn't affect me alone, so I wanted to talk with the friends about them, but also about every subject that touched me. It became routine, but it bothered me when people around me weren't up for it. Did this method solve all problems? I can't say it did.

I talked to Cemil a lot. I'd written my experiences down but kept the text to myself, then later, for security reasons, I had to destroy it. It was easy to tell Cemil about my escape from home, my marriage, and the divorce, tragic events that saddened, hurt, and angered me. Talking about them brought the feelings back to the surface. I didn't gloss over anything, but sometimes I felt like an actress. My words, my behavior, and my expressions reflected my feelings directly. I held nothing back, which surprised even me. I talked about my weaknesses, my vulnerabilities, my sorrows, my shame. I cried bitter tears, but not from shame or anger at my "fate." Here's what I said, so as not to be misunderstood:

Right now I'm not helpless. On the contrary, I think I'm on the right track. I feel stronger now. I'm just angry. When I look back, I see that none of it was necessary. I'm angry at my own weakness and at everything that held me back. Theoretically it may be true that struggle can lead to weakness, failure, and defeat. But there are some experiences that a person can't just deny. And you shouldn't deny them. Maybe it's inevitable that we experience things that leave scars behind. In life there must be experiences that cause pain—otherwise it would be boring.

Cemil was moved by these words, which I read to him through tears.

Why are you crying? You've solved the problem! Of course a revolutionary must be aware of his own progress, and of the possible consequences, since so much is at stake. The friends have told me a little about you, but not this much. I'm glad to know more about this affair now. But you really don't have to agonize about it anymore.

It wasn't a formal conversation, but I'd explained the events as if I'd been reliving them. To me, in my eyes, Cemil wasn't just a person— he was a stand-in for the organization. So I'd revealed myself to the organization. It wasn't that I'd opened my heart in a simple conversation. Our relationship could now develop more objectively. After all, rumors, and mistaken or exaggerated assessments and remarks, can lead to judgments that affect relationships.

During the time we worked together, Cemil always kept a certain distance. We shared the flat and the work, but he always acted toward me in a comradely and respectful way. He didn't discuss much with me. What was the reason for this disparity? Sometimes I wondered if it was my doing. Cemil normally didn't get into ideological discussions—he talked more about internal organizational matters, the daily course of work, or current developments. Sometimes he talked at length about subjects that had already been gone over several times. In such cases, he didn't push things forward and even sometimes aroused uncertainty. But he gave us all ideational strength. Wherever he went, he created an ambience of trust, seriousness, and straightforwardness, and all the friends, without exception, felt it.

Like the Green Line in Beirut Many demonstrations and rallies took place in Elazığ, mostly in or near Fevzi Çakmak. Whenever the fascists killed someone, Dev-Genç would turn up at the funeral, less out of revolutionary responsibility or desire for revenge than to keep their members in line using propaganda and agitation. At every demonstration, Gavur Ali would climb up onto some elevated structure and deliver a speech. The content was always the same and always unappealing. They used the funerals as assets that they otherwise would have lacked. If they had really been concerned with revolutionary values and traditions and had been true to the legacy of Mahir Çayan, we'd have respected them. But no, far more often they did the exact opposite of what Mahir and his comrades would have done.

They might have helped people understand the real problems and goals of the struggle, as well the nature of the enemy and the means to proceed, and thereby politicized them and set them in motion. But they missed the point. You don't honor a martyr by waging a war of words.

Even as the national liberation ideology was spreading and transforming the political discussion, Dev-Genç had internal problems. It introduced no basic new content, and its members were leaving in droves. The Turkish left's tradition of losing influence through constant splits emerged at this time. This group was notable for careerism and a narrow class perspective. Since it lacked a suitable leadership or vanguard, its regional structures developed according to the preferences of local activists. The local chapters increasingly varied from area to area. So was it with Dev-Genç in Elazığ, where Gavur Ali shaped the group.

On this day the fascists had shot someone who was on his way from the city center to Fevzi Çakmak. Most of the attacks happened on this street—it was like Beirut's "green line."[121] The city center and the Kültür neighborhood were under fascist control. The leftist groups had retreated to other neighborhoods and thereby entrenched the split within the city.

The person killed was a Kurdish worker. We took part in the funeral, bearing the coffin, along with a huge crowd of people, to a village cemetery beyond Fevzi Çakmak. We repeatedly shouted, "Martyrs never die!" All the groups shouted, "Down with fascism," and each group had its own slogan. Ours was "Down with colonialism!" After the funeral, we returned to the neighborhood and dispersed. But the other groups kept marching, and pretty soon shots were heard. At first we thought the police had attacked. A few of us ran toward where the shots had come from, to find out more.

We heard that Ali Rıza Kaçar had been shot. That was strange. He had been with Stêrka Sor, but rumor had it that he had left after the shooting of Alaattin Kapan: a hard blow for this group of agents, but it avenged Haki Karer. We had distributed flyers in Elazığ clarifying that group's true position. After the Kapan shooting, they distributed unsigned flyers in a few coffeehouses. We did some research and found out who had distributed them and who was still operating in the group's name. Ali Rıza Kaçar had said he had nothing to do with them anymore. So was his murder an internal settling of accounts? The rumor mill was working overtime. At first we thought his own people had killed him. When we asked people coming from the crime scene, they said, "It wasn't the police, it was Gavur Ali!" There were eyewitnesses. This episode ensured that an uproar would arise and bloody clashes among the different groups. It all alarmed the residents, who thereafter stayed home whenever a demonstration took place.

When I first came to Elazığ, none of the other groups had organized any women's activities. Young women were active only as individuals. But now a transformation was under way. Female cadres arrived from elsewhere, and women attended meetings of different groups. In the city squares, groups competed for female members, as I had seen back in Dersim. Their way of dressing was a bad imitation of leftist groups in Dersim. Many young women were interested in revolutionary work, and the leftist groups tried to win them over. Sometimes we met in the same home—they tried to recruit the women with whom we worked. Sometimes they did the exact opposite and punished with contempt the families that were associated with us.

The shot backfired Every day our numbers grew, and our range of activities broadened. We were now represented in almost all the neighborhoods. We tried to avoid repeating the mistakes of the other groups. Women's interest and participation were growing. We set up women's education groups everywhere and expanded our outreach into the schools. Around this time the students at the Teachers School were transferred to Mardin, so the school could be turned into a secondary school. We had already formed ties with many of the students and given them insight into our ideology. I assumed that some of them would reach out to the friends again. And I learned from their occasional visits to Elazığ that they did maintain the ties.

Whenever talk turned to the Teachers School in Elazığ, the students always mentioned Çetin Güngör (Semir). His family lived here, and we were in touch with them, especially his sister, who was, however, under a lot of family pressure and so couldn't contribute much to the work. Especially my cousin Makbule told me about Çetin Güngör. The Girls Art School and the Teachers School were in the same neighborhood, separated only by a street.

The boarding students, because of the repressive school system, were always stressed out and so were all the more interested in the opposite sex. Sometimes the repression led to extreme behavior. Semir, as the only male student at the school, was at the epicenter of female interest. He'd learned there to be very relaxed in the presence of women.

Semir didn't fit in with his family at all. Attending the school and later doing revolutionary work ruptured his connection to them. He was always moving around in Dersim. His theoretical level was high, so he was often invited to speak at seminars and other discussion forums. He was well known for it. He'd honed his skills not in organizing work or in practice but in agitation and had learned how to work within the prevailing political atmosphere.

For us, it was important to reach out to students at the Girls Art School, young women from all the Kurdish regions. But the fascists were also active in such places. Working under the smokescreen of religion, they enjoyed the covert or overt support from the school administration and so were able to build their sphere of influence. So we had to lay the basis for revolutionary work at the school and then let the students themselves lead it. We'd recruited a few members from the external students in Kırkdutlar and Yıldızbağları. They gave us information about the situation in the schools, and through them we tried to gain a foothold. The fascists were also recruiting in the Health School, the Trade School, and Euphrates University, so it was urgent for us to get involved there too.

I met Cahide Şener and a few other girls when Cemil and I visited the Sarıkayas. Cahide came from Siverek, while the others were from Çüngüş and Çermik. Cahide's father came from the Karakeçeliler tribe, who are of Turkish descent, and her mother was of Armenian heritage. Siverek was home to many tribal conflicts. To organize a woman from these feudal structures would be an important step.

Cahide introduced herself as the daughter of a mufti.[122] Her clothing signaled that she came from a religious family, but we weren't interested in that. We talked about many things with her. She told us about Siverek, the DDKD there, and her school. She was interested in the Kurdish issue and so had ended up at the Sarıkayas. She herself had no organizational tie to the DDKD. She was trying to understand the conflicts among the various Kurdish groups. She knew about us only from hearsay. She'd noticed the DDKD's agitation against our movement, and that induced her to reach out to us. She seemed articulate and intelligent. According to her, the fascists had brought hundreds of young Kurdish women into their ranks by using religion. Cemil and I asked her a lot of questions. Beaming at us, she exclaimed, "I've finally found what I was looking for!" We were glad too, since the schools offered much potential for our work.

"As the women's organizing continues, the work will get easier," I said. "If we have these women, we can easily gain a foothold in the school." We agreed with Cahide that we should meet every weekend. "Bring a few girls who you trust and who have good prospects for development. We'll organize the school with you."

Nadire Turgut, Saniye, Leyla, and a few other young women were at the Atatürk High School. We put Nadire in charge of the work there, unofficially and tentatively. At the Health School there were external students who we could reach through Nesrin and her sisters. I visited them sometimes. There were also young women from Dersim and Erzincan, and I knew the Dersim women's families a little, which made the outreach easier. The school administration had built a reactionary network here: many of the teachers were religious, and important MHP collaborators were active in the school. They forced the students, even those who were Alevi, to perform ritual prayer and fasting. Anyone who tried to resist was threatened with bad grades. And many of the teachers tried to exploit girls they liked. They had turned grade-giving into a weapon.

The students were often compelled to inform on each other to the school administration, which created an atmosphere of mistrust. The younger ones were most fearful. For students in the upper classes, their personalities had already been formed by the existing system. The external students knew more about the outside world and could have followed the developments, and were easier to get hold of. But they were very cut off. When I visited them, we talked about many things, at least beginning to guide their thoughts in other directions.

On weekends Cahide came to our basement flat with Güler and Havva. They had received permission to be away from the dorm for three days because of holidays. They were impressed by our way of life and the subjects we talked about. The first "revolutionaries" the three of them had ever met were members of DDKD or other nationalist groups. Now when they drew comparisons, our way of life came off well. Even more than the content we tried to transmit, they were impressed by what they saw. We talked about staying in touch and working together. May 1 was approaching, and I suggested they organize a celebration in the school. I emphasized how important it was to organize a small nuclear group but also to reach as many people as possible and aim to build a large circle of sympathizers. They would have to reach out to those who seemed less committed and explain the Kurdish liberation ideology to them. They should position themselves politically in contrast to all others and work toward establishing themselves through revolutionary action. I discussed in detail what they should pay most attention to.

Cahide listened with interest, signaled her agreement, and offered suggestions. She was smart and a quick student. She was also a good organizer. We were sure she'd develop fast, and even though she was a boarding student, she soon produced contacts for us and got more students interested in our work. During the next period she would report to us regularly, either in writing or verbally, about the situation in her school.

Moreover, having seen the state of our flat, she sent us blankets, food, and other things from the school. These were small things, but just the fact that she had thought of it was meaningful. We trusted her to do good work. She impressed the teachers as well as the students. At the Girls Art School, needlework, among other things, was taught, and here she showed talent. She got good grades, was praised by the teacher, and was in a position to teach others. A person regarded as exemplary in daily life is in a good position to influence others politically.

Our work at the school continued. The students used their study periods for the educational work and discussions. The May 1 celebration had good results. A few of the young women broke with the fascists. Of course Cahide's role didn't go unnoticed. She had long been a favorite of the female teachers, but the division of the students into right and left and the associated unrest disturbed the school administrators, who reprimanded Cahide.

Occasionally I went to the school grounds as a visitor. Trying to be inconspicuous, I sat with female students in small groups and answered their questions. But when these visits were noticed, I had to stop. But then, it was not only safer but better to let the students do the organizing work themselves.

We were in regular communication with external students and kept each other current with new developments and insights. Our work bore fruit: we were soon the school's largest and most influential political group. We positioned sympathizers in the school's various work areas, like cooking, library, and study hall, until they were usually on our side. During the homework period, they could lead discussions and read flyers. The kitchen soon provided for most of our own subsistence needs and cleaning supplies. They diverted many essential items, from salt to soap, to us, which considerably reduced our financial straits living in that flat.

During this time Meral Kıdır arrived in Elazığ, having finished her education in Mardin. One day Cemil brought her over, saying, "I've brought you a new friend." We hugged like two girlfriends who'd known each other for ages. When Cemil left us alone, we laughed and wondered that we both felt this closeness to each other. We'd never seen each other, although we'd heard of each other. Elif, a young Turkish woman from Miseli, had told me about her on her vacation, saying, "We have another Turkish friend, called Meral."

Elif herself had not impressed me: she'd stayed overnight at the Sarıkayas, then gone to Mişeli, where, disconcertingly to the village, she went swimming in a bikini in the Keban Dam Lake. The village was near the city and wasn't reactionary, but you had to consider certain things. Activities of revolutionaries were observed closely, and the people knew that not everyone could lead a revolutionary life. I'd seen Elif again when she drove by Elazığ to Mardin. I told Meral, "She has no fixed personality. She talks too much, she's a real chatterbox, and her behavior is self-indulgent." Meral agreed.

Meral was small and vivacious. Up to then I'd worked and lived mostly with male friends, which had not been a problem and hadn't hindered my work. But working with a female comrade was much nicer. I was glad to no longer be the only woman. Meral explained that her recent time in Mardin had been hard—"I couldn't do anything except read"—but in Elazığ there was a lot to do. Our sphere of influence was broad now and she could be active in many different areas. Later Sakine Kırmızıtaş, who had spent a long time in Mardin, joined us. She happily took the initiative and was eager for action. After a while she went back to Mardin because female friends were needed there.

Several of the young women we knew who had gone to Mardin for school returned to Elazığ and enthusiastically enrolled in our education work. It much improved the group's quality. Meanwhile almost all the local educational institutions had become centers for the national liberation struggle. All our new cadres came from these schools and then built bridges to other parts of the society. The state had tried to sway the teachers-to-be in favor of Kemalism: it instituted an abbreviated school term, in order to bind the young people to the state and obstruct their development as revolutionaries. But that had been an enormous mistake—the shot backfired.

Around this time we received our "manifesto" from the friends.[123] Some of us had already read and discussed it, and now we distributed it further. The title had been kept secret. We wrapped envelopes around it that said, *This must not be removed.* No explanation was needed: everyone who received the document handled it with an awareness of responsibility. Many valuable comrades, as I recall, kept the manifesto at home without knowing the title.

The manifesto became the most important source of our educational work. All the friends had the duty to understand the particularities of our revolution in historical context. Concepts that were used by others had to be given content so that they had specific meaning. Only this could ensure the raising of revolutionary consciousness and the necessary personality transformation.

Such a moment will come   Hikmet Tekin, the mayor of Bingöl, was shot, but he survived. He was to be taken by helicopter to the state hospital in Elazığ, and if possible, we were to try again there. Everything happened quickly. Chaos reigned in Fevzi Çakmak and near the hospital, as ever more people converged there, and police vans careened with wailing sirens through the streets. Shots were heard. As the helicopter bearing the wounded Hikmet Tekin landed atop the hospital, the friends carried out a further action. The attack in Bingöl had caused joy and excitement, and it was to be completed here in Elazığ. The purpose was to make clear the groups' revolutionary commitment. If an action was to be carried out, it must be absolutely successful.

The crowd dissipated into the side streets. Back at our flat, I looked around at the books and other materials. I didn't touch them—there was no opportunity to hide them. I locked the door and went back outside. Everyone was looking anxiously toward Kum Deresi [Sand Stream], an area beyond the cemetery. Several helicopters circled overhead. Never before had the enemy demonstrated such strength. What did the friends have to do with Kum Deresi? Could it be about another group? The friends were nowhere to be seen. I went to the Sarıkayas, but none of them were there. Mother Zencefil told me, "Cemil was just here. The friends have done an action. One group went over to the neighborhood, and another toward Kum Deresi. The police are chasing them. It's dangerous, the dogs will catch the young people."

So it was true! A friend and I headed toward Esentepe, to watch close up. Police had occupied the whole area.

The long, dry streambed consisted only of sand and gravel. On the side, toward Esentepe, it was difficult to get out. On the other side lay a flat field, where you could climb out. A little farther along lay a village where mainly fascists lived. The helicopter continued its aerial surveillance. On the ground, police were everywhere, and the friends were nowhere to be seen. The police had shot at a few rocks, and at first I thought the fragments were corpses lying on the ground. We were still far away and couldn't make anything out. If we'd had binoculars, we could have had some clarity, but where could we have obtained binoculars? The people here were poor!

The noise of the choppers and the shots scattered a herd of sheep that had been in the field. A group of civil police at a strategic point coordinated the search operation by radio. We sent a few children closer to listen in.

The chaos and the shooting went on for several hours. Toward evening, clouds darkened the sky, and a light rain began, limiting the enemy's mobility. We had no idea what was happening with the friends. The uncertainty was unbearable. Consumed with worry, we went back to the Sarıkayas, to ask if they'd heard anything. The news broadcasts were saying that the enemy had pursued the group but lost their trail as darkness fell. That was good news—everyone was unharmed. There was no information about anyone being captured.

We were all worried about Duran, who had come to Elazığ a few days earlier, and tried to figure out where he was. Someone said he'd been in the neighborhood's hospital during the action, while another reported seeing him at Kum Derisi. In the absence of accurate information, we speculated. Suddenly, amid all the excitement, he turned up, having survived the four hours of shooting from beginning to end.

The friends, he told us, had fled the police, heading for the streambed. Duran had seen them running and went in that direction but he didn't reach them. Amid the tumult, he hid in a hollow on the edge of a slope. Coincidentally, the police had chosen exactly this spot to coordinate their deployment. Since they directed all their attention at the fleeing friends, they didn't notice him. But Duran had overheard all their conversations. They were so close, he could even hear their breathing. Excitedly he reported now what had happened.

> It lasted about four hours, until it got dark. I didn't know what to do. It was almost unendurable—at times I even held my breath. But I had to choose between getting through those four hours or spending four years in prison. I decided for the four hours. And after the police left, I immediately forgot the torture.

We listened to him with surprise and joy. One friend joked, "If they'd caught you, you'd have been in the joint for more than four years. But yes, four years is a long time too!"

While the friends who had carried out the action were fleeing, it began to rain. That gave them an advantage, since the enemy had to call off the pursuit. But they had to trudge for hours through mud. By the time they reached Baskil, their shoes had crumbled. Hüseyin Taze had had the worst of it—his feet were split open and bloody.

In Baskil, the teacher Medine Vural took the friends to her home and cared for them. Some of the friends had relatives living in the village. They were ready to help and hid them in their houses. That night they sent us news via a driver from the village. Saim Durson, who had been following the crowd, was arrested but then released on bail. No weapons or documents were found on him.

After a while the group left Baskil. We tended Hüseyin's wound in our flat, using whatever means we had. It was the first time I'd ever done that. He hadn't been shot, but his wound was still significant.

While I was wrapping it, I felt his pain. It was an unavoidable part of the struggle that comrades would be wounded, die, or end up in prison. But I couldn't stand it if someone had even a bloody nose. Just the thought of death or a wound in a friend was hard for me. A lot of the friends said, "Calm down. Nothing's happened to us yet! There'll be moments when we'll have to fight alongside the corpses of comrades. We'll take their weapons and carry on."

I didn't contradict them. This aspect of the struggle was indeed unavoidable. A revolutionary had to be ready to pay a high price. But it was one thing to be ready for anything and another to feel pain. Was it possible to feel great joy at achieving a goal without admitting deep pain at the losses? When a person loves, one inevitably feels great emotions. Isn't that the meaning of love and connectedness? How can a wealth of intense feelings be separated? Some intense feelings induce us to fight, while others obstruct success. The nature of class struggle can't be changed. Everything and everyone there is involved in the war. Hatred of the class enemy surely doesn't demand a bloodbath. Yet in the struggle for a free future for humanity, human losses are unavoidable.

Impressed by these events, I scrutinized myself and came to the conclusion that one must be able to endure difficult situations and pain without considering them as normal. What kind of pain makes us stronger, and what kind weakens and immobilizes us? That was the crux of the matter. But this insight didn't change my emotionality. After all, theoretical answers weren't enough.

Our work became ever more wide-ranging. We no longer confined ourselves to young people and intellectual circles. Our actions against state institutions won sympathy for the national liberation struggle. We expanded into other neighborhoods and a few villages. Our meetings had ever-greater participation, and new regional committees were founded.

In Yıldızbağları many workers sympathized with us and got in touch. We organized evening meetings to meet them and try to figure out whether the basis for forming workers' committees was there. The people in Palu tended to favor the MHP. Many tradespeople were Sunni Zaza, who constituted much of the MHP's base. In Yıldızbağları I worked mainly with Ali Gündüz. Women participated in the meetings too, so it was better with both of us.

Deaf Metin was involved with youth work. Hamili organized crucial military actions. But this division of labor wasn't strictly enforced, as everyone was ready to carry out the work. Ali Gündüz and I sometimes drove to other districts, like Karakoçan and Hozat. Karakoçan had once been part of Bingöl province but later was shifted to Elazığ. The villages around Keban sympathized with us and we had many contacts. In Maden we had only individual sympathizers, we didn't succeed in organizing the people there. We had few groups in the Hozat district.

In Hozat we sometimes stayed overnight with a certain family. The grandmother's descriptions of the Dersim genocide touched me deeply. Crying, she told me how in 1938 two young women at the Hozat spring had been abducted and raped: "I can still hear their cries. They hid in the pantry of a house. They were very beautiful young women. The soldiers burst into the house and found them, then attacked them like animals." The old woman faltered and seemed to lose herself in the past. Then: "They were raped several times. Their cries are unforgettable." It wasn't hard to persuade people like her, who had experienced the Dersim genocide, about the necessity of our struggle in Kurdistan.

In Hozat, Dev-Genç tried to reorganize under the name Dev-Sol,[124] but it didn't achieve much influence. TİKKO was active here too. And we had contacts there. Early on, Cahit was our representative in Hozat. He was a teacher and beloved in his community. We organized several meetings and discussions with our sympathizers. In the family home where we stayed, the daughters belonged to different factions, while the sons were with us. One of the sisters was with TİKKO, the other with Dev-Sol. We had discussions with young women from other leftist groups who were receptive to revolution. Hozat was a small district where people were quickly influenced by events. The women were very active. A recent incident here had led to upheavals among the people: soldiers had raped a young woman, leading to street protests. The population was changing. Many went to work in Europe or in the large Turkish cities. The social and political standards were rather progressive. Our trip to Hozat helped us assess the possibilities for revolutionary work there and prepare for it.

Çemişgezek [in Dersim] had a different social structure. The fascists were organized here, and after 1938 Turkish families had settled here, as in Pertek. The MHP benefited from that. But in Karakoçan, cosmopolitanism predominated.[125] Mazlum and Delil Doğan were from Karakoçan—they were known as revolutionaries and had influence in the boarding school. At this time actions against several informers in Karakoçan were being planned. Not long before, a police van had been shot at, leading to tension, and searches and ID inspections were constant.

To avoid the danger of a house search, we stayed in a different place every night. Once we stayed with Mazlum, a son of our Şavak neighbors in Dersim. I knew from that time that he was a revolutionary. Earlier our contact had been limited, but now, happily, we were comrades. Both brothers had married women from their own tribe. The wife of Mazlum looked older than he, which surprised me. She was a quiet, sedate woman with no apparent ideas about politics, but she behaved very respectfully and hospitably toward us.

Finally we went to a house where many friends, like Rahime and Baki Kahraman, stayed. Ali Gündüz learned there about the situation in Karakoçan and the state of the friends' development. I listened, riveted. Later for security reasons we were taken to a house near the reform school, outside the city. It would be easier for us to disappear from there, should an unexpected situation arise. On the way the friends pointed out the house of Mazlum Doğan—now empty—and the flat where Kesire had stayed for a while.

The house where we were to sleep belonged to Gönül Tepe's family. I was happy to visit her. Unlike her uncle, her mother was very warm, and the oldest daughter was relaxed. Gönül was vivacious. She had two other siblings—the family was large. We discussed various topics. Gönül asked one question after another and described the situation in the city and their contacts with other young women. She wanted to leave the city and work professionally. She kept pointing out that the police were aware of her and that Karakoçan could become dangerous for her.

That had already been considered. Very soon more friends would be needed to organize the students during their vacation. Women could connect better with other women. I pulled Gönül aside. "You have an anarchistic soul," I told her. She laughed—she liked it. Her sister wanted to join us. Their mother didn't take our conversation seriously, but at times her face fell, as if she were silently wondering, *Have they come to take my daughters away?* To soothe her, I said several times, "It's not necessary for everyone to leave their family. People can fulfill their obligations from home too."

The food was great, and we talked until late into the night. In bed, Gönül and I kept on talking. With her warm personality, she often played a leading role in clashes with the fascists in Bingöl. She had the potential to develop further and the capability to work anywhere politically. But we had to find an advocate for the activities in Karakoçan. After talking with Cemil about it, I concluded that Gönül was mature enough.

After these visits, Ali Gündüz and I returned to Elazığ. We had left behind some literature in the flat, in which names were listed. During the whole trip, I had been annoyed by my own negligence. The flat could be searched at any time. Normally I didn't keep written notes. I couldn't shake my unease, although Ali Gündüz was less bothered.

When we got on the bus, there were no free seats. A young man offered me the seat next to his mother. That was a good thing, because not long afterward, at Kovancılar, an ID inspection took place. I signaled Ali with hand signs. We agreed that we didn't know each other and that the woman next to me was my relative. Her astute son bent over to her and said in Kurdish, "She's the daughter of your brother and is called Ayşe." The woman nodded her veiled head in agreement. We sat next to each other for a short time, and I tried to talk to her, but she spoke Kurmancî and I spoke Zazaki, and she didn't understand much Turkish. Just before the ID inspection, she laid her hand confidently on my shoulder and stroked my hair. I liked her. Her veil was an advantage too, since in the eyes of the gendarme, it would raise her credibility.

The bus was stopped. The soldiers raised their weapons. The commanding officer said, "Everyone get out, ID inspection. Leave your things in the bus."

Since we two were the only women, we got out last. The officer said, "Oh, women too? Make way for the ladies!"

The woman laid her hand on my shoulder, then took my hand. "She's my niece," she told the officer. I pretended to be looking for my ID in my purse.

"Okay, that's not necessary," he said. "You're a civil servant?"

"Yes, I'm a civil servant," I said. He looked me over from head to toe. My clothing was orderly. The officer thanked us and said, "Please pardon the disturbance, madame."

We got back on the bus while the other passengers were searched. The officer boarded the bus and inspected the compartment. The woman got nervous, and I tried to reassure her. But the officer was just putting on a show to demonstrate his own importance.

After the inspection, the bus continued on its way. The woman said a prayer of gratitude, relieved that all had gone well. The young man looked at me, smiling. He and Ali Gündüz were relieved too. It wasn't good to be traveling without an ID. Formerly women's IDs weren't even inspected, but that had changed. I'd been lucky. In the future I'd have to be more careful.

We didn't spend much time thinking about precautions back then. As long as the enemy wasn't attacking us that very instant, we tended to be careless. Then an inspection like this one would make us aware of our negligence. It was urgent that I get an ID. Once again I thought of the documents I'd left behind in the flat. Such mistakes just couldn't be allowed to happen. As soon as we got to the flat, I destroyed the documents.

"Who is this man?" The chairman came to stay with us in the basement flat. It was damp, almost intolerably so during the cold season. We'd installed a small stove in the front room, near the entrance, but since we didn't have any wood, it was pretty useless. Sometimes we burned wooden boxes that we bought at a shop, which warmed the place up a little, briefly.

All the objects in the apartment came from Bingöl. The most valuable thing was the curtains, so at least the flat looked good from the outside. We owned only the essentials: a twin bed in the front room, another in the back room. We kept the bedclothes clean, as well as the flat as a whole. Sometimes before going to bed, we ran a hot iron in a handcloth over the beds, to get rid of the dampness and warm the sheets. The chairman remarked, "The beds are clean but a little damp."

During the period he stayed with us, I was mostly out during the daytime, taking care of my work. He would be alone in the flat. One day when I came home, he was cleaning the place very carefully. Wherever he cleaned, there was no dirt or disorder. In the morning he ate bread with onions.

Nothing that had to do with life was a matter of indifference to him. Everything was part of his struggle. He radiated a magnetism that changed everything. While he was in Elazığ, he moved from one flat to another several times. He talked and excited interest in everyone he met.

His very presence pulled things together. During our free moments, we lounged in the flat and pored over newspapers and books. Sometimes the chairman looked up from his newspaper and asked those present for their opinions on the most important reports. One day a friend named Memo stopped by to visit. Memo participated in the revolutionary work in Elazığ but was a bit of a joker. For him, the placidity of the flat was exceptional. He tried to loosen things up a few times, but no one went along with it. Finally he sat down and pretended to read a newspaper. The chairman watched him.

Memo hadn't had much schooling and didn't like to read. He was more of an activist. He just skimmed newspapers and asked questions about the photos. He was clearly bored as he paged through the newspaper lackadaisically, unaware of how loudly he was rustling the paper. Suddenly the chairman pointed to an article. "What does this say?" he asked. Memo was caught—he couldn't answer. He repeated the headline, lamely, but that was all he could do. The chairman said, "Read the newspaper properly. It's not enough to read headlines."

For the rest of the evening Memo was silent and thoughtful. As he was leaving, he said to me at the door, in irritation, "Who is that man? Why'd he jump at me that way? People who want to read will read, and whoever doesn't won't." I didn't answer, since his questions had to do with the chairman. We explained such things to no one.

Later, after the chairman left Elazığ, Memo found out who it was who had rebuked him that day. Like a kid, he stamped his feet in rage: "Why didn't you tell me? Okay, from now on, I'll read, and I'll even do it happily!" Actually he didn't go on to read much, but at least he tried to keep his word for a while.

Cemil encouraged me to read the new draft program and to research the history of Communist parties. I read up on the Vietnam Workers' Party, the Bolshevik Party, and the Communist Party in China. I took notes. Meral and I wrote an article on the subject, but it was a little vague. The movement was becoming a political force. It needed cadres who had wide-ranging knowledge and could respond to current events.

The way the chairman did research was exemplary and came to be regarded as distinctive about our movement. It involved learning from leftist movements in other countries. What constituted a party, how did parties work, how could that model be adapted to conditions particular to Kurdistan? We discussed these questions. Ali Gündüz, Hüseyin Topgüder,[126] Deaf Metin, and all the other friends in the revolutionary work had to grapple with these topics.

Hüseyin Topgüder, from Palu, had been a leading cadre for the KUK[127] before coming to us. Our relations with the KUK were strained, especially in Mardin, where we had to publicly clarify the class nature of such petit-bourgeois nationalist groups. We focused on the ideological struggle, and violent clashes were sometimes unavoidable. But the enemy also tried to weaken us through such groups. Then members of the KUK defected to us en masse. Our clear, knowledge-based ideology, which accorded with the many aspects of Kurdistan's reality, influenced more and more people. Every upstanding person who understood the necessity of revolution and was aware of the specific conditions in Kurdistan simply had to become a member of our movement.

Friends who came to us from other groups brought their own traits and habits with them. Hüseyin seemed stolid and calm, but he actually loved to talk. He had a high level of theoretical knowledge and knew what it meant to belong to an organization. But he was clearly shaped by the KUK. The Kurdistan Revolutionaries were very different: they were militant and versatile and even talked in a different way, yet they shared connectedness, respect, and love. Hüseyin was as valuable as other comrades, and I sensed a certain closeness in him from the common work, although distance persisted between us. Haydar Eroğlu was livelier, more spirited and spontaneous. He organized our sympathizers at the Atatürk High School. He could sway people with his fine rhetoric.

Through other friends from Palu, we reached the shopkeepers in the city center. Organizing them had been one of our main tasks for a long time. In many shops we could hide weapons and prepare actions. Our serious actions against informers and fascists forced many of them to leave the area. Our movement was known for its practice. Whenever the subject of revolutionary violence came up, people first thought of the Kurdistan Revolutionaries. We were called UKO or "nationals." Our flyers bore the headline "Kurdistan Revolutionaries," although almost no one used that label.

Ali Gündüz was educated in theory and an able organizer. At first he focused on winning over members in the university but later broadened his range. He was more successful than Deaf Metin. Metin's theoretical level was high too, but when interacting with people, he was fussy and moody. Of course, his deafness played a role. Often he couldn't understand what was being said at first, and the person he was talking to would have to repeat it. He spent most of his time in coffeehouses.

Those in Elazığ, especially in Fevzi Çakmak, functioned like meeting rooms. We sought out other groups' headquarters, and the discussions that developed were very effective for us.

People kept trying to present our politics as contradictory, like so: "The UKO rejects democratic institutions and legal work, but they always go to others' meetings and have even started some themselves. That's illogical." For the other groups, their headquarters were their essential arena of operation, so they advised us to embrace their politics or else stay away. Our position was that the enemy had destroyed the conditions for democratic work in Kurdistan, so how could one then speak of democratic institutions?

When the discussions turned to this issue, the friends said, "In Kurdistan we can't even found a bird-protection association. What do the associations you've founded really stand for? Think about that." The leftist groups founded theirs on bylaws to promote culture or uplift, and they considered their existence an exercise of democratic rights, but that was nonsense. We had no qualms about using their clubs as a means to an end. Some of ours were banned as soon as they were founded—the enemy didn't allow us to exercise democratic rights. The leftist groups didn't want to see that happen to them. But we still went to existing meetings to discuss and to inform people about our ideology.

The founding congress In our work and discussions, we were preoccupied with founding a party. Cemil looked over our notes and addressed a few points. He talked about democratic centralism, the way classical Communist parties functioned, and the question of how to manage such an organizational structure among ourselves. His view was that centralism must assume greater significance.

Through discussion, we concluded that the preconditions for revolutionary organization in Kurdistan were different from those in other places and that we had to adapt to our particular needs. Cemil analyzed the level of our struggle and its impact on the society. He raised questions, then answered them himself. I realized that these discussions were intended to prepare us for something, but I didn't know what. I could only guess that it would mean changes in our organizational structure. But I didn't ask, and revolutionary conspiracy and discipline didn't allow for speculation.

Then one day Cemil said to me, "Get ready—we're going." Hüseyin Topgüder came with us [in a bus]. Ali Gündüz was already en route with another group. It was the end of November and very cold. I didn't have the right clothing. And for security reasons, I didn't want to travel wearing the clothes I'd been wearing in Elazığ. Hints were dropped that the journey ahead would be long, so I got some spare clothes from Cemile, who was a teacher—a coat and shoes—and Semra gave me pants and a sweater. Then we hit the road.

The bus stopped in Maden for a break. The architecture there was interesting: the town was built on a rocky slope, and the houses were stacked on top of each other. At the foot of the slope lay a riverbed. From where we stopped, we could see the whole village.

Toward evening we reached Amed. At a previously arranged meeting point, Hüseyin split off from us. I rode on with Cemil to a house in Bağlar.

I still didn't know why I was traveling or where. But I didn't ask questions. Saime Aşkın opened the door to us, and the chairman was inside. We shook hands. Next to his seat were a few books: a history of the Russian Social Democratic Workers Party and Lenin's *One Step Forward, Two Steps Back* and *What Is to Be Done?* I picked them up and looked at them.

The chairman asked, "Have you done your research and thought about this subject?" He pointed to various passages and continued his concentrated reading. Every now and then he asked a question or raised an issue. But his attention was elsewhere. I was careful not to distract him and paged through the book as quietly as possible.

Saime was reading a book too. She'd welcomed us to the founding, but we hadn't said anything more to each other. Soft music played from a radio on a shelf next to her. Saime had ties to TİKKO and was in the Teachers School. She had more theoretical knowledge than the rest of us. I'd recently seen her in Dersim and knew her only superficially. It was especially important for women to be ideologically trained, since women with political consciousness made a special impression and attracted interest. Later she would go to Urfa, where she worked as a teacher and remained active for the organization. Kemal Pir and the others would be arrested in the flat where she was staying; she could no longer stay there and would be moved elsewhere.

But where was Kesire? I'd thought I'd see her here. Food was served, two dishes and a fresh salad. Cemil joked, "Is this feast special for us?"

"No, we always eat this way," Saime answered. "There's no problem."

Cemil had been thinking of the bulgur and noodle dishes we normally ate. In Elazığ we could afford only limited nourishment. But then, we were extremely frugal—some called us stingy.

The chairman ate quickly as always—I'd first observed his way of eating in a cafe in Elazığ. He also had a distinctive gait, walking with firm, controlled steps. While we ate, Kesire came in and said hello. I half turned to give her my hand, but she strode past me and sat down on the sofa, looking somewhat aggrieved. She'd come from the bathroom and didn't want to eat with us. Then she went back into the other room. The chairman said, "We'll leave as soon as we finish eating."

So we wouldn't be staying here. Had we changed the accommodations for security reasons? A mood of depression hung in the air. I'd sensed it when I saw Saime, and Kesire's behavior confirmed it. It wasn't because the chairman was present and everyone was trying to be quiet for his sake. I could only observe and draw my own conclusions. I didn't understand what was going on but also didn't want to think about it much more. The chairman was looking at his books even while we were eating. He asked questions and made comments. He could do several things at once. Then the doorbell rang. "The car's here," someone said. The chairman rose and said, "Let's go."

The chairman, Cemil, Kesire, and I got into a taxi. Cemil sat in front. In the backseat, the chairman sat on the right, Kesire was in the middle, and I was on the left. The driver drove carefully, often turning off the car's interior light. The chairman sometimes asked for the names of the places we were passing. Kesire didn't utter a word.

Kesire and the chairman seemed to belong to different worlds. Or did I err in my perception? Why didn't they talk to each other? Probably they had to act "formally," I told myself, searching for explanations for the strange mood. Maybe they had too much to do. But something didn't seem right between them. Of course I didn't mention it—that would have been like a sin—just the thought made me uncomfortable. Maybe I was just imagining it. Kesire didn't talk a lot anyway. I tried to tell myself I was mistaken but couldn't shake the feeling.

We finally reached Fis, a village in Lice that lay at a crossroads, to the left of the main road. It had many gardens. We pulled up in front of a fairly large, prosperous-looking mud-brick house.

The grounds were inspected, and nothing could be seen. The house was in a remote location—the villagers would hardly notice who came and went here. The darkness was another advantage. Together we went into the house, which had a living room, warmed by a stove, and two bedrooms. The owners would stay overnight somewhere else, but they brought us food. The father was tall and had graying hair and smiled at everyone. The mother was shorter and chubby, wearing a tidy headscarf. Their small children came too. Seyfettin, who kept walking in and out, sent them on their way and warned them not to bother the guests.

Other friends had arrived before us, and we shook hands. Still more friends came. It was exciting. All the cadres were here, the brains of the movement, so to speak. *This must be an important meeting*, I thought exultantly, *for so many people to come together.*

I knew most of those present or had seen them at least once: Mehmet Hayri Durmuş, Mazlum Doğan, Duran Kalkan, Ali Haydar Kaytan, Baki Karer, Resul Altınok, Şahin Dönmez, and Ali Gündüz, among others. Some I didn't know. Mehmet Karasungur wasn't there. When I asked why, Resul said, "For security reasons. He stayed away to avoid attracting notice."[128]

More friends arrived around midnight. Everyone was tired from the journey, and the meeting was to start the next morning. We were told not to leave the house if possible, and only in the darkness. Kesire and I were not to leave the house for any reason, let alone go to the village. It got very late, and we had to get at least a few hours of sleep. Kesire and I slept in one of the rooms. Warmth penetrated to us from the living room stove and from the adjacent stable. The other bedroom was ice cold, with a concrete floor. The friends spread out there and in the living room. Resul said, "This room is too big for just the two of you. At least let comrade Abdullah sleep here."

Kesire answered superciliously, "No. No one sleeps here but us."

I was astonished. Why shouldn't the chairman sleep here? The room really was too big for two people. Why was Kesire so dismissive? Maybe Resul had offended her somehow, but no, she'd sounded indifferent. Finally I admitted she was right. It was better this way, at least for the family who lived here. But I remembered that at Amed and during the journey, Kesire seemed angry and resentful. She never spoke much anyway, but this was an extreme. Her face looked tense. We shared a mattress—as Kesire said, "It's warmer this way." It was better to have only two in the room, she insisted again.

In the morning, the official founding congress began. Friends filled the wooden benches along the walls and sat on the floor. Hayri and the chairman sat in front at a small table, with the draft program "Understanding the Right Way," which we all had read already, and a few other papers.[129] A device on the table would record all verbal contributions, but later it was decided not to record everything for security reasons, and not everything was transcribed. The chairman nominated Hayri to lead the discussion. That was accepted, and the founding congress began under Hayri's leadership.

The chairman delivered the introductory speech. First he explained the meeting's historical significance and its necessity. Then he discussed the conditions under which the national liberation struggle had emerged. He talked about the ideological vanguard, the structure of the organization, the foundations of our struggle and its stage of development, the situation of the cadres, and the position of the enemy and his attacks on us. In a clear voice and in accessible language, he discoursed on the international political situation and the various systems.

Sometimes he paused and raised his eyes to the ceiling, as if studying a fixed point. He kept adjusting his glasses with his index finger. Even in Elazığ it had occurred to me that he suffered from sinusitis—he sneezed a lot and got headaches. Cold seemed to worsen his health. But since we were at an official meeting, care was taken to avoid disturbing his concentration, even when he didn't even wipe his nose.

The atmosphere was very serious, and the chairman's analysis made it even more so. During his tours around Kurdistan, he'd spoken to meetings about political developments, but now his remarks were even more searching and comprehensive. Once again, as I listened to him, he opened new horizons for me. His words inspired us to become part of the new organization, to fulfill the necessary tasks, and accept our responsibilities for it. In the conditions prevailing in Kurdistan, we had to build a Leninist organization.

The chairman listened to the other contributions. Later Hayri read out the draft program and the bylaws. A few small changes were proposed, to which Mazlum paid special attention. After we adopted them both, we took a break. The meeting hadn't begun with a moment of silence—it had just been forgotten, although a few friends criticized that. The meeting resumed after the break, and the agenda items were quickly taken care of. Hayri explained why the friends Kemal Pir and Mehmet Karasungur hadn't been able to come. Kemal Pir was in prison, so he was named an honorary delegate. We couldn't waste any time— that would have been risky, since so many comrades had gathered in one spot. But Şahin spoke to almost every agenda item in long, detailed, and somewhat repetitive excurses. He talked more than the chairman did. People were soon murmuring with irritation whenever he got up to speak.

Most interesting to me were the local area reports. They were delivered verbally by the delegates and elaborated by others from the area. Then the delegates evaluated and criticized them. A few reports discussed ways of working. I shared my views on our work in Elazığ and referred to its shortcomings with regard to women. The friends didn't even try to draw their wives and sisters into the revolutionary work, I said, but instead waited for a female comrade to come along and organize the women. This was true even for the leading cadres, which was astonishing as well as wrong.

Resul laughed at my words. I didn't understand why. Did he like my criticism, or was he making fun of me? It unnerved me. Had I said something wrong? I hadn't prepared a speech. Actually I had been waiting for Kesire to take the floor. She had more experience and consciousness than I did and should have spoken before me, but she was silent. Out of respect for her, I stayed silent too for a long time, while the various agenda items were addressed. Her behavior discouraged me.

Most of the male friends were leading cadres who dominated the discussion. I couldn't compete with them. *These friends have a great responsibility,* I told myself. *They know what they're talking about, and their assessments are appropriately complete and multilayered. I've nothing important to contribute, so I must say nothing.* But the contents of the discussion would affect all of us ultimately, so I thought I had to speak up. If Resul laughed and made fun of me, well, that wouldn't stop me.

I'd taken a chill during the journey. My head was pounding, and I heard a rushing in my ears. I could hardly sort out my thoughts and pay good attention to the speeches, yet the intense meeting demanded the greatest concentration.

At one point, the chairman noticed that Resul Altınok had nodded off in his seat and was snoring softly. He glared at him so sharply that we all turned to look. It was unthinkable. "Hugely important things are being discussed here," the chairman said, "and here you are sleeping like a bum. That's not going to work. Wake up, and act as the seriousness of the situation demands!"

I'd never seen him so angry, not just because someone was asleep but because it expressed a certain attitude. But I wished he hadn't used the word "bum." It all happened very fast, and for a second everyone hushed. Then before the chairman could continue, Mazlum rose and, to everyone's amazement, said, "It's important to participate in this meeting with the necessary seriousness and awareness of responsibility. But I criticize Comrade Abdullah for his choice of word. Certain words shouldn't be used."

It was astonishing. Mazlum was acting responsibly and expressing his criticism respectfully, yet it felt strange, even unpleasant somehow. He was certainly right, but he'd criticized the chairman! Later in Elazığ I talked to Cemil about it. It befit Mazlum's character to criticize in a comradely way and in the context of revolutionary responsibility, no matter where he was or who it affected. This very trait accounted for his strong tie to the chairman. They complemented each other.

The chairman listened attentively to Mazlum, then said mildly, "Okay, the criticism is justified. I'll make a note of it." Then he returned to the subject he'd been discussing.

In Elazığ I'd written down some of my thoughts about experiences in other liberation struggles. There had been women's units in Vietnam and in Bulgaria. I had talked a lot with Meral about the women's movement and even wrote a piece titled "The Place and the Significance of Women in the National Liberation Struggle."

Meral often harshly criticized patriarchal relations among the friends in their daily lives. It was positive and justified to some extent but was not always realistic. She sometimes behaved in a sectarian fashion toward her own sex. We had formed an extensive network in Elazığ with around a hundred women, and our struggle influenced many more. In general, women in Elazığ were notable for their disputatiousness and rebelliousness. We had thought we could mobilize them easily.

At the bottom of our draft article on the formation of women's units, Meral, half in jest, had written "Down with male imperialism!" Cemil read it with surprise. Later he said, "We're tired—why don't you make some tea," and we shot back, "Make the tea yourself!" Then he understood better what it was all about. Our reactions were sometimes extreme, because we were still looking for the right orientation. In my notes, I was grappling with the issue of creating propaganda and action units.

Now at the congress the discussion continued, but I didn't feel prepared to express my opinion. During the break, I beckoned to Kesire, went into the other room, and showed her my notepad. "This is a sketch I wrote in Elazığ, and it contains proposals. All this time I couldn't say anything. Look—if you think it's appropriate, I'll raise it."

She read over the text. "Your ideas are good," she said, "but isn't it a little early for this? Are we really strong enough to form such units?"

"Yes, we are," I said, "at least in Dersim, Elazığ, and Bingöl, where many women are involved. Maybe in Amed too."

When the meeting resumed, I was still undecided. I couldn't get Kesire's question, about whether it was too early, out of my head. I didn't have the nerve to speak up. But she had also said that my ideas were good. I wished she'd speak up herself. But no, her lips stayed sealed. She didn't say anything on a single subject. Sometimes she talked with Mazlum or Duran, and especially with Baki Karer, but overall she spoke very little.

But Şahin talked incessantly, as if he couldn't let an opportunity pass. I whispered to Kesire, sitting next to me, "He talks so much—can't anyone stop him?" The male friends, too, sometimes murmured. No one said it aloud, but everyone was thinking, *That's enough, we don't want to listen to you anymore!* To everyone's annoyance, Şahin talked on every subject and repeated the chairman's remarks in his own words. But the chairman listened to Şahin serenely. *What is motivating this ambitious behavior?* I wondered, but actually it was clear: it was sheer careerism.

Finally the time came to choose the central committee. The chairman was unanimously elected as general secretary. Friends were nominated for central committee, but most of them modestly declined, adding, "I'll respect the friends' recommendations and decisions."

The chairman asked: "Comrade Hüseyin Topgüder, what do you think? Can you do it?" Hüseyin answered abashedly, "No, I'm new to this movement. Other friends should be nominated."

Cemil said he didn't deserve to be on the central committee because he was responsible for certain events in Antep. Modesty can be a good thing, but this was overdone. None of the leading cadres considered themselves worthy enough to step forward. Everyone wanted to yield to others. Gloom and silence fell. In the end Şahin was nominated, as was Mehmet Karasungur in absentia, so these two were elected. A proposal to increase the number of members was deferred to the central committee's first meeting.

What name would the party use? Out of several suggestions, the meeting adopted PKK (Partiya Karkerên Kurdistan [Kurdistan Workers Party]). Finally we had a name, which inspired joy and excitement. The party flag was chosen, and other such things determined, so we could declare the founding of the party.

After the two-day meeting ended, the participants left in groups. I rode back with the chairman, Cemil, and Kesire. We stopped at the same apartment, but this time stayed overnight. The chairman retired into a room with Cemil. Everyone was tired, and we didn't talk much. Şenay was there too—I'd last seen her in Ankara. We talked a little, and she looked haggard, as if she'd been through a hard time. As a cover for her work, she'd married İsmet from Bingöl. Initially the marriage existed only on paper, a formality to make the work easier and also to enable Şenay, who was from Yugoslavia, to stay in Turkey. But a relationship had emerged, for which neither of them was prepared, and over time it took a negative turn that was difficult for them both. The relationship was based neither on love nor on a voluntary union. Şenay ultimately left the movement, as neither of them had had the strength to use the relationship properly.

Kesire sat quietly on the sofa, immersed in thought. Mats were arranged on the floor, and Şenay, Saime, and I lay down. Finally Kesire joined us, crossing her arms under her head, still thoughtful. "Why aren't you sleeping?" I asked. "I'm not tired," she said. If it had been anyone else, I probably would have been satisfied. But Kesire was the close friend of the chairman, so her emotional state affected me.

The next day Cemil and I drove to Elazığ—a livelier journey. I shared my thoughts about the meeting with him and also about Şahin's behavior. I added my impressions of Şahin from İzmir and Bingöl and my brother Haydar's experiences with him. Cemil thought Şahin's behavior was careerist too. When I got to the episode about my brother at the police station, he said, "Really?" and fell silent for a few minutes.

"I also didn't find your position correct," I added. "None of you wanted to be nominated for the central committee—you all backed out." And by the way, I asked, what happened in Antep?

"Actually the episode didn't have to do with me directly," Cemil explained,

> but I was in charge of the area at the time. The two people who murdered Haki [Karer] were spreading rumors that there were two tendencies in our movement, one that supported the chairman and another that supported Haki. Many upstanding friends believed this story and were duped. Much more happened, and I could tell you about it, but the point is that these two did a lot of damage. In the end, they were punished, and many of those who fell for the rumor rejoined us. Antep is a place where we could be very successful. Haki was very influential there—he'd chosen it for a reason. But his death had consequences. It all could have been prevented if the necessary measures had been taken promptly. Every member has to be able to handle such problems, otherwise a pair of criminals like these two can destroy the organization. It can happen anytime. There are still people around who believe them—maybe they'll try something in Dersim or Elazığ too. Some people are just gullible.

As I listened to Cemil, I remembered some things Ayten had told me at Zeki's in Bingöl. There had been a lot of tumult in Dersim at that time, and it affected many people, including Ayten and Resul. Ayten had said, "The only people one can trust are the chairman and, in Dersim, Ali Haydar Kaytan." But she hemmed and hawed and wouldn't come out and tell me whatever was bothering her.

"What do you mean?" I pressed her angrily. "Be straight with me— what's going on? Is that the official view of the friends? I don't like Resul very much either, but he's in charge of this area for the party. If there is something against him, the movement will intervene. If there's something I should know, tell me now."

Ayten knew well that the organization's internal affairs were to be discussed only with the people directly affected. But if she knew something, or if everyone else knew something, then she must tell me. Finally she spewed out all kinds of nonsense:

> Sevim Kaya might be going to Ankara to talk to Hamili. You know, he's in prison. She'll tell him about the situation and find out what he thinks. Türkan visited Ali Gündüz in the prison in Dersim. They're trying to find out these comrades' opinions on certain points, so they can rid the organization of agents and suspects. They're looking for help. It's idiotic! No one understands how dangerous it is, and worse, they let themselves be used. They try to connect different events, true or false, and assess

individuals and episodes accordingly. Something in their minds pushes them forward. Cemile is suspected of involvement in Ali Haydar's arrest—she was even observed going to the police station. Rumors are spreading about Haki's murder, that it wasn't Stêrka Sor that killed him but someone in an internal dispute. They say they'll investigate to see if it's true. I'm telling you all this because I trust you. No one will know I've told you. It should stay in the strictest confidence—

"I don't understand a thing you've just said," I responded.

According to you, everyone in the movement is a traitor. These are serious charges you're making, unless it's some kind of joke. None of it sounds credible to me. I'm committed to the movement's official thought and analysis, and I'll stay that way. What you're saying is very strange.

Ayten seemed to regret that she'd talked to me. Hadn't the friends in Dersim taught her to keep her mouth shut? Her father was known as a bad man, and her family's social milieu was strange, but so what—this wasn't about her family. She'd made some very serous claims. Were these her own thoughts? Later when I was in Dersim, I wanted to meet Ali Haydar Kaytan to tell him about it.

Meanwhile I'd also seen Kıymet and my cousin Fadime Yıldırım and other friends, and what I'd observed of their behavior had astonished me. They'd been staying in Kıymet's house—some of them were being sought by the police because they'd beaten up a fascist—and during their stay, Kıymet had a negative influence on them. They began to make fun of things that were actually of great significance for us.

And they regarded Kıymet's marriage as a model, revolutionary and unique. What was so exemplary about it? That she'd taken on traditional male roles? One day when I was there, she'd said to her husband, "Zülfo, get up and make tea right now. Why is that child crying? Change the diapers!" Did she think this commanding tone constituted women's liberation or revolutionary behavior? Some of the young women seemed to have lost their marbles. To Fadime, I said, "What's going on with you? You've changed so much!" She just said, "That's true."

I had to share these developments with the friends, so I sought out Ali Haydar. I got my chance when a friend offered to drive me and some others to a wedding in a village, and "friends would gather there." Would Ali Haydar be there? I asked. The friend said he didn't know, but I went anyway.

Halfway there the van stopped, and I spotted Ali Haydar. He asked me, "Are you going to the wedding?" I said yes, and that I'd been looking for him and wanted to talk to him. He seemed rushed, nervous, and impatient. "I have to go back and settle a few things. Come with me. Something's happening," he said. I got in his car and told him what Ayten had told me in Bingöl and about how Fadime and the others were acting. "They're going off track," I said. "Okay, we'll talk more about it later," he said, and we drove to Erol Degirmenci's house.

It was the anniversary of Haki's murder, and flyers had been produced for wide distribution. We wanted to memorialize Haki in a dignified way and to counter the enemy propaganda that was being spread. I was assigned to distribute the flyers with Kazım Kulu and Gülistan. We canvassed in several villages, driving from Milli to Güleç.

During this time a meeting was held to finally clear up the confused events in Dersim, to cut short the attempt to stir up a provocation before it could do any further damage. Clearly the enemy attacked in various ways, as soon as he found our weak point. This made the class struggle within the organization all the more important. People had suspected most of the movement cadres of being traitors and presented themselves as the only saviors. The movement was forced to put its own members under the microscope, to learn their weaknesses and take appropriate measures. Some things one simply has to live through in order to understand them.

As Cemil described the situation in Antep, it reminded me of these recent events in Dersim. Taking the necessary measures meant supporting the organization's principles and defending its ideology against others. But we also had to be alert to what was said and done internally, and to what end. I realized how naïve I was sometimes.

"But we're not marriage brokers!" The founding congress opened up a new era for us. We were now PKK members. We had founded a party with a program and bylaws. I continued to be galvanized by this inspiring congress. While it was going on, I'd followed the discussions, but only afterward did I grasp their meaning. I didn't consider myself special for having been there. On the contrary, I was embarrassed by my own low level compared to the others. But more than anything, I felt pride and joy. The problems, the life, and the struggle no longer seemed onerous to me. The life was so beautiful and stimulated me so much that I could not imagine ever being finished with it.

No aspect of the life seemed strange to me. I didn't feel overwhelmed. It was as if I'd never lived any other way. Yes, the turmoil I'd experienced left behind traces, but what thrilled me and what now constituted my life was the powerful beauty of the revolutionary struggle. I had no concern for where this struggle would take me or how it would unfold. There was so much to do at every moment. What counted were conviction, connectedness, and confidence. Nothing else mattered.

Cemil was assigning tasks for the work in the next period, and then he would presumably leave the area. The committee in Elazığ consisted of five people: Ali Gündüz, Hüseyin Topgüder, Metin Güngöze, Hamili Yıldırım, and me. We also had subcommittees. At one meeting we discussed who would take on which tasks. Our work district was extended to include Pertek, Çemişgezek, Hozat, Karakoçan, and Malatya. Süleyman Aslan was put in charge of Malatya. He went there and was active for a while. Later Aytekin was mentioned, and a few others. The outlook for a successful effort there was good. We told no one about the party founding or the congress—it was to remain secret for a while. But the new energy that infused our work suggested that some organizational changes had been made.

In Elazığ, people tried to stir up trouble, as in Antep and Dersim. Once again, it was about two people who had been shot in Antep. "The local cadres are discriminated against," they complained. "The cadres' responsibilities are always imposed on them from without. But it's the local cadres who do the work. That's not fair." A few friends talked about how narrow-minded this accusation was and the actual reasons for the allocation of tasks. But we didn't take the matter seriously anymore. Later a real problem seemed to develop out of it, and Cemil warned us to be careful: "The enemy might attack directly."

We discussed the enemy's strategies, which certainly would include physically attacking certain cadres to destroy the organization. But our suppositions weren't specific. "The enemy might also attack us without destroying us." Cemil said. "You mean throw us into prison?" I asked. "Yes, of course. We have to be ready for anything."

Several of our friends had spent time in prison, while others were in jail still, among them now Ali Haydar Kaytan, Hamili [Yıldırım], Ali Gündüz, Kemal Pir, Dilaver and Kemal Coşkun. D— A— and others were the first. Then the shooting of Mustafa Çamlıbel had led to the arrest of more than ten friends. The trial was under way. The accused had succeeded in keeping the organization out of the charges, but the enemy didn't let up and imposed harsh punishments on them.

D— A— was transferred from Ağrı to the prison in Niğde. An escape attempt from Ağrı had failed. What could have gone wrong? We had only few ties to the prisoners, just the exchange of correspondence, but we gleaned some information from it. [D— A—'s] wife kept all his letters. He wrote poems to her, which embarrassed her but also made her happy. She was very emotional. She didn't want to join the movement but held back as a mere young woman who liked us, gave us material aid, and sometimes collaborated with us.

Our landlord lived above us. I worried about the young women coming from outside our neighborhood—we had to avoid arousing any notice. Hatun, our landlord's daughter, took an interest in our work. Her father was a Kemalist from Pertek, and her mother was one of the sad, oppressed women. Her older sister Yeter had run away with the man she loved, after he'd asked her parents for her hand and been refused. The two met secretly on a mountain to make plans. The girl thought about her family and knew that running away would give rise to a slew of hateful rumors. She wanted to try one more time to persuade her family to accept her marriage. The young man agreed, and next day the girl came home. Their plan failed, and the young man left the village and went to another city. "He dishonored her and then disappeared!" it was said in the village. The girl collapsed and begged her parents to believe her: "It's all not true, he never touched me." But no one believed her.

Yeter was actually still an "intact virgin" but couldn't persuade either her family or the villagers of it. Her father thought her honor had been ruined. He didn't know how to find the young man. If he caught him, he'd shoot him. So the best thing, he thought, would be to "purify" the girl. "She has lost her honor," he said, so he shot her. To protect the father from prosecution, her death was said to be a suicide. A virginity test was performed on the corpse, and it was discovered that she'd told the truth.

Now the whole family collapsed in grief, and the father had a bad conscience. The mother agonized that she'd believed her daughter but had done nothing out of fear of her husband. She could have said, "Come to your senses—she's still our daughter. She told me everything,

I'm her mother, she doesn't keep anything from me. Leave her in peace." But he'd have beaten and debased her. Through her silence, she became an accomplice, a partner in the murder of her daughter. Even after years passed, she still felt guilty and behaved coldly toward her husband.

She treated her other daughter, Hatun, more carefully. At their home in Tozkoparan, Hatun was influenced by leftist groups, initially by the PDA. Our dialogues had no apparent impact on her, but she was eager to learn more and had the potential to develop quickly, so I persisted with her.

In the basement of the house across from us lived students at Fırat University who came from different places. Among them was Ali from Kars, who was one of our friends. I don't know how their relationship came about or how far it had advanced, but in any case Ali told me he and Hatun had fallen in love and wanted to marry. Accompanied by other friends, we went to her parents' flat, where we made the usual small talk between tenant and landlord, then got to the reason for our visit.

When the word *Kurdistan* came up, Hatun's father reacted as if to an allergy. Kurds had been inseparable from Turks, he lectured us, ever since the Ottoman Empire. He even went so far as to insist that Turks suffered under the oppression of Kurds. His chauvinistic interpretation of history coincided with that of Turkish racists. He worked himself up into a state, but we didn't let up. After a while the man weakened, listened to us, and even admitted we were right on some points. Then when he found out that Ali came from Kars and was a Sunni, he said, "I'm not giving my daughter to a Sunni." But the fact that Ali studied at the university made him interesting to Hatun's parents. Finally the father said, "Well, I've seen him around once or twice, and he seems like a well-brought-up man." Maybe he'd give permission after all. We left it at that for now, since we were more interested in winning over the whole family. If the young woman worked out for us, she'd enter the revolutionary work and solve this problem as well. So we decided not to insist on a decision but to let time handle the matter.

Such relationships were considered a way to separate a young woman from her family. But sometimes a relationship could become a problem to be wrestled with. Around this time the elder sister of Sakine Kırmızıtaş was having problems with the marriage she desired. She was one of our members and a teacher. She turned to us because she wanted our approval for the marriage. Cemil said, half in jest, "If this keeps up, we could open a marriage bureau. Really, they should do what they want—we're not marriage brokers."

Meanwhile everyone connected to us brought their problems to the party and wanted us to regulate their affairs. That happened spontaneously but was also correct: they perceived the movement as trustworthy, and they wanted to adjust their lives to it. Of course we couldn't solve every problem right away. But this new situation forced the cadres to contend with many different questions and to broaden the range of their work. The aspiration to find solutions to the issues of daily life shaped individuals and allowed them to grow.

The pain people feel   During the semester break, I toured around Kurdistan. At the Girls Art School and the Health School, I met dozens of young women. Over the break, they were going home to Siverek, Çermik, Çüngüş, Maden, Keban, and elsewhere. Our relations with some of them gave us cause for hope. We had prepared to organize in their milieu or at least be available as mediators. We held a meeting in an apartment in Yıldızbağları with some 80 young women. Cahide had organized the nearby Girls Art School, the Teachers School, and the Trade High School. Nadire had mobilized the Atatürk High School and its surroundings, and Makbule took care of the Health School. In the afternoon we managed to bring all the young women to the flat in groups. If space hadn't been a problem, more than a hundred women would have been present.

We wanted Cemil to address the group, but he declined. Out of all the participants, no one stepped forward to speak. After a long discussion, Ali Gündüz was finally chosen, but he admitted, "I'm really self-conscious."

He and I got it going. When we walked into the room, all the friends rose. The sight of them waiting for us so seriously and expectantly was beautiful. A few had expected Cemil, but even for them it wasn't so important which friend appeared. Everyone was thrilled that so many young women had come together. Many met each other here for the first time. In all our educational groups, each individual woman had assumed she was the only one.

Ali gave the speech that we had sketched out. First he touched on the political developments and special features of the current period, then he highlighted the importance of women's participation in the national liberation struggle in Kurdistan. He spoke powerfully and well, even on subjects he hadn't prepared for. Now and then he turned and asked Meral and me whether he'd left out anything important. We took notes and reminded him about a few points. The speech wasn't comprehensive, but it was good enough for a beginning.

A few questions were asked, and then the meeting broke up. Everyone left exultant. We were proud of ourselves. A turnout of this many young women was nothing to disparage. Later people in many neighborhoods talked about the meeting. Before the meeting, at most ten young women would come together, in that neighborhood, to discuss something or study together, but now the number kept growing. Families became concerned for their daughters, as our activities and the relations that grew out of them were still considered dangerous. The parents' fears were palpable, and many tried to keep a tight rein on their daughters. But then they realized that their own daughters weren't alone in showing revolutionary tendencies—dozens of intelligent and nice young women thought the same way. They couldn't all have lost their minds.

To connect the meeting's participants to the organization, we needed to strengthen our ties to their home places. So I took a trip to get to know them and their families and to mobilize those who seemed able to stand on their own two feet, or else to maintain connections in different ways. Especially for the women who decided to join the revolutionary work, I wanted to get to know their families and win over the people around them, too. That was part of the plan.

First we decided to drive to Maden, and our first destination would be Siverek. Cahide and Havva and many other female friends were in the bus. Havva was thin, quiet, and introverted, but she listened closely to everything and tried to grasp what was going on. During the journey Cahide planned what we would do and who we should look up. She and Havva tossed around various names. It was gratifying that she took the initiative. She'd given me a rough idea about her family and even written a little autobiography. She'd told me about her parents and described her elder sister. I encouraged her and others to do this: "Each of us should write something about the women in their home places, about their particularities and ways of life." A few of the friends did as I asked. I learned more, from their texts, about the women of certain regions and about the female friends themselves. It was highly instructive.

To finally see Siverek, a famous place in Urfa province, was wonderful. The district city lay on a plain. It wasn't very developed, but it was large.

"Your city is bigger than Dersim," I said to Cahide, "but we have mountains and forests and a wonderful natural environment."

Cahide laughed. "Ah, then I'll go to Dersim and work there!" She wanted to see it as well as do revolutionary work. She was clearly preparing herself to become professionally active. I thought, *She has the best potential to develop quickly.*

The house belonged to her family. Like most houses in Siverek, it had only one story. The front wall reminded me of a prison yard. In the side streets, women were wearing the long garments typical of the region. The walls around the houses were very high—I asked why. Cahide explained the tribal structures and blood feuds endemic to Siverek. Blood feuds! So the houses had been transformed into fortresses, with high walls for defense!

Cahide's family was large and got many visitors. Her mother Emine had big eyes with bluish rings beneath that reminded me of Armenian women's eyes. Cahide's elder sister had them too. All the women looked similar, and most were chubby. They served us sweets—Siverek was famous for them. Cahide had told me her family earned their livelihood that way, selling homemade sweets. Her father didn't work, only the women did. It was rare in Kurdish society for a man to live off the labors of his wife. The father was also a drinker, inclined to gambling and womanizing. The family knew all about it, and Emine didn't like it much but couldn't do anything about it. One of Cahide's sisters was married to a cousin, Ramazan, and they had a child. Then Ramazan had taken a second wife. The first wife couldn't stand it, even though she'd initially agreed to her husband's second marriage, and got a divorce. All that seemed wholly normal to them, as they were accustomed to such problems. So this was an ideal place to make women into revolutionaries.

I said to myself, *At least a few of them will become militant. Once Cahide makes a start, others will follow.* Cahide knew how to make her voice heard in her family. Since she was educated, she enjoyed a certain respect. She'd been living away from her family for some time and was now in her last year at school. She'd soon become a teacher. That gained her respect in her family, as was evident in housework, shopping, and our meetings.

She introduced me to them as a schoolmate named, once again,

Fatma. But the family saw right away that our relationship was special. That first night her sister Nevin went through my purse and found my ID. In the morning she told Cahide my name wasn't Fatma, it was Sakine. Cahide lit into her in a fury—what had she been thinking, to go through the purse of a guest? Nevin had been curious, but I didn't care for her behavior, as it suggested a poor upbringing. The nieces of Mehmet Karasungur had done the same thing and smoked out my true identity. Did girls always have to be so curious?

The next day Cahide invited over a few young women who were politically interested or involved with other leftist groups. It was normal for her to have a lot of visitors since she'd been away from home for so long.

One woman, Naciye, was lame and walked on crutches. She sympathized with the DDKD. She'd been around and had some experiences, but she didn't know much about the reality of Kurdistan, so she was kind of tiresome, making conservative points and trying to rile me. The way she talked about certain concepts, it sounded as if she'd memorized them—I wasn't sure she even understood their meaning. She didn't let anyone talk against the DDKD. She denigrated us as "quixotic" and "aggressive" and "adventuristic," the way many leftist groups did. It was irritating. We talked for hours. Apparently she had complexes that motivated her to bad-mouth us.

The others were more mature and listened to us. Cahide was upset about the way the discussion unfolded and tried to mollify me. But I was so mad that I lost my temper for a moment and snapped, "Get out—you twist everything! You're trying to sabotage the discussion!" I nearly hit her with her own crutches.

When the meeting ended and the guests left, we learned afterward that they'd been arguing in the street. The others said the DDKD members had been wrong and scolded them for their behavior. Meanwhile I was in a foul mood. "Why did you invite such people?" I demanded of Cahide, who explained, "She wasn't like that before. She seemed open to new things like the other girls. She never talked that way. If you'd reacted more calmly, it wouldn't have reached the point it did. You got angry much too fast."

Cahide was right, I'd done myself in, and her criticism restored me to my senses. "Did the other women get the wrong impression?" I asked. "No," she said. "Naciye will definitely come back tomorrow, or she'll invite us to her place. She'll think things over at home. She's actually quite sensitive. She acted that way because she really doesn't understand a lot, and she thinks highly of herself and thinks she knows better. But up to now she's talked only with people at my level. She was seeing you for the first time. Probably she also resented that you attacked her and the DDKD." Cahide obviously knew her very well.

It is important, in a discussion, not to let yourself be provoked. That was a lesson for me. These women were actually easy to influence. You had only to find the right approach to draw them in. I realized my mistake. That I let myself get upset so easily was a serious fault and led to my bad mood. I would meet people like Naciye often, and I couldn't afford to let them all infuriate me to the point of tossing them out. I pledged earnestly to pay attention in the future and not to let myself be provoked.

Soon thereafter Naciye invited us over. Happily, Cahide's hypothesis was right. Naciye admitted she'd made a mistake in our previous discussion and apologized. We talked for a long time. Afterward she said she was no longer with the DDKD. She wanted to get to know our movement better, she said, and was moving toward supporting us.

Cahide took me to visit other families in Siverek. And we visited her aunt, a lovable, smart woman. Even at her advanced age, she was robust and educated and interested in politics. Cahide looked like her, I noticed. The Karakeçili tribe were of Turkish origin, but they'd lived with Kurdish culture for a long time and had accommodated to it. The aunt made her living selling candy too. She had three sons, Ramazan, Mehmet Emin, and Şiyar, as well as a daughter. Uncle Şiyar lived in their home, and a nephew, also called Şiyar. The nephew was Ramazan's son. Since his mother had divorced his father, he was connected to both sides. They lived together and quarreled a lot, but they maintained their connection as relatives. Their quarrels weren't violent. But Emine didn't like Ramazan. It annoyed her when he visited, and the fact that he'd taken a second wife after marrying her daughter offended her. The aunt was unhappy with the situation but didn't show it—she tried to stay on good terms with everyone.

At first it was difficult to sort through this family's chaos—their web of relationships was so absurdly entangled. It wasn't enough to explain that the existing social order brought about such family structures, since ultimately it could contain anything.

Up until a few years ago, the family had been working in cotton fields in İzmir, Denizli, Aydın, and Manisa. The children had been brought in to do the seasonal work too. It wasn't easy to commute from Siverek to Aydın or Manisa, to harvest cotton and plow fields. But that was one aspect of life in Kurdistan, and many families depended on such work.

Such stories cut very close to me. Our people's poverty and the sorrows they had to endure fortified me in my struggle. It was of the utmost urgency to organize the people. Our society was fragmented, and people could be pitted against one another and exploited. Preventing that was our most important task.

The more I got to know Cahide's family, the better I liked them. Yes, they were very tangled up, in ways that often made me angry, but I thought, *They know about life in all its difficulties, so they are the ones the revolution wants the most.* Even the aunt could collaborate as a militant. I told her about Gorky's book *The Mother.* In the depths of my soul, I was certain that the mothers of Kurdistan would prove to be even more courageous.

The other family members had little to do with the father, Koço. He was like a guest in the house. They were accustomed to his absences. Then he would come home and pocket their hard-earned money, which aggravated them. "If only he'd just leave!" they would say, but he didn't, not least because of the money. When he drank and behaved badly, his children suffered the most. They even wished for his death and thought about how they could contribute to it. They were ashamed of him. Emine despised her husband when he was drunk. She was disgusted by him and refused to accept her fate. Yet she still considered him her husband, and a divorce was out of the question. She'd taken to selling candy so as to be economically independent of him and to care for her children. She now had an occupation, and her sweets were the best in all of Siverek. That first day she'd set out a large tray for me, and the candies really were delicious.

Cahide and I talked a lot, and I tried to persuade her to leave this life to become a revolutionary. She wanted to, which gave me hope. I introduced her to a few friends in Siverek who worked toward the revolution. "During your vacation, you'll be able to build a circle of interested people," I said. She already had many contacts—it was just a matter of deepening her relations with those who were open to change and development. Before I left, I said, "It's not a question of whether you have enough theoretical knowledge. You'll develop that further in the work. That's how it is in this movement. I learn from you and from everyone I'm involved with. I don't understand fully even the most important points. It's not easy to be a revolutionary. Life is our teacher. At first it's enough just to really want it, to be committed and straightforward." Cahide listened to me attentively as she always did, then said, "I've learned a lot from your life."

From Siverek, I went to Cermik and Çüngüş, and Cahide came along. Actually I needed her to join me, since she knew Güllü's and Serap's families as well as others from her school. It would have been better for her to spend the time in Siverek, but I needed her. Serap, Güllü, and a few more younger women gave me hope.

Güllü came from Cermik. Her brother and her extended family had been with the DDKD, but now they were with us. Hüseyin Durmuş worked in this area—I was glad to see him again. After he got to know Güllü and the other young women, he said, "Good, now we can use their home. That way we won't attract any attention."

I knew Güllü's family since her mother and her brother had once come to Elazığ. Güllü had had surgery and lived with us for a while afterward. I had introduced her to Cemil, saying he was my elder brother. Her mother was impressed by how much we'd cared for her daughter. Now we had long discussions in this large family's home. With Güllü's support, we'd be able to have a meeting in Cermik.

Afterward we drove to Çüngüş. Serap's father was a mufti, and her younger sister went to the same school as her. The mother was Turkish, the father Kurdish. Other Kurdish groups were active in Çüngüş as well. Their members were mainly teachers and civil servants. Both places had a good outlook for organizing the people. Local cadres were an advantage there. The level of discussion was high. The youth were educated. The people who worked for the authorities and other state institutions were mostly local. If we organized well, we could infiltrate the state structures and use them for our struggle.

I returned to Elazığ sooner than I'd planned. There wasn't enough time for me to go to Maden and the other places I'd wanted to go, like Hani. But classes would soon resume in the schools, so I'd be better off waiting till summer vacation to continue my tour.

Ali Gündüz was now in charge of Malatya—he commuted there [from Elazığ]. I had done propaganda work with Aytekin in Elazığ, but later he was transferred to Malatya. So we were newly active there, and the prospects were good.

Action in Elazığ in response to the Maraş pogrom[130] The pogrom in Maraş of December 1978 was in every respect a warning: the enemy showed how far he was prepared to act against the Kurdish people. Its purpose was to ensure that the Kurdish people never awoke from their sleep to struggle in an organized way. But conversely, it made the use of revolutionary violence all the more important. The people were becoming more militant. The national liberation struggle continued to grow and sink deep roots. The enemy attacks led to a hardening of positions, as people were forced to acknowledge with which class and which power they would move forward.

The state had developed a plan for an anti-Kurdish pogrom and chose a place where sectarian discord already existed. It stoked up this discord long enough to lead to a massacre. Then it declared a state of emergency. Using this tactic, the enemy sought to strike a blow at all revolutionary tendencies that could threaten it.

The national liberation struggle, in Kurdistan as well as in Turkey, worked to prepare the society for a revolution. The movement soon became a force with supporters in many regions, and it assumed an ongoing, determined vanguard role. In the wake of the Maraş pogrom, it showed that it would not be easily annihilated. The people of Kurdistan had found the path to resurgence. The fire of freedom was spreading. A boil had burst, and despite the bleeding wound, a resistance movement had emerged.

The enemy had attacked directly. How would we respond? We discussed this question intensively and came to the conclusion that our organizational structure could best be protected by means of an ongoing struggle that included revolutionary violence. That corresponded to the chairman's approach. Only in this way had a handful of cadres, despite all the obstacles, gradually gained a foothold in Kurdistan as well as popular acceptance of our ideology. With the Maraş pogrom, the enemy had exposed the situation clearly. He had carried out this massacre in order to suppress our struggle. Hence the movement must prepare to mount attacks in kind.

Future attacks clearly wouldn't be limited to Maraş—if successful, they would spread to other places. But the enemy didn't achieve his desired outcome. Many fascist cadres deployed by the enemy were killed. The people were outraged. Some Elazığ fascists who had participated in the Maraş pogrom were killed or wounded. Medical treatment centers were set up for them in Elazığ, in a foundry and elsewhere. Retaliatory actions continued, targeting 11 fascists in just a few days. The Elazığ group gained confidence—this was what reprisal looked like. They attacked the places where the wounded fascists got medical care. Flyers in the name of the Kurdistan Revolutionaries were distributed, saying that the actions would continue and demanding a reckoning for the Maraş pogrom.

The Turkish leftist groups objected to our activities. Instead of opposing the state of emergency that was called, they took the position that our revolutionary actions were far more dangerous and insisted that we were the cause of state repression. They were especially fearful for their own associations. Due to the repression, they couldn't carry out any more demonstrations in the street, or try to manipulate people with slogans and speeches. It caught them unprepared because their concept of revolution was vague and had no real goal.

Once the state of emergency was declared, many leftists vanished from the scene, fleeing to their villages, to their homes, or even to Europe to protect themselves. Instead of welcoming our activities, supporting them, and regarding them as a sign of strength, they legitimated the state's attacks by propagandizing against us. Once they showed their true colors, support for them crumbled, especially in Kurdistan. The people saw for themselves who was doing the fighting, who was telling the truth and putting it into practice.

Our overall struggle, as well as the anti-Kurdish pogrom in Maraş and the actions in Elazığ, was having noticeable effects everywhere. Even at the MHP congress in Elazığ, some young men rose to declare, "We're not Turkish nationalists, we're Kurdish nationalists." We would later get in touch with these young Kurdish men from Palu. They produced their own flyer. Reşo, the group's leader, broke with the MHP—and a 200,000 lira bounty was placed on his head. The day he broke with the MHP, he brought his revolver along. Our first meeting felt strange to me. He had been a fascist yet was now a comrade. The enemy used the MHP to try to poison the minds of Kurdish youth, but our struggle was effective with the MHP base. Similar things happened in Erzurum and Bingöl. More than 70 people shifted over to us, a splendid thing! Hüseyin worked with Reşo and his group, since he too came from Palu.

Everywhere, in homes and in coffeehouses, people were talking about us. We heard tales about our doings, most of them exaggerated. In ordinary conversations we heard people say things like "Bravo! They nabbed them right in the city center!"

After the founding congress, our committee became official, and so we began to found subgroups. In Elazığ we had a lot of cadres, so we discussed transfers. It was important to place each cadre according to his or her abilities. Most worked in their own neighborhood or in the school they attended. Friends were sent to a few areas as advocates, which was not a problem. But downtown was most important. All day we discussed how to organize there, and how many and which friends should be active.

Ali Gündüz was the regional secretary, in charge of coordination. Hamili [Yıldırım] was in charge of the military committee, Deaf Metin of youth, and Hüseyin Topgüder of the workers', peasants', and shopkeepers' committee. I took responsibility for the women's committee and for media, propaganda, and agitation. Hasan Serik came to Elazığ after a while—it had been decided that we should print, and distribute flyers and brochures here. We were told to work together, but not about how to begin to do that. Hasan took Aytekin's place.

Our first joint action was an internal letter signed "PKK Central Committee." Hasan and I could type with only two fingers. He said I should write, and I said he should. Finally he did it. He read aloud, and I typed. Then we had to duplicate the piece, which we did in the village of Mişeli. I'd driven there before with Kurdo, who was good at such things.

Hasan didn't know what the signature "PKK Central Committee" meant, but he didn't ask either. Years later at the Fifth Party Congress, he told me he'd been too proud. "My feudal pride prevented me from just asking," he said, as I laughed. He realized only that the organization's structure had changed.

Hasan stayed only a short while, then left for work in Antep. Deaf Metin caused difficulties in choosing members of the subcommittee. He didn't like any of the nominees for a subcommittee that was answerable to him. We had to make some changes and came to the conclusion that he just couldn't always get things done. At one meeting Ali criticized him harshly. He rebuffed the criticism as a personal attack, but when we all said we agreed with the criticism, he had to back down.

I trust women   In Dersim a clash erupted between the HK and us after they murdered our friend Mahir Can in Kars. [Other PKK militants] Aydın Gül and Metin Turgut had been shot in Dersim. This news ripped through Elazığ like wildfire.

Hamili and a few other friends grabbed weapons in Elazığ and drove to Dersim. We knew that some leading HK cadres collaborated with MİT,[131] which overtly directed events like those in Dersim. The HK leader was Hasan Aydın, director of the Tunceli Teachers School. Without this support, the Kurdistan Revolutionaries wouldn't have been attacked in Dersim, and their cadres wouldn't have been murdered.

The ideological conflict was harsh and unrelenting. The other leftist groups had difficulty finding a correct position on the Kurdish question since they were all pervaded by Kemalism and social chauvinism. But from the outset, the HK had distinguished itself by distorting our ideology. So we couldn't just ignore them. We had to expose their true face to the public.

We all reacted emotionally to this most recent murder and wanted to retaliate in Elazığ instantly. They were killing off our most valuable cadres one by one! We could prevent it only by deploying revolutionary violence in retaliatory strikes. The local people said, "The revolutionaries are shooting each other." The Turkish left as well as the enemy spread the rumor that the murder was an internal vendetta between leftists.

We had to demonstrate that that rumor was false. Through meetings, flyers, and seminars, we tried to explain to the people how the HK and similar groups, in the name of revolution, used violence against revolutionaries. We had to show who they served in so doing, and which side supported them. Of course we had to be careful not to let ourselves be provoked. Some of the HK cadres had become spies, we explained, and people must not let themselves be misled by them and should take a position against them. Mostly we got through to them.

The HK, in turn, published flyers insisting that we had defamed them. In our internal discussions, we agreed that to solve the problem over the long term, we had to proceed prudently. It would be unrealistic to wage a general street war against the HK, directed as they were by the enemy. Instead we had to drive them into a corner and then wage a political struggle. Otherwise many innocent people, who had no idea of the basic problem, could be hurt.

The HK mobilized its base against us. Many people didn't see through it or realize that they were being manipulated. We had to defend ourselves against their attacks and try to turn them to our advantage.

Around this time, Meral was transferred to Dersim. She wasn't thrilled. "I like you," she said, "and I don't want to leave our intensive work here, but I have to do it." All the problems in Dersim had continued. The organized women's groups there were no longer active. Kıymet and her group had become a real problem, acting as if they had everything under control when in fact, as only a few friends understood, she had rendered our groups dysfunctional. It was good that Meral would be there now. With her theoretical knowledge and her quick understanding, she could counteract Kıymet. Of course, she didn't let it show that she really didn't want to go to Dersim. Later she wrote a poem about this "separation." She read it to me with tears in her eyes. It was a beautiful, touching poem.

Our collaboration in Elazığ hadn't been perfect, marked by inexperience and superficiality, but overall I considered it positive. We interacted lovingly and respectfully and had supported each other as comrades. I still miss her, after all this time. In the organizing work she'd displayed weaknesses, but theoretically she was proficient and could influence people.

One day Cemil said we had to build a women's movement in Kurdistan. To create the foundations for it, we had first to analyze the historical and social dimensions of the women's question theoretically, and then we could implement women's organizing practically. Since the chairman as well as the central committee supported this work, I thought we should start right away. I was to work with Ayten and Meral as the committee. It was great news, and I was thrilled. To build the women's movement! Had my conversations with Kesire at the founding congress played a role? Kesire had mentioned to me the same books that Cemil now mentioned: "You can start with the Roman legal system. There are a lot of books and resources that you can use for your research."

I said we could get the right books through our friends at the university. Ayten was very happy too. This new area of work would even offer us the opportunity to travel through Kurdistan. But it wouldn't be easy to research the theory and practice of the women's movement worldwide from past to present, absorb the necessary knowledge, and draw conclusions for Kurdistan. The task before us was as difficult as it was beautiful and important. I had no fears and no doubts that we would succeed.

It was the most beautiful and most necessary work that I could imagine. I was impatient and wanted to start right away. The brief tour that I'd taken during the vacation had shown me the social structures and women's viewpoints in a few places. Based on that, I outlined a work program. I took to asking all the female friends I met about the state of the woman work in their areas.

As the woman work in Dersim, Elazığ, and Bingöl took shape, it became a source of hope. It could serve as a model, as educated female cadres could then be sent to other places to organize more women. Yes, my ideas were rather utopian, and Ayten said, "You are rushing it." But without utopias, nothing can function. I was certain that if we took our task seriously and fulfilled it, the women's movement would develop. It was a very good feeling that gave me hope. At the present moment, of course, we were far from grasping this task in all its dimensions. But the chairman's view of the woman question gave us strength: he'd said from the beginning, "I trust Kurdish women. They're so oppressed that if they become revolutionaries, they have a fantastic development ahead of them." He thereby bolstered our confidence and our will to fight for our own freedom.

After a while Cemil left Elazığ, and Şahin Dönmez arrived. He was on the central committee. Ever since the congress, he'd been busy traveling to the different places and inspiring work there. We talked in the home of Rızaiye, where Hamili was also staying. Şahin elaborated on the distribution of tasks in the woman work as Cemil had done. We were talking alone. He went at great length into the theoretical background of the woman question. I interrupted him to explain that I'd already discussed it with Cemil. He looked a little piqued and broke off, saying, "That may well be, but I'm saying it to you officially."

The enemy attacks   It was March 1979, with Newroz[132] just around the corner. The friends who had gone to Dersim, including Hamili, returned to Elazığ with their weapons. Everyone expected that certain actions would take place at Newroz, an important day for the people. A series of actions were planned. Hamili was in charge of selecting attack targets and naming the friends who would take part. He worked with Zeki on the local committee. Since it had previously been decided that the press and publicity work would be centralized in Elazığ, we wrote a flyer that we then duplicated and sent out to the various regions. Only after we were finished did we receive a flyer from the central committee. We rushed out couriers to stop the distribution of our flyer. They didn't differ much in content, but there had to be only one flyer. Since we were late, we had sent many places only the text, so they could copy it locally. But the central committee's flyer didn't reach certain areas in time, and our draft was distributed instead. This episode helped us see that we had to define how press and publicity would be handled and how much self-initiative would be allowed.

On the night of Newroz, we did simultaneous actions in 11 places in Elazığ. Among the targets were coffeehouses and clubhouses used by fascists, a police station, and a few fascist shops. We deployed dynamite, bombs, and firearms. We had never before carried out such a concentration of actions. It was the first time we had celebrated Newroz this way in Elazığ. We all rejoiced at our great success. None of us could sleep that night. But the actions also exposed the hitherto inconspicuous homes where we had been staying.

Around this time Şahin went to Ağrı and then returned. Soon afterward a group of friends were arrested. Ali and Hamili were sitting in a coffeehouse when civil police came in and carried out an ID inspection. They took Ali but said nothing to Hamili. Then Aytekin, Rıza, Hüseyin Taze, and Zeki Budak were also arrested. When we heard about it, we scrubbed our apartment. We had been storing piles of placards, flyers, and brochures there. We hurriedly shipped off material intended for other places.

How had these arrests come about? No specific event seemed to account for them. Had there been any warning sign that we missed? A day earlier we got hold of a list of people who were being sought by police. In addition to Deaf Metin, Ali, and a few others, my name was there. We were exposed.

But it wouldn't be so easy for the police to find out where we were staying. We had always been very careful on the way to the flat. But we often met friends in coffeehouses or in the immediate area, and that was pretty careless. Recently we'd been warned several times. After the Maraş pogrom, Cemil had given the first warning: "It's very possible the enemy will attack directly and there will be arrests. We have to be careful." Then we'd talked about safety measures, but what kind? We tended not to take the police seriously. From now on we would limit the meet-ups in coffeehouses. But the friends didn't adhere to this policy, which in the end would cost us dearly.

At Newroz, nothing happened at first. The planned actions were successful. The arrests took place in the lead-up to May 18. The arrest of Rıza from Elazığ seemed especially portentous to us. Clearly the arrests wouldn't stop there.

I talked it over with Şahin. He said, "Don't worry—nothing's going to happen." We decided to give up the flat and get rid of most of the stuff that was there. At night we hid the remaining flyers and placards on the roof. Adjacent to our building stood another house, so close you could cross from one roof to the other. "If something happens, we can always escape over the roofs," we told ourselves.

I had good relations with the neighboring families—they liked me and had no suspicions. The flat was on the fourth floor. Visits weren't observable. Sometimes families came to visit, including the mothers of Güllü and Cahide. We looked entirely normal.

Şahin was very relaxed about it. If he hadn't been there, we would have taken more serious precautions. In the past we'd told Cemil that if worse came to worst, we'd retreat to the country. But Şahin kept saying there was no danger.

One day we were in Süleyman Aslan's flat. Once again we talked about the security situation. Deaf Metin was nervous. Şahin's nonchalance infuriated him—Şahin didn't take our concerns seriously at all. His attitude annoyed me too.

The next morning Şahin said we should prepare for a meeting. At that point, I blew up. So many friends had been arrested, everything was so uncertain, and he wanted to have a meeting?

Hüseyin Taze was released, and I went to see him right away. He looked haggard, sober and tense. The friends had been tortured. Hüseyin said Ali Gündüz had had it particularly hard. "No one talked," he said. "Ali Gündüz and Aytekin held out." Police took Rıza to a house in Esentepe, so we concluded that he hadn't stood firm. The police wanted to know where the weapons and ammunition were being hidden. But Rıza hadn't received weapons from us. I sent a message right away to Şahin.

The next day the meeting Şahin had called took place. Many friends found it unreasonable to meet at this moment. No one said so directly, but the discontent was palpable. Once again Şahin talked for hours. It was infuriating—it reminded me of the founding congress. The whole time I was restless, since my thoughts were with the friends who'd been arrested. Lots of papers had been hidden in Hamili's flat.

I wanted to meet with Hamili that evening. He'd sent me a message and suggested we meet in our flat, which I couldn't understand. Secretly I thought, *The friends are really getting us into trouble.* It was May 17. That night placards were to be hung and flyers distributed. On the assumption that the next day strict police inspections would be carried out, we had already shipped out our material to several groups, to cover all the neighborhoods. Hamili was to come to the flat, once he'd taken care of this task. Ayten and I waited for him for hours. Exhausted from the excitement of the recent days, we fell asleep. Normally I would have just napped, but since I had a splitting headache, I wrapped a cloth around my head and lay down. We didn't hear the doorbell ring when Hamili arrived.

He was uneasy that we didn't open the door, yet there was light in the flat, and he knew we were waiting for him. So he climbed up to the transom above the door to try to open it. He loosened the nails and the sealing on the glass panes. Just as he was forcing his upper body through the transom, the noise woke me up.

I leaped to my feet and ran to the door. The sight I beheld froze me in my steps. Shocked, I asked, "What's going on!" Had Hamili lost his mind? I woke Ayten, who was also astounded. But then, even though we were furious, we began to laugh. Instead of opening the door for him, we scolded him. "Where were you the whole time? Why did you make us wait so long?" To which he responded, "Why didn't you open the door?" Then we opened it.

He explained why he'd tried to enter through the transom. We were embarrassed that we hadn't heard the doorbell, but there was nothing to be done now. We discussed whether to remain in the apartment. He told us what was going on in the streets. We turned out the lights and peered out the window. Police vans were rolling through the streets. Hamili said he'd been careful on the way over here.

"But why did you choose this flat as the meeting point?" I asked. "We could have met somewhere else!" He blamed me for not showing up at a previously arranged meeting. I couldn't stand it any longer and just decided to leave. But then I gave up that idea. I was indecisive. We turned out all the lights again and watched the neighborhood from the window. We were very edgy. Cahide and Gönül had been in the flat all day and had cooked for us, but none of us felt like eating anything. It was dangerous to leave the flat at night, and I had no viable ID, so we decided to spend the night in the flat, then leave first thing in the morning.

Hamili was a member of the local committee and lived near here, and judging from the information we received, he hadn't informed to the police. But it had been reckless for him to enter this flat. It was like gambling. Before we went to bed, I inspected the flat one more time and hid some papers under the linoleum seat of a chair. There was also a typewriter, some carbon paper, and other materials for duplicating texts, which I now had no place to hide. In the attic were placards and flyers. The only book was a history of the Bolshevik party. One book was not a big problem, but I was nervous anyway.

I tossed and turned all night. My headache didn't let up. Şahin's laxness had contributed to it. I still didn't understand why Hamili had tried to enter the flat through the transom. And I kept thinking about Ali Gündüz, Aytekin, and the others. They'd been brutally tortured, Hüseyin Taze had said.

Would Rıza Sarıkaya keep his mouth shut? He knew about this flat, but he didn't know where Hamili usually lived—that was where our archive was. Should we take it somewhere else? But where? The questions pounded in my head unrelentingly.

In the early evening, I had slept so deeply that I didn't hear the doorbell. Now morning was approaching, and I couldn't sleep at all. But it made no sense to get up while it was still dark. Should I get up and pace around in the living room? That was a habit of mine. Lots of times I went for walks in the evening without anyone noticing. When the friends saw me walking back and forth, they would laugh and ask, "Didn't you move around enough today?"

The hours crawled by, and slowly the traffic noise increased outside. Sirens could be heard, coming nearer. Then I heard some car doors slam. I thought about getting up to see what was happening. If I hadn't hesitated just then, we could have fled to the adjacent building in time. But how was I to know it was the police? Then there was a pounding on the apartment door. My worst fear had been realized. It was not normal door-knocking.

"That's the police," I said, leaping up. I was wearing a nightshirt. I grabbed a random pair of pants and pulled them on. I looked around. I stuffed the typewriter and the other things into a plastic bag. I burned some papers in the bathtub. The bathroom was directly across from the apartment door. I woke Hamili and Ayten: "Get up! Police." Both were startled. Hamili moaned, "Are you sure?"

He surveyed the room too. He had a switchblade knife that he carried in a pocket. I left only the book behind. I tossed the plastic bag, with everything inside, out the kitchen window. We had recently laid a board from our window to the window across the way, in case flight was possible that way. But the plank was very thin. We couldn't use it to cross over.

The police kept hammering at the door. "Open up! Or we'll break the door down!"

I feigned a sleepy voice. "Who's there?" I asked.

"Open up, it's the police!"

"Okay, I'm not dressed, just a minute!"

We hadn't taken any precautions, and now the enemy was at the door. I tried not to reveal any fear in my voice. It was so stupid. What was that again about revolutionary alertness, and making arrangements, and the need to be able to anticipate things? Damn! I tried to appear calm anyway.

To Ayten and Hamili I said, "We know each other from Dersim. You brought Ayten here for hospital tests. You're newlyweds. You eloped. Yes, if they ask the family, it'll all come out anyway—it's not important. Me, I'm separated from my husband. Sometimes my siblings come to visit."

The story accounted for the men's clothing in the flat. Suddenly I noticed what kind of pants I'd put on. They were much too loose and were frayed in many places. It was unpleasant for me, but I had no time to change. At that moment one of the police managed, like Hamili the previous evening, to start coming into the flat through the transom.

"Just a minute, I'll be right there. What's going on? Why are you doing this? Was I supposed to open the door in my nightgown? One second, I'll open the door!" I said. To the others, I whispered, "Okay, anything else? We won't make any statement. You've just come to visit. We know each other from Dersim."

Then I opened the door. They rushed in like a pack of hounds and rooted through the flat. "Just a minute—we want to be present when a search is made," I said. They found a typewriter, the history of the Bolshevik Party, some blank pages, and a piece of carbon paper. They found a page with the title "To Our Heroic People," with a few lines.

They classified it all as evidence. I protested, "Why are you taking the typewriter? And that book is available in stores—it's not forbidden to read! Why are you taking that?"

I knew my protests would have no effect and would change nothing. But I wanted to influence them psychologically. Anything was better than waiting in silence and fear. I talked the whole time and kept intervening: "Be careful, don't get anything dirty! Oh, you're mixing everything up! Even during a search, some proprieties should be observed!" I watched their reactions. "Do you have a search warrant?" I asked. "I want to see it!"

One of them laughed grimly. The one with the radio device in his hand said, "Of course we do. Come on, we're going."

A couple of the cops were familiar to me. We'd probably seen each other around the neighborhood. As we descended the stairs, the landlady saw us. With eyes wide open, she said, "She is our best neighbor and tenant! Mr. Police, where are you taking the poor thing?"

Outside it was quiet. We climbed into the car. They put us three on the backseat. The one with the radio sat up front.

In the car I whispered one more time, "You're just visiting, you brought Ayten to the hospital. Otherwise we'll make no statement. We have to stay calm, and it'll be fine."

Suddenly I noticed the car behind us. Rıza was sat on the backseat. I whispered, "Bastard!" No one had known about this apartment. And Ali hadn't been able to hold his tongue. I couldn't stop thinking about Rıza. It had been so clear with him.

The car headed toward the prison. We three communicated via looks. Hamili was pale, his lips were white, and his pulse pounded visibly in this temples. He looked as if he wanted to say, *If I hadn't come over last night, none of this would have happened.* Yes indeed, he'd been the one to bring this calamity on us.

Zap Valley, February–April 1996

Notes

1 The Kurdish Democratic Party was founded by Mustafa Barzani in 1946 and has been led since 1979 by Massoud Barzani.

2 Erik Zürcher, *Turkey: A Modern History*, 3rd ed. (London: I.B. Tauris, 2009), p. 255.

3 Ibid., pp. 254–255; Paul White, *Primitive Rebels or Revolutionary Modernizers? The Kurdish Nationalist Movement in Turkey* (London: Zed Books, 2000).

4 David McDowall, *A Modern History of the Kurds*, rev. ed. (New York: I.B. Tauris, 1977), p. 408.

5 Ibid., p. 411.

6 Nicole Pope and Hugh Pope, *Turkey Unveiled: A History of Modern Turkey* (Woodstock, NY: Overlook, 2004), p. 134.

7 Ibid., p. 136.

8 McDowall, *Modern History*, p. 407.

9 Ibid., p. 409.

10 Ibid., pp. 409–410.

11 Joost Jongerden and Ahmet Hamdi Akkaya, "Born from the Left: The Making of the PKK," in Marlies Casier and Joost Jongerden, eds, *Nationalisms and Politics in Turkey: Political Islam, Kemalism and the Kurdish Issue* (New York: Routledge, 2011), p. 126.

12 White, *Primitive Rebels*, p. 29.

13 Quoted in Jongerden and Akkaya, "Born from the Left," p. 128.

14 Dersim (in Turkish, Tunceli) is a mostly Kurdish city in eastern Turkey. It was, writes McDowall, "notoriously defiant. No fewer than eleven military expeditions had tried to quell its inhabitants since 1876. It had given trouble in 1925–26, and in 1927 four thousand troops had been sent to subdue the Kutch-Ushagh tribe. From 1930 the state began a policy of deportation, disarmament, and forced settlement of nomadic tribes to control it" (*Modern History*, pp. 207–208).

15 Nasreddin Hodja was a thirteenth-century Seljuk Sufi known for funny stories and satirical anecdotes.

16 A band tied with the traditional headscarf.

17 Ayşe Şan (1938–1996) was a Kurdish singer.

18 The parents' names were Ismail and Zeynep Cansız. In June 1934 the Turkish state enacted a law enabling itself to forcibly transfer populations, most notably the Kurds, from their villages and urban neighborhoods to Turkish-speaking areas. The law's intention was to obliterate Kurdish settlements

and therefore identity. In 1937, the government initiated a military operation to reorganize Dersim, a largely Alevi Kurdish city and province, massing 25,000 troops around the city. Kurds soon rose up to resist, to which the state responded with aerial bombings and gas and artillery barrages. Military forces moved through the area rounding up rebels and burning villages. "An estimated 40,000 Kurds perished, and thousands more were deported or expelled; the remainder were put under the supervision of local garrisons" (McDowall, *Modern History*, pp. 207–208).

19 Turkish for "lifeless." In Turkey surnames were required only after 1935.

20 A long-necked lute.

21 The Demenan tribe had participated in the Dersim rebellion.

22 Alevism is one of the two main branches of Islam in Turkey, the other being majority Sunni Islam. It is the largest minority faith in Turkey. Alevis are relatively mystical and differ outwardly from Sunni Muslims in that they fast, not during Ramadan, but during the Ten Days of Muharram (the Shiite commemoration of Imam Husayn bin Ali's martyrdom at Karbala in A.D. 680); they do not prostrate themselves during prayer; they do not attend mosques; and they ignore many Muslim practices like obligatory formal almsgiving, although they have a strong principle of mutual assistance. They are technically a type of Shi'ism, but they differ greatly from the Shi'a communities in other countries as well.

23 In Dersim, both a legend and a massif.

24 A cheese made from skim milk.

25 The eponymous Pir Sultan Abdal (c.1480–1550) was a medieval Alevi poet. He became an Alevi saint, symbolizing community cooperation and opposition to injustice.

26 For the TİP, the Turkish Workers Party, see "Translator's introduction."

27 The phrase has the sense of "Toward a better future. TİP."

28 Rayber was the nephew of Seyid Rıza, leader of the Dersim resistance. Instead of participating in the resistance, he collaborated with the state, took part in the killing of Seyid Rıza's son, and came to symbolize betrayal in Dersim.

29 Sheikh Said (1865–1925) was a Kurdish sheikh of the Sunni order who in 1925 led a rebellion against the new Turkish government of Mustafa Kemal Atatürk. The rebellion was crushed, and Sheikh Said was executed. He has become a symbol of Kurdish resistance.

30 In 1921 Alişêr Beg, the son of an Alevi chief in western Dersim, led a rebellion against the Kemalists in Ankara. Besê was the wife of Seyid Rıza and a fighter in her own right.

31 This dessert, known as Noah's pudding in the Alevi faith, is prepared and shared only on certain days of the year.

32 Aşure is the tenth day of Muharram, the first month of the Islamic calendar. On this day Alevis commemorate the death of Imam Huseyn bin Ali in A.D. 680. The dessert *aşure*, served on that day, is composed of grains, fruits, dried fruits, and nuts.

33 Mahir Çayan co-founded the THKC in 1970; see "Translator's introduction." On May 17, 1971, Çayan, the socialist author Hüseyin Cevahir, and other TKHC guerrillas kidnapped the Israeli consul. On May 23, the consul's body was found in Istanbul. On May 30 Çayan and others entered a house in Istanbul, in Maltepe, and took hostage Sibel Erkan, a young girl.

34 On June 1, 1971, police and soldiers attacked the house in Maltepe and captured Çayan. Among those they killed was the Hüseyin Cevahir.

35 Deniz Gezmiş (1947–1972), co-founder of THKO, was a Marxist-Leninist revolutionary student leader who emulated Che Guevara. See "Translator's introduction."

36 Deniz means "sea" in Turkish and *gezmis* means "the one who traveled." The young Sakine Cansız misunderstood the name *Deniz Gezmiş* as *denizleri gezen adam*, "the man who traveled the seas."

37 In both the Turkish and the German editions, the word used here is a cognate of the English word *boycott*. But what is described here sounds more like a rebellion than a boycott, so I've used the word *rebellion*.

38 Kemal Burkay (b. 1937) is a Kurdish writer and politician. In 1965 he joined TİP (the Turkish Workers' Party) and later founded and led the Kurdistan Socialist Party (PSK). After the 1971 military coup, he fled Turkey for Syria and Lebanon, returning in 1975. Then in March 1980, six months before another military coup, he fled Turkey again and was granted refugee status in Sweden. There he lived until July 2011, when the Turkish government invited him to return. In 2012 he became president of HAK-PAR, a Kurdish nationalist party in Turkey.

39 See "Translator's introduction."

40 Ibid.

41 The surviving guerrilla, Ertuğrul Kürkçü (1948–), hid during the Kızıldere shootout and was taken alive on March 31. He was sentenced to death by a special court, but in 1974 his death sentence was commuted to 30 years in prison. He was released in 1986.

42 The mud-brick house can be seen in the film *Sara: My Whole Life Was a Struggle*, dir. Dersim Zerevan, 2015.

43 Yılmaz Güney (1937–1984) was a celebrated actor of Kurdish origin who went on to become a film director. Despite spending many years in prison, he made numerous films that explore conditions in Turkey's poorer regions and urban neighborhoods: *Umutsuzlar* (*Hope*, 1970), *Ağıt* (*Elegy*, 1972), *Acı* (*Pain*, 1971), *Endişe* (*Worry*, 1974), and *Zavallılar* (*The Poor*, 1975). His most acclaimed film was *Yol* (1982).

44 Aşık Mahzuni Şerif (1940–2002) was an Alevi folk musician and poet. Zamani was a Kurdish troubadour from Dersim who sang about social and revolutionary issues faced by the peasants and working class.

45 Mustafa Bülent Ecevit (1925–2006) was a charismatic social democratic politician of the CHP (see note 46). In 1973 the army allowed a general election and a return to civilian administration. The oppressed classes,

including Alevis and Kurds, saw in Ecevit hope for new politics and for greater rights and gave him their votes. Ecevit stated that his mother was of Bosniak ancestry and his paternal grandfather was of Kurdish ancestry. His nickname Karaoğlan, literally "dark-skinned boy," was the name of a fictional boy, living during the Genghis Khan period, known for being adventurous and brave.

46 The CHP or Republican People's Party, Cumhuriyet Halk Partisi, was founded by Mustafa Kemal Atatürk, the first president of the Turkish Republic. It is the oldest political party in the Turkish Republic.

47 Tunceli is the Turkish name for Dersim.

48 In May 1974 the new somewhat left-of-center government declared a general amnesty that freed many militants and intellectuals who had been arrested and imprisoned after the March 12, 1971, coup.

49 *Almancı* are people who go to Germany (Almanya) as guest workers.

50 Nazimiye is a district in Dersim.

51 The Turkish Communist Party (TKP) was the oldest leftist party in Turkey, formed in 1920. It had little appeal to the 1960s and 1970s generation because it was hardline pro-Moscow and because of its doctrinaire focus on the industrial proletariat as the moving force of the revolution.

52 The Turkish word *dernek* (like the German *Verein*) is normally translated as "association." Finding that word clumsy in this context, I have rendered it "political club" throughout.

53 Alparslan Türkeş (1917–1997), former army official and a far-right, neofascist politician, founded the Nationalist Movement Party (MHP) and the Grey Wolves paramilitary organization.

54 Kurdistan Democratic Party of Iran.

55 İsmail Cem (1940–2007), a journalist of the Turkish center-left, wrote about economic and social factors contributing to underdevelopment in *Turkiye'de Geri Kalmışlığın Tarihi* (*A History of Underdevelopment in Turkey*), published in 1970.

56 *Şalvar* refers to the traditional Kurdish baggy trousers; a *kefiye* is a traditional Kurdish scarf.

57 Mustafa Barzani (1903–1979) was the founding leader of the Kurdish Democratic Party (KDP), in the Iraqi part of Kurdistan from 1946 to his death. He was the father of the current KDP head, Massoud Barzani. The Republic of Mahabad was the only Kurdish nation-state ever to exist. It was founded in northwestern Iran, in an area occupied partly by Britain and partly by the USSR. It existed from January 22 to December 16, 1946. Mustafa Kemal (1881–1938), known as Atatürk after 1934, was the founder of the Republic of Turkey and its first president. The 1920–1921 Koçgiri rebellion, in Sivas province, demanded an independent Kurdistan.

58 Peshmerga (Kurdish, "Those who look death in the eye") are Iraqi Kurdish fighters. The concept existed since the 1920s. The armed militias of the KDP and the PUK are most often called Peshmerga today.

59 A *raxt* is a traditional ammunition belt; a *şutik* is a hip cloth.

60 Kurdish for "Forget not, forget not the path of Lenin."

61 A traditional round dance.

62 Mazgirt is a district in Dersim.

63 In 1972 İbrahim Kaypakkaya (b. 1949) co-founded the Communist Party of Turkey/Marxist-Leninist (TKP/ML) as a Maoist insurgent group. Its goal was to carry out an armed struggle, a People's War against the Turkish state. At 24, Kaypakkaya was one of Turkey's most prominent Marxist theorists. He became the group's first leader. On 24 January 1973, Turkish military forces attacked Kaypakkaya and his comrades (including Ali Haydar Yıldız) in the mountains of Dersim. Kaypakkaya was wounded badly, and the military left him for dead, but he survived.

64 PDA: Proletarian Revolutionary Enlightenment (in Turkish, Proleter Devrimci Aydınlık), founded January 1970.

65 TİKKO: Türkiye İşci ve Köylü Kurtuluş Ordusu, the Workers' and Peasants' Liberation Army of Turkey, the armed wing of the TKP/ML.

66 Julius Fučík (1903–1943) was a Czech Communist author and journalist who died by hanging in Plötzensee prison in Berlin. A collection of his prison writings, *Reportáž psaná na oprátce*, was published posthumously in 1947.

67 Maxim Gorky (1868–1936), a noted Russian novelist, published *The Mother* in 1906. It is the story of Pelageya Nilovna Vlasova, a woman who toils in a Russian factory. After her husband dies, her son Pavel gets involved in revolutionary activities and brings books home. His illiterate mother has no interest in politics and is wary of the changes in Pavel. But her maternal feelings for him move her, and though uneducated, she overcomes her political ignorance and gets involved in revolution too. The novel inspired Bertolt Brecht's 1932 play *The Mothers*.

68 Nickname for Ecevit.

69 On the Grey Wolves and Türkes, see "Translator's introduction."

70 The word *kirve* literally means "godfather," who officiates at a Turkish circumcision, but it also refers to an important tie between families, especially among Alevis in the Dersim region. The word *bacı* means "sister." By using these terms, the vocabulary of ordinary people in peasant and rural communities, TİKKO was attempting to demonstrate that it was part of regular society.

71 Uncle Hıdır and Aunt Tonton are the parents of Metin. Although author calls them "aunt" and "uncle," they are not blood relatives.

72 Mazlum Doğan, like the author, would be a founding member of the PKK. Cansız elsewhere said that "Comrade Mazlum had told his comrades to take a close interest in me, saying that I could be a good revolutionary fighter. He told them they were wrong about me." See "The PKK Foundation in Sakine Cansız's Words," ANF News, November 27, 2015, http://bit.ly/2nPUrFI.

73 Sakine wrote elsewhere of the radical students living in the mud-brick

house: "It was a good coincidence for me that some comrades were often visiting a house near our house in this period of revolutionary impressions and searches. Fuat, Mazlum and Şahin Dönmez visited students living in that house. Left-wing groups were dominant in these gatherings. They would pay special attention to us, giving us magazines to read. But I never felt satisfied with their revolutionary ideology, as I felt like there was something else I was looking for and was going to find. Despite our shared sympathy and interest in revolutionaries, I felt unready and declined to take a part in this movement. Their way of life had an impact on us. Other people living in the neighborhood described them as 'quite different.' They had a seriousness in their relations, their visits, their way of dressing, and everything else. I formed a relationship with those people, but I was always anomalous in their circle as I was making a point of different issues. I was living a contradiction, with the revolutionary impression on one side and with other issues in my mind on the other. Neither I nor the comrades could make sense of my situation." See "The PKK Foundation in Sakine Cansız's Words," slightly edited here for clarity.

74 D.K. was a member of the Apocu group, most likely Duran Kalkan. This was a house meeting, an example of the Kurdistan Revolutionaries' face-to-face strategy (see "Translator's introduction"). It is the winter of 1974–75.

75 The novel *Cement* by Fyodor Gladkov (1883–1953) was published in 1925.

76 Halkın Kurtuluşu, or People's Liberation, a regrouping of members from the THKO tradition. Formed in 1976, the HK was oriented toward Albania and China rather than the Soviet Union.

77 Misak-ı Millî (National Pact or National Oath) was the political manifesto of the Turkish independence movement after the First World War, in 1920. Territories that weren't occupied at that time were claimed as homeland of the Turkish nation.

78 Leyla Qasim (1952–1974) was a Kurdish activist who fought the Iraqi Ba'ath regime, for which she was executed.

79 Urfa (Şanlıurfa) is a city and a province in Kurdish southeastern Turkey.

80 See "Translator's introduction."

81 Referring to the coup of March 12, 1971.

82 Deniz Gezmiş was said to have uttered this slogan at his execution.

83 Mustafa Timisi (b. 1936) headed the Unity Party (TBP), formed in 1966 as an Alevi party of the center left. It would be dissolved after the 1980 military coup.

84 Kurdish for "father of dogs" (instead of Atatürk, "father of Turks").

85 Ali Haydar Kaytan, from Dersim, would be a founding member of the PKK.

86 Kesire Yıldırım, born in Depe (Karakoçan), would be married to Abdullah Öcalan from 1977 to 1987.

87 Cities in the Kurdish east; the earthquake was in 1966.

88 Mustafa Suphi (1883–1921) was a co-founder and general secretary of the

Turkish Communist Party (TKP). In 1921 he was murdered by agents of Mustafa Kemal.

89 The March 12, 1971, coup; see "Translator's introduction."

90 "Yellow unions" were formed to counteract the "red unions" promoting socialist or social democratic ideas. They rejected the union struggle and sought friendly relations with employers, who supported them morally and financially.

91 *Özgürlük Yolu* (*Freedom Road; Kurdish Rîya Azadî*) was the journal of the 1970s Kurdish party TKSP (Socialist Party of Kurdistan Turkey).

92 The Lice earthquake took place in September 1975.

93 The group that formed in 1973 around Abdullah Öcalan. See "Translator's introduction."

94 Zazaki speakers would not be able to understand Kurmancî.

95 Some Turkish Maoist organizations of the 1970s organized marriages for their members. See Pope and Pope, *Turkey Unveiled*, p. 131.

96 Halkın Birliği, or People's Unity.

97 Kemal Pir (1952–1982), of Turkish heritage, would be a co-founder of the PKK in 1978.

98 An ethnic group native to the southeastern Black Sea coast, with its own language and culture.

99 That is, to the Kurdish east. At a 1976 meeting in the Ankara neighborhood of Dikmen, the Kurdistan Revolutionaries decided to shift their operations from Ankara to Turkish Kurdistan. Here too they established that Öcalan would be chairman, and Haki Karer second in rank. See Jongerden and Akkaya, "Born from the Left," pp. 123–142; and Jongerden and Akkaya, "The Kurdistan Workers Party and a New Left in Turkey: Analysis of the Revolutionary Movement in Turkey Through the PKK's Memorial Text on Haki Karer," *European Journal of Turkish Studies* 14 (2012): 1–20.

100 A comprador is, generally, a person within a country who acts as an agent for a foreign organization engaged in investment, trade, or economic or political exploitation. In Marxism, the term *comprador bourgeoisie* was applied to the trading class in regions outside East Asia.

101 Orhan Bakır, an Armenian, was born Armenak Bakırcıyan but later adopted a Turkish name to avoid anti-Armenian prejudice. In Diyarbakır he worked with an Armenian priest to find Armenian children who had converted to Islam after being orphaned during the genocide. He was a central committee member of TKP/ML TİKKO. Bakır would escape from Buca prison in 1977.

102 The main square in modern Istanbul.

103 Haki Karer (1950–1977) had worked with Abdullah Öcalan since their year (1974) in the ADYÖD and had been a roommate of Öcalan and Kemal Pir. He was second in rank to Öcalan in the Kurdistan Revolutionaries. He was killed in a coffeehouse in Antep (Gaziantep), allegedly by a militant from Stêrka Sor, a small Kurdish leftist organization known by the name of its magazine, *Stêrka Sor* (Red Star). Stêrka Sor, founded by Alaattin Kapan

and mainly active in Antep, sought to unite Kurds in an independent Kurdish state. See Mehmet Orhan, *Political Violence and Kurds in Turkey: Fragmentations, Mobilizations, Participations, and Repertoires* (London: Routledge, 2015), p. 110. After Haki Karer's murder, the Antep branch of the Kurdistan Revolutionaries collapsed, and the Kurdistan Revolutionaries denounced Stêrka Sor as a satellite of Turkish Intelligence. See Jongerden and Akkaya, "Born from the Left," p. 130.

104 In March 1977 the HK murdered the Kurdistan Revolutionary Aydın Gül in a Dersim high school. He was very young (b. 1959), only a high school student, and is considered one of the PKK's first martyrs. His murder and that of Haki Karer had profound consequences. According to Jongerden and Akkaya, "before the killing of Haki Karer, the PKK had defended armed struggle ideologically but without [making] any serious attempt to organize one. After 1977, the organization of armed struggle became important as a means of self-defense and to overcome 'obstacles.'" It should be understood that the Kurdish movement had no nonviolent avenues of political expression.

The Kurdistan Revolutionaries also decided that they needed to establish a political party. "As such," write Jongerden and Akkaya, "the formation of the PKK became the promise to continue the struggle of the martyr Haki Karer, as well as a symbol for Turkish–Kurdish brotherhood (Karer being a Turk). See "Born from the Left," p. 130. See also White, *Primitive Rebels*, p. 30.

105 Beş Parçacılar was another name for Stêrka Sor.

106 Perhaps the work meant here is *Draft Theses on National and Colonial Questions* (1920), at www.marxists.org/archive/lenin/works/1920/jun/05.htm.

107 Ali Rıza Altun was detained in Diyarbakır prison from 1980 to 1992 (see Volume II). He remains a member of the Kurdish freedom movement today.

108 Gönül Atay would be detained in Diyarbakır prison along with Sakine Cansız (see Volume II). In 1989 she left the PKK and fled to the Turkish embassy in Damascus.

109 Hikmet's poem "Like Kerem" is reproduced at this point in the Turkish edition but not in the German. An English translation of the poem can be found at www.brighteningglance.org/like-kerim.html. Thanks to Mustafa Gundogu for this link.

110 Amed is the Kurdish name for Diyarbakır, the largest Kurdish city in Turkey and the de facto capital of Kurdistan.

111 The PKK's founding congress, held on November 27–28, 1978.

112 The founder of Stêrka Sor.

113 Seko is short for Sakine.

114 Mehmet Karasungur (1947–1983) was a founding member of the PKK.

115 Selim Çürükkaya (1954–) left the PKK in the mid-1990s, after his brother

crossed over to the enemy during a battle. He fled to Germany, where he denounced the PKK and published a book called *The Dictatorship of A. Öcalan* (1997).

116 Thin cakes made of dried pulp of apricots, plums, or mulberries.

117 Aram Tigran (1934–2009) was an Armenian-Kurdish singer born near Diyarbakır. He was the only member of his family to survive the 1915 Armenian genocide. At 12 he fled to northeastern Syria, where a Kurdish family adopted him. His mother had been Kurdish. In 1966 he went to Yerevan, where he worked for 18 years at Radio Yerevan.

118 Mustafa Çamlıbel, a member of *Özgürlük Yolu* group, a rival of the PKK, was shot in Doğubeyazıt. White, *Primitive Rebels*, p. 157.

119 Zazaki for "Likely he's an ox from Kars."

120 Cemil Bayık had worked with Öcalan since 1974 and would be a founding member of the PKK.

121 During the Lebanese civil war (1975–1990), the Green Line separated predominantly Muslim West Beirut from the predominantly Christian East Beirut.

122 An Islamic legal scholar.

123 In 1978 the draft program of a forthcoming organization was distributed to a few cadres including Sakine in Elazığ. The Kurdistan Revolutionaries had been researching the history of parties and revolutions in other countries, and "we were discussing how those parties had been established." The cadres were told to study the document. See "The PKK Foundation in Sakine Cansız's Words."

124 Devrimci Sol (Revolutionary Left), founded in 1978, was a militant Marxist-Leninist organization.

125 Karakoçan is a district of Elazığ on the border with Dersim. Most of the residents are Kurdish Alevis who consider themselves descended from people in Dersim.

126 Hüseyin Topgüder would participate in the 1978 founding congress.

127 KUK, or Kurdistan National Liberators (Kürdistan Ulusal Kurtuluscuları).

128 Each of the 22 participants was considered a delegate representing a particular region: for example, Cemil Bayık, Sakine Cansız, and Hüseyin Topgüder represented Elazığ. For a full list, see Jongerden and Akkaya, "Born from the Left," p. 138.

129 The founding declaration was issued under the title *Kürdistan Devrimin Yolu* (*The Path of the Kurdistan Revolution*). The party announced itself as "national-democratic" and "revolutionary." It sought to create an alliance of workers, peasants, and intellectuals that would destroy colonialism—by all forces, Turkish and otherwise, occupying Kurdistan. It would combine class struggle with the struggle for national liberation, to seek the creation of a democratic and united Kurdistan based on Marxist-Leninist principles. This declaration was accepted as the party program. See White, *Primitive Rebels*, p. 18.

130 In December 1978 in the hill town of Kahramanmaraş (formerly Maraş), neofascist Grey Wolves attacked, tortured, raped, and massacred Alevi Kurds. "For two days and nights, the town was plunged into an orgy of violence and terror. At least 107 people died and more than a thousand were wounded. Babies were ripped from the bellies of pregnant mothers and dead men strung up from electricity poles. Five hundred shops, mostly opened by Alevis, were burned. Motorized military units came to put down the violence. ... In thirteen provinces martial law was immediately declared" (Pope and Pope, *Turkey Unveiled*, pp. 134–135).

131 Millî İstihbarat Teşkilatı, the Turkish intelligence agency.

132 The Kurdish New Year, March 21.

Index